Beyond Subsistence

Beyond Subsistence

Plains Archaeology and the Postprocessual Critique

Edited by Philip Duke and Michael C. Wilson

The University of Alabama Press
Tuscaloosa

The paper on which this book is printed meets the minimum requirements of American National Standard for Information Science-Permanence of Paper for Printed Library Materials, ANSI Z39.48-1984.

Library of Congress Cataloguing-in-Publication Data

Beyond subsistence : plains archaeology and the postprocessual critique/
edited by Philip Duke and Michael C. Wilson
p. cm.
Includes bibliographical references (p.) and index.
ISBN 0-8173-0799-0 (acid-free paper)
ISBN 978-0-8173-0799-8 (pbk. : alk. paper)
ISBN 978-0-8173-8364-0 (electronic)
1. Indians of North America—Great Plains—Social conditions.
2. Indians of North America—Great Plains—Antiquities. 3. Social archaeology—Great Plains—Philosophy. 4. Environmental archaeology—Great Plains—Philosophy. 5. Great Plains—Antiquities. I. Duke, P. G., 1953 II. Wilson, Michael, 1948
E78.G73B49 1995
978'.00497—dc20 9411820

Contents

Part III: Commentary

Illustrations and Tables

FIGURES

TABLES

Preface

In October 1989, the editors of this volume chaired a symposium titled "The Post-Processual Paradigm in Plains Archaeology" at the 47th Annual Plains Conference in Sioux Falls, South Dakota. This symposium was the first formal attempt to debate the relevance of the postprocessual approach to Plains archaeology. Papers were presented by P. G. Duke, M. C. Wilson, A. Kehoe, N. A. Mirau, and R. A. Krause. Because of the success of the symposium, as indicated by the supportive and critical comments we received, we decided to solicit more papers from like-minded colleagues and publish the collection. The extra time needed by the new contributors is the primary reason for the delay between the original symposium and its final publication.

Besides wanting to demonstrate the potential of postprocessualism to Plains archaeologists, we hope this volume will be of interest to archaeologists in other areas. Thus far, most postprocessual studies have concentrated on ethnographic and historical data drawn from "complex" societies, which is not surprising in light of their heavy use of symbolic and structuralist arguments. Nevertheless, if the postprocessual approach really does have a place in standard archaeological practice, clearly it must have some application to prehistoric hunting-and-gathering societies and to ones for which the richly networked social relationships so loved by postprocessualists have not yet been defined.

The authors in this volume come from different intellectual backgrounds and have different objectives for their research. They therefore exemplify a trend that is important in the development of all new paradigms or research strategies, viz., although a particular paradigm's *founder* may directly convert his or her own students, the particular path of a paradigm's development is ultimately determined by *second-generation* scholars who, often entirely independently, arrive at the paradigm from different intellectual routes. This *intellectual hybridization* is, we believe, one of the strengths of postprocessualism.

However, despite their differences, all the authors are unified by a willingness to step outside the existing intellectual boundaries of their own areas and to consider alternative approaches and frameworks of interpretation. Marcus and Fischer (1986: x) have noted that a period of experimentation is characterized by eclecticism; the play of ideas free of authoritative paradigms; critical and reflexive views of subject matter; openness to diverse influences embracing whatever seems to work in practice; and, finally, a tolerance of both uncertainty about a field's direction and incompleteness in some of its projects. Broadening the field of research strategies—the adoption of what geographer Edward Taaffe (1974) called "cautious and pragmatic pluralism"—will encourage more varied interpretations of a wider range of evidence. The bottom line, for now at least, is that we all need a plurality of strategies; the fact that some will ultimately prove more useful than others will not completely invalidate the less useful ones. If we may be permitted to make an analogy with biological evolution, it has often been stated that the most highly specialized animal or plant groups are the most vulnerable to environmental change and hence the most likely to become extinct. Scientific inquiry faces its own threats from a shifting cultural environment that periodically resorts to fundamentalist religions or alternative belief systems that have attempted to repudiate science; surely the calls from within for scientists to follow a straight and narrow philosophical path create an increased vulnerability to shifting external societal pressures.

All of the authors willingly acknowledge the tentativeness of their conclusions, and all realize that such tentativeness is but the first step to a greater understanding of the past. Without preempting arguments developed in more detail later on, the contributors of this volume see postprocessual archaeology as an addition to, rather than a total replacement of, existing theoretical stances. In this sense, they enact the spirit of the actual term: *postprocessual*, rather than *antiprocessual*, archaeology. Of course, many of the contributors do take positions severely at odds with the processual program. However, they take these positions not so much from any sense of ideological purity but simply because in their opinion the particular postprocessual approach works better than any other. At the same time, postprocessual archaeology has the potential to bring back from the theoretical wilderness certain approaches that fell from favor in the processual paradigm, such as induction and the historical method. All the contributors believe that a responsible archaeology should be accessible to members of the public and should not be written just for other professionals. The introductory chapter of this volume in particular is written with this goal in mind—despite the danger of oversimplifying our arguments—so that interested laypeople can get at least its flavor.

We have not tried to make the chapters in this volume follow any single postprocessual theme or program, preferring instead that the contributors eclectically explore the ramifications of postprocessualism for their own particular areas of the Plains. Our reasoning is as follows. First, postprocessualism stands against a single program of research, preferring diversity in both goals and methods. Second, this volume is the first of its kind to address Plains archaeology, and it would be both unwise and unproductive at this early stage to close down debate and argument prematurely. We would argue fervently that the very diversity of the chapters is one of the volume's great strengths. This volume must only be considered a beginning, but we hope it encourages other Plains archaeologists to consider our arguments and their potential relevance to their own work.

We are extremely grateful, first and foremost, to the contributors for their commitment to alternative ways of looking at Plains archaeology. Melissa Connor and Ian Hodder provided specific commentaries on the essays, and we thank them for their perceptive and constructive comments. Guy Gibbon and an anonymous reviewer provided critical and accurate comments that greatly improved the overall substance and tone of the volume. We sincerely thank them for their contribution. Finally, we wish to acknowledge with gratitude the help and advice we have received from Judith Knight and other members of the staff of The University of Alabama Press.

P. G. D.
M. C. W.

Beyond Subsistence

Introduction

Postprocessualism and Plains Archaeology

Philip Duke and Michael C. Wilson

On the prehistoric Plains, a culture area that has persisted without change in boundaries for over 11,000 years, there was at first only a Man (called Early Man). So utterly rational a Being cloned Himself, becoming a Man among Men. All of these Men were adult, utterly rational, and adaptively expedient. Women and children (and irrational Men) were to come much later. Each of them carried His cultural templates in a skin bag fastened around His waist. These Manly Men among Men seldom made mistakes (except sort of, when fluting projectile points made out of flawed material, so that the material actually was at fault). Other observable errors were probably random events or sampling errors.

These Men among Men were careful to discard tools that were not so worn out as to mask their original use, and in most cases they were concerned enough about their archaeological signature that they used any given tool for only one kind of task. They thought that the whole world should be coated with red ochre, and they started to do it, but didn't finish.

Although they were as strong as Conan the Barbarian (their muscles are better described as "thews"), they did much of their job passively; whenever environment forced them to change, they obediently did so, without shaking fists at the Almighty. Mostly, they wandered around behind large, furry animals, many of which they killed. At first, they liked to throw big rocks at the animals from hilltops, but soon they tired of this and devised stone spikes to stick into the animals. These Manly Men lived in perfect balance and harmony with Nature, well below the carrying capacity of the land, and when they had completely wiped out one prey species they would switch to another. Everything they did was for an adaptive reason.

These Men among Men all had the same personal name, because they were all alike. We have strong reasons to believe that they were all called Norm. "Hey, Norm, get a load of those buffalo." "For sure, Norm."

One day, the Early Period ended, and the start of the Middle Period was announced by the Almighty (in a later speech He used the word "Archaic," but was apparently daydreaming of a holiday in Florida). The news of this new period spread like the biggest prairie fire ever seen, and the Men among Men scrambled to update their technologies. They were in such a panic that they didn't have much time to talk to one another, the result of which was increased diversity and regionalization. As if this wasn't enough, at some point, for obscure reasons, women appeared; children were soon to follow. The arrival of women was signalled by the appearance of pottery (or perhaps even earlier by grinding stones), and the arrival of children by small and/or substandard artifacts. Tiny stone spikes made by Early Men were, of course, for ceremonial purposes and do not mark the presence of children. The adaptive value and precise purpose of women (and children, for that matter) has never been agreed upon by archaeologists, most of whom are Men among Men.[1]

During the last thirty years, archaeology has undergone a theoretical and methodological revolution as it has assimilated various philosophical concepts into its basic panoply of analytical tools; indeed some philosophers have even entered directly into the archaeological arena (e.g., Watson 1976, 1990; Salmon 1982; Wylie 1982; Patrik 1985; Hanen and Kelley 1988; Kosso 1991). For some archaeologists, the borrowing has been superficial, an example of "intellectual potlatching" (Johnsen and Olsen 1992: 420); for others it has even been threatening (humorously exemplified by Flannery [1982]), and certainly a concern exists that as a result of all this assimilation archaeologists, instead of becoming better archaeologists, are simply becoming poor philosophers. However, the proliferation of archaeological books and articles explicitly dedicated to theory building and its philosophical base suggests that philosophy has become an unavoidable—perhaps even welcome—topic of archaeological conversation.

One result of the interest in philosophy has been a controversy regarding the constitution of archaeological knowledge. The contemporary debate on this issue can be categorized, for didactic purposes at least, into a struggle between processual and postprocessual schools, both of which have often conceptualized themselves as mutually exclusive. These categorizations are extremely useful because they provide well-defined theoretical positions that archaeologists can then adopt wholesale or modify and they provide a convenient shorthand for describing overall approaches to archaeological interpretation.

Despite the usefulness of these terms, it is obvious that most archaeologists, for whom theory is simply a tool to facilitate the interpretation of their data, will not always so categorize themselves. Rather, they will eclectically borrow whatever methods and theories seem most appropriate for their particular set of data (cf. Abrams [1982] for a defense of this position in sociology). Although some archaeologists may frown on this borrowing (cf. McGuire [1992: 8] for such a critique), most archaeologists, we suspect, place finding out about the past above ideological purity. Indeed, we hardly need to emphasize that eclecticism can only succeed if a full availability of options exists; this is one of the purposes behind this volume.

This chapter serves as a prelude to the others in the volume. It examines the status of theory on the Plains before it discusses how postprocessual approaches can contribute to a better understanding of Plains archaeology. Any attempt to introduce something new must, of necessity, involve a criticism of what has gone before. However, in drawing on archaeological studies both of the Plains and elsewhere to make our points, we must stress that no malice is intended; archaeology has had altogether too many ad hominem attacks masquerading as scholarship (cf. Pailes 1981). Individual studies were chosen precisely because they are, in our opinion, the best representatives of their particular genre.

Archaeological Theory on the Plains

If symposia offered at annual meetings of the Plains Anthropological Society are a rough gauge, explicit theory building is not of overwhelming concern for most Plains archaeologists. We do not wish to imply that Plains archaeology is antitheoretical (every aspect of archaeological interpretation is predicated on theoretical positions), merely that these positions are rarely stated explicitly. Plains archaeology does, of course, have a history of theory building. One needs only to think of the paramount importance of Strong (1935) and Wedel (1938) in developing the direct historical approach and its impact on the rest of American archaeology (cf. Steward 1942). Similarly, Wedel's (1941, 1953) early concern with the environment as a primary determinant of human behavior on the Plains stood in stark contrast to much contemporary American archaeology, which was characterized by "the anti-evolutionary [and] anti-environmentalist philosophies which long dominated American anthropology" (Willey and Sabloff 1974: 197).

Perhaps, as Patricia O'Brien (personal communication) has observed, this rarity is simply because many Plains archaeologists have been born and raised on the Plains themselves, an area whose specific culture and world view encourage the pragmatic and practical over the theoretical. Contemporary Plains archaeologists demonstrate a continuing reluctance *explicitly* to engage in theory building, but at the same time, as is shown by this volume and many other studies, they are not unaware of the changes sweeping the discipline or reluctant to incorporate them into their investigative armory. The pragmatism that has always characterized Plains archaeology will no doubt continue to place the goal of understanding the past above model building for its own sake, but this end does not mean that it is theoretically conservative.

Elsewhere, one of us (Duke 1991) has argued that archaeology is currently dominated by three paradigms: culture history, processualism, and postprocessualism, with different areas and schools placing different emphasis on them. In Plains archaeology, culture history is clearly the most embedded, and, despite early processual arguments to the contrary, this paradigm still provides the primary organizing structure of archaeological data on the Plains and elsewhere. However, at the risk of taking this paradigm for granted, we wish to concentrate on the latter two and their potential for explaining the archaeological record because these two paradigms have taken the most clearly drawn sides in the contemporary debate on theory.

If processualism is characterized by a commitment to ecological functionalism *and* to hypothetico-deductive reasoning, processual archaeology has not been that prominent on the Plains. However, many studies have utilized elements of the paradigm, and so its influence has clearly been seen. Perhaps the earliest is Deetz's (1965) study of Arikara ceramics, in which a strict hypothetico-deductive set of arguments was adduced. Deetz's study was a short-lived transplant from elsewhere, and he did not follow up with further Plains studies. Computer analyses, such as that by Calabrese (1974), demonstrated the utility of multivariate statistical techniques, and these projects follow on from studies like Deetz's.

A clearly processual position has been taken in Reher's ecologically based work (e.g., Reher 1977); this work provided an exciting example for other workers on both the Northern and Southern Plains. Studies by Greiser (1985), Bamforth (1988), Johnson (1988), and Kelly and Todd (1988) follow some of the best advice offered by processual archaeology in putting all their theoretical cards on the table for all to read.

The emphasis on human-environment relations continues, as exemplified by a recent synthesis of Southern Plains archaeology (Baugh 1986), among many others, and it is perhaps the single most important explanatory model in use on the Plains today. Perhaps the most explicit convergence of animal and human behavioral studies is found in Frison's (e.g., 1974, 1978) classic studies of bison and human ecology. Some of his theoretical positions were clearly in the same mold as processual archaeology, but it is not clear that the influences on his work can be directly traced to that paradigm. Frison studied under James Griffin, as did Binford, but much of his most insightful work can be traced to his own roots as an experienced Wyoming rancher and student of animal behavior, as well as to the tradition of taphonomic studies in vertebrate paleontology at the University of Wyoming under the general supervision of Paul McGrew (e.g., Voorhies 1969). Despite the apparently obvious connections between Frison's studies and processual archaeology, the former did not generally adopt the specific processual methodologies being advocated by Binford and other processualists at the time.

Despite the continuing dominance of a generally ecological-functional emphasis to interpretation, postprocessual themes are not entirely foreign to Plains archaeology, as Connor notes in her overview in this volume. As just one example, Rogers' (1990) study of changes to Arikara material culture during the contact period is replete with the kinds of arguments found in any classic postprocessual study. Significantly, this study was not conducted under an explicit postprocessual umbrella.

The advocacy of postprocessual approaches made in this volume implies a dissatisfaction with some elements of contemporary practices, and, consequently, in this section we wish to identify some areas of weakness. We have borrowed Wobst's (1978) term to identify what we consider to be five *tyrannies* that bedevil archaeology on the Plains (and elsewhere) and that are addressed, implicitly and explicitly, by the individual chapters of this volume.

1. *The tyranny of the ethnographic record.* Overapplication of modern ethnographic models can obscure the novelty of the past (Wobst 1978). As Trigger (1984a: 281) notes, "If the only significant difference among societies is the stage of development they are in, archaeology has nothing new or valuable to offer anthropology. It can merely illustrate concretely the past history of specific regions and determine when they passed through different stages of development." The expectation that every possible cultural variation is *frozen* in a modern culture somewhere in the world is tantamount to the expectation that modern cultures, aboriginal or otherwise, are "living fossils."

Plains archaeology, in common with that of the rest of North America, uses ethnographic analogy. However, the use of ethnographically studied societies simply as analogies for the understanding of archaeological data comes dangerously close to neocolonialism (cf. Trigger 1980: 671, 1984a: 294), and it has been argued that the imposition of a methodological and epistemological division, marked by European contact, between prehistory and history reinforces the pernicious notion of a primitive *them* and an advanced *us* (Duke 1991: 109). The correct epistemological relationship between the past and the ethnographic present must be reached in an accommodative and *interpretive* process (described more fully below), with neither one a priori being considered superior to the other in terms of being closer to a perceived reality. Archaeologists must put into practice their awareness that, although the prehistoric past can be partially understood through the ethnographic present, the latter is still a product of the former and can only be fully understood as such.

2. *The tyranny of ethnocentrism*. Efforts to use the ethnographic record, problematic as Wobst (1978) has shown them to be, have been in part sincere attempts to avoid the practice of imposing one's own cultural values on the past. The presence of a potential ethnocentrism is found in two examples. First, it can be argued that processualism is itself a Western cultural document inadvertently hiding ethnocentric biases about the way cultures should work. Theories that depend on notions of efficiency in resource exploitation are, in part, statements about how societies, especially our own, should work, rather than how they do. Moreover, in applying neo-Darwinian principles to the explanation of human cultural behavior, these theories tend to devalue the humanity of the societies under study (Ingold 1992). Second, the search for *comfortable* solutions in archaeology stands in stark contrast to the culture shock experienced by ethnographers, and it documents the continued imposition of the analyst's own values on, or at best the maintenance of an *arm's-length* relationship with, human beings, who are made to resemble mathematical functions rather than cultural entities. Indeed, in some recent studies that have been conducted on the Plains (e.g., Johnson 1988), people per se are almost invisible as cultural entities, lost in a sandstorm of explicitly scientific data.

3. *The tyranny of institutions*. In most of North America, archaeology has been institutionally yoked to cultural anthropology because of its placement within the discipline and departments of anthropology. Archaeology has been discouraged from developing fully its ability to comment on the *long-term* power of *material culture* (its two unique contributions to human understanding) because of anthropology's necessary involvement with the short term and its frequent avoidance of the mundane aspects of material culture. Obviously, moving archaeology out of anthropology departments, even if that were a feasible option in these days of budgetary woes, is not simply the answer. Rather, archaeology must continue striving to develop its own unique potential in the study of human behavior despite the influences of its precise institutional location.

4. *The tyranny of temporal units*. Temporal divisions of the past are driven by the notions of tripartism and oppositional dualism that are a consequence of Indo-European and Semitic influences on Western thought

(cf. Dumezil 1968). Often, these heuristic units take on a life of their own and drive subsequent interpretations. The plethora of periods divided into Early, Middle, and Late should tell us that we are imposing our own cultural values on the past; surely not everything inherently develops in three stages. Threefold systems also arise from our cultural interest in duality: we establish dualities and add the "Middle" category to deal with "boundary problems" between the other two. This action, of course, creates two new sets of boundary problems where only one existed before, so the next step is a fivefold system (see, for example, the African Stone Age, with its First Transitional period and Second Transitional period). The creation of Early Middle and Late Middle prehistoric periods on the Northwestern Plains clearly shows our infatuation with binomial and trinomial systems; note that we consistently balk at "Middle Middle." The obvious solution is to parachute in a name from another system; if we bring in "Archaic," we can immediately break it up into Early, Middle, and Late all over again.

5. *The tyranny of the culture area.* Culture areas, as established early in the present century, are seldom challenged by modern scholars (cf. Scaglion [1980] for a review of the concept's application on the Plains). These areas, although in most cases well founded, represent an ethnographically driven classification. What is dangerous is that we project them back in time, as if they were as fully developed ten thousand years ago as they are in the ethnographic present. We talk of the Paleo-Indian period "on the Plains," meaning the Plains culture area. Culture areas were quite possibly dramatically different in the past.

Postprocessualism

It is argued in this section that these tyrannies can be reduced by addressing them within the context of a postprocessual strategy. However, it might first be appropriate to describe briefly its major principles. It must be stressed that postprocessual archaeology does not take a strict programmatic position. Thus, the following principles must not be seen as *sine quibus non* for a postprocessual approach.

1. *The role of the environment.* Postprocessualism denies the primacy of the natural environment as a deterministic factor in cultural change, preferring instead to see environmental change as only a precondition for cultural change (Hodder 1986). Postprocessualism uniformly rejects the view of human culture only as a means of passively reacting to outside stimuli, such as the environment.

2. *The importance of the individual.* Binford (1989: 49), representing the processual position, has argued that as "a modern archaeologist . . . I can quite literally gain insights into an order of reality that was unknown to participants in ancient cultural systems," thereby implying that individuals are less important than the system controlling their behavior (cf. Flannery 1967). Shanks and Tilley (1987a: 35–36) have criticized the widespread relegation of human beings in mathematical models to the point of virtual nonexistence, arguing instead that an appropriate model for cultural change must attempt to embody the specific cultural context as perceived by the individual actor, a position that tends to the emic pole as opposed to the more etic processual emphasis. Saitta (1992a: 66) has argued that approaches like postprocessualism can "restore the human element to what can become, on a systems-ecological approach, relatively bloodless models of human behavior."

People create themselves, in the cultural as well as the physical sense. The acts of individuals are not solely determined by a cultural code because the culture is itself constructed in those acts, in the same way that a particular landscape is constructed and activated through the perceptions of the people who occupy it (Wagner 1974: 135–136). Postprocessual archaeology's concern with the individual stems from a concern with how contemporary political and social change can be brought about (a position almost certainly initiated by Britain in the 1980s where, despite government rhetoric, the individual was seen as increasingly powerless), and from a desire to see the individual as something more than a powerless pawn either of powerful social groups or of governing laws of nature. The concern with the individual in the past is manifested in the attempt to recognize *internal* causes of change, especially those that are related to struggles for social and political power. Clearly, we cannot focus to any great extent on empirical individuals, named or otherwise (cf. Hill and Gunn 1977), and this is certainly not the intent of postprocessualism. We assume that we deal in norms after all (cf. White 1949: 233–281), and these norms represent groups of people who are, presumably, subject to some degree of leadership and following. Rather, postprocessual archaeologists argue that the individual can cope with the social milieu through the control, manipulation, or subvention of dominant structures, and this argument gives a different perspective to investigating cultural change than that proposed by processualism.

3. *Explanation and understanding.* Processualists adopted a strongly programmatic epistemology that reduced explanations to a set of deterministic external phenomena, adaptive and therefore often ecological in nature, in a search for cross-cultural lawlike generalizations. Initially, the

search for these laws was to be made within the context of a strictly deductive Hempelian methodology, regardless of the fact that the methodology was by the 1950s already becoming discredited in philosophy (Lamberg-Karlovsky 1989: 6). Further, processual archaeologists succeeded in loading the debate on archaeological theory in such a way that its own positivist-based system was conceived as the only way of gaining legitimate knowledge. Thus, the debate for processualists at least became very black-and-white: processual archaeology (truth) versus the rest (fiction). For processualists, the touchstone of scientific competence was an appropriate methodology, which yielded truth.

In this regard, it is worthwhile making a distinction between *understanding* and *explanation*, one first made by the nineteenth-century philosopher Johann Gustav Droysen (Johnsen and Olsen 1992: 421). The former is the objective of postprocessualism: it involves the notions of intentionality and hermeneutics and is appropriate for the historical and social sciences. Explanation, on the other hand, is associated with the natural sciences and aims to identify strictly causal relations between phenomena, an objective akin to that of processual archaeology. This distinction suggests that both knowledge and explanation are worthy scientific objectives, but neither has privilege over the other in any absolute sense. Indeed, it can be argued that attacks from one paradigm on the other's goals are, therefore, misdirected (cf. Saitta 1983a).

4. *Archaeology as contemporary politics.* Of broad interest to all social scientists today are matters such as the empowerment of minorities and the social repercussions of scientific and technical innovation. The beauty (and danger) of archaeology is that, although the data can be manipulated only within certain limits, nevertheless great flexibility exists in the questions that are asked and therefore the specific type of past constructed. The creation of the past is subject to modern societal norms and is also a compelling document of them.

Postprocessual archaeology explicitly acknowledges the unavoidably political content of interpretation and indeed has advocated that archaeology contribute to contemporary political debate (Hodder 1986; Shanks and Tilley 1987b). This role is most clearly seen in the rise of a feminist agenda in archaeology (Gero and Conkey 1991); it has even been claimed that the rise of postprocessual archaeology has depended on feminism and a feminist archaeology (Hodder 1991: 10). However, if archaeology is serious about contributing to greater social equality, which we assume to be the objective of the call to political action, it must not stop at gender. Archaeology must look at all minorities and socioeconomic classes; it might be that many female archaeologists already have a highly privileged position in society and their discipline. What is required is a full awareness of different perspectives in the development of a truly gender-unbiased archaeology (cf. Bahn 1992).

5. *A contextual approach.* The meaning of artifacts, and thus their roles in guiding human action, can be understood only by placing them within their contexts and association of use (Hodder 1986). Contextual analysis "attempts to *read* or interpret the evidence primarily in terms of its internal relations rather than in terms of outside knowledge. In particular an emphasis is placed on internal symbolic relations rather than on externally derived concepts of rationality" (Hodder 1990: 21). Material culture provides the environment within which individuals find their places and learn the places of others. Yet it also produces new situations and is, with language and gesture, one of the media through which individuals attempt to achieve their personal goals. This feedback harks back to the language-culture and landscape-culture relationships discussed respectively by Whorf (1956) and by Wagner (1974). From the cognitive anthropologists we have long since learned that if an informant looks at a sea that we call "blue" and calls it "green," he or she is not necessarily trying to mislead us. The color systems of the informant's culture might not distinguish blue and green as separate colors. By the same token, many of the distinctive categories we impose on the archaeological record may not have been recognized as meaningful by the prehistoric peoples being studied.

As we have already noted, a fundamental paradox exists with which we must all come to grips: the paradox of culture shock. Archaeologists have tended, above all else, to seek *comfortable* solutions. This predilection seems to be a good scientific attitude, embodying the desire to reduce the mysteries of the universe to familiar systems of understanding. It is an attitude that is laudable for studies of the physical environment, but it may well be counterproductive for studies of the cultural past. Again, that irritating word *arbitrary* springs forth from the analytical underbrush, for the arbitrary element of culture cannot be hidden by the foliage of physical laws or cultural lawlike generalizations. The paradox arises from the contrast between modern culture contact and the culture contact between archaeologists and paleocultures. On the one hand, comfortable answers for cultural anthropologists working with other cultures come rarely, and they come only after an agonizing period of alienation (for an entertaining example, see Barley [1984]). Much of archaeology, on the other hand, reflects a more rapid transition from first encounter to "comfortable solution." Alienation per se is brushed aside as an inconvenience. The danger of this action, and the essence of the paradox, is that the archaeologist may never experience culture shock and that the categories that are reconstructed are those of his or her own culture.

6. *Historical explanation.* During the past three decades much vitriol has been hurled by some archaeologists at historical analysis. Processual archaeologists, for example, in trying to make archaeology a science (or to restrict archaeology to a scientific approach), rejected traditional culture history. However, such a methodology does not necessarily involve the dangers flagged by processualists. The first danger was that in remaining idiosyncratic, historical explanation could not, by definition, apply itself to the sort of generalizations that were specified as the "real" objectives of archaeological explanation. Second, evaluation of a historical explanation was said to rely too heavily on an evaluation of the explainer, which involved factors that were not at all scientific (e.g., the analyst's personal reputation, position, or visibility within the academic community). The continued use of historical methods has been repeatedly championed by Trigger (1978), and the introduction by Hodder (1986) of Collingwood's (1946) conception of history, as well as of various hermeneutic procedures, has resuscitated the validity of historical understanding and intentionality (Johnsen and Olsen 1992).

Of particular interest is the definition of long-term structures of meaning that are defined from the specific historical trajectories of artifacts (Hodder 1987a, 1987b). Central to this objective is the archaeological tradition, but it is necessary to clarify the difference between culture-historical and postprocessual notions of this concept. Culture-historical definitions of tradition are *content driven,* in that morphological homogeneity defines membership of the tradition. In contrast, postprocessual traditions are *meaning driven,* and homogeneity of meaning constitutes membership. Thus, postprocessual traditions can crosscut existing culture-historical traditions. Similarly, culture-historical traditions may encompass several changes in the meaning of the artifact without any corresponding change in artifact morphology. Explicating this distinction would have improved Duke's (1991) analysis of long-term structures of *mentalité* in the archaeological record of the Northern Plains.

Not all archaeologists operating under the postprocessual rubric uniformly adopt these six elements, and already different varieties of postprocessualism emphasizing different elements can be defined. For example, Patterson (1989) has defined: (1) the contextual approach identified primarily with Hodder (1986, 1991); (2) an emphasis on social power and domination, associated with the writings of Shanks and Tilley (1987a, 1987b); and (3) an emphasis on ideology, as expressed, for example, in the writings of Leone (e.g., 1978). Watson and Fotiadis (1990) have separated postprocessualism into Marxist (and neo-Marxist) and cognitive/symbolic/structural approaches. Preucel (1991) has identified *hermeneutic* and *critical* emphases. The former is essentially Hodder's (1991) interpretive archaeology, whereas the latter is concerned with neo-Marxist concepts of social power and the oppressive or emancipatory roles of the past in the maintenance or disruption of contemporary social relations.

Because of its internal variation, as well as its inherent avoidance of exclusive methodologies, the exact paradigmatic status of postprocessualism may be questioned. However, given the eclectic approach to theory taken in this volume, we are not especially concerned whether postprocessualism is termed a paradigm, a research strategy, or just an approach. This lack of concern with the precise classificatory status of a postprocessual archaeology is perhaps also behind Trigger's (1989a) avoidance of the term (*postprocessualism* is not even listed in his index), in favor of more restricted ones such as neohistoricism, idealism, neo-Marxism, and contextual archaeology.

Watson (1991) has portrayed the debate between the processualist and postprocessualist camps, as represented in some of the writings of Binford and Hodder, as akin to a gladiatorial combat, but it is encouraging to note that increasingly researchers are for practical purposes investigating how the two approaches can legitimately be combined. For example, Rogers (1990: 228) stressed the need to consider "cultural relevance" with "economic, social, demographic, and other factors," in explaining the changes to Arikara material culture as a result of European contact. Duke (1991) has combined culture-historical, processual, and postprocessual approaches in a Braudelian *Annales* model and applied it to Northern Plains prehistory. Watson (1991) has identified at least five areas of reconciliation between the processual and postprocessual positions. Preucel (1991: 28) maintains that processual, hermeneutic, and critical approaches must be seen as complementary. Saitta (1992a) has demonstrated the complementarity of processual (economic) and postprocessual (social) models in several contemporary studies of the Anasazi of southwest Colorado and has elsewhere argued for the application of explicitly middle-range theories to radical archaeology (Saitta 1992b). Even Hodder (1991) has now advocated an explicitly *interpretive* archaeology in which a "guarded objectivity," drawing on processual, ecological, evolutionary, behavioral, and positivist archaeology, has a role to play, together with hermeneutic and reflexive approaches: "processual archaeology needs to be subsumed within a relation to critique and hermeneutics, and postprocessual archaeology needs to react to the charge of methodological naivete" (Hodder 1991: 13). Kosso (1991), from a detached philosopher's position, has argued for a methodological similarity between middle-range theory and hermeneutics. It is important to acknowledge, therefore, that postprocessual archaeology can legitimately be seen as a logical descendant of processual archaeology and not necessarily as a paradigm opposed to it.

Earlier, we identified tyrannies current in Plains archaeology. How then can postprocessual archaeology contribute to their solution? First, postprocessual archaeology has shown the potential to develop the unique attributes of archaeology: the study of material culture using a long-term perspective. Recent analyses by Duke (1991, 1992) are preliminary attempts to apply this approach to the Plains and to solve the tyrannies of institutional placement and the ethnographic record. Second, the recognition of meaning-driven rather than content-driven units is an attempt to move archaeology away from traditional taxonomic units, both spatial and temporal. Third, the explicit recognition of the political content of archaeological interpretation attempts to reduce ethnocentrism. Similarly, although a completely emic approach is untenable with archaeological data, the advocacy of contextualism and the definition of "inside" history (Collingwood 1946) removes archaeology, at least a little, from a purely "outside" and etic position and provides for an examination of intentionality in human action.

The following chapters explore some of the issues we have raised here. We have structured the chapters into three general categories. The first group considers general conceptual and theoretical issues raised by the application of postprocessual arguments to Plains archaeology. Alice Kehoe situates the development of Plains archaeology into the wider social and cultural as well as specific disciplinary contexts of North America. She argues that processual archaeology's popularity is partly explained by the wider infatuation of American society with science during the 1960s and 1970s. One of the political bases to archaeology is thus exposed. Larry Zimmerman considers the ways in which archaeology and Native American concerns can be reconciled without reverting to a futile hyperrelativism. Through an examination of two case studies, Zimmerman shows that it is not necessary for archaeologists working with Indians to reject historical or archaeological methods or to abandon their own version of the past. Rather, we must offer archaeology to Indian groups as one means by which they can interpret their past for their own use and empower themselves in relationship to the dominant culture. Mary Whelan looks specifically at the development of Plains archaeology from a feminist perspective, basing her critique on a wide range of examples drawn from throughout the Plains. Whelan suggests that an understanding of the processes that created the diversity of historic gender systems, and the influences on these processes of technological change, economic reorganization, and population fluctuation, is a substantive contribution to Plains archaeology that goes well beyond contemporary feminist goals.

In the preface, we argued that paradigms are strengthened by the contributions of scholars from different backgrounds. Patricia O'Brien's chapter is an excellent example. Steeped in a culture-ecology background, O'Brien nevertheless raises some fundamental problems with this model, such as its implicit ethnocentrism and its version of causality. She explores these problems through an examination of the social and cultural dynamics of the Steed-Kisker phase of the Eastern Plains and in so doing proposes a new cross-cultural type, the homestead neighborhood.

A common complaint made against theoretical debate in archaeology is that it is often conducted in the rarified air of academia and is thus often seen as irrelevant by many archaeologists who work in government or cultural resource management. The chapter by Monica Weimer introduces the postprocessual critique to the day-to-day procedures of federal government archaeology. Weimer makes the point that too much emphasis has been placed on environmental variables in developing management plans. Rather, she argues, archaeologists must move away from a narrowly scientific and environmentally deterministic methodology and consider culturally particularistic and idiosyncratic factors in developing models for site location and plans for the management of these sites. Her arguments stand in sharp contrast to the explicitly processual landscape approach recently advocated by Rossignol (1992: 4–5), for example.

The next section comprises specific case studies that utilize various postprocessual concepts, implicitly and explicitly modifying them in accordance with the demands of the specific data and area being analyzed. The political and intellectual basis of postprocessualism is Marxist and neo-Marxist. David Benn's chapter returns to these elemental roots in proposing a Marxist-oriented explanation of the origins of intensive agriculture on the Eastern Plains and adjacent prairies. Benn argues that such theories as optimal foraging are inappropriate because they rely on assumptions of rationality that are specific products of modern Western society. Benn rejects neo-Darwinian theories in favor of ones that emphasize social relationships and ideology. Richard Krause examines the construction and use of earthen mounds in the Eastern Plains. Krause criticizes the processual interpretation of these sites as incomplete because they are viewed simply as passive reflections of social stratification. Rather, in relying on the concepts of *sacra* and *communal cult institution*, Krause argues that these mounds were actively used in the creation and manipulation of social power and authority.

James Brooks presents an interpretive narrative history of the Northern Plains as expressed by the Hidatsa and Crow. His chapter interweaves multiple and parallel narratives (the archaeological record, ethnohistory, ethnography, and tribal memory) into a single, comprehensible text predicated on the position that no single form of knowing should be given privilege. Brooks challenges the traditional viewpoint that the ideational world is subordinate to the material; instead, such practices as the vision quest were not simply "the superstructural validation of infrastructural conditions" but rather potent and creative tools by which individuals could renegotiate their social and cultural positions.

Tipi rings, or stone circles, are one of the most numerous site types on the Northern Plains. Archaeological studies of these sites have tended to concentrate on their adaptive features, overlooking the very rich ethnographic documentation on the tipi's symbolic importance. In a chapter that takes the reader into the literature of cultural geography, Michael Wilson examines how Plains tipi rings can be viewed as a text that offers great insight into the archaeological record of the Plains as a richly contextual and symbolic mnemonic device. In relying on a wide range of sources, including similar sites from Tibet, Wilson's chapter is suggestive of the rich potential for a contextual and interpretive archaeology.

If tipi rings are the most numerous types of sites, then medicine wheels, the focus of Neil Mirau's chapter, are one of the least so. Mirau's study is predicated on the importance of context, both prehistorically and contemporaneously. Mirau chides those archaeologists who concentrate on only one or two aspects of medicine wheels and then extrapolate their preferred explanation to all similar structures. Mirau suggests that the desire to create uniformly applicable explanations is a result of the archaeologist's own world view. Rather, the potential variability in meaning is what must be acknowledged and explained, and this goal can only be accomplished by examining medicine wheels in their full contexts. Mirau's analysis of medicine wheels demonstrates why the content-driven categories of traditional archaeology must be reconciled with the often contradictory meaning-driven categories that are the logical product of a postprocessual analysis.

The chapter by Miranda Warburton and Philip Duke synthesizes the ethnographic record of the rich symbolism of Blackfoot projectile points and shows how the meanings of artifacts change according to their specific context of use. The ethnographic evidence is then contrasted to traditional ways of analyzing projectile points from the archaeological record. Their chapter offers ways by which the archaeological analysis of this tool may be taken beyond the prevailing concentration on such aspects as function and ethnicity.

The final section comprises commentaries on the previous chapters. Melissa Connor looks at these studies within the context of Plains archaeology. She concludes that the essences of postprocessualism—eclecticism and symbolism—will strike a chord of sympathy in many Plains archaeologists, especially those who are not totally wedded to a processual approach. Connor further argues that Plains archaeologists have always prided themselves on their interdisciplinary skills and that postprocessual approaches should be used to complement, rather than to replace, existing approaches. Ian Hodder situates the chapters within the overall field of postprocessualism. He makes the important point that postprocessual archaeology needs to work through its positions in detailed studies and along different lines as it is accommodated to particular traditions of scholarship in specific areas such as the Plains.

Note

1. The idea regarding "Manly Men" is used with both credit and apologies to Greg Keeler, professor of English, Montana State University, and is an allusion to his gender-bashing satirical song of that name, from the album, *Nuclear Dioxin Queen* (1989, Mastodon Productions, P.O. Box 6272, Bozeman, Montana 59771).

Part I

Conceptual and Theoretical Perspectives

1

Processual and Postprocessual Archaeology

A Brief Critical Review

Alice B. Kehoe

There was a time when words such as "metaphysics" and "premises" drew hostile stares from Plains archaeologists, a pipe-smoking crowd in khaki pants. Laying out points and sherds from their latest River Basin Surveys digs, they thrashed over whether this handful was *Talking Crow* or *Scalp Punctated*. *That* was archaeology, a no-nonsense man's world.

Then came the New Archaeology. Some fellow from somewhere East—Michigan? No, couldn't be, Jimmy Griffin was Michigan, a real guy—Chicago? That's it, he was getting Paul Martin all worked up—this fellow started saying archaeology is anthropology or it is nothing. It has to be science that's hypothetico-deductive nomothetic and we must let the past speak for itself, not use ethnographic analogy or any analogy because then it wouldn't be testable. Fellow said it was called *processual archaeology*. And about that time, River Basin Surveys folded up. The Smithsonian even stopped publishing those *Bureau of American Ethnology Bulletins* in their institutional olive-green bindings.

Processual archaeology came in when the projects, on which the first postwar generation of archaeologists built their careers, ended. These men—Marie Wormington was the only woman who was acknowledged—formed a cohort much like an age-grade society, let us say the Brave Dogs. The generation coming up after them constituted the next society, let us say the Kit-foxes. Each society had its emblems. The Brave Dogs' "jeans had been through the mud and the barbed-wire fences of countless field seasons, . . . hat had faded in the prairie sun, . . . eyes had the kind of crow's feet known locally as the High Plains squint. [One] could tell . . . an archeologist by his boots [and the] bourbon and water in . . . his hand" (Flannery 1982: 267). And, of course, there was a not-yet-gilded

Marshalltown stuck through his belt. The Kit-foxes waved a banner labeled "processual archaeology" and ritually presented research questions in the form of rigorously structured, testable, generalizable hypotheses. Some time during the 1970s they cut their unkempt long hair and beards and changed their scruffy shorts for tweed jackets.

The Brave Dogs had come up at the end of that "kind of golden age for archaeology in the United States" (Quimby 1979: 110), the Works Progress Administration (WPA) era. They had served in the armed forces during World War II and started careers funded by the Army Corps of Engineers' massive campaign to conquer the Missouri River. The next generation found no ready-made projects. Kit-foxes were funded as individuals competing for National Science Foundation grants.

Where the Rainbow Ends

The matter of source of funding is a critical although generally ignored factor in the emergence of the New, or processual, archaeology in the 1960s. American archaeology had taken off in the 1930s with WPA efforts to devise labor-intensive, minimal-capital projects. To get a job as an archaeologist with the WPA, one had to demonstrate some ability in managing teams of manual laborers and have a little experience with excavation technique. After World War II, the big money for American archaeology came from the Missouri River engineering scheme. Plains archaeology, which had been struggling against the dictum that the Plains were uninhabited before the horse (Wedel 1977: 8–9), suddenly became the center of research. River Basin Surveys differed from the WPA projects in requiring greater competence in archaeological investigation from its supervisors because the rationale for the projects was recovery of data about to be destroyed. River Basin archaeologists were expected to salvage archaeological data efficiently and thoroughly within the time constraints of the engineering scheme and to prepare reports presenting these data in standard archaeological monograph format. One's career depended on the presentation of highly comparable data from which a master history of the Missouri Basin could be synthesized after the destruction of its sources.

With the close of River Basin Surveys, archaeologists were no longer sought out to supervise archaeological projects. Instead, the archaeologist had to initiate a project and compete not only against his peers (I use the male pronoun deliberately; women were strongly discriminated against [Gero 1983]) but also against their diverse claims to significance for their projects. Archaeology being a field—rather than a library—discipline, the shift of principal funding agency to the federal endowments in the United

States logically placed it under the National Science Foundation rather than the National Endowment for the Humanities. The crux for a successful career was to cast one's projects as significant science.

The New Archaeology was new in that it responded to a major shift in funding sources, from essentially humanistic programs oriented toward historical questions to programs expanded from institutionalized science. This shift was part of the triumph of *Big Science* in the United States following the achievement of nuclear power. Science was believed to hold the keys to social as well as technological breakthroughs that marked the culmination of man's quest to dominate nature. For example, in *Science and the Social Order*, Barber (1952: 259) informed readers that "the social sciences, like all science, are primarily concerned for analysis, prediction, and control of behavior and values." Discourse in the mode of science was the discourse of power.

When Lewis Binford began publishing in the early 1960s, he signaled his intention to be at the cutting edge of the field by highlighting his acceptance of Willey and Phillips's (1958: 7) recently articulated theme: "archaeology . . . is compelled to[ward] . . . an actual convergence with cultural anthropology and the possibility of an eventual synthesis in a common search for sociocultural causality and law." Binford built on Willey and Phillips's last line, "causality and law," moving it into the discourse of science. This mode of discourse—speaking of rigor, testing, and deduction, and embellishing texts with statistical tables and graphs—enabled archaeologists to win a share of Big Science support. Binford became the leader of ambitious archaeologists, shoving aside Willey and Phillips, who had failed to see that their humanistic discourse (traditions and horizons) was no longer instrumental in gaining support.

How this New Archaeology happened to be called *processual archaeology* is somewhat an accident. The term *process*, as in *process philosophy*, was fashionable in the 1950s and 1960s (Lucas 1983). Process was linked to modernist concepts of nature as perpetual transitions within a deep structure of determining natural forces, concepts promising eventual human control over fate as natural-science research revealed these forces and the determinative factors (Ross 1991: 317). At this time, radiocarbon dating had revolutionized archaeology by providing a technique that made chronological ordering a relatively simple standardized procedure rather than a challenging goal. Gordon Willey and Philip Phillips responded to the opportunity for a magisterial reordering of American archaeology with a publication that would not only constitute an Establishment response to Walter Taylor's *A Study of Archaeology* (1948) but, at the same time, would map out the field. On page 5 of their final version of

Method and Theory in American Archaeology, Willey and Phillips (1958) introduced the term "processual interpretation, which might conceivably cover any explanatory principle that might be invoked"—a rather blatant hegemonic move! Binford lifted this mantle from Willey and Phillips to his own broad shoulders.

For the journeyman archaeologist, another avenue had opened. The dedication of Carl Chapman and a few others willing to brave political battles had won legislative hearings for heritage protection, climaxing in the Moss-Bennett Bill. Throughout the 1970s, what had once been salvage archaeology grew into a multimillion-dollar commitment eliciting the formation of private as well as public contracting enterprises employed to mitigate site destruction. Bureaucratic management of these contracts normalized archaeological procedures and reporting. Defined as business documents adhering to legal guidelines, these reports had no place for humanistic reflection or philosophical argumentation: they were to be strictly empirical, and what it meant to be empirical was not problematical. As that icon of the period, *Dragnet*'s Joe Friday, intoned, "The facts, just the facts." Both major sources of support rewarded positivist proceedings.

The situation in Canada offers a useful comparative perspective. Confederation structure in Canada gives the provinces somewhat stronger power than the states in the United States, resulting in more attention to provincial interests. Translated into archaeological funding, regional concerns have not been so easily ignored when national funding is disbursed. Canada differs also from the United States in never having been caught up in an overweening ambition to be master of the world, never assuming the national scene is isomorphic with the universe. Struggling always against Big Brother's hubris, Canadian researchers are a bit cautious about jumping on bandwagons rolling along south of the border. In Canada, national pride usually incorporates a consciousness of difference between the Canadian and the American. Without ignoring trends, Canada's funding of scientific and other scholarly research through its Research Council has avoided the worst excesses of trendiness. In archaeology, Cultural Resource Management development has kept up with and, on occasion, proceeded more quickly than Cultural Resource Management in the United States; the provinces' regard for their heritages has more clearly guided archaeological work since the 1970s than have states' heritage policies in the United States.

Processual Archaeology

Processual archaeology built on a cultural evolutionist framework and included an environmental determinist causality and a systems theory assuming equilibrium as the normal state (Leone 1972: 19). These guiding assumptions (cf. Donovan, Laudan and Laudan 1988: 9–10) reflect three successive periods of recent intellectual history: the mid-nineteenth, early twentieth, and mid-twentieth centuries. As Gibbon (1989: 140) insists, "Rather than a sharp break with tradition, the early 1960s' effort is seen as a last gasp in the attempt to preserve an entrenched position."

The evolutionist framework was derived from the universal histories of the eighteenth century, which were accepted, although already labeled "conjectural histories," in the early nineteenth century. By the 1830s, Comte had articulated the positivist philosophy of unilinear evolutionary progress. Daniel Wilson (1862) developed his pioneering, widely read *Prehistoric Man* on the basis of the vitalist evolution published by his mentor, Robert Chambers (1844), titled *Vestiges of the Natural History of Creation*; Wilson's paradigm persists in contemporary American archaeology (e.g., Wenke 1990). That the New Archaeology's evolutionism is unilinear is evidenced in its consistent use of Service's schema of bands-tribes-chiefdoms-states (this in spite of Service's own repudiation of the schema in 1967 [Service 1971: 157]). Hull (1984) discusses the persistence of nineteenth-century metaphysics under cover of varying referents for the term "species" (including *Homo sapiens*). Hull asks (1984: 17), "Why do genuine scientific laws continue to elude the sciences of 'man'?" His answer shows contempt for "those permanently wedded to the covering-law model of scientific explanation," (1984: 33), who failed to realize, he argues, that "those putative theories and laws limited *necessarily* to a single species [*Homo sapiens*] . . . are at most true descriptive statements, possibly theory-laden, but not themselves laws or theories. They lack the requisite generality and extrapolatability" (italics in original). From Hull's principles, it is clear that any unilinear evolutionary description of human history is fundamentally metaphysical rather than scientific. This condition was cloaked, in the New Archaeology, by what Mayr calls "window-dressing" (1982: 850–852).

Environmental determinism, preferring natural forces to human volition as causal agent, follows logically from the positivist and anti-idealist metaphysic that has characterized bourgeois American thought since the early nineteenth century. Trigger (1989a: 289–303) places New Archaeology's environmental determinism within, and as flawed as, the non-Darwinian evolutionist perspective. Kingsland (1985: 8), analyzing ecologists' work, perceptively notes that the oft-reiterated importance of searching for "patterns" will "minimize the importance of history" and thereby move the work toward the science pole of that ill-founded popular antithesis, science versus history. I could, in addition, point out the political effect of masking imperialist conquests and exploitation by reading the archaeological record as a story of environmental stimuli and stresses. If the record of the Late Prehistoric period on the Plains is read thus, rather than as a history of Mississippian state penetration, the genocidal horrors of United States penetration, conquest, and exploitation (Moore 1989) of the Plains Indians will be sleeping dogs let lie. At the least, focusing on environmental factors allows archaeologists to utilize methodologies from the sciences and produces sets of citations heavily weighted by references published as science, creating for readers an instant impression of science—a nice touch for proposals submitted to the National Science Foundation.

Systems theory became popular in the mid-twentieth century, promoted by Shannon and von Bertalanffy as a means of introducing more rigor into analyses of complex phenomena. Systems theorists modeled series of equilibria representing normative states of populations and sought to identify "disturbing" factors, which processual archaeologists have usually assumed to be more or less direct environmental changes, confirming their image of archaeology as a natural science searching to identify broad regularities or laws. Systems theory was popular in ecology, the obvious ally of an archaeology inclined toward postulating environmental determinism. Kingsland (1985: 128) remarks that the introduction of mathematical modeling convinced many ecologists that "ecology was on the way to being an exact science." Systems theory is one type of mathematical modeling, and its use lends this aura of science.

I cite Kingsland's study of our sister science because ecology has been swinging along a track parallel to archaeology. Like archaeology, ecology has clearly revealed socioeconomic influences affecting the popularity of its dominant theories. Simberloff (1982: 88–89) pointed out that the National Science Foundation's Ecosystem Studies program had twice the money and half the proposals of the General Ecology Program, which suggests a state bias toward the normative, reductionist approach congruent with bureaucratic values. In ecology, as in archaeology, the presuppositions of this approach—that the whole is a recognizable bounded set of interacting parts, that equilibria are norms, that variation is deviation from a norm—have increasingly been called into question; the ecosystem, for example, is seen to be a model with tenuous justification (Simberloff 1982; Kingsland 1985: 8).

Normative, reductionist, essentialist thinking is on the wane in many fields. Neo-Darwinian biology reasserts the critical, central significance of chance. Heisenberg's Uncertainty Principle is extended to highlight the indeterminacy of anthropological, sociological, and psychological observation. In literary studies, deconstruction trumpets the fragility of the text.

These movements have in common a resurrection of skepticism, a rejection of positivist assumptions. Their popularity is a sign of academics' recognition of the naïveté of the promises claimed for positivist science beginning with Comte in the 1830s.

The Postprocessual World

Now we have postprocessual archaeology, its name echoing "postmodernism." Postprocessual archeology is an eclectic movement incorporating efforts to reorganize artifacts' roles in communicating social understanding, efforts to recover evidence of societal roles including gender, the selective use of Marxist principles, and reflexivity. All these ideas drawn from the humanities represent a swing away from the focus on science in processual archaeology. *Time* magazine recently noted that "federal support for the NSF has yet to match the level of the go-go '60s when measured in constant dollars." The United States lost its commanding position in the world and with it lost its simple faith in, and willingness to tithe for, *Big Science*. With less money for science, ambitious archaeologists will look elsewhere for support from humanities funding. To tap these monies, their proposals will exhibit postmodernist themes.

It is difficult and false to disengage socioeconomic factors from scientific paradigms. Speaking strictly of their intellectual aspects, normative processual archaeology embedded a nineteenth-century social evolutionism developed by Saint-Simon, Comte, Spencer, and Morgan from eighteenth-century Enlightenment universal histories. Science, or more precisely industrial technology (Barnes 1985: 15–16), is the index to Progress (for example, archaeology demonstrated that the more evolved Neanderthals used the relatively industrial Levalloisian technique to produce standardized flakes more quickly and efficiently). Leslie White championed this set of assumptions, and through his teaching at Michigan, it was carried into archaeology by Binford and his followers. It is no coincidence that this set of guiding assumptions has been strongly associated with white Anglo-Saxon Protestant men, the dominant class in all English-speaking nations; both nineteenth-century social evolutionism and White's distinctive evolutionary schema (Barrett 1989) legitimize their dominance (Trigger 1989a: 109, 118, 145, 290).

What happens when this dominance fades? Postprocessual archaeology asserts the singular value of the societies we study rather than typologizing them or premising an evolutionary trajectory in a manner suspiciously like the Enlightenment glorification of its own European culture. Postprocessual archaeology embraces a contemporary rather than obsolete concept of what science is, recognizing the indeterminacy of observational data (Trigger 1989a: 379–382). Given this openness to relativism, postprocessualist archaeology cannot resist acknowledging what Barnes and MacKenzie (1979: 53) refer to as the "instrumental interests in terms of which scientists construct and evaluate knowledge-claims." The emergence of postprocessual archaeology reflects societal shifts on two levels, directly mirroring societal concern with pluralism and accommodation to non-Western power and responding to the funding source shifts that themselves reflect a societal need to deal with peers in foreign cultures. Controlling iron or even uranium mines is no longer the means to dominance. Eric Larrabee (1966, cited in Greenberg 1967: 26) complained years ago, "The only thing wrong with scientists is that they don't understand science. They don't know where their own institutions came from, what forces shaped and are still shaping them, and they are wedded to an anti-historical way of thinking which threatens to deter them from ever finding out." To understand postprocessual archaeology, we must think historically.

The New Archaeologists are now paunchy graybeards, and another ambitious set seeks to distinguish themselves. Hard science has become tarnished. It and its sibling, social engineering, failed to maintain Western dominance. The perceived general worsening of human life proved progress illusory. Public recognition will accrue to those who focus not on technology but on social power and its manipulation (e.g., Ian Hodder). Postprocessual archaeology is humanistic because human relationships are now recognized as critical instruments to success; it is eclectic because it operates in a universe composed of competing First, Second, Third, and Fourth worlds. It gains support because it is seen embodying appropriate concerns; it speaks today's language.

Conclusion

Plains archaeologists seldom paid much heed to philosophical labels. Americanist archaeology's guiding assumptions made the Plains distinctly uninviting to theorists because unilinear evolutionism and environmental determinism told us that Plains societies were simple and uninteresting. Why would archaeologists work on the Plains? To earn a living. Maybe they lacked the panache to get tenured as prestigious universities' research leaders. Maybe they just liked kneeling outdoors in that ever-blowing wind, solving the puzzle of how people once lived on the prairies (those were the fellows who kept their Marshalltowns shiny without gilding). Working on the Plains was seen as a decent, respectable job but not as an avenue to eminence as a theoretician—for that, one should work either on early hominids or complex societies. Plains archaeologists might appear to be everyday processual archaeologists, particularly insofar as Cultural Resource Management formats were established under that framework, yet few could be said to be seriously committed to that label.

Postprocessual archaeology presents a more pleasant vista for Plains archaeologists because its relativism and eclecticism let the archaeology of bison hunters appear interesting. No longer need they be dismissed as simple. Neo-Darwinian evolution asserts the intriguing value of every species and society, and neo-Darwinian evolutionary questions are easily accommodated under the postprocessualist umbrella. Questions of human relationships, symbols and semiotics, class relationships and infrastructure/superstructure, cosmologies and appropriate technologies can all be accepted. What should be avoided is any claim that postprocessual archaeology *must* use Critical Theory to see class conflict or *must* picture sex-gender classes, or ethnicity, or whatever seems to be selling. Plains archaeologists, like other scientists and humanities scholars, cannot ignore fashion if they want to be given funds, but taking cognizance of fashion need not mean blind fad-following. New Archaeologists made their discourse look scientific, and the postprocessualists make theirs look humanistic. Perhaps the challenge to Plains archaeologists is to build a discourse that persuasively encompasses our range of data.

2

We Do Not Need Your Past!

Politics, Indian Time, and Plains Archaeology

Larry J. Zimmerman

In his recent lecture at the University of South Dakota, William Means, Oglala activist and coordinator of the International Indian Treaty Council, chastised archaeologists for what he called "a ridiculous construction of the past." In his view the Sioux, as well as other American Indian nations, were put in North America by the Creator. He told us, "If you want proof, just read Jeffrey Goodman's [1981] book, *American Genesis,*" which proved Indians originated here and that they did not come across the Bering land bridge. He avowed: "We do not need your past!"

Means's sentiment is similar to that expressed by many Indian people who tell archaeologists, "You got it all wrong." When archaeologists hear comments like this, they are prone to label the speaker as militant, ignorant, or antiscientific. In doing so, archaeologists fail to recognize biases in their own methods of interpreting (pre)history and cut themselves off from a potentially useful world view that might broaden (re)constructions of the past.

The intent of this chapter is to examine some variations between archaeological and Indian views of the past and of time and to show how these views have been important in two cases involving archaeological interpretation on the Plains. Views of time and the past can be documented from both published sources and transcripts of meetings between Indians and archaeologists, especially those about the reburial issue. The particular cases involve the Yellow Thunder Camp in the Black Hills of South Dakota and investigations by the Northern Cheyenne into the historical archaeological case of the Dull Knife breakout from Fort Robinson in 1879. Both show how interpretations that considered the Indian view resulted in a past that satisfied both groups and worked to augment the archaeological record. Both also demonstrate that archaeological research is not a value-free science; the pasts archaeologists construct have an impact on the people they study.

How Can There Be Different Pasts?

Most archaeologists agree that archaeological research has at least four major goals. The first goal is to construct culture histories, to determine where particular cultures fit in place, time, and relationship to each other. The second goal is to document the lifeways of peoples of the past—patterns of subsistence, residence patterns, technologies, religious beliefs, and other cultural practices. The third goal is to examine cultural processes, those factors that influence how a culture might change through time and the mechanisms supporting or prohibiting that change. Finally, archaeologists try to construct cultural meanings, what the elements of a culture meant in the lives of peoples.

When they discuss these goals, archaeologists often say they are "reconstructing" the past. Many believe that they are truly reconstructing the events of the past; the chronologies they build, the lifeways they write about, the processes they investigate, and the meanings they establish are believed to be somehow a reflection of the way things actually were. Those persons who seriously study the past recognize, however, that archaeological reconstructions are actually only archaeological constructions. What archaeologists present are models of the past or hypotheses about it. Ultimately, most archaeologists agree that the past cannot be proved; rather, one can only offer hypotheses about it that are more or less feasible than others. In other words, more than one past can exist.

Some people might ask, "Isn't the past, the past?" Those who are scholars of the past recognize that different pasts can indeed exist (Lowenthal 1985; Zimmerman 1987). Individuals, for example, create their own pasts as they record the events of their daily lives in a diary or journal. They pass the events through a filter of what the individual feels is important at the time because of mood, desires, or stresses of the moment. To another who views the life of the diarist, the events that seem to be significant might be very different or certainly might be interpreted differently. So it is with scholarly disciplines that study the past, especially archaeology.

If archaeologists learned anything during the New Archaeology's discussions about the philosophy of science, they realized that one's research is ruled by disciplinary paradigms that dictate research designs, even specific research questions. In other words, how archaeologists view the past determines how they learn about and understand the past. The record of the past is really their own construction, extremely mutable and subject to influences as diverse as disciplinary paradigm shifts or the needs of the broader society in which they function as scholars. No issues are more critical to archaeology than views of time and past and how archaeologists come to develop or "know" them (cf. Zimmerman 1987).

Archaeological Time

At no time during the history of archaeology was an archaeological view of time better articulated than during the New Archaeology period. Indeed, the very term *process*, a hallmark of the period, implies that time is linear. Archaeological time is fundamentally a Euroamerican, literalist approach that Littlejohn (1983) would describe as rationalist and empiricist. Crucial to this view are archaeological divisions of time into a past, a present, and a future. Leone (1978: 28) suggests that the construction of times apart from the present moment stems from the construction of a dual world. This duality consists of the present, which is direct and immediate, and of another world that is not so available but is well articulated and distinct from the here and now. This "not-present" is segmented into a past and future. Processual archaeology, in particular, placed an emphasis on discovering an eternal reality with a goal of making lawlike statements about reality that transcend all time and human events. This goal was pursued by analyzing components and subparts of a phenomenon or event and by seeking causal, mechanistic explanations for it. In this way time became a past, present, and future in which events are linked in linear fashion.

For archaeologists the present is the least significant, viewed as an event that we know by our role in it and, because it is only momentary, a link between past and future. Thus, past and future are more important and the present is nearly insignificant. This view is amply demonstrated in the current Society for American Archaeology's antilooting campaign slogan, "Save the past for the future."

Some scholars might point out that archaeologists consider the concept of "ethnographic present," but that notion also emphasizes the past as more important than the present. Sometimes described as "the time at which a group was first studied by an ethnographer" (Kottack 1991: 93), archaeologists use the ethnographic present as a baseline, not considering events occurring after that time because of "contamination" by outsiders.

Especially important in North American archaeology, ethnographic present locks Indian culture into the past and may even subtly push archaeologists toward an acceptance of the usually mistaken idea that the cultures they study are extinct (see statement by Meighan below), rather than cultures that simply adapted and changed.

Much the same applies to the use of ethnoarchaeology. Often associated with the origins of New Archaeology, ethnoarchaeology looks at cultural practices of contemporary cultural analogs of prehistoric groups, again to ascertain what happened in the past. The practices of the present are of incidental interest; the focus is the past or the development of general statements about human behavior transcending time or individual cultures. In point of fact, the archaeological uses of ethnoarchaeology primarily have been applied to contemporary hunting-and-gathering groups such as the !Kung (Yellen 1977) or Nunamiut (Binford 1981) and rarely applied to others.

For archaeologists the future remains an unknown that is yet to be formed, but it is recognized to be influenced by the past in unknown ways if it can be mediated properly through the present. This idea is summarized in the paraphrase, "Those who are ignorant of the past are bound to repeat it." The past, on the other hand, can be known because it has already happened. To know the past, however, requires it to be discovered or modeled, largely through written sources and archaeological exploration and interpretation. From the past one may learn or discern what actions should be taken in the present to obtain desired effects in the future. What happened in the past is interpreted through the hindsight of the present and becomes an "artifact of the present" (Lowenthal 1985: xvi). When archaeologists write the past, it becomes "a fixed, unalterable, indelibly recorded" entity unto itself.

Archaeologists know of no other way to be able to write this past except to excavate, analyze, and place events into sequences and then draw meaning from them. This view is typified by Meighan (1985: 20): "The archaeologist is defining the culture of an extinct group and in presenting his research he is writing a chapter of human history that cannot be written except from archaeological investigation. If archaeology is not done, the ancient people remain without a history and without a record of their existence."

In this common archaeological view of time and past, the past and present are related in a linear fashion, with historical retrospection and "periods," "phases," and "traditions" serving as conceptual and linguistic partitions. Developments begin and end, and events in between follow in a linear fashion. The approach is intellectual, with the past evident in the study of remains recovered by excavation and analysis (Watson, Zimmerman, and Peterson 1989).

Indian Time

Indians have directly challenged archaeological views of the past. To them the idea that discovery is the only way to know the past is absurd. They might agree with Miller and Tilley (1984a: 3) who recognize that "archaeology may be held to tend toward 'fetishism': this idea as used in critical approaches suggests that relationships between people may be represented as though they were relationships between objects." This fetishism is a nearly precise opposite to a traditional Indian treatment of natural objects as sentient or animate. It is a key to Indian rejection of an archaeological past. These extremes would seem to allow little compromise (cf. Fagan 1991: 189–190).

In a critique of Euroamerican approaches to history, Deloria (1977) says that history and archaeology are a theoretical house of cards built on evolutionary theory in which objects or events, but not people, are put into chronologies, with meaning somehow drawn from the chronology. He contends that Indians focused on people and how they experienced their lives; they know what their lives mean. Conceptually and pragmatically, the past lives in the present for the Indian oriented toward traditional practice and belief, with the present viewed as the only "real" event. Past events provide exemplars for present action, but because human nature does not change, the situation is only different as to its observable factors such as people involved or locations. The past, therefore, is the present (cf. Lowenthal 1985: xv). Indians know the past because it is spiritually and ritually a part of daily existence and relevant only as it exists in the present. A specific future is unknown and of little immediate concern except that, for a future to occur, time must be renewed by proper ritual adherence to natural law. The past and present are not separate but are in a continuous process of becoming. The past is a unifying spiritual "knowledge" that is not and cannot be constrained by any versions of time made by human beings.

These ideas do not mean the Indians were without a view of chronology or tried to avoid its use, but "lacking a sense of rigid chronology, most tribal religions did not base their validity on a specific event dividing man's time experience in a before and after" (Deloria 1973: 113). The critical issue is that "truth" was revealed in mythical times, specifically at creation, given by the gods and effectively became natural law, with time as eternal, cyclical, and endlessly repetitive (Eliade 1985: 112). As Viola Hatch, a Southern Cheyenne, stated at the Peacekeeper reburial conference (U.S. Air Force 1985: 58): "We do not have a set of guidelines written on a piece of paper to show us how to live. We got it from the Great Spirit. He told us one time, we learned it, followed it to this day."

These approaches are supported by primary orality, the nearly complete emphasis on the spoken word by traditional cultures. In most traditional Native American cultures, "learning or knowing means achieving close, empathetic, communal identification with the known" (Ong 1982: 45), and "word meanings come continuously out of the present, though past meanings of course have shaped the present meaning in many and varied ways, no longer recognized" (Ong 1982: 101). Although the past is recognized as being important, its relevance to the present is determined by what is happening now. The mechanism for knowing the past is oral tradition, which recounts the mythic and makes the past and the present the same. Oral tradition therefore takes precedence over any other kind of knowledge about the past/present, including that generated by Euroamerican historical or archaeological techniques.

Esther Stutzman, a Coos, effectively phrases the differences in approach to knowing the past (Ross and Stutzman 1984: 6): "The past is obvious to Indian people, as it does not appear to be obvious to the white man." Cecil Antone of the Gila River tribes elaborates: "My ancestors, relatives, grandmother, so on down the line, they tell you about the history of our people and it's passed on and basically, what I'm trying to say, I guess, is that archaeology don't mean nothing. We just accept it, not accept archaeology, but accept the way our past has been established and just keep on trying to live the same style, however old it is" (Quick 1986: 103).

Finally, the attitude toward discovery of the past is well summarized by Athabascan Ernie Turner who says, "Human bones are not able to talk to the scientists and leave them information. Culture talks to us and gives us messages from the past. Spiritual communication is not a theory, it is a fact. I am not sure what the bones tell [the archaeologists] of the spiritual beliefs of my people. Even if the bones do communicate, I'm not sure what they tell you is true" (Anderson, Zieglowsky, and Schermer 1983: 28). Simply stated, the past and the present are essentially the same in content and meaning, although details may differ. As a tradition-oriented Indian, if you know the oral history of your people as passed down, you need use no other mechanisms to "discover" it.

Implications for Archaeology

Quite obviously, such disparate views of the past and how to know it present difficulties for communication between Indians and archaeologists. Nowhere has this been more evident than in the reburial issue, but it is also evident when Indians reject other archaeological constructions of the past. Archaeologists are often at a loss when confronted with rejections of widely accepted notions like that of the Bering land bridge migrations and Indian origins. Although details remain to be debated about New World settlement, the basic outline is quite clearly documented. How can Indians so adamantly resist its apparent truth?

The answers to this question are not entirely evident but seem to relate to the notion that past and present are the same. If the past lives in the present for Indians and does not exist as a separate entity, then archaeologists stating that the past is gone or extinct send a strong, although unintentional, message to Native Americans to the effect that the latter themselves are extinct. Acceptance of the past as archaeologists construct it would actually destroy the present for Indians. By accepting the archaeologists' view of time and past, the Indians, to paraphrase Ong (1982: 15), would have to die to continue living.

Is there any way, then, that archaeologists and Indians can communicate at all? A way may exist if each is willing to recognize that the view of the past has legitimacy in its own context. In particular, archaeologists must recognize that oral tradition contains important elements of truth and may contain specific information useful in construction of an archaeological past, especially when questions of meaning arise. Indians, on the other hand, need to recognize that archaeological constructions contain their own kinds of inaccuracies but are not necessarily false in their entirety. Rather, archaeologically generated data can be put to use in dealing with specific questions about the past that might be useful in questions of land rights or in efforts to revitalize culture. In point of fact, both groups have made progress in an understanding that they can be allies. Two brief case studies might be useful to demonstrate how such an alliance can work. The cases on the surface may seem to be different in views, construction, and uses of the past. In one, the Yellow Thunder Camp case, oral tradition is used to challenge Euroamerican views about Lakota origins and the date for presence of the Lakota in the Paha Sapa, the Black Hills. In the other case, archaeological technique is used to support Northern Cheyenne oral tradition about one of their recent culture heroes, Dull Knife, in his dramatic escape from captivity. In both cases, however, oral tradition is the primary way of knowing the past, with archaeology used to bolster tradition and thereby "correct" white versions of the past. For both, a "correct" version of the past is important for continuation of a Lakota and Cheyenne present.

Yellow Thunder Camp

In early April 1981, on the advice of holy men, a group of American Indian Movement activists, primarily Sioux, and their supporters established a camp on United States Forest Service land in the Black Hills outside Rapid City, South Dakota. The land was called the Yellow Thunder Camp, and the Indians filed claim for the 800-acre tract with the Pennington County Registrar of Deeds. On April 22, they filed a Special Use Application form for the construction of eighty-three permanent structures to be used for education, residences, and religious practice. Using various federal statutes, they made their case to the secretaries of Interior and Agriculture that the 800 acres should be withdrawn from the public domain as had other land for several Christian churches in the Hills. In August their special use permit application was denied by the Forest Service.

A protracted legal struggle followed. The camp occupants remained on site and actually built several structures. Federal marshals tried to evict the Indians and participated in planning a government attack on the camp. Several arrests of Indians on minor charges angered camp residents because the acts were seen as harassment, and someone killed a non-Indian near the camp. The case went to federal court in late November 1982 and dragged on until 1985, when the presiding judge ruled in the camp's favor. Archaeology played a key role in the case.

During the late 1970s, the professional archaeological community in South Dakota had become increasingly irritated by the Black Hills National Forest (BHNF) cultural resource management policies. Essentially, in the eyes of the Council of South Dakota Archaeologists (CSDA), the BHNF was neglecting the resources. Of particular concern was the use of poorly trained and supervised paraprofessionals to survey timber sales. Even when presented with evidence that their program was finding substantially fewer sites than professionals found in similar areas, the BHNF refused to change policies. CSDA members were most frustrated in their efforts to effect change and began to seek alliances with other groups concerned about the management of the BHNF. One of these groups was the Indians (Zimmerman 1982, 1985).

In an effort to forge an alliance and to meet CSDA guidelines about the treatment of human remains, Robert Alex, then state archaeologist of South Dakota, agreed that twenty-six human skeletons from the State Archaeological Center identified as Sioux could be returned for reburial. The International Indian Treaty Council interred the remains in the Black Hills, near Yellow Thunder Camp (Zimmerman and Gregg 1989: 93), which added weight to arguments that the camp residents had made that the location of the camp and that all the Black Hills were sacred.

One of the key issues raised by the government attorneys in the case related to the date of the presence of the Sioux in the Black Hills and their view of the sacredness of their Paha Sapa. Using the known archaeological record and historical documentation, an expert witness for the government contended that the Sioux had no claim to the Black Hills because they did not discover the Black Hills until the late 1770s. He also claimed that the Hills were not sacred in traditional Lakota religion until the concept of holiness of the Black Hills was invented by tourism promoters shortly after World War I. The consultant, James Hanson, noted: "For 900 years, roughly, the Lakota practiced their religion without any reference to the Black Hills" (*Sioux Falls Argus Leader* 1982: C1). The government also developed a case that the Black Hills had been little used by any groups in prehistoric times.

These contentions infuriated the Sioux, even many who did not support Yellow Thunder Camp. Their oral history contended that the Black Hills were the center of the universe. The history stated that the Sioux had come from the underground in the Black Hills, and several elders and holy men believed that the precise location was near Yellow Thunder Camp.

Indeed, examination of their oral history does suggest that the Sioux came from underground, "in the region of the pines" (Powers 1977: 55, 79). This region might be interpreted as the Black Hills. Other stories, however, suggest that the event happened near a great sea far to the east, which some might interpret to be the Carolinas (South Dakota Writers Project 1987).

Moreover, little was known about the archaeology of the Black Hills until the intensive cultural resources surveys required in the 1970s. Indeed, the prevailing belief in the period before the 1970s was that the Hills had never been used except on the outer edges. With more intensive survey, however, archaeologists began to recognize a long habitation of the Black Hills back to at least late Paleo-Indian times. The government case provided the alliance the CSDA had been seeking. Lakota oral history and archaeology began to coalesce.

In the nearly three years that passed between the time the government finished its case and the defense was able to present theirs, the Yellow

Thunder Camp attorneys built a substantial case to counter the contentions about Sioux origins and beliefs regarding the Black Hills. They also used other tactics. Among the first approaches taken was to join with the archaeologists in their charge that the BHNF was not doing an adequate job of identifying and protecting the cultural resources of the Black Hills. The BHNF had conducted two cultural resources surveys in the Yellow Thunder Camp area using paraprofessionals as part of the Victoria and Commissary-Balser Timber Sales. The Yellow Thunder Camp attorneys asked for two independent professional assessments of these surveys and found both to be inadequate, noting that they were conducted by paraprofessionals and that fewer sites on the tract were found than might be expected. When the BHNF received these reviews, it did commission a professional survey of the 800 acres of Yellow Thunder Camp (Cassells 1982).

During the survey of the camp, Plano Associates located two substantial sites and five isolated prehistoric finds, as well as a number of historic sites missed by the paraprofessionals. One site, 39PN540, contained a substantial quantity of lithic material including a projectile point estimated by Cassells (1982: 24) to be from A.D. 200–1750. Site 39PN542 was another lithic scatter of undetermined age. One of the isolated finds was a Duncan projectile point dating to the Middle Archaic, 3000 to 5000 B.P. (Cassells 1982: 32).

Although these finds were limited, they were nonetheless important. First, they demonstrated the weakness of the poorly supervised BHNF paraprofessional approach to survey. For the Sioux, they were a vindication of the notion that they had been in the Black Hills for millennia. The Yellow Thunder Camp attorneys used both ideas as arguments in court. For the former, various cultural resources specialists were brought in to testify about the weaknesses of the BHNF system. The latter idea was more important for the Lakota.

Several archaeologists testified that the understanding that the Sioux crossed the Missouri after 1750 was based solely on historical accounts by non-Indians who had seen the Sioux only after that date. Given that the first white incursion into South Dakota had only occurred a few years before, it was feasible that the Lakota could have been present in the Black Hills at an earlier, unknown date. Also, they testified that substantial human habitation had occurred in the Hills at a very early date and that they could not give the tribes a "name," only an archaeological taxonomic label. They could not deny that the groups might have been ancestral to the Lakota.

The attorneys used oral tradition to provide additional evidence. In particular, Lakota tribal historian Charlotte Black Elk testified about Lakota star lore to document a long Lakota presence in the Hills. Specifically, she testified that Lakota legend about certain positions of the stars must have put the Lakota in the Black Hills near the Harney Peak area nearly seven thousand years ago.

Neither the testimony of the archaeologists nor the historian could be refuted by the government, although all realized that neither by any means proved the Lakota had been in the Black Hills earlier than A.D. 1750. What the testimony did accomplish was to link evidence in such a way as to say that the notion was feasible. The Lakota were happy that their oral tradition was corroborated, however minimally.

In the end, Judge Donald O'Brien found in favor of the Yellow Thunder Camp, but the case was overturned on appeal. Archaeology and oral tradition were not mentioned in any of the opinions rendered about the case, but the trial testimony did have an impact on BHNF. Since that time the agency has been far more responsive about concerns for cultural resources in the Black Hills.

The Northern Cheyenne and the Dull Knife Outbreak of 1879

The second case involves historical interpretation of the "outbreak" of Dull Knife and his Northern Cheyenne people from Fort Robinson, Nebraska, on January 9, 1879. The story has been well documented by books such as Sandoz's (1953) *Cheyenne Autumn* and the military hearings about the outbreak. Northern Cheyenne oral tradition tells a somewhat different version of the episode, however. During the summer of 1987, the Northern Cheyenne Tribe of southeastern Montana collaborated on a project with archaeologists from the University of South Dakota Archaeology Laboratory in an effort to substantiate Northern Cheyenne oral history concerning the Cheyenne outbreak. Dull Knife Memorial College, a community college on the Northern Cheyenne reservation, was in the process of acquiring a 365-acre plot of land near Fort Robinson. The plot was of particular interest to the college because it contained the escape route taken by Dull Knife's band during the outbreak. The escape route had been a point of contention for years, with white accounts establishing one route and Cheyenne accounts supporting alternate routes. The college hoped that the use of archaeology might shed some light on the controversy. Ultimately, the college and the Northern Cheyenne Tribe wish to construct a commemorative path along the escape route and perhaps build a visitors' center to tell their story. They recognize that their past overlaps and partly conflicts with the white past of the same incidents. In building the center their wish is not to share their past but to provide a correct version of oral tradition for their own people and those whites who might be interested.

That the versions of the escape story vary is not surprising. The flight of the Cheyenne from Indian Territory is an account of courage and daring, one that caused great confusion for the Euroamericans of the period. That story bears retelling, especially where Cheyenne tradition differs from white history.

The Flight from Indian Territory and the Outbreak. Considerable confusion surrounded the Medicine Lodge Treaty of 1867, ratified by Congress in 1868. The most significant misunderstanding, and the one that ultimately led to the Cheyenne outbreak, was that many of the chiefs who signed the treaty did not understand that they and their people were to be moved south to Indian Territory. In November 1872, a party of chiefs from several Northern Plains tribes traveled to Washington to express their desire to President Grant to stay in the North. Dull Knife and Little Wolf of the Northern Cheyenne were present at this meeting. Their firm refusal to move south caused Grant to allow them to stay, but only temporarily. However, with the Custer Massacre at Little Big Horn in 1876, Dull Knife and Little Wolf knew they were in for trouble despite the fact that they and their followers were not involved in the battle (Ashabranner 1982: 37–39).

Fearing the repercussions that were sure to follow the defeat of Custer, Dull Knife and Little Wolf sought refuge along the Powder River in the Big Horn Mountains. Soldiers under the command of General R. S. Mackenzie discovered and defeated the Cheyenne, destroying their food supply and killing many horses. This defeat was significant for the Cheyenne because the loss of this battle caused some among them to consider surrender for the first time.

Under Dull Knife, the Cheyenne eventually surrendered to General Mackenzie at Fort Robinson in western Nebraska in April 1877. The government's intention was to consolidate the Northern and Southern Cheyenne tribes, although the tribes had by then evolved into somewhat different peoples, living in totally different environments. After much deliberation, the Cheyenne finally consented to move south to Indian Territory on what they considered a trial basis. The journey was a difficult one, taking seventy days.

Immediately on their arrival at the Darlington Agency (Fort Reno) near present-day Oklahoma City in August 1877, the Cheyenne were racked with sickness. Exposure to the unfamiliar southern Indians, combined with exhaustion, insufficient food and clothing, and unfamiliar climate, caused the Cheyenne to die off. Only one doctor was stationed for the more than five thousand Indians living at the Darlington Agency at that time. He was given almost no medical supplies, and none arrived for almost a year. More than two-thirds of the northerners were soon sick with fever and plague. That winter, forty-one Northern Cheyenne died (Grinnell 1915: 400–401; Board of Indian Commissioners 1880; Sandoz 1953: 11).

Mounting pressure from Dull Knife's and Little Wolf's people, combined with the chiefs' own miseries (Dull Knife had contracted pneumonia), caused them to flee north to their homeland in September 1878. They made no secret of their desires and plans to leave. In council with Indian Agent Miles, Dull Knife stated simply, "My friend, I am leaving," and left the room with his family. Little Wolf went so far as to ask that the soldiers allow the Cheyenne to get a few days' journey from the post before setting out after them. He said that some of his people wished to remain, and they did not wish to bloody the ground of their future home. He stated that when the inevitable fighting began, he wanted it to begin away from their relatives and friends who had chosen to stay (Ashabranner 1982: 42).

The 353 Cheyenne staged a remarkable running battle, with the military never able to overtake them. Although the Indians were still in extremely poor physical health and had few horses, scant provisions, and relatively few firearms, they managed to elude the soldiers for many miles and had only four major encounters. After the band crossed the North Platte River in Nebraska, they split into two groups; one was led by Dull Knife, and the other was led by Little Wolf. Little Wolf wished to return to the Powder River country. Dull Knife mistakenly figured that his group would be safe at the Red Cloud Agency near Fort Robinson, but he did not know that Red Cloud had been relocated to Pine Ridge. Little Wolf's band settled into the Sand Hills of northwestern Nebraska for a relatively peaceful winter. Dull Knife's people were not so lucky.

In late October 1878, the Third Cavalry from Fort Robinson located Dull Knife and persuaded him to surrender. The surrender was not without incident. When the young men of Dull Knife's group learned that everyone was being conducted to Fort Robinson, they incited the people to scatter and dig rifle pits for a last stand; eventually, however, the entire group was rounded up and led to the fort.

On the way to Fort Robinson, a seemingly trivial event took place that would have disastrous consequences. Leaf, the wife of Bull Hump (Dull Knife's son), jumped from a wagon and hid in the snow as the convoy moved past. Once the Indians were settled in at the fort, she entered the camp disguised as a male Sioux scout and convinced Bull Hump to come away with her. Dull Knife's people had a decent time for a month or so, having the run of the fort and permission to hunt (from which many believe that reconnaissance of the terrain was secretly conducted). One day, the cook discovered the absence of Bull Hump by having one cup too many at breakfast time. Although he kept Bull Hump's flight secret for a day, the cook finally alerted Captain Wessels, the commanding officer.

Although both Bull Hump and Leaf were recaptured, the Cheyenne were locked into their barracks and told they would be sent south to Indian Territory again. Dull Knife flatly refused and stated that they would all die before returning to the "land of sickness." Shortly thereafter, Wessels cut off the Indians' food rations in an attempt to starve them into submission, a plan that failed. He then cut off the water supply, but still the Cheyenne refused to consent to the journey south. After five days with no food, three days with no water (accounts vary on the exact number of days for both), and the imprisonment of Wild Hog, Crow, and Strong Left Hand—all three influential leaders—the Indians had enough.

On the bright, moonlit evening of January 9, 1879, Dull Knife's people broke from the barracks. Although they had only five rifles and an assortment of old pistols, the group staged a running battle that saw nearly half of them killed and scattered along the way. They fought their way across the old parade grounds, down to the bridge over the White River, and headed upstream. Some of the young men carried saddles and forged ahead to steal horses from the Bronson ranch on Dead Man's Creek (Sandoz 1953: 204, 221, 225). However, Bronson's ranch and those for miles around had been alerted to the possibility of the breakout. Therefore, all stock had been gathered and was under heavy guard.

At some point along the White River, approximately 2 1/2 miles west of the fort, the Indians crossed the river again and headed for the sandstone bluffs (it is at this point that the group crossed the land now owned by Dull Knife Memorial College on which the survey was conducted to ascertain the exact escape route). They made their way to the cliffs and through one of two cracks in the rocks that would allow passage. Those who survived to the top of the ridge were pursued for eleven more days—much to the embarrassment of the soldiers—and were finally destroyed in a small buffalo wallow on Antelope Creek, almost 25 miles from Fort Robinson. Only a handful from this last stand lived, and they were taken back to the fort. Sixty-four Cheyenne were killed during the outbreak. The surviving male leaders (Crow, Tangle Hair, Strong Left Hand, Wild Hog, and Porcupine; Dull Knife and his family had escaped death by hiding in a cave) and their families were sent to Dodge City, Kansas, for trial, and the remainder were sent to the Pine Ridge agency of the Sioux. Dull Knife and his family made their way, undetected, to the house of William Rowland, the half-Cheyenne interpreter for the fort. From there they were taken to the Pine Ridge Agency. Eventually, the remnant of Dull Knife's band settled on the Tongue River Reservation in southeastern Montana (Stands-in-Timber 1967: 236–237; Grinnell 1915: 426–427).

Controversy Regarding Escape Routes. The major concern of the Northern Cheyenne regarding this project was that the escape routes consistently discussed by military and local history accounts designate an area for the escape routes of Dull Knife's band that is incongruent with Northern Cheyenne oral tradition. The military accounts, and even a roadside historical marker, all present as the escape route a long, barren ridge rising to a crest north and west of the fort. The Cheyenne have long disputed this route. Rising Sun remembers his grandmother, who escaped in the outbreak, showing him a route going to the west-northwest following a drainage. The Northern Cheyenne contend that their people would not have been so foolish as to try the open ridge. Their people were weak from starvation, and some were sick. They would certainly have chosen the more protected, easier route. They contend that if the ridge were used at all, only a few decoys might have been sent that way to draw attention from the others.

Fieldwork on the tract of land consisted of a joint venture involving a survey crew of four people from the University of South Dakota Archaeology Lab and three representatives of Dull Knife Memorial College and the Northern Cheyenne Cultural Committee. Four days of intensive survey were conducted on the site. The fieldwork was coordinated with the representatives of the Northern Cheyenne tribe, who provided geographical guidance while maintaining the spiritual and religious integrity of the project. Prayers and storytelling were incorporated into the research being conducted by the crew from the university. Special reverence for the land and artifacts recovered was practiced to the satisfaction of both groups.

Metal detectors were used to locate metal artifacts such as bullets and shell casings, the most likely artifacts to remain from such an episode. McDonald et al. (1991) document the complete artifact assemblage from the survey. Numerous lead balls, bullets, and shell casings were recovered from the areas that Cheyenne oral tradition says were escape routes. No such items were recovered from the area that the military had identified as the escape route.

Although numerous other possibilities could account for the presence of artifacts (or lack of them) from the time period in all the areas, the survey at least showed that the Cheyenne version of the past was feasible.

Although some might argue that the "past" of the Cheyenne is as "historical" as the white view, the important concern for the Cheyenne in this case was that the primacy of their oral tradition, a story of nearly mythic stature, was validated. The Cheyenne were satisfied with the results of the survey and believed that their version of history had been substantiated.

Conclusions

These two cases document the limitations of the archaeological record on the Plains and show, to some degree, the political content of archaeological discourse. At the same time, both also show the inherent and imputed weaknesses of oral tradition as sole evidence for cultures trying to make their case to the dominant society about either land issues or history. Both also show, it is hoped, that a combination of the two can be a powerful tool usable by both archaeologists and Indians. Much of the distrust of archaeology by Indians results from Indians and archaeologists defining time and the past differently, especially in terms of how the past becomes known. Indians emphasize the present and its importance, whereas archaeologists, especially processualists, pay little heed to the present and emphasize the duality of past and future. Indians do not have to investigate the past because it comes to them from oral history, whereas archaeologists must excavate, analyze, and interpret to know the past.

Some archaeologists may believe that the import of these cases is minimal and wonder why the Indians made such major issues out of what would seem to be minor ones, especially in the Dull Knife case. Why would the Northern Cheyenne be so adamant about correcting what seems such a minor variation in the escape story? When asked why it was so important, Northern Cheyenne Bill Tall Bull said, "We finally figured out that the victors wrote the story of our people and if we wanted it right, we now have to tell it ourselves." Perhaps there is much more to the matter: cultural survival. Again, the Indians' concerns stem from their regard for the present, not the past. As noted earlier, the present and past are fundamentally the same. Oral tradition provides a spiritual guidance, a natural law, that transcends units of time made by people. Oral history, in other words, is the underpinning of traditional culture. Time is renewed by adherence to that tradition. If (pre)histories written by outsiders contradict the oral tradition of the people, those (pre)histories are as dangerous to the people as any other threat from outside.

In regard to the reburial issue, for instance, many archaeologists have wondered why Indians have been so forceful about pursuing the issue when they are faced with so many seemingly more difficult problems, such as alcoholism, health problems, or unemployment. We have wondered why they would even worry about whether their ancestors came over the Bering land bridge.

What we have failed to realize is that our constructions of the past, if they are accepted as truth by Indians, tear away at the very fabric of their culture. If they accept archaeological views of the past as true, Indians may be forced to the conclusion that their own are not true. This is fundamentally what Ong (1982: 15) meant when he said that Indians must die to continue living. This is also what many Indians mean when they say, as Potawatomie archaeologist Ben Rhodd (1990: 374) did, "that you [Euroamerican archaeologists] place yourself in the position of opening to the world an imbalance of nature and its course. The balance of all things that grow and live today is dependent on the ones that have gone before us."

On the other hand, Indians do not disbelieve everything we archaeologists say or think our methods are inadequate. To the contrary, they believe that we can provide detail about the past. They are therefore willing to use *archaeology if they see it can provide pertinent information for correction* of Indian or non-Indian versions of their past or supplement it. They must correct or reshape the past (i.e., the present) if their culture is to survive.

Archaeologists can earn respect for their discipline among Indians only if they are willing to share power with Indians and put the discipline to Indian use, not just to archaeologists' use. This statement does not mean that archaeology has to give up its version of the past; in fact, we have a right to it. Rather, it means that we must not promote our past as the only reasonable view. We must also stop suggesting that we are preserving the Indian past and implying that there is no other way of knowing the distant past than through archaeology (as in the Meighan quotation above). We need instead to offer our archaeological expertise to them for their use with the information gathered for their interpretation. We may find that at least some of the archaeological record on the Plains is in surprising concordance with much of Indian oral history and that our view of the past can be clarified by theirs.

Acknowledgments

Many of the ideas about time and the past in this chapter were developed in lengthy discussions with Patricia M. Peterson and the late Norman

Watson. The chapter has also benefited from comments by Mike Wilson, Phil Duke, Larry Bradley, and Randy McGuire. Work on the Fort Robinson project was funded by Dull Knife Memorial College; other research for the essay was supported by a General Research Fund grant from the University of South Dakota.

3

Beyond Hearth and Home on the Range

Feminist Approaches to Plains Archaeology

Mary K. Whelan

If papers presented at national and regional conferences are any measure, archaeologists have recently discovered gender, both as a topic of research and as a characteristic of researchers.[1] Because the explicit archaeological consideration of gender is relatively new, only limited progress has been made toward outlining methods for the recovery of information on gender or theories for understanding the significance of gender in regional prehistory (Conkey and Spector 1984: 2; Conkey and Gero 1991; Conkey 1991a; Wylie 1991a, 1991b). Yet even these tentative steps have begun to elicit a backlash, as Wylie observed, and a challenge to feminist archaeologists to "deliver the goods" (Wylie 1992: 16), a reasonable request that clearly has not been easy to fulfill.

The importance of feminist research on gender became clear to sociocultural anthropologists during the early 1970s. Advances in descriptive ethnography and theory followed quickly, illustrated by the number of monographs and articles published in that decade (Rosaldo and Lamphere 1974; Reiter 1975; Quinn 1977; Tiffany 1979; MacCormack and Strathern 1980). When Conkey and Spector surveyed the state of archaeological gender studies in 1984, however, they decried the absence of self-conscious works about gender in the past. To date, still relatively few archaeological contributions to the study of gender have been published (Hodder 1984; Marshall 1985; Gibbs 1987; Ehrenberg 1989; Spector and Whelan 1989; Gero and Conkey 1991; Kornfeld 1991; Walde and Willows 1991). This situation is in marked contrast to the still rapidly growing bibliography of gender studies in sociocultural anthropology (Mukhopadhyay and Higgins 1988; Moore 1988; Morgen 1989; di Leonardo 1991).

Current interest in an explicit archaeology of gender is intertwined with two broader trends in the discipline: the growth of postprocessual archaeology and the increased participation of women in the field. Processual archaeologists have spent more than two decades defining archaeology as a science that produces objective knowledge about past truths (Wylie 1991a; e.g., Watson, LeBlanc, and Redman 1971, 1984; Binford 1983). Although processual archaeology has expanded our understanding of the past in many ways, feminist critics have pointed out that the structure of science itself is androcentric and ethnocentric (Bleier 1986a; Keller 1985). Scientific conclusions are partial, not impartial (Minnich 1982), and many have begun to question the meaning of objectivity or truth in complex social settings (Bleier 1986b; Conkey and Spector 1984; Etienne and Leacock 1980; Fedigan 1986; Gero 1985; Handsman 1990; Haraway 1986; Zihlman 1987).

Specific criticism of ethnocentric bias in archaeology has come from a number of scholars (e.g., Leone 1982; Trigger 1989b; Hodder 1982a, 1986; Wylie 1985). In addition to challenging positivist notions of scientific objectivity, these analyses have argued that partisan ideological agendas are built into many archaeological scenarios (Leone 1981; Trigger 1984b; Wilk 1985; Wylie 1985; Leone, Potter, and Shackel 1987). One example is the treatment of men and women in most processual studies: archaeologists have tended to replicate modern Western gender roles and relationships in their (re)constructions of past male and female lifeways (Conkey and Spector 1984; Gero 1985, 1991; Bender 1989). Men, and presumed male activities, are presented as dominant and important, whereas women's activities are frequently not reported or are trivialized (Spector and Whelan 1989; Gero 1991; Watson and Kennedy 1991). Archaeologists have projected the present onto the past and in so doing have provided a legitimation of the present by making it appear to be the logical outcome of cultural processes in the past: "Since we are members of a capitalist society with an ideology of its own, and since we know that one way ideology operates is to make the present look inevitable by making the past look like precedent for modern conditions, then to what degree does our modern archaeology create the past in its own image? This is not a new question, but it does raise the possibility that archaeology may serve modern economic or political functions" (Leone 1982: 750).

Gender has been a contentious issue in American culture for decades. During the 1960s an expanding women's movement raised the visibility of gender issues and sparked significant pressure for social change. These contemporary social issues do have an impact on the production of archaeological knowledge, not surprisingly, because the present shapes the point of view of all archaeological practitioners (cf. Wylie 1985: 138; Fowler 1987). The issue is not that gender has been ignored in archaeological research but rather that gender has been incorporated into archaeological (re)constructions in androcentric and ethnocentric ways (Conkey and Spector 1984; Kornfeld and Francis 1991). As we loosen the grip of the present on our models of the past, we allow the diversity and richness of prehistoric cultural systems to emerge. Only with critical, reflexive attention to gender as a "useful category of analysis" (Scott 1986), a position cultural anthropologists have consistently argued for, can less partial and more inclusive statements about past gender systems be made (Conkey and Spector 1984; Spector and Whelan 1989; Conkey and Gero 1991).

The advent of feminist studies of prehistoric gender systems relates to the politics of the present in another way, through the impact of increasing numbers of women in the field. American archaeology is a profession practiced by predominantly middle-class men of European-American descent (Kramer and Stark 1988; Stark 1991). It naturally reflects the (partial) experiences of that select group. As *other* voices gain entry into the field (e.g., Native Americans, people of color, women), their perspectives as *others* enlarge archaeology's interpretive realm. Because much of the feminist re-vision of an archaeology of gender involves expanding our view of women's roles, as well as men's and women's relationships in the past, it is not surprising that growing interest in research on gender coincides with the increasing participation of women in the field.

The "field" in question has a double meaning. Gero (1983, 1985) identified gender-linked patterns in the fieldwork experiences of North American men and women, which she argued were the result of the exclusion of women from certain career specializations and funding opportunities. Women were less likely to pursue, or to get funding to carry out, field excavation projects. Instead, they tended to select (and receive funding for) projects involving laboratory work or museum collection analysis. Gero (1983: 51) related this situation to current American gender stereotypes concerning proper male and female work.

After examining specializations among male and female archaeologists in South America, Gero dismissed the argument that personal preference, rather than culturally constructed gender roles, could account for the archaeological division of labor in North America. Intuitively, one might assume that Latin machismo would exaggerate the trends seen in North America. Surprisingly, in South America, both women and men chose field projects, completed field-based dissertations, and wrote journal articles in comparable numbers. There, class background, rather than gender, tended to structure the division of archaeological labor (Gero 1983: 53–54). Yellen (1983) reviewed statistics concerning the projects funded by the National Science Foundation's archaeology division during the fiscal years 1978–1981 and agreed with Gero's conclusions but has analyzed more recent data (fiscal year 1989) and found more equity in male and female project funding at the doctoral dissertation level (Yellen 1991).

It appears that gender is integral to American archaeology, although not usually as a topic of scholarly investigation. It influences who has access to fieldwork opportunities, whose voices are heard telling stories about the past, and what roles men and women in the past are allowed to have played. The time has come to reexamine the significance of gender in our field, as well as the vocabulary used to construct the gendered worlds of the past. Plains archaeology is typical in that gender has rarely been the focus of research, but implicit assumptions about gender roles and relationships have clearly influenced archaeological (re)constructions of prehistoric Plains cultures. From Paleo-Indian to Late Prehistoric times, hunting by men has been the most heavily emphasized aspect of the Plains archaeological record. Simple, universal gender roles have been assumed as well: men did the hunting and the tool manufacturing, and women did the gathering and the domestic chores. Kornfeld and Francis (1991) comment that this initial structuring can lead researchers to forgo an investigation of gender because (presumed) male tools and activities are so much more visible than female. They rightly insist that gender systems be problematized, rather than assumed as simple, universal constants.

A gendered Plains archaeology will need to pursue a number of lines of inquiry. First, ethnographic and ethnohistoric data document a wide range of activities by women and men in Plains Indian societies (Wood and Liberty 1980; Albers and Medicine 1983; Kehoe 1983). Tracing the antiquity of these systems in the Historic, Protohistoric, and Late Prehistoric periods would be of considerable value. Beyond modeling women as active members of society, however, archaeologists must attempt to elucidate the nature and significance of gender relationships in different regions and time periods. Drawing on recent methodological and theoretical advances, archaeologists can use data to explicate the nature of prehistoric gender relationships in Plains societies and the factors involved in the development of various historic Plains sex-gender systems over time. A particularly useful approach links labor relationships (division of labor, task organization) and technology (e.g., Duke 1991; Wright 1991; Brumfiel 1991). How did technological change, economic reorganization, or population fluctuations affect gender relationships? These important aspects of social processes should be at the heart of an archaeology of gender.

What Is Gender? Definitions and Derivative Observations

Gender, by definition, refers to behavioral, not biological, traits. It includes the culturally proper ways of moving, speaking, dressing, and acting in a given society. Gender systems should be viewed as complicated networks involving interactions among various categories of people. In this way gender systems are similar to kinship, economic, or prestige systems. Minimally, gender systems are composed of multiple (two or more) gender categories, the gender roles individuals within each category play, the rules for gender relationships among the categories, and the gender ideology that legitimizes the structure of each system (see Kessler and McKenna 1978). Gender systems therefore involve not only individual action but also relationships among individuals with similar and different gender ascriptions. These systems are social constructions, and, consequently, gender-appropriate behaviors vary widely from culture to culture (Mead 1935, 1950; Martin and Voorhies 1975; Ortner and Whitehead 1981; Gailey 1987; Collier and Yanagisako 1987; Jacobs and Roberts 1989).

A number of archaeologically significant observations follow from these definitions. First, gender should be highly visible in the material record. In order to function in a living context, gender categories must be marked not only behaviorally but also materially and spatially because it is normally important to recognize another actor's gender. Personal decoration and style of dress, as well as speech and body movement, become symbols of gender categories. Gender roles often involve the possession and use of specific material items and the occupation of certain facilities and spaces. A number of recent ethnoarchaeological studies have demonstrated the spatial and material richness of gender systems in living cultural contexts (see Braithwaite 1982; Welbourn 1984; Donley 1982; and Spector 1983 for examples).

Another archaeologically important observation is that gender systems must be approached as variable entities, differing among cultures and across temporal boundaries. Because gender systems are culturally constructed, not biologically given, a static, universal set of gender roles (men hunt, women gather) or gender relationships (men act in a dominant public sphere, women in a subordinate private domain) is simplistic and inaccurate. The first step in any archaeological study should be to investigate the number of gender categories, their natures, and their interrelationships in a given region and time period.

A final point to consider is that gender and sex may not be synonymous. Western culture tends to recognize only two categories of gender, each derived from a corresponding category of sex (Kessler and McKenna 1978; Martin and Voorhies 1975). Like kinship systems, however, gender systems need only loosely refer to a biological basis. The cross-cultural elaboration of gender categories and roles extends far beyond the Western model of two sexes giving rise to two genders. Considerable evidence indicates that more than two genders are frequently recognized in non-Western cultures (Martin and Voorhies 1975; Whitehead 1981; Callender and Kochems 1983; Medicine 1983; Blackwood 1984; Williams 1986; Roscoe 1987, 1988; Gailey 1987; Jacobs and Roberts 1989). Notably, many of these multiple-gender societies have been identified in the North American Plains (Callender and Kochems 1983; Blackwood 1984; Albers 1989; Roscoe 1987). The existence of multiple-gender societies emphasizes that sex (as Westerners would define it) is not always the determinant factor for gender.

Multiple-gender systems can operate even if only two sexes are recognized. Sex may be an important category, but gender attribution often involves choices among a variety of socially defined categories quite separate from sex (Whitehead 1981; Callender and Kochems 1983; Medicine 1983; Blackwood 1984; Williams 1986; Roscoe 1987, 1988; Gailey 1987; Albers 1989; Jacobs and Roberts 1989). For the archaeologist, then, gender and sex must be investigated separately if for no other reason than to bring the cultural construction of gender to the fore and alert researchers to the possibilities of misinterpreting past gender systems.

To accomplish this goal, we must carefully delineate the notion of gender as distinct from biological sex. Sex and gender, although conflated in our own cultural tradition, are not equivalent concepts. Given the ethnohistoric and ethnographic literature on gender in Plains societies, it is clear that multiple genders were recognized in many groups. A simplistic (re)construction of typical "male" hunters and "female" gatherers belies the complexity and importance of gender relationships in many Plains cultures.

Promising Methods and Topics

To proceed with a feminist archaeology of gender we first have to develop the methodological and theoretical tools necessary to recognize gender systems archaeologically. One of the stumbling blocks that seems to have retarded progress is the question of methodology. How can we ever hope to identify gender categories, recognize gender ideology, or describe changing gender relationships in past societies? In fact, a variety of methods can be used to aid in the recovery of information about prehistoric gender. After Binford's (1962) assertion that it is not the archaeological record that constrains our understanding of the past but rather the limited models and theories we use to interpret material data, great progress was made in the analysis of such previously inaccessible realms as kinship, status, political structure, and ideology[2] (McGhee 1977; Hodder 1982a; Spriggs 1984; Miller and Tilley 1984b). Gender systems are really little different from these other complex behavioral realms. Three methodological approaches need to be explored more fully as we begin researching prehistoric gender questions: ethnographic analogy, mortuary studies, and the use of artistic representations; other methods are then addressed.

Ethnographic Analogy

A wide array of ethnohistoric and ethnographic materials exists for the North American Plains, spanning more than two centuries. Unfortunately, much of this work is problematic because of the androcentric nature of the data collection and presentation: "In keeping with the pervasive European idea that women constitute the passive, inferior, and hidden side of humanity, Plains Indian women are rarely visible as individuals or a category of people in the early journals of traders, missionaries, explorers, and government agents" (Albers and Medicine 1983: 3). Similarly: "In the ethnographic writings of anthropologists, Plains Indian women are also generally ignored. With few exceptions . . . the contributions of Plains Indian women rarely receive more than passing reference in ethnographies devoted to the more 'vital' and 'valorous' accomplishments of men" (Albers and Medicine 1983: 4). Still, if used judiciously, ethnographic analogy can greatly facilitate the investigation of prehistoric Plains gender systems. Albers (1989) and Medicine (1983) have documented the variety of gender roles and relationships in existence throughout the Plains. In many cases gender roles beyond "female" and "male" have been described, such as the manly hearted woman (Medicine 1983; Blackwood 1984), and the berdache (Blackwood 1984; Albers 1989).

Recent works by Guenther (1991), Hughes (1991), and O'Brien (1991) are examples of archaeological attempts to use ethnographic analogues when analyzing prehistoric Plains assemblages. After constructing a gendered model of hunting camp activities (unfortunately, relying more heavily on Nunamiut data than on Plains Indian data), Hughes uses artifact, faunal and feature distributions to identify five male and female activity areas at a Besant site in eastern Montana. On the basis of the ethnographic information, she identifies two exterior hearth areas (male), two interior "kitchen" hearth areas (female), and an interior tool manufacturing area (male) near one of the "kitchen" hearths. In light of Gero's

(1991) reanalysis of the gender of stone tool manufacturers and users, Hughes's model is probably too conservative. Still, it provides some insight into the role that ethnographic analogy can play in interpreting Besant activity areas.

Guenther (1991) utilizes ethnographic information drawn from a variety of Plains societies to interpret features and artifact distributions at the Archaic Horse Creek site. The ethnographic descriptions link gendered behavior to the archaeological materials, thus adding a welcome human dimension to the site description. Although this approach is useful, ultimately it limits our understanding of the past rather than expands it. Unless gender roles and relationships are somehow problematized (not assumed), prehistoric gender systems that differed from historic descriptions will not be identified.

A much stronger and more compelling case is made by O'Brien (1991). Drawing on ethnographic descriptions of Pawnee cosmology, she argues that the structure of Pawnee religious and gender ideology dates back at least six centuries. Excavations at the fourteenth-century C. C. Witt earthlodge and burial mound complex in Kansas uncovered features, faunal remains, and artifact distributions showing remarkable similarities to ethnographically described Pawnee lodges as well as suggestions of the Morning Star ritual at Witt Mound. The strength of the material correlates found at the archaeological sites supports her projection of aspects of historic Pawnee gender roles and relationships into prehistoric times.

Although scattered and difficult to winnow, ethnohistoric accounts also provide a great deal of specific information on gender roles, gender relations, and gender ideology. Historic documents are of particular interest because they contain descriptions of gender systems that were functioning in prereservation times. However, these documents should not be taken as directly representative of prehistoric situations because of the disruptive and homogenizing impact of Euroamerican colonization (Leacock 1978, 1983; Etienne and Leacock 1980; Weist 1983). DeMallie (1983) was able to outline the structure of nineteenth-century male and female gender ideologies and relationships in Lakota (Teton) society based on his examination of the ethnohistoric evidence. Spector (1983), adopting an archaeological perspective, modeled the material and spatial dimensions of gender roles for nineteenth-century Hidatsa men and women using ethnohistoric and ethnographic accounts. The most appropriate archaeological uses of their conclusions would obviously be as models for Historic, Protohistoric possibly Late Prehistoric Lakota and Hidatsa culture sites. However, feminist studies of Plains Indian women make a more general contribution; by focusing on the dimensions and varieties of women's as well as men's roles and relationships, the potential analogies on which archaeologists can draw are greatly expanded.

Ethnographic and ethnohistoric documents are also important sources of information about kinship systems and village organization. All too often, although we classify societies as "bands" or "tribes," the underlying model structuring (re)constructions of subsistence activities, labor allocation, social relationships, and decision making is often based on state-level American society, that is, male-headed, nuclear families where men go off to "work" each day (i.e., hunt), and women stay home to cook and raise the children: "This uncritical projection of aspects of our 20th-century Western gender system back into the remote past implies that gender configurations are unchanging and immutable, built into the species like erect posture or large brain size" (Spector and Whelan 1989: 67). Unless it is defined as synonymous with sex (a position rejected here), gender is not a biological fact of life but a cultural category open to manipulation and change. When gender is viewed as a functioning part of culture, changes in gender systems should be expected in all Native American cultures during the past twelve thousand or more years. The application of universal gender roles or gender relationships implies that gender is biologically, not culturally, determined. Thus, although ethnographic and ethnohistoric data are useful in expanding our knowledge of possible gender systems, independent investigation is needed before conclusions can be drawn concerning prehistoric gender systems.

Prairie ecology does structure economic forms in fundamental ways. Animals are critical resources in this "sea of grass" because many prairie plant species are not digestible by humans (Ewers 1955; Bamforth 1988). Consequently, the harvest of animals is a major focus of Plains economies. However, there is a decidedly androcentric cast to the manner in which subsistence tasks have been described and differentially valued. The collection of meat resources may have been a mostly male activity, as documented in historic and ethnographic accounts, but it was certainly not universal. Women in Plains Indian societies commonly fished, trapped, and collected small game (Albers 1989), and women in certain cultures did have the option of participating in large game-hunting efforts with men (Landes 1968: 165). Furthermore, certain game-harvesting techniques such as netting were probably not gender-specific tasks but involved everyone in a community (Sundstrom 1989: 162–166). Now that net fragments have been recovered from a Late Paleo-Indian site in Wyoming (Frison et al. 1986), the model of all-male hunting parties needs to be reevaluated.

Accompanying the man-the-hunter model is an often implicit valuation of male and female roles—an androcentric celebration of male hunting tasks with a corresponding denigration of female gathering or processing tasks. Economics, as a cultural domain, involves not just production but distribution, processing, and consumption. Archaeologists have tended to overemphasize the productive aspect of this sequence. Produced items are not consumable until they have been processed into food, a transformation structural anthropologists have highlighted as the movement from raw to cooked, from natural to cultural. The significance of this transformation should not be overlooked. Duke (1991, 1992), for example, is one of the few archaeologists who has tried to explore the relationships between producers and processors. Instead of searching for clues to identify which gender actually performed a task, he argues that archaeologists should identify activities that were likely to have been gendered. On the basis of historic documentation he concludes that, regardless of who actually performed the labor, production (hunting) and processing (cooking) were likely to have been gendered activities in prehistory. The insight he provides is in suggesting that instances of rapid technological change in either of these domains (illustrated by stylistic changes in projectile points, on the one hand, and scrapers and ceramics on the other) would signify changes in the gender system, especially in gender ideology and gender relationships. He discusses this aspect with regard to technological changes in several Late Prehistoric Northwestern Plains phases: "The care and detail invested on points from the Avonlea and late Old Women's Phases . . . are interpreted in the light of the symbolic role such objects played in a society with a long tradition of hunting large-game; these points were tied into notions of power and prestige associated with killing. . . . The same type of symbolic importance does not seem to have been attached to Besant and Samantha points" (Duke 1992: 105).

Processing artifacts do not seem to have undergone similar elaboration or rapid change in style and consequently do not suggest that individuals utilizing them were actively seeking to gain prestige in this arena. However, Duke (1991) suggests that the adoption of ceramics may have indicated not a functional change in cooking techniques so much as an appropriate vehicle for the negotiation of gender relationships between producers and processors.

Gender and Mortuary Evidence

A second method appropriate to the investigation of gender in prehistory is mortuary studies.[3] Burial data have the potential to reveal information concerning gender categories and gender relationships, although the distinction between gender and sex must be kept clearly in mind. Mortuary studies are significant aids in the analysis of gender not only because the skeletal remains can be sexed but also because discrete clusters of artifacts and aspects of burial mode can be associated with particular individuals irrespective of sex. Once mortuary patterns have been isolated and the individuals associated with these patterns identified, then the meaning of the patterns can be interpreted.

Gender difference is only one of a number of possible explanations for mortuary patterning; other options include membership in kin or ethnic groups, status positions, or economic specialties. In order to conclude that an archaeological pattern signals gender and not one of these other categories, sex should be considered. Careful interpretation is required to unravel the intertwined strands of sex and gender in mortuary patterning, however. As mentioned above, gender, like kinship, has a biological referent. Beyond a universal recognition of male and female "packages," different cultures have chosen to associate very different behaviors, interactions, and statuses with men and women. Further, in many Native American societies, options existed for adopting gender behaviors outside those usually associated with one's sex, that is, for changing one's gender (Callender and Kochems 1983; Medicine 1983; Blackwood 1984; Albers 1989).

Sex is one variable that can indicate gender categories, but it should be examined only after artifact patterns are identified. In this way, notions appropriate in the archaeologist's culture will be less likely to intrude on the analysis of the data. Too often, androcentric and ethnocentric assumptions about gender roles and sex-linked behaviors distort archaeological interpretations. For example, when Tuck (1976: 90–91) examined the Maritime Archaic burials from Port au Choix, Newfoundland, he interpreted artifacts associated with male skeletons as personal possessions of the deceased, which reflected the gender roles they played in the society: marine mammal hunting and fishing. However, this same logic did not apply to his interpretation of the heavy woodworking artifacts mainly recovered from female burials. Rather than assume (consistent with his previous methodology) that these artifacts reflected women's roles in construction activities (e.g., boat building?), he suggested that these tools were gifts donated to the women by male relatives (Tuck 1976: 91). No other artifacts were treated in this way by the analyst. To re-create Western male-female gender roles and relationships among prehistoric Maritime Archaic people denies cross-cultural variability as well as change through time. Thus, although it may seem unusual to conceptualize gender apart from sex, that distinction is in fact important when using mortuary data to investigate past gender systems. Western gender categories too easily intrude into archaeological analyses, distorting the interpretation of sex-linked artifact distributions.

An illustration of how mortuary data can be used to investigate past gender systems comes from the nineteenth-century Blackdog Cemetery site (21DK26) in southern Minnesota (Whelan, Withrow, and O'Connell 1989; Whelan 1991). The Blackdog Cemetery was so named because of its likely association with Blackdog's Village, an Eastern Dakota summer village located near the mouth of the Minnesota River. Blackdog's Village was occupied from at least 1815 until 1851; artifacts from the Blackdog cemetery indicate that individuals were interred there between 1835 and 1855 (Whelan, Withrow, and O'Connell 1989). Analysis of skeletal remains suggested that between thirty-nine and forty-one individuals were present in the twenty-four burials at the site (O'Connell, Whelan, and Withrow 1989). Careful analysis of the skeletal remains indicated the following distribution of sexes and ages: six women and six men, with twenty-seven to twenty-nine indeterminate; and sixteen adults and sixteen juveniles (less than eighteen years of age), with seven to nine indeterminate. Because comparable numbers of male and female, and adult and juvenile, burials were recovered, simple correlations of artifacts with sex and age variables were calculated. On the basis of these correlations, no evidence was found of artifacts associated solely with women or solely with men. Task-specific artifacts that might have indicated gendered divisions of labor were not recognized. In other words, gender defined as isomorphic with sex was not visible at the Blackdog Cemetery site. This finding probably indicates that mortuary contexts were not the primary arena in which the Dakota signaled adult gender roles, rather than that such roles were absent from the culture.

However, when examined without reference to sex, certain artifact patterns did reveal likely gender categories. The distribution of three artifact types that held historically documented ritual significance (pipestone pipes, mirrors, and pouches) was analyzed and found to be limited to seven people, the majority of whom were male (six of seven individuals). The predominance of one sex (male) in this group suggests that possession of these artifacts did signal a gender category because sex played an important but not exclusive role in defining membership. The woman in this gender category was relatively young, twenty to twenty-five years old, and her burial contained more artifacts of more different types than any other at the Blackdog site. Rather than dismissing her as unusual, or explaining the inclusion of the items with her as gifts from men, I suggest that she was a fully participating member of this gender category, as much as any of the men. Although it may have been statistically more usual for males to possess and utilize these items, women obviously were not barred from access. I would argue that this finding is an archaeological example of ethnographically known cases where an individual adopts an alternative gender category in adulthood at the urging of a parent after receiving a vision or having a dream (Medicine 1983; Blackwood 1984; Albers 1989).

Gender relationships may also be visible in the Blackdog materials. An analysis of the total number of different artifact types found with each individual was undertaken as a way of measuring status. The study assumed that higher status corresponded to a greater number of duty-status relationships and, consequently, a greater participation of diverse people in the mortuary ceremony at an individual's death (Binford 1971; Tainter 1978; Brown 1981). The result would be a greater number of mortuary offerings with higher status individuals. The results of the status analysis at Blackdog suggest that, in general, male and female statuses were comparable. The mean number of artifact types per sexed adult burial was 13.6, the median was 12, and the range was 3 to 34 (Whelan, Withrow, and O'Connell 1989). Three females and three males were in the upper half of the distribution ($n > 13$ types), where one female and one male had the two highest counts ($n = 34$ and $n = 30$, respectively). Similarly, three females and three males were found in the lower half of the distribution ($n < 13$ types). Because no status differences were apparent when the number of artifact types was used as a measure, gender relationships between females and males at Blackdog may have been complementary and relatively equal (Whelan, Withrow, and O'Connell 1989). This view is consistent with ethnographic and ethnohistoric information that describes the Dakota as egalitarian.

Mortuary data have great potential to advance the archaeological study of gender systems because patterned information can be associated with individual people. Once patterns have been recognized, sex can be used as a variable to distinguish gender categories from other possible categories. Artifact distributions that coincide completely with one sex or another likely identify gender roles. Patterns in which the majority of, but not all, individuals are of one sex may also signal gender. In the latter case, the existence of gender as a cultural category apart from biological sex is demonstrated. Gender is what you act, wear, and use, not what your genes dictate.

Gender and Artistic Representations

Artistic representations (e.g., petroglyphs, pictographs, and decorated portable objects) provide a third vehicle for the elucidation of prehistoric gender systems. As with mortuary studies, artistic representations are significant because they illustrate particular decorative patterns, artifacts, and behaviors associated with discrete individuals. Certainly, a number of difficulties exist with this method. For example, gender is only one of the socially constructed categories (with ethnic affiliation, age, or status) that might be symbolized in artistic representations. By linking sex to artifact or decorative patterns, however, it should be possible to isolate gender from other social categories. Obviously, the purposes for which the representations were made will affect the kinds of categories found in rock and portable art.

If communication with other people was not an intention of the artist, then information delimiting different categories may not have been included. The detailed richness of many rock art sites suggests that interpersonal communication was important (e.g., Keyser 1977, 1979, 1987; Sundstrom 1989). Rock art is not equally distributed throughout all areas of the Plains, nor are figurines or other human representations. Furthermore, difficulty in dating rock art, and thus attributing representations to specific cultures or time periods, also hampers analysis to some extent. Where artistic representations exist, however, they provide a valuable source of new information on prehistoric gender categories. Because both patterned information and sexed individuals are available, it is at least theoretically possible to study gender through rock and portable art. As argued above, gender is defined as arbitrary behavioral categories constructed by cultures and communicated through patterns seen in artifacts as well as behavior. Recognition of these patterns should precede attempts to sex the individuals so that androcentric and ethnocentric expectations do not bias the interpretation of the data.

Cucchiari (1981) and Bender (1989) have both attempted to derive gendered information from Upper Paleolithic portable and rock art. Cucchiari (1981) speculated that gender and kinship systems developed simultaneously during the transition from the Middle to the Upper Paleolithic period. Children were exchanged between groups to maintain viable population levels in small bands, and this strategy brought about an elevation of the status of women because of the increasing awareness of, and importance placed on, the female role in reproduction. This strategy resulted in the first formal kinship systems, as well as a female ceremonial cult, exemplified by the Upper Paleolithic "Venus" figurines. Cucchiari goes on to argue that the exchange of children was used as a model for a later exchange of women and sees this as leading to gender inequality and ultimately male dominance. Although his ideas are at times problematic, he does utilize material data and suggests that changes in Paleolithic material culture and cave art reflect changes in the social and gender systems of Paleolithic cultures.

Bender (1989) also tackles the interesting issue of the development of inequality, especially gender inequality. She argues that domestication need not be seen as a necessary precondition for "institutionalized social inequality." Instead, the author suggests that instances of hunter-gatherer inequality should be examined, and she cites Upper Paleolithic artistic representations from Western Europe as a case in point. Using changes in the location and accessibility of cave art over time, Bender argues that categories of difference are first being highlighted (the emergence of numerous "styles") and then regulated. She speculates that ritual became more complex as larger social groups were involved, and access to ritual knowledge was limited to delimit group boundaries. Men at this time assumed a gendered role as hunters who controlled social reproduction and so, by extension, women's gendered roles. Again, these ideas are somewhat problematic as an explanation of gender inequality per se, but her use of artistic representations is innovative.

Little work has been conducted on gender and rock art in the Plains, but a number of likely sites exist. For example, the petroglyphs and pictographs at Writing-On-Stone, Alberta (Keyser 1977, 1979, 1987; Magne and Klassen 1991) and at various locations in the southern Black Hills (Sundstrom 1989) provide many detailed renderings of anthropomorphs engaged in activities and associated with specific material culture items. Their potential for a gendered analysis is considerably enhanced because a number of the representations can be sexed.

Although the published information is insufficient to allow a gendered analysis here, the Writing-On-Stone sites clearly include both male and female as well as (most commonly) indeterminate sex individuals. If distinctive artifact or decorative patterns can be worked out for those figures that do show sexual traits, those associations might be extended to some of the indeterminate individuals. Keyser argues that much of the older, Ceremonial Art is religious, perhaps executed in connection with vision quests (Keyser 1977: 51). Because female figures are illustrated in some Ceremonial Art, it is possible that women artists were depicting their own vision quests. Keyser's assertion that most of the unsexed individuals were probably male is androcentric and hinders research on gender in archaeology: "Anthropomorphs are the most common rock art motif at Writing-On-Stone. Nearly 700 were recorded occurring at 46 of the 58 sites. . . . A variety of phallic representations identify many anthropomorphs as males, and depictions of the vulva identify single anthropomorphs . . . as females . . . , but the sex of most of the anthropomorphic figures is not indicated. It is likely that most of the anthropomorphs without sexually distinguishing features represent males, reflecting the higher status of males in those aspects of Plains Indian culture (warfare, religion, and hunting) that are the subject of this rock art" (Keyser 1977: 23). As argued above, the impact of colonization on gender systems in North America was significant (Etienne and Leacock 1980; Leacock 1983; Weist 1983). Rather than project this scenario onto the past, a more interesting research approach would be to investigate the Writing-On-Stone representations as examples of precontact gender systems that may have been significantly different from historic period systems. In this way, the effects of colonization might be gauged by contrasting documented gender roles and relationships with information extracted from Late Prehistoric rock art localities.

Magne and Klassen's (1991) recent multivariate analysis of Writing-On-Stone offers some useful revisions to Keyser's classificatory scheme. Magne and Klassen, after running a cluster analysis of attributes found on 185 anthropomorphs, conclude that neck style (e.g., V neck, horizontal) is not the meaningful division that Keyser suggested (Magne and Klassen 1991). Instead, they identified a Classic Style of anthropomorphic representation (prehistoric) that was related to, and gradually developed into, a Historic Style. Within each of these classes they distinguished subdivisions based on neck form, degree of artistic elaboration, and activity of the figure. If the classic-to-historic transition is temporally controlled, what is the meaning of the other subdivisions? Do categories such as V neck or horizontal neck, elaborate or simple designs, and active or inactive figures represent differing genders, ages, or statuses? An investigation of these possibilities is now viable. The Black Hills rock art sites contain information on gendered activities of considerable antiquity. Sundstrom's (1989: 167) analysis of the technology visible in the representations suggests that many scenes date to Middle Archaic times. She discusses several implications for gender roles and relationships based on the Black Hills data (1989: 162–168). In particular, she interprets complex scenes with animals, people, and straight and looped lines as depictions of enclosures and nets, suggesting hunting drives, netting, and impoundment techniques. Individuals of both sexes and several ages were visible in the scenes, indicating community involvement in hunting rather than all-male hunting parties (Sundstrom 1989: 162–168).

Other Methods

Archaeologists have avoided addressing issues of gender directly, rarely examining instances of technological change, innovation in subsistence strategy, or realignment of settlement patterns from a gendered perspective (but see Duke [1991], and Kornfeld and Francis [1991]). Yet these very topics may best demonstrate the significance of gender systems in prehistory. Marxist archaeologists in particular have argued for more attention to periods when technological innovation resulted in changes in the relationships of production (Spriggs 1984; Gilman 1984; Bender 1985, 1989). Changes in the forces of production (tools, techniques, labor pool, land, knowledge) are subjects routinely investigated by archaeologists. Culture history is replete with descriptions of changes in technology, settlement pattern, population density, and environmental conditions. If one accepts that changes in the forces of production would necessitate corresponding changes in the relationships of production (people's relationships to each other, to tasks, and to property), then occasions of culture-history change (i.e., changes in the forces of production) would at times be likely to show evidence of changes in gender systems (relationships of production) as well. Having predicted such periods in culture history, analysts might fruitfully apply the methods discussed above to an analysis of changing gender systems.

One other method for the analysis of gender warrants attention: the contextual approach advocated by Hodder (1986, 1987b). Contextual archaeology has been applied to gender studies by three researchers: Ian Hodder (1984), Margaret Conkey (1991a), and Liv Gibbs (1987). An understanding of the meaning of patterns visible in the archaeological record is achieved by examining multiple lines of evidence, looking for variations or echoes of a pattern seen in multiple contexts (e.g., habitation structures and mortuary sites). Hodder (1984) utilized this logic successfully in his interpretation of Neolithic burial and house forms. The analysis by Gibbs (1987) was similar in that she used burial material, hoards, rock carvings, and settlement data to document the development of a Neolithic female gender role associated with agriculture and domestic activities. These works are especially persuasive because of the consistency the authors are able to identify among multiple lines of evidence.

Conkey (1991a) used a contextual approach in her analysis of Upper Paleolithic aggregation sites and arrived at a number of interesting, gendered conclusions. Her findings are particularly relevant to Plains archaeology because of the prevalence of multiple-band aggregation sites in Paleolithic France and in Plains sites of several time periods. In essence, she proposed that large, Upper Paleolithic aggregation sites represented social settings in which the need for new ways to categorize people would arise. Although face-to-face egalitarian interactions among kin could regulate decision-making and labor-allocation processes at the small-band level, activities involving multiple bands would require new social strategies to help regulate interaction in larger group settings. Quoting

LaFontaine, Conkey argued that the function of categories based on sex or age was to create a social order "beyond the household" (Conkey 1991a: 67). Thus, gender was a category of relevance primarily in situations requiring the division of a large aggregate into smaller units along nonband (or nonethnic) lines. The unity of the aggregated group would not be threatened because divisions were not made along ethnic or cultural (i.e., band) lines; instead, divisions were made so that the resulting task groups contained members from all bands. In this way, gender or age distinctions became part of a broader cultural process whereby categories of difference were created by people to serve social and political ends. In Conkey's Paleolithic example, she pointed out that aggregation sites occurred in locations where two or more abundant resources existed, creating scheduling conflicts for a small group. All resources could be utilized and shared by a larger social aggregate if several smaller groups fused, then redivided into work parties that were sex-based, age-based, or both (Conkey 1991a: 68–69). This view led her to speculate that other activities (manufacturing of lithic and organic tools, secondary use of these items to produce other goods such as cordage or nets) visible at these sites might have also been carried out by tasks groups organized along sex or age lines rather than along band or ethnic and cultural divisions. Items so produced could be exchanged, functioning as symbols of alliance that could structure future aggregations and exchanges.

Multiple-band aggregation sites are common in many parts of the Plains from Paleo-Indian to late Prehistoric time periods. In fact, Bamforth (1988) has argued that these same scalar stresses (i.e., the periodic aggregation of small groups into large groups) that Conkey discusses were operating in Plains societies from Folsom times onward. Parallels between the two areas include increasing population densities, more prevalent multiple-band aggregation sites, and increasing stylistic variability (as demonstrated in lithic tool style changes, for example) over time. If tool style diversity is seen as an expression of, and manipulation of, changing corporate identities, Plains aggregation sites can be analyzed as locations where complex social and political interactions took place. Here, as in Paleolithic France, gender and age may have been important categories "beyond the household." These sites should be examined, using the methods discussed above, as locations where gender systems may have been defined and redefined over time.

Gender on the Plains

Gender is not invisible in archaeology; it structures our field both explicitly and implicitly. Unfortunately, if gender is not made a formal topic of research, androcentric and ethnocentric readings will dominate the field as contemporary American gender ideology is projected into the past. Plains archaeologists must expand the amount of methodological and theoretical work focused on the prehistory of gender and also begin to evaluate critically the ethnocentric and androcentric assumptions hidden in the interpretations we make of the past (Conkey and Spector 1984: 28). The rewards of a self-conscious investigation of past gender systems are considerable. Only archaeology can answer questions about changes in the cross-cultural status of women over time, questions about variations in gender roles in cultures before the advent of stratified societies in the world, or questions about changes in the interaction among genders over time. Gender relationships are a significant component of social life in most societies, and gender systems can be an important factor in promoting cultural change or resisting that change (Handsman 1990). Creating an archaeology of gender will not require completely new methods or theoretical orientations, but it will require a reeducation of archaeologists, as advocated by critical theorists, to sensitize individuals to the ways in which the modern world appropriates the past for its own ends.

A feminist approach to gender can restructure the way processual archaeology normally represents Plains prehistory. Although gender need not be investigated solely from a feminist perspective, studies on gender that eschew the feminist literature ignore an extensive body of cultural, ethnohistoric, and theoretical scholarship that provides models of diverse sociocultural systems. The outcome of a feminist approach is a multifaceted past, stressing the importance of diversity in our models of prehistory. As do many postprocessual approaches, a gendered prehistory seeks to offer alternative interpretations of the past. Thus, engendering Plains archaeology is not limited just to making women visible (although this is a worthwhile goal) but also includes expanding archaeological consciousness about the form and significance of Native American gender systems.

Notes

1. Some examples include the 1987 Plains Anthropology session on "Gender Issues in Plains Anthropology"; the 1988 National Science Foundation conference on "Women and Production in Prehistory," Wedge Plantation, South Carolina; the 1988 Society for American Archaeology session on "Post-Processual Archaeology"; the 1989 Society for American Archaeology session on "Women in Archaeology"; the 1989 Chacmool conference on "The Archaeology of Gender"; the 1989 Society for Historical Archaeology session on "Gender and Historical Archaeology"; and the 1990 Society for Historical Archaeology session on "Gender and Historical Archaeology."

2. It is telling that, after Binford's exhortation to processual archaeology in 1962, some of the most significant progress in understanding complex behavioral realms has been made by postprocessual archaeologists. It seems clear that processual methods are most successful when applied to explicating the process of systems change, but when the question is understanding the meaning of past lifeways, particularly when historical contexts and individual action become paramount, the more humanistic postprocessual approaches (e.g., Hodder 1986) have been more successful.

3. Reburial and repatriation laws have significantly changed the amount of mortuary analysis that can be undertaken by archaeologists. Although I do not advocate scientific investigation of sensitive materials in the face of Native American opposition, many mortuary assemblages still exist in research collections and should be examined from a gendered perspective before reburial if possible. Furthermore, when mortuary sites are accidentally exposed or rescued, gendered analyses should be attempted.

4

Taxonomic Determinism in Evolutionary Theory

Another Model of Multilinear Cultural Evolution with an Example from the Plains

Patricia J. O'Brien

In the 1960s Demitri B. Shimkin said "anthropology is pre-Linnean." Two theoretical observations are embedded in such a statement. First, anthropology lacks a broad theoretical model, such as biological evolution or atomic theory, to explain cultural dynamics and change. Second, it lacks a comprehensive taxonomic system inherent in such a model. This chapter examines two issues: (1) present systems of cultural taxonomy and a means of increasing the number of taxa, and (2) another model of multilinear evolution associated with this enlargement. In this effort, the chapter builds on the work of Steward (1955, 1960).

At the core of any scientific paradigm are the formal taxonomic categories that demonstrate the hypothesized developments and transformations associated with it (see Hempel 1965: 139–141, Kluckhohn 1960: 134–136, Mayr 1982: 144–148). In the nineteenth century a cultural taxonomy of savagery-barbarism-civilization was defined in association with a theory of cultural evolution. In the twentieth century White (1959) revived this unilinear scheme, and other unilinealists, particularly Service (1962), developed the bands-tribes-chiefdoms-states scheme that dominates much of American archaeology today. Although Steward's notions of "cultural ecology" and "levels of socio-cultural integration" have been used by many scholars in association with this evolutionary model, his concept of multilinear evolution has been neglected. One exception is the work of Sanders and Webster (1978), who propose several evolutionary trajectories using a four-taxon scheme, which incorporates Fried's (1967) notions of egalitarian and stratified societies with the concepts chiefdom and state.

This study will build on Steward's theory of multilinear evolution, but its focus is taxonomy. The taxonomic problems inherent in our present models are seen by examining the literature on the origins of complex systems: the city in the 1960s and early 1970s, and "chiefdom/state" from the mid-1970s to present. One finds scholars defining these taxa and then showing that the people under study met it. The result has been a proliferation of definitions: for the city, for example, Childe (1950) outlined a ten-trait definition, Adams (1966) advocated a three-part processual one, Sjoberg (1960) used a single criterion, and Rowe (1963) established a series of five idealized community types.

One reason for this lack of definitional concurrence is that it is implicitly assumed that "civilization," "cities," or "states," whatever they are, are of one cloth. In Morgan's (1963: 12) nineteenth-century scheme the cultural diversity of noncivilized peoples could be subsumed not only by the taxa savagery and barbarism but by their subtaxa labeled upper, middle, and lower. However, he never suggested there might be upper, middle, and lower civilizations. Furthermore, this nonconcurrence comes from a tendency to use taxa in one instance as if they are species or genera and in another context as if they are orders; that is, taxonomic levels are confusing, leading to endless arguments of taxonomic assignment. This lack of definitional agreement, however, is symptomatic of deeper issues.

Ernst Mayr, the leading Darwinian theorist, outlined six assumptions about the natural world that biologists had to overcome before Darwin's theory could be accepted. Three assumptions involved the replacement of scientific ideas and three necessitated overcoming metascientific ideas (Mayr 1972: 987–988). For modern theories of cultural evolution it will be argued that four assumptions are present: (1) the problem of too specific or too general taxa; (2) the concept of "preformism" or finalist theories suggesting a built-in plan; (3) the idea of progress; and (4), most importantly, ethnocentrism. The first concept hinders development of a larger theory of cultural evolution because either the uniqueness of cultural systems is emphasized or taxa are so broadly defined as to defy precise delineation. The result, either way, obscures the significant variables necessary to understand culture change and diversity. Additionally, although a scheme like bands-tribes-chiefdoms-states is an improvement over savagery-barbarism-civilization, it is unilinear and unconsciously implies the notion of progress. It still ethnocentrically places our system at the apex, and it often has the preformist idea that the succeeding system, evolving out of the previous system, is "preformed" within it.

This chapter examines Steward's notion of cultural taxonomy and shows how it allows us to address these issues, including the creation of a new model of cultural evolution. This approach is illustrated by isolating a new cross-culture type, the homestead neighborhood.

Stewardian Cultural Taxonomy and Cultural Ecology

Steward (1955: 22) created the concept of the cross-culture type as a means of precisely identifying and classifying recurring phenomena. He also outlined the culture cores of a number of them: the patrilineal hunting band, the composite hunting band, and the multilineage village community. His students, Lefferts (1963) and Hellawell (1963), defined the core of the matrilineal hunting band and delineated an agriculturally based type called "incipient lineality," respectively. Steward's (1955: 37, 87–92) cross-culture types are defined by their culture cores. The core is defined as "the constellation of features which are mostly closely related to subsistence activities and economic arrangements. The core includes such social, political, and religious patterns as are empirically determined to be closely connected with these arrangements" (Steward 1955: 37). Thus, Steward suggested that the economic, political, religious, and social spheres of a culture were the prime loci for taxa formation. He further observed (1955: 42) that cultural ecology is the methodological tool for isolating constellations of core features that arise from environmental adaptations and represent similar levels of integration. He also stated (1955: 24) that *innumerable culture types have yet to be recognized.*

To Steward cultural ecology was the heuristic means of isolating culture cores associated with the definition of cross-culture types (1955: 39–42). He showed how the core of each was the product of relationships between subsistence and economic patterns, and the specific political, social, and religious institutions that defined the type. He noted (1955: 40–41) that cultural ecology involved three fundamental procedures or strategies: (1) to determine the interrelationship of exploitive or productive technology with the environment; (2) to outline those behavior patterns involved in the exploitation of a particular area by means of a particular technology; and (3) to discern the extent to which behavior patterns entailed in exploiting the environment affected other aspects of culture. Basically, he suggested that a given environment, when exploited by a given technology, resulted in a specific cross-cultural type. Cultural ecology, then, is a form of technoenvironmental determinism, but whether it is a "polite" form of economic determinism is doubtful, particularly if limited to Steward's original three procedures. These procedures have been systematically explored by many scholars, but their purpose, the isolation of cross-culture types, has been neglected.

Although Steward (1960: 180) believed limitations to cultural ecology existed when dealing with large complex systems, he was successful in outlining one cultural ecological aspect of a complex state system in a study of rubber tappers and fur trappers (Steward and Murphy 1977). That research showed the impact on an unstratified native cultural system when a specific resource (rubber or furs) controlled by a native society was part of a national or international trading network. Steward and Murphy showed the transformation of the native society into individual families that are then linked to a larger nation.

As Steward's work drew to a close, he not only failed to define cross-culture types dealing with complex societies but also seemed to doubt the potential of cultural ecology to deal with such issues: "The process of cultural-ecological adaptation becomes increasingly subsidiary to other processes which underlie state formation, for local societies cease to be independent structures that are organized primarily for survival in situations of very direct man-to-nature relationships and become subsocieties, or part-societies, whose interaction with the environment is increasingly modified by a special relationship to the larger society and culture" (Steward 1960: 180). Such a statement means we have to look beyond cultural ecology to other processes to explain cultural change. That there are complex systems whose character has a cultural ecological basis is possible, to some even apparent, but unfortunately these cross-culture types have not been rigorously defined.

Steward defined his types by their culture cores, and cores were isolated by focusing on four areas of culture: the social, political, religious, and economic. In selecting these areas Steward implied that they were the key elements for taxa formation. Thus, it might be useful to examine them more directly for that purpose, particularly by using symbolic notation, which clarifies their relationships.

Steward's original culture core and its cultural ecological model can be symbolized in the following manner: E (subsistence activities and economic arrangements) → (empirically cause) certain specific types of S (social), P (political), and R (religious) patterns, i.e., E → S, P, and R. However, by representing this model in symbolic notation the following combinations are clearly possible:

(1) E → S, P, and R
(2) S → E, P, and R
(3) P → E, S, and R
(4) R → E, S, and P

If one manipulates the symbols further one can arrive at the following combinations:

(5)	S and E	→	P and R
(6)	S and P	→	E and R
(7)	R and P	→	E and S
(8)	E and R	→	S and P
(9)	E and P	→	S and R
(10)	S and R	→	E and P
(11)	S, E, R	→	P
(12)	S, R, P	→	E
(13)	E, R, P	→	S
(14)	E, S, P	→	R
(15)	E, S, P, R	→	"type"

This notational rearrangement allows one to see in a clear formal way that more taxa can be isolated. It also implies, however, that several different causal models are possible. Whether Steward was aware of the potential for a more diverse taxonomy by enlarging and transforming his definition of the culture core is unknown, but his ideas clearly have that potential, as well as the capacity to generate several new causal models. In methodological terms the models implicit in sets 1 through 4 could be called social ecology, political ecology, and religious ecology, as well as the oft-explored cultural ecology.

The New Ecologies or Causal Models

Theoretically, additional taxa are possible, but also present is the potential for new ecologies, or causal models, to isolate these new types. As noted, in outlining the procedures of cultural ecology, Steward was in reality talking about technoenvironmental determinism. Logically, based on the symbolic manipulation of the elements of the culture core, there should be a social, political, and religious ecology as well as cultural ecology. The word "ecology" might be a poor choice, but "determinism," which is what is implied, may be too strong. Therefore, it is proposed to use the word "causation" because it is not too rigid. Thus, we are saying that some cross-cultural types are "empirically caused" by social, political, or religious (ideological) factors.

The notion of religious ecology or ideological causation implies that ideology creates particular cross-culture types. By ideology is meant a belief system, and such systems have two foci: the supernatural and the natural. The supernatural involves a series of concepts and beliefs that forces above the natural order exist that control or override it. The natural involves the belief that the behavior of human beings and the world can be empirically explained by natural laws (what we call science) without recourse to supernatural agents. Both of these perspectives are used to create a series of ideologies that serve as guides for human behavior and for the operation of cultural systems. For present purposes the ideologies will be labeled *sacred* and *secular*.

The position that ideology causes culture change is subject to debate, but Rappaport's (1971) essay "The Sacred in Human Evolution" shows this area of life is paramount in some circumstances. Indeed, Steward (1977: 180–187) argued for "ideological determinism" in 1941 when he described the transformation of Carrier Indian culture by religion. He showed how these Indians changed not their methods of production but their concepts of ownership and wealth because of their interaction with Northwest Coast Indians; he then showed how that system of wealth, facilitated by the European fur trade, was changed and directed along new lines by their conversion to Catholicism. He argued (1977: 186) that Catholic ideology transformed the native system and said the Carrier economy, although permitting several different social systems, was not its determinant.

The most obvious example of ideology transforming social, economic, and political institutions is in utopian societies (see Morgan 1976). Utopias, whether sacred or secular, strive to build a more harmonious society, an ideal society without imperfection, with justice, order, tranquility, peace, and, at the same time, a society that allows the individual to flower (Plath 1971: ix–xvi). Utopian visions may operate at a local or an international level. Although many sacred utopias are unstable and as social systems do not survive their founding or second-generation membership, some have become successful and highly adaptive in creating viable cultural systems. Two examples are the Amish and the Hutterites.

Secular ideology is the other aspect of ideological causation, and the best examples are the "isms" of the twentieth century, Marxism, fascism, and nationalism. The dynamic character of ideology is especially seen in cultures under crises. Human beings repeatedly use ideological mechanisms in response to severe or potentially mortal outside threats to their culture. Prime examples are the nativistic revivals of the North American Indian and the messianic cargo cults of Melanesia.

Successful cultural systems and potential culture types whose core is determined by ideology can surely be found over time and space. What is called a "divine elite ancestral theocracy" has been proposed, which includes the Benin, Dahomey, and Yoruba in West Africa; Shang China and Kofun/Yamato Japan in Asia; the Chimu and Inca in Peru; and Cahokians of the American Midwest (O'Brien, 1993a). The culture core of the type is characterized by the following systems: (1) economic system: well-developed agricultural economies with extensive trade, a specialized labor force, and special raw material extraction areas; (2) social system: well-developed and pervasive lineage systems, generally patrilineal; family lines are very important not only to the ruling class but to all families; (3) religious system: religious ideology focuses on two elements: a deep-rooted worship of ancestors, especially those of the ruler, and a strong emphasis on fertility rituals and general societal and world well-being; and (4) political system: political authority is vested in a sacral ruler, a royal family, and attendant nobles. Conspicuous aspects of this system and its ideology are massive human sacrifice at the death of a ruler and a royal cult of the ruler's remains. It is argued that this cross-culture type derives its unique form from its pervasive emphasis on ancestor worship and its transforming effects on other areas of life.

The full parameters of ideological determinism remain to be worked out, but the role of the "true believer" (Hoffer 1951) will be significant. Also important will be the relationship between the ideology's ceremonial cycle and patterns of daily living; the interaction between ideology and neophyte recruitment and societal leadership; the impact of ideology on the economy via food taboos and usury; and its impact in social areas via kinship, marriage rules, and communal life-styles.

Social ecology, or social causation, means that kinship, social organization, or both determine the form of some culture types; that is, political, economic, and religious institutions are embedded within social structure and are arranged and transformed by it. The literature of social anthropology (especially in Africa) reveals cultures with agricultural, mixed farming and stock raising, or pastoralist economies, which have underdeveloped political institutions and nonelaborated religious hierarchies. It is believed that the character of such societies is the result of their social structure.

Established cross-culture types are rare, however, due to the neglect of the application of Stewardian taxonomy to that literature. Sahlins (1961) came the closest when he argued that the "segmentary lineage," exemplified by the Tiv of Nigeria and the Nuer of Sudan, could be used as a "predatory" means for expansion. Exploring the literature on segmentary lineage systems, he observed that it "is a mechanism for large-scale political consolidation in the absence of any permanent, higher-level tribal organization" (Sahlins 1961: 97). To Sahlins, the segmentary lineage has six elements: lineality, segmentation, local-genealogical segmentation, segmentary sociability, complementary opposition, and structural relativity (Sahlins 1961: 99). These elements operate to integrate a large number of people into a "specifically intertribal environment, in competition between societies of the tribal level" (Sahlins 1961: 118). Predatory land expansion occurs and is successful against small, weakly integrated band societies, but where it encounters chiefdoms or states the lack of large-scale economic and political (especially military) integration causes it to collapse (Sahlins 1961: 118). Clearly, within this system social organization is the dominant vehicle for expanding the system.

Another example of social causation might be found in the age-set villages of the Nyakyusa in Africa (Wilson 1949). Here villages of specific age-sets operate to provide basic agricultural subsistence. Chiefs and headmen are present, but political authority is vested in the age-grades made up of villages of male age-set mates with an attendant headman. The age-grade system of the Masai in East Africa and possibly the age-grading of some American Plains Indians might be additional examples of this process.

Some "big-man" social systems, representing what Burling (1974: 14–17) called "diffuse leadership," are systems based on the acquisition of political power through achievement by an individual who is not able to pass that power to the next generation. Similarities of some aspects of "big-man" systems at state levels of integration may be found in the caudillo systems of Latin America and the retinue leaders of Germany (Blanksten 1951: 34–38; Burling 1974: 159; Wolf and Hansen 1967). Another example of complex systems based on kinship and social ties are oligarchies. Central and Latin America provide modern examples, and ancient Greece and Rome offer historic ones.

The worldwide diversity of societies with underelaborated political and religious organizations, or complex ones where kinship structures dominate economic and political relationships, needs to be examined and, where appropriate, new cross-culture types isolated. Scholars will have to show which social patterns of the types specifically affect their economic, religious, and political features. For example, what is the impact of kinship on complex bureaucracies, on the military, and on economics? Is Greenfield's (1977) "patrimonial state" a relatively recent (post-fifteenth-century) example of the use of social principles to create a kind of culture type? Additionally, some very complex societies might be understood more clearly by examining how political behavior is grafted on kinship in the foundation of royal families, lineages, or clans (see Burling 1974: 17–25).

Political ecology, or political causation, means some culture types are the result of political behavior and decision making. Political ecology has two aspects: warfare and politics proper. That is, it must be determined which cross-culture types are a product of war and which are a product of politics. Marc Bloch, the French historian, most successfully defined a complex culture type, feudal society, and argued that it was caused by war (Bloch 1961: 441–447). He (1961: 446) defined the core of feudal society as follows: "A subject peasantry; widespread use of the service tenement (i.e. the fief) instead of a salary, which was out of the question; the supremacy of a class of specialized warriors; ties of obedience and protection which bind man to man and, within the warrior class, assume the distinctive form called vassalage; fragmentation of authority—leading inevitably to disorder; and, in the midst of all this, the survival of other forms of association, family and State, of which the latter, during the second feudal age, was to acquire renewed strength—such then seem to be the fundamental features of European feudalism." His analysis showed that endemic warfare, resulting in the disintegration of centralized state systems, was responsible for feudal society as a type.

The other aspect of political ecology is politics proper. It deals with the institutional organization within a culture that mediates conflict between groups, deals with the allocation of resources and wealth, and focuses on lawmaking and the imposition of sanctions on lawbreakers. Public consensus can be achieved by allowing all adults to have input, some adults to have input (via age-set, lineage, and caste systems), or specific elites to have input (e.g., "big men," chiefs, kings, presidents). Additionally, political behavior tends to be either structurally dispersed or, more commonly, centralized.

It is a truism that political elites are a product of the centralization of political decision making. Indeed, the whole question of "voluntaristic" theories of the origin of the state (see Carneiro 1970: 733–734) is appropriate here. The causal character of "centralizing" in creating a culture type is illustrated by what Wittfogel (1957) and Steward et al. (1955) called "hydraulic civilizations." The original cause (much debated) was identified as irrigation, but Mitchell (1973) demonstrated that it was not irrigation per se that led to hydraulic civilizations but rather the societal decision to centralize political institutions that led to the coordination of irrigation activities.

The full ramifications of political causation await elaboration, and the many culture types derived from it are yet to be delineated. Still, it will obviously be of great importance to isolate the impact of the following: (1) warfare on such systems (e.g., features such as slavery, concubinage, specialized warrior groups, pillaging, raiding, and military juntas, whether as in modern Latin American or Africa or as among the ancient Greeks); (2) political decision making through centralizing or decentralizing processes that result in "democratic" institutions or "totalitarian" ones (see Arendt 1958); (3) Machiavelli's, Shen Pu-Hai's, and Nizam Al-Mulk's rules or principles of government and bureaucratic operation and the formation on specific cross-culture types (see Machiavelli 1952; Creel 1974; and Al-Mulk 1960); and (4) elected elites, hereditary elites, or self-appointed elites on types.

This review of the potential implications of Stewardian taxonomy reveals several things. First, a more diverse taxonomy is possible. Indeed, *in theory*, we could have at least fourteen new cross-culture types (counting just formal permutations), but actually many more must have existed. Second, we have three new heuristic methodological approaches to isolate those culture types: social, political, and religious (ideological) ecology. These causal models are like cultural ecology, and it might be interesting to examine any given culture using them along with cultural ecology to determine best fit. Third, Steward's notion of cultural ecology is, in reality, a type of technoenvironmental determinism. It has also become a mechanism to explain change (like natural selection in biology) for most cultural ecologists. Therefore, we can logically ask whether it would include economic determinism in its more traditional form when we are dealing with more complex cultural systems or whether economic determinism is a separate model in this paradigm. Finally, given the various permutations of Steward's definition of the culture core, it follows logically that we could have multiecologies; that is, the symbolic model E, P $\rightarrow$ S, R implies that cultural and political ecology in combination create other cross-culture types. That issue, however, will not be explored here.

A New Cross-Culture Type: The Homestead Neighborhood

Having outlined a theoretical means of expanding our cultural taxonomy, it is appropriate to illustrate its perceived utility, which can be achieved by defining a new cross-culture type, the neighborhood homestead. This type is derived from prehistoric data from the Great Plains, specifically associated with the Steed-Kisker phase, which dates around A.D. 1000–1250, although the type may also include the Central Plains tradition peoples who are contemporaneous with it. Additional examples of the type are found in sub-Saharan Africa and possibly in South America. The homestead neighborhood type proposed here is a substantiative example of political ecology.

The Steed-Kisker phase in northwestern Missouri in and around metropolitan Kansas City was first defined by Wedel (1943) based on a number of traits: a four-posted earth lodge; shell-tempered, incised ceramics with designs like arcs and zigzags, but especially sunbursts; and small, triangular-notched projectile points. The majority of burials were extended, with only an occasional grave good; more rarely remains were flexed, semiflexed, or bundled. Using ceramics, lithics, and burials, Wedel postulated a migration of Middle Mississippian people associated with Cahokia near East St. Louis, Illinois (about 420 kilometers east) into the Kansas City area. Since Wedel's work various scholars have studied the complex: Barnes (1977), Calabrese (1969, 1974), Finnegan (1977), McHugh, Gardner, and Donahue (1982), O'Brien (1972a, 1974, 1977, 1978a, 1978b, 1981), O'Brien and McHugh (1987), Shippee (1972), and Wood (1968). The synthesis that follows is based on these researches and is admittedly interpretative, even speculative. It is a construct of Steed-Kisker society and focuses on the social, political, religious, and subsistence and economic features of that society.

Steed-Kisker people lived on farmsteads and raised maize, beans, squash, sunflower, and marsh elder. They also used wild plants like amaranth, chenopods, and wild sunflower. Protein was obtained on hunts into the Ozarks and maybe west onto the Plains, but local fauna, fish, and mollusks were widely used. Deer and bison were the most important prey, and domestic dog was present. Evidence from the distribution of tool classes within and between individual farmsteads (O'Brien 1972a) indicates that specific families manufactured pottery and engaged in bow, arrow, and spear production; leather and hide processing; and the processing of hematite for trade with groups on the Central Plains.

Important economic relationships with other people are shown in trade: conch from the Gulf of Mexico probably by way of Cahokia along with its pottery and Burlington chert tools; hematite from central or southwest Missouri; and Dakota sandstone and Niobrara, Nehawka, and Florence chert tools from the Central Plains. Although not documented because they are invisible in the archaeological record, produce in the form of animal hides, jerked meat, and grain is believed to have moved through the system. Fundamentally, Steed-Kisker facilitated the movement of goods and people up and down the lower Missouri River and especially monitored the movement of goods between the Central Plains and the Midwest (O'Brien 1988, 1993b).

Social structure is best reflected in house structures, attendant limited activity areas, and settlement system. Sites were farmsteads consisting of houses with nearby storage facilities or trash areas. Storage and trash dump sites also existed. A string of family farmsteads spaced from 2 to 5 kilometers apart (depending on their nearness to the Missouri River), dotted the streams and rivers. An analysis of the burial areas associated with these farmsteads shows they were family cemeteries because most individuals buried within them were genetically related. Population density was relatively low for a farming society, probably eight to twelve persons per square kilometer.

These data would suggest that the local population was organized at a family level of sociocultural integration, with the farmstead being the permanent social unit. No evidence of any large settlements (villages or towns) has been found in the 6,500-square-kilometer region, but the lack of evidence is not for want of effort. The region has undergone four extensive, systematic surveys on three of its largest drainages (the Little Platte and the Big and Little Blue rivers), and extensive collecting by two local amateur groups. If a village site was present, it is surprising that it should have been missed given all this professional and amateur research.

Data on religion are derived from ceramic designs, burial modes, and a possible shrine. Burials, associated with individual farmsteads, reflect a simple social order and probably represent family lineages. Single individuals (men and women of all ages, adolescents, children, and infants) were buried in extended, flexed, semiflexed, or bundled condition. The dead had minimal grave goods. Most had none, and a few had a fragment of a pot or a whole pot or a tool or a few tools. Occasionally burials had more exotic items (e.g., a child was found buried with a conch shell necklace, and other individuals have been found with one or two conch shell beads or a conch shell necklace or a conch pendant). Thus, perhaps we have a society whose people believed that afterlife was a reflection of the present one and whose lives were basically egalitarian with only slight differences in wealth occurring between families.

The designs found on the ceramics are religious symbols, the most common being a radiating sunburst in a cross pattern. They are associated with the Southern Ceremonial Complex (see Brown 1976, Hall 1972, Howard 1968). Brown (1976) has noted that motifs of the Southern Ceremonial Complex are symbols of important themes in the religion and society of Middle Mississippians. One motif is associated with elites whose prestige was conferred through warfare, another is associated with the war captain's role, and a third is representative of the mortuary-temple complex that pervaded Middle Mississippian society. Brown observed that there are other symbol groups, not as widespread, whose meaning is not clear, including the chunky game. These themes are not present in Steed-Kisker ideology.

Hall (1972) identified a "Ramey symbolism," consisting of forked-eye motifs, nested chevrons and arcs, scroll and feather designs, and marine conch designs. He interpreted them as symbols of rain, water, the rainbow, and the thunderbird with lightning. He did not see them solely as rain symbols but rather more as continuity of life concepts. Howard (1968) noted that the sunburst or sun circle and the four-quarters cross were important symbols associated with a sacred fire, the sun, and the four-log fire. They belonged to what he called a "fire-sun-deity" complex at the core of the Great Busk or Green Corn ceremonies. Howard (1968: 150) thought the Southern Ceremonial Complex elements were part of an ancient state religion. These are Steed-Kisker themes.

Because Steed-Kisker lacks the warfare and elite-mortuary themes but has those of fire, fertility, and continuity of life, religious ideology most likely focused on the fertility of the corn, agricultural products, and probably on the fertility of people and the world in general. Indeed, the warfare and elite-mortuary rites with human sacrifice were probably what the Steed-Kisker migrants were escaping. The sun shrine (McHugh, Gardner, and Donahue 1982; O'Brien and McHugh 1987) was probably the focus of these simple rituals for groups of farming families.

The lack of a village level of integration in Steed-Kisker has some interesting theoretical implications. Wedel (1943: 210–211) proposed that Steed-Kisker resulted from people migrating into the Kansas City locality from the Illinois River–St. Louis (Cahokia) area. Two possibilities are viable with this scenario. First, these farming migrants were politically tied to Cahokia and functioned in a pattern similar to farmers moving onto the Plains from the eastern United States in the nineteenth century; that is, they would be Cahokians, and their presence helped Cahokia control its western frontier and the lower Missouri River. Second, the people who migrated 420 kilometers up the lower Missouri River were deliberately leaving Cahokia, intent on creating an independent polity, Steed-Kisker, outside of Cahokia's control. Archaeologists working on the Central Plains and in Missouri have argued and explored the various ramifications of this intrusion and its implications, but they have not reached a consensus. Still, two new pieces of data help to clarify the issue: (1) Middle Mississippian temple mound towns exist on the lower half of the Missouri River, and (2) Cahokia's boundary markers may have been found. They seem to point to Steed-Kisker's independence.

Although no systematic site surveys have been conducted along the Missouri River between the Steed-Kisker and Cahokia localities, amateur surveys do reveal scattered Middle Mississippian artifacts in the north-central Ozarks area (O'Brien 1978a, 1981). This apparent lack of population on the floodplain relates not only to the chronic heavy flooding of the Missouri before federal channel control at the turn of the century but also to the fact that the temple mound communities, extant on the lower Missouri River, were destroyed in the 1850s before the development of modern archaeology survey (O'Brien 1993a).

Broadhead (1880: 355–356) noted that railroad construction cut through two mounds on the flats west of the Berger Station (Berger, Missouri). This site controlled traffic moving down the Gasconade River into the eastern Ozarks as well as traffic on the Missouri. He also illustrated (1880: figure 2) a temple mound located on the north side of the Missouri River bottom 2.5 miles west of Cote San Dessein, which is just opposite the mouth of the Osage River. Thus, this town was in a position to monitor movements west up the Missouri River and the mouth of the Osage. A Cahokian connection in this region is suggested by Whelpley's (1914: 352–355) report of a Union County, Illinois, Mill Creek flint-notched hoe found in Boone County just west of Cote San Dessein. Cobb (1989) argued that these hoes were distributed by Cahokia elites. These data, in fact, document a Middle Mississippian occupation of the lower Missouri River valley and fill the landscape halfway between Cahokia and Steed-Kisker with Mississippian people. Further, no evidence of defensive structures exists in the Steed-Kisker area, as is true for the region between it and central Missouri. The data show a broad belt of sparsely populated land separating the permanent Steed-Kisker people and the central lower Missouri River valley Middle Mississippians.

In an unpublished paper (O'Brien n.d.), I proposed that Cahokia's boundaries could be defined by a series of petroglyphs, particularly a sun circle (cross in a circle) glyph. If these proposals are correct, Cahokia's western border is located near Rocheport on the Missouri River because sun circle petroglyphs are found nearby (Truener 1880). Rocheport is 70 kilometers upriver from Cote San Dessein, which would suggest that Cahokia controlled the two temple mound towns to the east. From Rocheport west to greater Kansas City, only highly scattered Mississippian remains are occasionally found. The area is empty of towns and villages. If these data are correctly interpreted, Steed-Kisker society was politically independent of Cahokia.

Thus, Steed-Kisker seems to be a culture of farming families. It was a social order with only slight differences in social status and wealth, reflecting a basic egalitarianism. It was a culture without evidence of connections to a larger political entity but in which the religious concepts, although derived from the Southern Ceremonial Complex, focused on matters of concern to farmers: fertility and success in crop production, with the war and elite-mortuary elements of Cahokia left behind. Steed-Kisker society is unique not simply because of its artifacts and traits but because structurally it represents a family level of integration, in a Stewardian sense, of farmers. Theoretically, this view is most interesting because agriculturalists are typically integrated into larger systems.

Discussion

Steward differentiated a family level of integration among hunters and gatherers who lived in harsh and marginal environments, which did not allow for permanent relationships beyond the family level. Those relationships that occurred were of the most intermittent and unstable kind. Occasionally Steward called the type an ad hoc band, whereas Service (1962) referred to them as "anomalous bands." Generally, scholars have not explored the potential for a family level of integration among agriculturalists, although Johnson and Earle (1987: 62–90) have examined the Machiguenga of Peru (farmers) and Nganasani of Siberia (herders) in that light. Still, even they have not attempted to define these peoples as a Stewardian cross-culture type. The Steed-Kisker data raise the possibility of this theoretical type here.

Serious problems exist with the notion of a culture type of agriculturalists organized at a family level of integration. In general, all agricultural populations must have some means of regulating access to agricultural lands and a way of marrying off their children, and they often must have defended that land and its resources from neighboring peoples. These facts, coupled with the idea of being tied to the land, with attendant decreased mobility, would present difficulties to the successful functioning of a cross-culture type at this level. Some possibilities, however, do exist.

Steward and his students discussed family levels of integration, lineage levels, community levels, national levels, and how at each level populations interact in different ways. Service (1962) too talked about levels of integration (band-tribe-chiefdom-state), and his state level is roughly equal to Steward's national level. Murdock (1949: 80) presents some possibilities because he noted that a fixed residence, as with sedentary fishing populations or farmers, allowed the community to assume the form of either a village (a cluster of buildings near the center of an exploited territory), a neighborhood (with families scattered in semi-isolated homesteads), or some compromise between the two.

This concept of neighborhood is important. Could one have culture types integrated at a neighborhood level? Using Steed-Kisker, we would have a culture of subsistence farmers who controlled the resources associated with their farmsteads and participated in common rituals at neighborhood shrines. This view, of course, would mean that the neighborhood would form a higher level of integration. Its political structure would seem to be underelaborated, and the relationships would be basically egalitarian with an emphasis on skills and abilities. Within this society the individual would achieve status rather than be ascribed to it, and each individual farming family would participate within the neighborhood, contributing the products of their specific skills and talents to make up the greater whole. Ethnographically, cultures of isolated farmsteads exist that are organized into "neighborhoods." The Tonga in northwestern Rhodesia provide an example of this culture (Colson 1960: 57–93, 1962; Reynolds 1968: 10–40), as do the Chiga in western Uganda (Edel 1969), and the Kipsigis in Kenya (Peristiany 1939).

The Tonga have the greatest identification with the *cisi*, translated "neighborhood," and within them are unstable "villages" and isolated homesteads. However, the neighborhood has great stability and is highly endogamous. Its members are linked by common interests, such as good weather and abundant harvests. The people form work parties, use unoccupied and uncultivated land and its resources in common, respect local shrines, and recognize the shrine's authority. Political structures are undeveloped, and leadership is dependent on personality and personal ability.

In colonial and postcolonial times villages were and are present, but they are very unstable because their authority rests with a headman who is appointed by modern administrators. Because archaeological data are lacking, it is unclear whether villages existed in both the precolonial and preslaving days, but early colonial information on the decentralized nature of the society suggests they were not present.

Major differences between the Tonga and Steed-Kisker are the population size and economics. The Tonga have a higher density of people (from five to fifty people per square kilometer in their 19,700-square-kilometer territory). In addition to their crops the Tonga keep domestic animals such as cattle, goats, sheep, donkeys, chickens, and pigeons.

Among the Chiga the basic social unit is a patrilineal household whose independence is based on its flocks and fields. Again, unlike the Steed-Kisker peoples, the Chiga keep livestock in addition to raising crops. No formally organized political entity exists. Occasional references are made to the existence of small hamlets and villages, but like the Tonga, they are fluid and continual shifting of their memberships and boundaries occurs. As with the Tonga, the Chiga have been subject to slaving and European colonization, so their original settlement patterns are unknown; nevertheless, the lack of tribal organization may be very ancient. The patriarchal households belong to lineages, and lineages belong to clans. However, these kin-based segments crosscut the hamlet/villages today, and all of them are subject to fission.

Modern Kipsigis society has homesteads, hamlets, villages, shires, provinces, and tribes, but the homestead is the basic unit. Homesteads are scattered around the countryside. Presently, a high population density exists (thirty to forty persons per square kilometer), and a few adjacent homesteads form hamlets and several form villages. Villages, interestingly, have no spatial distinction. Shires, a grouping of villages stretching over 4 to 10 miles, have war leaders, a ceremonial leader, and a great judge. The patrilineal household is basic, with individuals tied into a clan system; additionally, men are grouped into age-sets. Again, political authority is underdeveloped even though the government has appointed headmen and other officials. In spite of the high population density, spatially concentrated population clusters are rare, and the spatial arrangements of homesteads strung across the land several hundred meters apart are reminiscent of Steed-Kisker.

By this very brief ethnographic description we can see that agricultural cultural systems exist where the basic social unit is the family homestead. The members of these homesteads are linked into larger networks by way of lineage, clan, and age-set groupings. Peoples' greatest interaction is with their immediate neighbors, and political authority is diffuse and underdeveloped. The spatial distribution of these populations today is diffuse except in those areas where modern governments have attempted to gather people together for administrative purposes. Populations are dense, much denser than for Steed-Kisker, but it is unclear whether this density is due to the added presence of livestock, the cessation of slaving and warfare, or both, following modern colonial intervention. It is also unclear whether the scattered, diffused settlement pattern is the product of a strategy against precolonial slavers, is a very ancient system, or is even a pattern evolved from an earlier fragmented complex society.

If the system is truly ancient, it might represent an example of the hunter-gatherer compound settlement that acquired agriculture (as discussed by Flannery [1972: 8–10] for the Near East). Although agricultural economies provided the resources to develop complex cultural patterns at the village level and beyond, and have done so in most parts of the world, no inherent reason exists for this situation to occur. Thus, it is possible that a people acquiring agriculture might prefer to maintain the egalitarian principles that marked their lives when they hunted and gathered. However, it is also possible that the dispersed settlement system represents a cultural adaptation on the part of village-level agriculturalists to external cultural factors, specifically slaving and war (ultimately, the archaeology of the Tonga, Chiga, and Kipsigis should answer this question). If this possibility is the case, this system would be another example of political factors creating a cross-culture type.

A strategy of dispersing a population across the land to counteract highly organized slaving and looting operations by militarily and politically dominant societies would make those expeditions less successful in a cost-accounting sense. Such a strategy could be important in a culture emphasizing individual self-sufficiency and egalitarianism. It might be a much more effective means of maintaining those values than to collect the population into villages and thereby create potential leadership elites. Flannery (1972: 25–27) makes a related point in his discussion of the development of villages rather than family compounds in the Near East.

If we accept the idea that a homestead neighborhood social organization exists as a cross-culture type among agriculturalists, then its broad features can be delineated as follows.

1. *Economy*. Such systems are found in environmental settings with varied agricultural potential, from good bottom land to marginal swidden land, where a variety of crops will grow. The addition of domestic animals for protein would allow for denser populations, especially when supplemented by the products of animals (meat, milk, blood, and hides), whereas a dependence on wild game for protein would inhibit population growth. Steed-Kisker, which has the lowest population density of the cultures discussed, had no domestic animals other than the dog.

2. *Political system*. The type would lack structural organization and would emphasize egalitarian principles. Kin-based systems such as clans or age-sets would be used to recruit warriors to defend the neighborhood, and leadership would be informal, based on kinship, age, ability, and personality.

3. *Social system*. The type would have individual families as the basic social unit, with differences in wealth and status due to numbers, ability, and resourcefulness, and with the sharing of products of special skills (e.g., ceramics, woodworking) based on informal reciprocity. Relationships between families would be based on kinship (probably lineages or clans), friendship, and proximity.

4. *Religion*. The type would have ceremonies dealing with fertility, maintenance of crops, rain and good weather, and the importance of animals (wild or domestic). The religious expert would probably be a shaman or part-time priest, and religious hierarchies would be underelaborated or missing.

How this cross-culture type arose is difficult to assess because of the lack of archaeological data in Africa. In the case of the Tonga, Chiga, and Kipsigis, it is possible that it developed out of a hunting-and-gathering base, but given what is known of the antiquity of agriculture in Africa and historical evidence of Arab slaving and warfare, it is more probable that the neighborhood system represents a response to external political pressures (especially the slaving and warfare that existed prior to colonial rule).

The Steed-Kisker data suggest this source, too. Although Steed-Kisker seems to represent a migration of some people out of Cahokia, it has no extended relationships with it and appears to be politically distinct. Although Wedel (1943) proposed that Cahokia was the source of Steed-Kisker, he never truly explored why his proposed migration occurred. The Cahokia site is representative of a very large and complex social system (O'Brien 1972b, 1989, 1992) in which warfare and slaving occurred at very high levels. Major satellite sites, such as Aztalan, are usually fortified, and massive human sacrifice has been documented by the excavations in Mound 72 at Cahokia (Fowler 1974). It would not be farfetched to suggest Steed-Kisker represented a minority in conflict with Cahokia's political and social elite. Thus, Steed-Kisker may represent (with its dispersal of population) the same basic response as the Tonga, Chiga, and Kipsigis, that is, to disperse and scatter from the dominant polity (either as a slave revolt, a disaffected social class, or the resurging independence of a conquered people).

Fundamentally, this culture type, which probably has warfare (and slaving) as its cause, is called the homestead neighborhood. This type has been identified among late prehistoric North Americans (the Steed-Kisker phase), and in sub-Saharan Africa among the Chiga, Tonga, and Kipsigis. It represents an egalitarian agricultural people's response to slaving and war by large statelike systems. In this culture type individual farmsteads are scattered around the countryside and are tied loosely to each other in joint political, social, and religious networks. This dispersal makes slaving and war operations less effective and is an adaptive response of a cultural system with an egalitarian nonhierarchical political structure. Beckerman (1980) makes an identical point for Bari settlements in Amazonia, and Boehm (1984: 40) further generalizes this notion.

A New Multilinear Evolutionary Model

The preceding discussion has focused on taxonomic issues, but these concepts can also be used to create a new model of cultural evolution. Many social scientists believe changes in subsistence or economic patterns are essential to understanding cultural development. For that reason the model proposed here will be based on two economic levels. Cultural evolution's return to respectability resulted in part from the obvious fact that people were once hunters and gatherers, then became farmers and pastoralists, and then lived in cities, which is one rationale for building an evolutionary model based on subsistence. It should be revealing, therefore, to compare the evolutionary types developed by systems based on the use of wild-food resources with those dependent on domestic food resources (i.e., hunting/gathering and farming/pastoralism). The implication here is that economics is the "deep structure" of cultural systems.

Figure 4-1 is an abstract scheme of hunting-gathering and agricultural modes of food acquisition, and it treats them like orders in biological evolution. The radiating lines ending with letters on each level indicate the

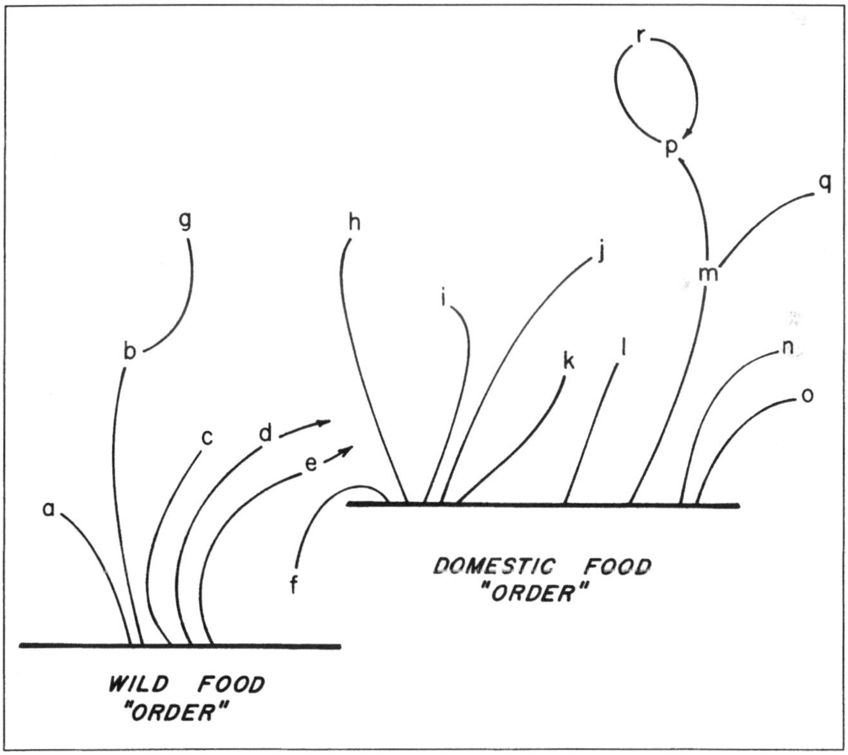

Figure 4.1. Cross-Culture Types (identified by letters) Developing upon "Orders" Defined on the Basis of Wild and Domestic Food Production

Stewardian cross-culture types possible for each general mode of subsistence. This "radiation" is conceived as being analogous to the radiation of genera within orders in biology. Whether this cultural radiation is adaptive to specific niches like some genera or species, or is more general, remains to be ascertained. Certainly Steward's family and patrilineal hunting bands are ecologically adapted, as are the multilineage villages of the American Southwest or the protolineal villages outlined by Hellawell (1963), but it is doubtful, or at least unclear at this time, that "imperial" or "state" systems have such a base.

The model proposed here differs from Steward's (1955) multilinear model in that his model emphasized parallel regularities and causality between the Old and New worlds. In *The Theory of Cultural Change* (table 4), Steward presents what is basically a unilinear scheme in the following order: hunting and gathering, incipient agriculture, the formative, regional florescent states, initial empire, Dark Ages, cyclical imperial conquests, Iron Age culture, and the Industrial Revolution. The multilinear aspects of his scheme are the parallelisms throughout the world denoted by specific areal cultural traditions.

The model proposed in this chapter (see Figures 4-2 and 4-3) is only generally tied to specific chronological development and would be tied to a specific culture only if it represented a unique cross-culture type. Under this scheme, band-tribal-chiefdom systems (actually the various cross-culture types encompassed in them) are not viewed as survivals or anachronisms but adaptations to conditions that may be either unique or recurring; if the latter, the associated type will appear over and over through time and space. Thus, some cross-culture types develop out of others, and some are very ancient and successful ways of life. The issue is to identify them and their parameters and to integrate them into a larger theory of culture change.

Conclusions

In order to achieve the modern synthetic theory of biological evolution it was necessary to develop a classification system (derived from Linnean taxonomy) that orders the basic diversity of the biological world in an array going from the simple to the complex. Populations are subject to continual change in which complex forms can be replaced by simple ones, or vice versa, in an endless process of adaptation to changing circumstances. Four mechanisms have been isolated to explain this continual

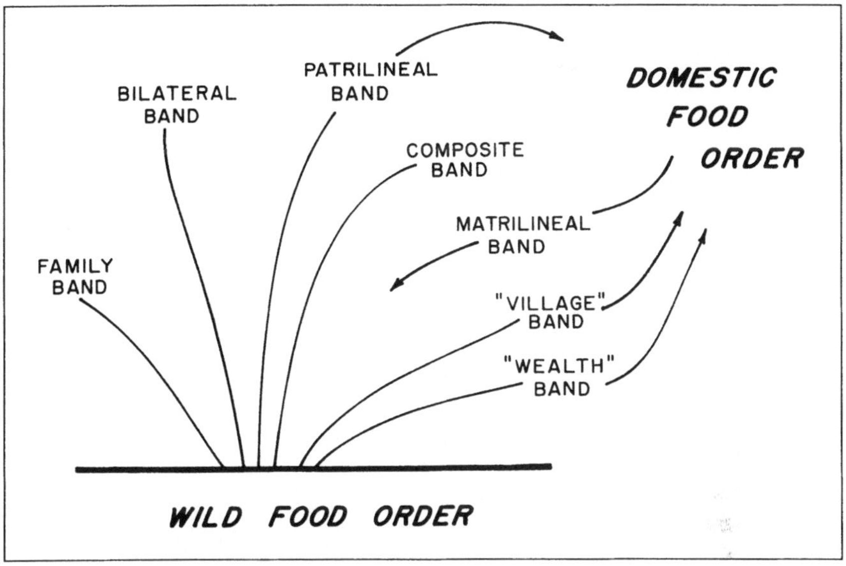

Figure 4-2. The Adaptive Radiation of Some Cross-Culture Types Defined by Steward. The "Village" and "Wealth" bands represent groups like the California Indians and the Northwest Coast Indians whose "types" remain to be defined.

change: natural selection, mutation, genetic drift, and hybridization. Through various combinations of these mechanisms, old forms are replaced by new ones in an endless, dynamic array.

This chapter suggests that a theory of multilinear cultural evolution can be created, based on Stewardian classification, which orders cultural diversity on two levels: wild-food collection and domestic food production. Furthermore, four (perhaps five if classic economic determinism is separate from cultural ecology) heuristic methodologies exist for isolating these types: (1) cultural ecology, or technoenvironmental determinism, where economic and subsistence features in interaction with environmental and technological features cause specific cross-culture types (the family or ad hoc band, patrilineal band, or incipient lineality); (2) political ecology, where warfare or political decision making causes specific types (Bloch's feudal society, Mitchell's hydraulic society, or the homestead neighborhood); (3) ideological ecology, where sacred and secular ideologies create specific types (a divine elite ancestral theocracy or an Amish, Nazi, or Marxist type); and (4) social ecology, where kinship or social organization causes specific types (predatory segmentary lineages or age-set villages). It is also suggested that very complex cultural systems have multiecological origins.

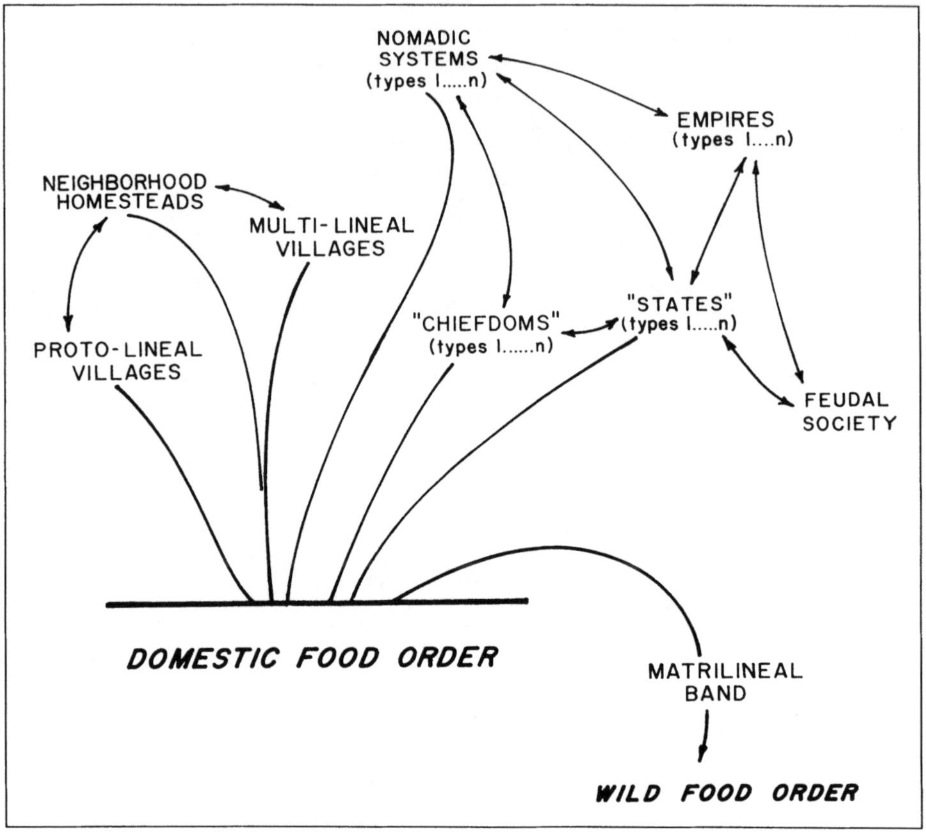

Figure 4-3. The Adaptive Radiation of Some Cross-Culture Types Defined by Steward and His Students. Some like Chiefdoms, States, Empires, and Nomad types remain to be delineated as cross-culture types.

Two other comments are appropriate. Some scholars may view the nondifferentiation of highly complex agricultural societies from less complex ones and their placement on the same evolutionary scale (see Figure 4-3) as incorrect. Two possibilities can be suggested in response: first, apes and horses are still mammals (i.e., we are being ethnocentric), or second, another level exists above the domestic food production, and if the latter, is it not possible that the level concerns what Wolfe (1977) calls the "supranational" level? He suggests that this level has a new, novel mode of production and that imperial states and colonialism are transitional subsystems of this higher level. Also, readers will note the apparent neglect of the idealism versus materialism debate. These ideas are not discussed here because this chapter focuses on cultural evolution alone. Clearly those issues relate to the different segments of the model proposed here and might even resolve some of that debate.

Finally, as mentioned earlier, Steward's notion of cultural ecology has become a causal model for most, if not all, cultural ecologists. It has become a mechanism to explain culture change such as natural selection in evolutionary biology. Is it not possible that the new causal models, "ecologies," proposed here, heuristic methodologies to isolate additional cross-culture types, may, if they prove empirically successful, become additional mechanisms to explain change in an enlarged and expanded theory of cultural evolution?

Acknowledgments

This chapter has benefited immensely from the often long and detailed comments of many friends. To them all I extend my heartiest thanks. They are archaeologists Dena F. Dincauze, Charles Di Peso, Gloria Fenner, Elaine Bluhm Herold, Alice B. Kehoe, Susan Kus, William A. Longacre, and Donna C. Roper; cultural anthropologists Janet Benson, Barry Michie, Martin and Harriet Ottenheimer, Demitri B. Shimkin, M. Estellie Smith, and Robert B. Taylor; sociologists Lonnie Athens, Lelah Dushkin, Eugene A. Friedmann, and George Peters; sociologists and historians John Langellier, Donald Mrozek, and Robin Higham. The Steed-Kisker section of this chapter has been read by Janet Benson, Barry Michie, and Harriet and Martin Ottenheimer. Their comments, suggestions, and criticisms all helped to hone and clarify the ideas presented herein. Finally, Dr. Elizabeth Colson kindly answered my questions on Tonga culture, and I hope I have not abused her answers by my interpretations. This chapter also benefited immensely from the comments of its various anonymous reviewers over the years and most especially from the first who has the greatest faith in it. To them all my deepest thanks. Additionally, I am most grateful to the editors of this volume, Philip Duke and Michael C. Wilson, both for their helpful and insightful comments on the manuscript as well as their acceptance of it.

5

Predictive Modeling and Cultural Resource Management

An Alternative View from the Plains Periphery

Monica Bargielski Weimer

A common criticism of nonprocessual approaches to archaeological interpretation regards the inadequacy of methodological applications (Binford and Stone 1988; Watson 1989). This failure to provide "cookbook" methods of analysis is at least partially defensible because one of the objectives of the movement is to offer alternatives to a strictly positivist point of view. Predictive modeling, the subject of this chapter, represents the apex of "recipe archaeology"; in effect, if certain natural environmental variables are present in particular proportions, a "site type" will result. Although it is by definition a research methodology, predictive modeling has been heavily funded in the last decade, both by the government and the private sector, to serve as an archaeological survey tool for cultural resource managers. This financial support has resulted in the development of local and regional databases, as well as aided recognition that archaeology is as equally a valid resource and discipline as forestry, geology, and biology and should be funded as such. However, in the last fifteen years, despite lip service to the contrary, predictive models have been designed almost exclusively around natural environmental variables. Additionally, statistical probabilities have been perceived to be adequate substitutes for on-the-ground inventories.

Both cultural and depositional factors contribute to the condition in which Plains archaeological assemblages and sites are found. Because the cultural data seem to be limited whereas natural environmental data are easily collected, cultural simplicity is often inferred, in spite of contradictory ethnological evidence. The application of ecologically oriented predictive models to Plains archaeological data serves to reinforce and exacerbate this misconception.

An analysis of archaeological inventory data from southeastern Colorado collected in the "traditional" fashion attests to the importance of the mind of the researcher in the initial phases of data recovery. Whereas predictive models can serve as an aid to information organization, a wholesale or even partial replacement of fieldwork by computer modeling could result in the neglect of irreplaceable and, in the Western Plains, rare cultural information.

In addition to developing computer skills, archaeologists can improve data recovery and interpretation processes in several ways. Attention to the extant methodological, as well as theoretical, archaeological and anthropological literature is a luxury for most cultural resource managers. Concurrent with the development of computer databases, funding priority should be assigned to the purchase of relevant books and journals. As knowledgeable anthropologists, rather than field technicians, archaeologists will naturally begin to consider the social, ideological, and political factors that might have had an effect on the archaeological record. Recognition that, as human beings, all archaeologists are subject to culture is a first step in understanding that our ancestors were affected by many of the same social, historical, and natural environmental forces that we are. The analysis of southeastern Colorado survey data demonstrates that empathy plays an important role in at least one aspect of archaeology—site discovery. Finally, acceptance of the concept that archaeology is simply the historically oriented branch of anthropology allows for an interpretive approach that synthesizes cultural process and interactive historic events. By examining how events shape our lives, as well as the lives of ethnographic peoples, we can develop a deeper understanding of populations for which no histories are recorded.

Predictive Modeling

Because an extensive collection of papers on predictive modeling has recently been published, only a general descriptive discussion of the methodology is necessary in the present volume. The reader is referred to Judge and Sebastian (1988) to obtain more detail. Predictive modeling is a technique whereby models designed to assess the probability of finding locations of human activity are generated and tested. Predictive models are inductive because they are derived from data gathered specifically for the purpose of model building. They can also be considered deductive because the research question, where will a site be found? is their raison d'être.

The process of building a predictive model involves the compilation of any data that might be relevant to the position of a site on the landscape within a specified region. For reasons that will be explored below, the variables are often natural environmental ones, although by definition sociocultural information should also be considered. Sufficient site inventory in the region of interest is also required so that existing correlations between loci and other variables may be documented. The results of the data gathering are fed into a statistical formula (these days into a computer via one of various Geographic Information Systems [GISs]). Projections of statistical probabilities of site occurrence are generated and can then be empirically tested.

Kohler (1988) traces the concept of locational modeling back to the work of Steward (1938, 1955), Stewart (1943), and White (1949). He notes that Steward was more interested in causality than correlation, as well as a consideration of *local* natural environments. Indeed, Steward's "culture core" concept was based on the idea that ecological relationships were the primary basis for cultural differentiation. Any features not directly related to environmental exploitation were considered secondary. The growth of settlement pattern studies, heralded by Willey's work in the Viru Valley (1953) and his 1956 collection of related papers, was the next theoretical step toward predictive modeling. In these relatively early works, demographic and social trends, as well as natural environmental determinants, were considered.

The ecosystemic view of culture, which interdigitates with the idea of process, was well established by the 1960s. The idea that systematic articulations between the material and nonmaterial aspects of culture are significant and could be investigated was inherent in Taylor's (1948) conjunctive approach, and Trigger (1989a) demonstrates how functionalist and processual concepts were being discussed as early as the 1930s. The work of Clarke (1968) established archaeology as a "science," and Binford's "discovery" of positivism served to propel ecologically oriented archaeological theory and method into the forefront of epistemological discourse. Quantifiable data were, and still are by some, perceived to be more "scientific" and testable than nonquantifiable data and therefore accurate representations of "truth."

The New Archaeology was introduced in the 1960s, and the late 1970s and 1980s were the "boom years" of locational modeling. The ecological and systems-oriented theoretical environment of the 1960s, along with the results of site catchment studies and previous settlement pattern research, profoundly influenced the development of systematized predictive modeling in the mid-1970s. Site catchment analyses, introduced in the 1970s, are based on the assumption that people will elect to locate sites near resources in order to exert minimum effort for maximum return (e.g., Vita-Finzi and Higgs 1970). Data collected for such analyses are quantifiable and statistically manipulable and thus "scientific."

None of the theoretical developments in American archaeology in the past three decades, particularly the ecosystemic perspective and related locational modeling, occurred in a cultural vacuum. A national recognition that the natural environment was being degraded and destroyed by technological expansion and population growth (the environmental movement) resulted in the enactment of the National Environmental Policy Act of 1969. This act requires that, before any federal undertaking occurs, the environmental effects of a project must be taken into account in an environmental impact statement. The Federal Land Policy and Management Act, enacted in 1976, established specific policies for compliance with the National Environmental Policy Act on public lands, with particular reference to the Bureau of Land Management (BLM) and the United States Forest Service. In conjunction with the 1966 National Historic Preservation Act, which requires that federal agencies consider prehistoric and historic resources previous to any activities on federal lands, the Federal Land Policy and Management Act obliged the government to systematize cultural resource management.

The Federal Land Policy and Management Act also initiated the development, within the federal government, of management plans designed to assess the status of resources, identify issues, and guide management of the public lands. Such planning documents require, as a foundation, complete resource inventory data. Gathering the data is a very expensive process, particularly in the western United States, where 291 million acres of public land are still in the public trust. Because of the cost, federal agencies and state historic preservation offices became interested in the economic utility of predictive models in the late 1970s (Kohler 1988). Data that had already been amassed could be incorporated into such models, and the resulting extrapolations could become essential tools in the development of management plans. In theory, on-the-ground inventory might be unnecessary in some cases, substantially reducing the bottom line in cultural resource management programs. The long list of projects reproduced in the Judge and Sebastian volume (Thoms 1988), which represents only a fraction of the extant work, attests to the funding that the federal and state agencies poured into the predictive modeling effort in the late

1970s and 1980s. The production of the Judge and Sebastian (1988) volume itself represents the financial commitment of the federal government to the methodology.

An Analysis of Predictive Modeling

The predictive modeling trend has resulted in some positive benefits for cultural resource management and American archaeology as a whole. Cultural resource specialists are better and more efficient resource managers if armed with complete inventory data. The development of predictive modeling schemes has encouraged the funding of data collection by federal and other agencies, as well as the creation of local, regional, and statewide relational databases. The adoption of GIS systems by many federal land management entities has also been beneficial to cultural resource management programs. In addition to producing accurate, high-quality maps, GISs allow numerous variables, including management-related ones, to be simultaneously analyzed. When generalizations are required, as during the planning process, predictive models are useful tools.

Additionally, predictive modeling has caused the federal government to acknowledge that theoretical and methodological development within the discipline is worth funding (witness the Judge and Sebastian [1988] book). Better archaeologists result from better theorists, as well as from the debate that theory sparks. Paradigmatic refinement allows better data analysis and systemization, but in addition, it encourages improvement and keeps the discipline alive.

However, government funding and the resultant misconceptions by nonarchaeologists have serious drawbacks. Wildesen noted that "[t]he problem is that some archaeologists have told some planners that our predictive models can be used as hard data, when in actuality it is our hard data on site location and significance that must be figured into the planner's cost-benefit ratio. To substitute a scientific hypothesis (our predictive model) for scientific fact (actual site location) as a criterion for a planning decision is to court disaster" (Wildesen 1974: 1–2; quoted in Kohler 1988: 34). Sixteen years later, the problem continues to be acknowledged (Sebastian and Judge 1988), although this author's experience has shown that it occasionally must be reinforced in the minds of planners and lay managers alike.

It is unrealistic to consider computer-generated statistical probabilities of site occurrences as an adequate substitute for on-the-ground inventories. Probabilities are sufficient only as very general indicators of what might be present in the field and consist of layers of assumptions, most of which do not apply to archaeological data. Statistical data are extrapolations from *random, adequately* large samples. Archaeological data are, by their nature, nonrandom. The fact that cultural information is patterned allows archaeologists to make comparisons and thus to begin to detect cultural differentiation and homogeneity. To randomize site data is to lose information.

Although adequate sample size might not be a problem with certain Plains site types (such as surface lithic scatters in southeastern Colorado), others (well-dated Paleo-Indian sites, sites with pottery present, and tipi ring sites with stratigraphic deposition) are all scarce enough to thwart rigorous statistical analysis. Furthermore, archaeological sites are often so spatially and temporally complex that they defy parsimonious classification. The reliability of statistically generated probabilities decreases with an increase in variability.

A problem specific to the application of predictive modeling methodology by federal cultural resource managers is that the land patterns of most public acreage (particularly BLM lands) are uneven in their relationships to environmental resources. An old adage in the BLM is that if the land is rocky, barren, and inaccessible, it is probably managed by that agency! If only public lands are inventoried for predictive models, it is quite likely that the results will be awkwardly skewed. Additionally skewing the data is the effect that historic Euroamericans have had on the aboriginal landscape. Although modern land use resulting in site alteration or destruction is a universal problem for archaeologists, it poses an additional difficulty for anyone attempting to create a statistical model based on random sampling.

Predictive modeling is, by definition, the formulation of *models*. In pure scientific hypothesis testing, hypotheses generated from such models, along with alternatives, are tested. If rigorous model testing is the goal, generated hypotheses should be *rejected*. Exhaustive ground coverage of every square centimeter must be conducted in order to reject all possible alternatives, and predictive modeling quickly becomes the extremely expensive endeavor it is supposed to replace.

Another serious problem that characterizes virtually all predictive modeling schemes is the universal lack of concern for any variables that are not directly related to the natural environment. Given the history of the methodology, arising from the environmentally oriented archaeology of the 1960s and 1970s, an emphasis on subsistence and economic variables is to be expected. This natural environmental determinism is recognized by practitioners of predictive modeling (Kohler 1988; Kincaid 1988), but it is not considered to be a major issue. Kohler (1988: 25) suggests that "[t]he task of locational modeling is to isolate those aspects of the environment that do influence settlement behavior and place them into perspective with non-environmental factors that also influence settlement behavior." However, since he also admits that archaeologists do not know how to use nonenvironmental variables, it seems that, given present methodology, the influence of such variables on settlement patterns would be difficult to determine, much less measure.

Finally, predictive modeling schemes are based on the assumption that the current environment parallels the paleoenvironment. Paleoenvironmental data indicate that climatic fluctuations, from minor to severe, have characterized the Plains periphery since the time of the earliest occupations (e.g., Benedict and Olson 1978). Although the physiographic effects of such climatic fluctuations are still in dispute, the impact of Euroamericans on the Colorado environment in the last century is startling and easily observed in historic photographs and stream-flow records.

Plains Archaeology and Secondary Data

The application of predictive modeling techniques to archaeological data in the Plains is difficult for several reasons. Plains archaeologists, especially those working in the western and peripheral areas, are in a serious analytical predicament because the sparse material assemblages found at many aboriginal sites seem to provide minimal information. As at any archaeological site, this paucity of aboriginal materials is probably the result of some combination of cultural, depositional, and postdepositional factors, ranging from the aboriginal need for portable, disposable objects as part of a seminomadic lifestyle to the site vandalism that undoubtedly started as soon as the first white visitors entered the area. Consequently, it is not surprising that environmental data are emphasized; they are easily collected and analyzed. However, this emphasis, along with certain aspects of the pioneering work of Wedel (1961), has led to a perception by some archaeologists that the natural environment was pivotal, to the exclusion of other factors, in the development of Plains aboriginal culture.

The assumption, based on the archaeological record alone, that the western Plains prehistoric aboriginal material culture, and perhaps even culture as a whole, was undeveloped, is a gross oversimplification. Unfortunately for the archaeologist, many of the historic and presumably prehistoric Plains assemblages are subject to relatively rapid decomposition.

As Wedel (1961: 302) notes, even the most stereotypical "diagnostic" artifacts of historic Plains culture (the use of bison for shelter and clothing, as well as for food; the dog travois; the conical skin tent; the use of dried meat and sign language) rarely contribute to the archaeological record.

As a result, Plains archaeologists must look for other evidence to supplement archaeological data. For example, the puzzling scarcity of ceramic materials in southeastern Colorado might be explained by a reliance on basketry containers. Certainly no shortage of basketry raw materials existed on the western Plains, and baskets are lighter and more portable (but also more prone to deterioration) than pots. Lowie (1954: 59) indicates that among historic Plains groups, "true baskets seem to have occurred only among the villagers and such peripheral groups as the Ute and Shoshone," both of whom might have lived in southeastern Colorado at some time in the past. Apaches were also basket makers and are known to have inhabited the area (Opler 1971; Gunnerson and Gunnerson 1988). Although a direct analogy cannot be made without further testing, it is possible that the basket-weaving ancestors of these historic groups produced some of the western Plains archaeological sites with relatively low occurrences of ceramics, and substantiating evidence could be sought.

The assumption that the nonmaterial aspects of prehistoric western Plains cultures were not complex, based on archaeological subsistence data and descriptive analyses of material culture assemblages, is undoubtedly inaccurate. Wedel (1961: 307) recalls that as far back as Wissler's time, the historic aboriginal cultures of the Plains were known for their "great material uniformity with notorious linguistic and political diversity." Ethnohistoric and ethnographic accounts of historic Plains groups confirm that elaborate systems of kinship, exchange, social relationships, and ideology were pervasive and characterized by distinct local variations.

Cultural artifacts and the contexts within which they are found can certainly provide information about such systems. For example, the process of pottery making among the historic Jicarilla Apache was ritualized from the gathering of the raw clay through the firing (Opler 1971). Even the details of decoration were dictated by ritual and could have had far-reaching effects. An Apache informant told Opler, "If he is going along a rocky ledge a man will find a way out, though it looks impossible, providing his wife, when she makes a basket or pot, doesn't enclose the whole object with the design but leaves a 'road' open. As long as his relatives make a 'road' on their baskets and pots, a man will be able to find his way out of a difficult place. If he is chased to a deep arroyo, he'll find a way to cross. His pursuers won't be able to pass the barrier. He'll be the only one who has a road" (Opler 1971: 31).

Knowledge of nonmaterial cultural systems can be essential to locating sites and translating the archaeological record. Again, historic Plains culture serves as an example rather than a direct analogy. According to Jicarilla Apache tradition, the Arkansas, Canadian, Rio Grande, and Pecos rivers were sacred boundary markers that enclosed their "holy land" (Stoffle 1984). Such information could both supplement archaeological data and call attention to potential areas of investigation (e.g., identifying and developing an understanding of Apache culture).

Ethnohistoric accounts can also be extremely useful. Levine (1984) demonstrates how military reconnaissance reports of the 1850s can be important in determining the ethnicity of the site occupants. Site attributes such as hearth size and the presence or absence of hide processing artifacts were used by Delaware guides to distinguish between the Comanches and the Kiowas. Although it is unlikely that any such specific information could be easily applied to prehistoric Plains sites, the information serves to illustrate that such "particularistic" attributes might advance the understanding of a particular cultural system and its material manifestations.

The Realities of Cultural Resource Management

Cultural resource management in the BLM, as in most other government agencies, is not research oriented. Instead, the goal is compliance with the web of laws, regulations, and policies that govern the program (e.g., the National Environmental Policy Act, the Federal Land Policy and Management Act, the Archaeological Resources Protection Act, and internal policies). Even if somewhat daunting to the uninitiated, this tangle of directives is ultimately beneficial in the protection and preservation of archaeological data as well as in the enrichment of existing databases. Although they can be destructive, nonarchaeological undertakings present opportunities for investigations that might not otherwise be funded.

What actually happens during archaeological survey? Following a prefield literature review, the archaeologist goes to the field with the intention of surveying as much of the project area as the topography allows. Time constraints usually necessitate that inventory methodology be devised on the spot on the basis of information gathered during the literature review, consultation with maps, and visual survey of the project area. Certain areas will be more closely scrutinized than others, whether by intention or not. Such intuitive "predictive modeling" is not based on computer-generated probabilities but on a combination of the experience of the archaeologist and the realities of the natural environment, which are most often not reflected by United States Geological Survey topographic maps or computer screens. Although perhaps not scientifically rigorous, such a methodology probably more closely approximates the processes by which the subjects of the investigation selected locations for various activities than by the computation of aspect angles and elevations.

In order to determine "scientifically" how sites are found during "unmodeled" inventories, data from actual fieldwork were analyzed. The fieldwork was conducted between September 1988 and October 1989 (an arbitrarily selected time period) by the Royal Gorge Resource Area archaeologist (BLM), and the data set consists of information from forty-three aboriginal sites found in the course of twenty-eight projects (see Table 5-1). At that time the Royal Gorge Resource Area encompassed the western periphery of the Great Plains, the foothills of the Rocky Mountains, and the Rocky Mountains themselves to the Continental Divide.[1] Aboriginal occupants of most of the area (excluding the park and Chaquaqua Plateaux) were clearly influenced by Plains cultures, with Western (Ute) influences dating to protohistoric and historic times.

Historic sites, of which an equal number were found during the one-year period, were excluded because they are associated with a different level of cultural complexity. Also excluded were sites associated with non-BLM and paraarchaeological[2] projects in an effort to standardize investigative bias. A total of 6,095.37 acres were inventoried during the twenty-eight projects, yielding a ratio of one site for every 142 acres. This relatively low density of aboriginal sites is common in the area.

A large percentage of the sites (49%) are less than 1 mile from a permanent water source, and most (86%) are found in areas with a slope of 5% or less, with none located on a slope greater than 15% (see Table 5-2). Neither the proximity to water nor the percentage of slope is surprising. Although personal analytic bias might have altered the slope values, the presence or absence of water in the project areas was entirely dependent on the nature of the project for which the clearance was needed.

Environmental zones included the foothills (piñon-juniper forests), the Eastern Plains, mountain parks, and montane areas. Again, the value of this variable was dependent on the location of the proposed project area.

Aspect values were based on the actual view from the site and were estimated in the field. It is unlikely that the presence of rocks or the specific locations of individual trees that might affect the aspect could be discerned by computer due to the gross scale often necessitated by GIS systems. As expected, in most cases the view was unobstructed (49% at 360°) or only partially obstructed (44% at 180°).

As expected, most sites were found at elevations between 6,000 and

Table 5-1. Site Survey Data, Royal Gorge Resource Area

Site	Proximity to H_2O	Aspect (°)	Slope (%)	Zone	Type	Date	Method	Elevation (feet)
5FN984	3,600 m./2.2 miles	180	0	PJ/Rip	IF	Unk	L	7,760
5FN985	3,600 m./2.2 miles	360	10	PJ/Fth	Q	Unk	L	8,000
5FN986	3,600 m./2.2 miles	360	10	PJ/Fth	Q	Unk	I	7,960
5FN988	2,500 m./1.5 miles	360	5	PJ/Fth	OA	L.Pre	K	6,320
5FN993	1,400 m./0.9 miles	180	0	Mntn	OL	Ar/Lp	I	6,640
5FN994	3,600 m./2.0 miles	90	0	PJ	IF	L.Pre	L	6,560
5FN995	4,600 m./2.9 miles	180	5	PJ	OL	Unk	L	6,480
5FN996	3,600 m./2.0 miles	90	5	PJ/Can	OL	Unk	L	6,360
5FN998	1,700 m./2.1 miles	180	3	Mntn	OL	Unk	L	6,720
5FN999	3,600 m./2.0 miles	360	5	PJ	OL	Unk	I	6,880
5FN1000	2,600 m./1.6 miles	360	5	PJ/Fth	OL	Unk	L	6,880
5FN1002	2,500 m./1.5 miles	360	5	PJ/Fth	OL	Unk	L	6,400
5FN1004	250 m./0.2 miles	360	10	PJ/Fth	OL	Unk	I	5,920
5TL267	2,200 m./1.4 miles	360	0	Mntn	OC	L.Pre	L	8,820
5TL270	4,000 m./2.5 miles	360	10	Mntn	IF	L.Pre	L	8,440
5PA564	250 m./0.2 miles	180	5	Park	IF	Unk	L	9,800
5PA571	1,800 m./1.1 miles	180	0	Park	IF	Unk	L	10,000

Table 5-1. (continued)

Site	Proximity to H_2O	Aspect (°)	Slope (%)	Zone	Type	Date	Method	Elevation (feet)
5PA572	2,400 m./1.5 miles	360	0	Park/H	IF	Unk	I	9,420
5PA573	2,600 m./1.6 miles	180	0	Park/H	IF	Unk	I	9,380
5PA574	2,400 m./1.5 miles	90	5	Park/W	IF	Unk	I	9,380
5PA575	2,400 m./1.5 miles	360	5	Park/H	OA	L.Pre	I	9,463
5LK754	250 m./0.2 miles	180	3	Riv/Mtn	OL	Unk	L	9,720
5CF551	50 m./0.03 miles	180	0	Riv/Mtn	OL	Unk	I	8,320
5CF552	50 m./0.03 miles	180	0	Riv/Can	OL	Unk	I	6,900
5CF553	75 m./0.05 miles	360	0	Riv/Mtn	IF	L.Pre	I	7,720
5CF555	5,900 m./3.7 miles	360	5	Mntn	MC	Unk	K	7,720
5CF576	20 m./0.01 miles	180	0	Riv/Mtn	OL	Unk	I	8,240
5CF578	20 m./0.01 miles	180	0	Riv/Mtn	OL	Unk	I	8,240
5CF579	550 m./0.3 miles	180	0	Riv/Mtn	OL	Unk	I	7,400
5CF580	400 m./0.2 miles	180	0	Riv/Mtn	OL	Unk	I	7,400
5CF581	1,000 m./0.6 miles	360	10	Hil/Mtn	OC	Unk	L	7,520
5CF582	200 m./0.1 miles	180	5	Riv/Mtn	OL	Unk	I	7,400
5CF583	1,100 m./0.7 miles	180	15	Hil/Mtn	IF	Unk	I	7,560
5CF584	100 m./0.06 miles	360	5	Riv/Mtn	OL	Unk	K	7,720

Table 5-1. (continued)

Site	Proximity to H_2O	Aspect (°)	Slope (%)	Zone	Type	Date	Method	Elevation (feet)
5CF585	1,000 m./0.6 miles	360	5	Riv/Mtn	OL	Unk	I	7,740
5CF586	2,000 m./1.2 miles	360	5	Riv/Mtn	OL	Unk	I	7,740
5CF587	1,200 m./0.7 miles	360	5	Riv/Mtn	OL	Unk	I	7,720
5CF588	600 m./0.4 miles	360	5	Spg/Mtn	OL	Unk	I	7,720
5CF589	1,000 m./0.6 miles	180	5	Hil/Mtn	OL	Unk	I	7,760
5CF590	1,000 m./0.6 miles	180	5	Spi/Mtn	OC	1980 B.P..	I	7,800
5CF591	200 m./0.1 miles	180	0	Riv/Mtn	OL	Unk	L	7,520
5LA5860	10,800 m./6.7 miles	360	5	Plains	OA	API?	K	5,110
5LA5861	10,800 m./6.7 miles	360	5	Plains	OL	API?	I	5,150

Site = Smithsonian site number.
Proximity to H_2O = proximity to permanent water; m. = meters.
Zone = environmental zone and specific topographic location, if appropriate:

PJ/Fth = piñon-juniper forest, foothills;
Rip = riparian;
Mntn = montane;
Can = canyon;
Park = mountain park;
Park/H = hilltop in a mountain park;
Park/W = woods in a mountain park;
Riv/Mtn = riverbank in the montane zone
Riv/Can = riverbank in a canyon;
Hil/Mtn = hill in the montane zone
Spg/Mtn = spring in the montane zone
Spi/Mtn = spires in the montane zone
Plains = plains zone.

Type = site type:
IF = isolated find;
Q = lithic quarry;
OA = open architectural;
OL = open lithic;
OC = open camp;
MC = multiple component.

Date = approximate relative date:
U = unknown;
Ar/Lp = Archaic/Late Prehistoric;
L.Pre. = Late Prehistoric;
Api? = possible Apishipa focus.

Method = method of site discovery;
L = luck; found during transects;
I = "intuitive" (see text);
K = previous knowledge.

Table 5-2. Site Characteristics, Royal Gorge Resource Area

Characteristic		Number
		Total Sites: 43
Water		
	Less than 1 mile from permanent water	21
	Between 1 and 2 miles from permanent water	13
	More than 2 miles from permanent water	9
Slope (%)		
	0	15
	3	2
	5	20
	10	5
	15	1
Aspect (°)		
	360	21
	180	19
	90	3
Elevation (feet)		
	Lower than 6,000	3
	6,000–7,499 (foothills)	13
	7,500–8,999 (montane)	20
	9,000–11,500 (subalpine)	7

9,000 feet above sea level. These data, particularly on the low end, are constrained by project location.

Aboriginal sites found by a combination of environmental indicators (e.g., proximity to water and slope) and experience (both academic and practical) were labeled "intuitive" and compared with sites discovered by "luck" (found during routine transects) and by "previous knowledge" of their locations (literature reviews). Nearly twice as many sites were found by the intuitive process (56%) as by luck (35%). Only four sites were relocated on the basis of previous knowledge.

Of the sites found by intuition (see Table 5-3), 54% were partially or nearly obscured (based on field analyses of aspect angles) and 46% were not obscured. Thus, in more than half of the cases, searching for sites based on a "feeling" led to their discovery, despite limited exposure, in contrast to the predominance of totally exposed sites (49%) in the sample as a whole.

The pattern of proximity to permanent water in the intuitive group (67% less than 1 mile from the source, 25% between 1 and 2 miles, and 8% more than 2 miles) was comparable to the main sample (49% less than 1

Table 5-3. Environmental Features by Method, Royal Gorge Resource Area

Environmental Feature	Luck	Knowledge	Intuition
Water			
Less than 1 mile	4	1	16
1 to 2 miles	6	1	6
More than 2 miles	5	2	2
Slope (%)			
0	5	0	10
3	2	0	0
5	5	4	11
10	3	0	2
15	0	0	1
Aspect (°)			
90	2	0	1
180	7	0	12
360	6	4	11
Elevation (feet)			
Less than 6,000	0	1	2
6,000–7,499	6	1	6
7,500–8,999	6	2	12
9,000–11,500	3	0	4

Totals by method: Luck, n = 15; Intuition, n = 24; Knowledge, n = 4.

mile from the source, 30% between 1 and 2 miles, and 21% more than 2 miles). This similarity might be a result of the location of projects or of "luck" sites actually being found intuitively.

A site that was found by the intuitive method produced one of the few absolute dates from the area (Bargielski 1990a). Site 5CF590, the Spires site, is an open campsite located in the vicinity of a relatively unique geologic landmark. Because of its location at the edge of a steep slope, the area adjacent to a group of limestone spires might not have been investigated as part of the normal transect pattern. However, because of experience in the area, the archaeologist located a roasting pit with a radiocarbon date of 1980 B.P. ± 80 (BETA-37998). The limestone spires are not mapped on the 7.5-foot United States Geographic Survey topographic map.

Although not comparable to a computer-generated predictive model, the results of this small experiment demonstrate several important points.

The data indicate that if only the aboriginal sites found by luck were recorded, more than half would have been missed. Clearly, predictive modeling is not based on chance but on probability. However, if the predictive model indicated that, on the basis of the information programmed into it, only a slight chance of finding cultural materials in a particular location existed, then location would likely be excluded from transect inventory. Even if an area was included (and what is the appropriate percentage? 50%?) and others were excluded "because the model said so," it is possible that more than half of the sites could be missed!

Another potential danger is that if aspect is factored into the model at the relatively gross level of a 7.5-foot United States Geographical Survey topographic map, the probability might be artificially reduced. More than half of the intuitive sites were characterized by aspects of less than 360°. Although some site types (e.g., refuge sites) might always be partially or completely obscured, which could be factored into a predictive model, the gross level of a GIS would still be unable to pick up the subtle environmental features that might be present.

Of much importance, however, is that this experiment clearly demonstrates that intuition is not simply a feeling but a significant product of the efficient mental computer of the archaeologist. If the field observations and methodological decisions of the Royal Gorge Resource Area archaeologist had been excluded from the fieldwork, a large percentage of sites in an area of low site density would not have been recorded, including at least one that is eligible for the National Register of Historic Places (5CF590). Although an analysis of the prehistoric aboriginal mind is neither practical nor desirable, the data indicate that consideration of past populations as thoughtful individuals not unlike ourselves is an important aspect of the initial steps of archaeological data recovery. Furthermore, the "scientific" test serves to prove empirically that the wholesale replacement of the archaeologically trained mind by silicon chips is not only inefficient but potentially destructive to an irretrievable resource.

An Alternative Approach to Predictive Modeling

Because of the enormous amount of time, energy, and money that has been invested into it, the methodology of predictive modeling should not be dismissed out of hand. If used carefully and thoughtfully, it is an important tool for cultural resource management as part of planning efforts and as an aid to archaeologists in explaining and demonstrating the significance of cultural resources to other specialists and managers. However, because it has progressed from simple research-oriented hypothesis testing to an accepted form of inventory, archaeologists must be prepared to ensure that predictive modeling does not become a wholesale substitute for on-the-ground survey and that the nonarch-aeological advocates of such abuse understand the reasons.

Instead of being viewed as the ultimate goal of cultural resource management, data forming a predictive model can be used to supplement the other important aspects of proper management. Because of its flaws, in particular the lack of attention to nonenvironmental variables that might affect site location, other methods, including the widely downplayed literature review, can be used in conjunction with relational databases. Archaeologists, particularly those immersed in cultural resource management, need to sharpen their skills as anthropologists and historians and then, by adopting a truly holistic approach, will begin to develop a deeper understanding of past cultural patterns of stasis and change. If, instead of viewing site occupants as variables to be analyzed by computer, archaeologists think of their subjects as human beings with minds that are as complex as their own and with lives as affected by historic events as those of modern populations, new insights into various cultural patterns of the past, including site location, might result.

Reallocation of funds from the development of more and better predictive models to the purchase of relevant archaeological, ethnological, and ethnographic reference literature is an important first step toward better cultural resource management and thus better archaeological research as a whole. Although the construction of direct analogues is not necessarily desirable, a thorough understanding of known cultural patterns, processes, and histories within a particular geographic area is essential to the initial diagnosis of archaeological sites and assemblages. The awarding of federal permits is partially dependent on a researcher's access to or possession of an adequate library of relevant resources; however, familiarity with current literature is not currently stressed in any but academic positions. An additional benefit of such a program might be a narrowing of the gap between cultural resource managers and academicians.

Cultural resource managers are often called on to handle several "related" programs (e.g., Bargielski 1990b). Obtaining more literature is useless unless time is allotted for study. Such reading time is usually assigned the lowest priority, yet it is essential to the development of new and relevant research questions.

In addition to reading the current literature, all archaeologists will benefit by sharing data and cultivating open communications. For example, some state and federal agencies have been developing and maintaining virtually identical computer databases for years. Instead of duplicating efforts, programmatic agreements among these agencies can save both money and time. The Colorado State Historic Preservation Office and the Colorado BLM have developed such an agreement, and BLM archaeologists may now perform their own literature searches and obtain site information through a modem. Such an arrangement both eases the workload of the staff at the State Historic Preservation Office and allows federal archaeologists to gain access to the most current information.

Third, attention to aspects of past cultural systems that were not strictly governed by the natural environment might help to explain previously unexplainable aspects of the archaeological record. Even *preprocessual* scholars recognized that the answers might, and probably do, derive from ideological, social, or religious decisions, perhaps in some combination with environmental ones, and that all are affected by the course of historic events. Steward (1955: 34) admitted that "the physical environment exerts but a permissive and limiting effect," and Wedel (1961: 291) said that "the Plains environment did not predetermine the direction in which native culture would have to go; rather, it offered certain options which at different times and places, and in varying degrees, were accepted and developed in different ways by the native populations."

Because of the low density of sites in most of southeastern Colorado and certainly in other areas of the Plains, the lack of a site in a particular location is often perplexing. The nature of prehistoric archaeological sites makes it unlikely that the riddle will ever be solved. However, only by considering the inhabitants of the sites as members of societies of individuals and not simply respondents to natural environmental stimuli will we begin to understand what appears on and in the ground.

Finally, as Hodder (1985, 1987a) has stressed, we should recognize that archaeology is a historical discipline. Certainly, some of our methods are scientific, in the sense of the application of physical and chemical principles. However, we do well to acknowledge that although the answers to "why" are virtually unattainable, "what happened" is not only approachable but is also what the public, the source of most funding, wants. Implicit in a consideration of historic events and historic traditions as essential parts of human cultural systems is a certainty that people are able to perceive the results of their responses to events and to behave accordingly. Rather than individuals changing within a stable system (Ebert and Kohler 1988), the results of individual decisions can change the system as a whole, thus causing process and history to interdigitate. For example, Wolf (1982) has shown how the narrow anthropological treatment of !Kung hunter-gatherers as a society without history excluded the consideration of how centuries of interaction and exchange with others in the region might have affected the !Kung system.

Both the descriptive and "particularizing" approach and the processual systemic view have important places in the development of culture histories and are quite compatible. In order to begin to understand how cultures changed, we must have a firm grasp of the contents and the details of the archaeological record. Artifacts, from the mere interior flake to the landscape as a whole, provide access to social, ideological, and political information as well as to subsistence patterns. Placed into temporal context, such data can narrate history; archaeologists are the interpreters. Accepting that interpretational bias cannot be avoided, the archaeologist can improve accuracy and relevance by being well informed and open-minded about all the details, regarding both the archaeological assemblage itself and the relevant histories of other groups that preceded as well as superseded the culture that produced the materials.

Conclusion

The intent of this chapter has not been to discredit the predictive modeling movement but to offer an alternative approach. Instead of the creation of more predictive models, the development of relational databases and adequate research libraries should receive funding priority. The gap between academia and cultural resource management, a consequence of, among various factors, the sudden need for numerous archaeologists in the late 1970s, is beginning to narrow with the employment of archaeologists with advanced degrees. The management of precious cultural resources will improve substantially if the managers are trained and knowledgeable anthropologists, not simply computer and field technicians. Attention to relevant literature is important not only for improvement in site identification techniques but also for the determination of site significance and interpretation.

Redefinition of archaeology as historical anthropology, although apparently semantic, has important implications. The analysis of archaeological materials often becomes an end unto itself, particularly in cultural resource management. Although the secretary of the interior's standards and guidelines require that compliance reports contain an interpretive or synthetic section, these efforts often become perfunctory, which is generally the result of time constraints. What is needed is not another set of cookbook instructions for interpretation but an overhaul in approach. A reacquaintance with the anthropological literature serves to remind us that cultural interaction and process are not exclusively subsistence related. Acknowledgment that historic events, ranging from human-caused through natural disasters, play an important role in the rates, seriousness, and types of change in human systems is equally important (see Schlesier 1990). Archaeologists who deal with preliterate populations, such as those in the Plains, would have to devise analytic methods that integrate local, particularistic temporal changes with patterns on a more regional level. Through such regional analytic schemes, a course of events might be recognized and a greater understanding of areal cultural systems acquired. As part of this historically oriented approach, funds for nonreactive excavation and testing would take precedence over those earmarked for predictive modeling programs. We should be moving in the direction of obtaining more, rather than fewer, details.

Because of the complexity and variety of the human mind and therefore human and human-related systems, it is unlikely that practitioners of archaeology will ever develop a single "ultimate" methodology. The introduction of new technology and related methods, such as predictive modeling, can vastly improve our analytic abilities, but only by improving our synthetic capacities can we become better archaeologists.

Acknowledgments

The author wishes to express appreciation to the editors for the opportunity to contribute to this volume, and to John Beardsley for some of the ideas in this paper and for the hours of banter that inspired its creation. Thanks also to John Beardsley and Stub Freer for providing preliminary review and to the anonymous reviewers for their insightful comments.

Notes

1. In 1991, the Royal Gorge Resource Area was expanded to include the entire eastern half of Colorado.

2. Paraarchaeologists are professionals in other disciplines who, after intensive training and under the supervision of a professional archaeologist, are allowed to inventory limited acreage.

Part II

Building Alternative Archaeologies

6

Social and Political Causes for the Emergence of Intensive Agriculture in Eastern North America

David W. Benn

It seems a long time ago that I was a graduate student at Madison, Wisconsin, and we were encouraged to take courses in environmental studies with the goal of learning about the ecological context of prehistoric human societies. My peers and I were under the tutelage of David Baerreis, who with Reid Bryson and his students was developing models of past episodes of climatic change from proxy data in seeds, bones, and pollen and relating changes in climate to prehistoric culture change. In those days our models of environmental effects on culture were simple, causal, and direct. With Griffin's (1960) climatic model of Hopewellian decline and the Baerreis and Bryson (1968) model of Mill Creek culture change fresh in our minds, we grasped at environmental causation when grains of maize turned up in flotation screens.

All of us have changed our views about the role environment played in prehistoric societies. Environmental determinism has passed out of nearly all the recent literature. The natural environment tends to be viewed as a constraining factor for human behavior, not a direct cause of culture change (Brown 1986: 323). Today, analyses of floral and faunal remains, which formerly were sideline specialties for many archaeologists like myself, have developed a degree of detail and sophistication that qualifies them as separate disciplines. An information explosion has been produced by specialists in floral analysis, especially regarding the evolution of domestic plants and the origins of agriculture. The newest theories about domestication of plants explain cultural adaptations and change with processual paradigms (Ford 1977; Smith 1987).

Background

Theories explaining the origin of agriculture in eastern North America proliferated as domesticated plant remains were discovered and dated. Practically all of these theories can be categorized as "prime-mover" and "system-serving" types of explanations (Nassaney 1987: 130) grounded in evolutionary theory. Prime-mover explanations seek single causal factors, such as population growth, environmental change, or technical innovations, as the impetus for culture change. The current trend is away from simplistic, prime-mover explanations toward system-serving explanations, which seek multiple causes for disruptions in the equilibrium of culture systems followed by change and a return to homeostasis. One positive aspect of system-serving explanations is that the development of agriculture can be tied to other culture changes, giving an overall picture of cultural "intensification."

The system-serving models gaining widest acceptance today are constructed on the anthropological theories of optimal foraging (Earle 1980; Christenson 1980) and risk management (Jochim 1981). The essential assumption in optimal foraging theory is that hunters and gatherers will minimize energy costs, particularly in subsistence pursuits, and maximize output (product). Theorists (e.g., Christenson 1980: 36) would prefer to include all aspects of life in their least-cost equations, thereby arriving at a "least-cost equilibrium," a sort of average acceptable cost for all types of work. Risk management theory interjects a social factor into the least-cost strategy. When the pursuit of least-cost resources is curtailed by competition from other forager groups, residential plans are modified (e.g., from residential mobility to logistical mobility in Binford's [1983] terminology). Accordingly, the logistics of obtaining needs are modified to incorporate more intensive exploitation of specific resources with more effective tools.

It is amazing how the evidence for intensive use of weedy plants, the domestication of native species, and eventually the development of maize agriculture fitted easily into the least-cost and risk management theoretical frameworks (cf. Christenson 1980: 50; Reidhead 1980: 177). From the perspective of an archaeologist living in the modern world of practical scientific inquiry, the "obvious" nutritional advantages of growing and consuming cultigens have been a powerful inducement for the formulation of explanations of why foragers became first horticulturalists and then agriculturalists (e.g., "push" and "pull" models in Stark [1986: 296–303]). Recent writers have tried to overcome the inherent bias of rationalism (adaptationism), which is characteristic of modern scientific thinking, by carefully tracing the genetic coevolution of indigenous and domesticated plants (Smith 1987) and by formulating coevolutionary models of social intensification, plant domestication, and population growth (e.g., Braun and Plog 1982; Brown and Vierra 1983; Asch, Farnsworth, and Asch 1979; Asch and Asch 1985; Ford 1985; Braun 1987; O'Brien 1987). The strongest point of the coevolutionary system models is that they are able to account for social and technical changes that took place over thousands of years: they do not portray the "invention" of cultivation as a rapid, necessary achievement.

I am uncomfortable with this modeling not because optimal foraging theory can be refuted (Brown 1986: 319) but because its assumptions lack a dialectical perspective. Optimal foraging theory depends on rational behavior (see Binford 1983: 231), but rationality is a hallmark of the Western scientific tradition, not of all kin-based societies (Shanks and Tilley 1987a: 51). The assumption that subsistence strategies are grounded on rational decision making comes from industrial societies and is misapplied to preindustrial social formations, where resource procurement strategies may be guided by a variety of subjective ideological beliefs (Kahn and Llobera 1981: 312–313). My other criticism of optimal foraging and risk management theories is that human beings are expected to make economic decisions based on perceived facts and an assessment of real needs when, on the contrary, human beings tend to view economic needs through a veil of social values (Geertz 1964). For instance, where is there a concept of exploiting human resources (labor) in optimal foraging theory? The absence of a dialectical perspective renders coevolutionary models of agricultural development positivist in approach and too reliant on neoevolutionary paradigms (Charles 1987), such as population expansion (Paynter 1989: 374–375), to be a sound basis for explaining human behavior in contexts of cultural change.

Current optimization models for agricultural intensification emphasize those ecological conditions that prompted human beings to develop seed crops. The weakness of this approach is that ecological systems encompass both positive and negative feedbacks that are part of long-term processes not immediately visible to human actors in the system. How are we to judge whether the positive or negative effect was the prime mover in cultural evolution? Indeed, why should we presume that aboriginals evaluated ecological processes as simple positive and negative outcomes? Models exist that build explanations of culture change from both sides of the ecological picture. Coevolutionists O'Brien (1987), Braun (1987), and others (Brown and Vierra 1983) view the fixed amount of natural food resources as the constraining element in the environment; as the theory goes, people developed cultivation to compensate for limitations in the natural system. However, Hall (1980: 432–433) presents an opposite argument he calls the "shmoo effect" ("the challenge of abundance") to explain the dissolution of the Hopewell system and the beginnings of cultivation during the Late Woodland period. I too view the natural environment as a fixed pool of resources, and all human beings perceive limitations in their specific forms of exploitation of natural resources. Thus, "risks" are a constraint that all human beings possess as a mental template derived from their economic activity. Generalized risks cannot be conceived as precipitating specific forms of culture change. Clearly, what is needed to address the problem of agricultural intensification is a social theory and related methodology that crosscuts all forms of human production (Kahn and Llobera 1981: 313).

Some theorists view culture change as a social process, meaning that social relations mediate all productive and ideational systems in the social formation. The social approach (Nassaney 1987: 131) sees culture change as generated by the internal dynamics of social relationships, which are embedded in the production system, and by contradictions derived from historical processes (e.g., Hindess and Hirst 1975; Friedman and Rowlands 1978; Bender 1979, 1985; Wolf 1982). Individual action and group variation are emphasized; the dominant view of society as goal-oriented in resolving problems—a Western industrialist ideology—is avoided (Nassaney 1987: 131). Social analysis by the methods of historical materialism developed by Marx (1906, 1973) is still being refined for application to anthropological topics (cf. Shanks and Tilley 1987a). The strength of historical materialist inquiry is that it can see through the disguise of social values to expose the exploitative relationship linking the sources of socially produced agricultural products to the consumption of surplus by elite members of society. This type of economic structure is a tributary mode of production (Wolf 1982), in which surplus material and human labor are controlled by and move centripetally toward dominant authorities (cf. Bender 1979, 1985; Marquardt 1985; Nassaney 1987). The purpose of this chapter is to investigate how the intensification of agriculture and the production of surplus value are related to the formation of political authority—processes often lumped under the rubric of "Mississippianization."

Subsistence Evidence

Smith (1975, 1978) set the tone for current investigations into the origins of maize agriculture by arguing that the Mississippians adapted to the meander belt zone in large alluvial valleys where linear bands of naturally renewable resources (aquatic, riparian, and forest) and arable soils existed. For Smith the process of Mississippianization began when human beings applied maize and native domesticates to this alluvial habitat, thereby intensifying the system of food production. Ford (1977: 179–181) extended this line of ecological reasoning through the Mississippi period. He described intensive maize agriculture as an environmentally immature system that Mississippian managers had to monitor and regulate with the intervention of ritual and food redistribution; thus, he identified the function of hierarchical administration in Mississippian societies.

Today, we know that Emergent Mississippian (cf. Kelly 1985) communities were not relegated to the meander-belt zone because they occur on older alluvial landscapes as well as outside the Mississippi River valley (e.g., House 1982: 45; Price and Price 1984; Markman 1986). Gibbon's (1974: 133) hypothesis that Mississippian traits appeared all across the eastern United States prior to the florescence of Cahokia is coming true. Figments of the *Mississippianization* process, such as population aggregation, specialized ceramic production, flake tool technology with the bow and arrow, village fortifications, and intensified maize-complex agriculture, appeared contemporaneously (Gibbon 1988) in the Plains area (e.g., Mill Creek, Initial Middle Missouri), southern Wisconsin (e.g., Oneota), the Ohio River basin (e.g., Fort Ancient), and the trans-Mississippi south (e.g., Baytown, Spiro). All of the Mississippian traits are aspects of a larger developmental process of which intensive maize agriculture is but one part.

An almost irresistible hypothesis concerning the development of maize agriculture is Hall's (1980) proposition that the tropical maize plant had to pass through a period of adaptation to the length of the photoperiod in the Midwest before it became a successful crop. The evidence for the gradual infiltration and use of maize during the Middle Woodland period in the eastern United States (Asch and Asch 1985) fits Hall's scenario. Because high-yield, eight-rowed maize was developed much earlier in Central and South America and introduced into North America (Lathrap 1987), it seems likely that a period of adaptation to northern latitudes also was necessary for the tropical eight-rowed variety to be developed into Northern Flint. Still, a great time lag exists between the availability of high-yield maize varieties and their widespread use during the Mississippi period (Watson 1988: 54–55). The ecological argument for the adaptation of high-yield maize in North America quickly becomes deterministic when it is applied as a primal cause in the broader context of social change.

The archaeological distribution of early eight-rowed maize outside the Mississippian core area in the central Mississippi Valley illustrates the contention that growing this plant does not correlate with the emergence of hierarchical administration (Watson 1988). In the Illinois and Mississippi River valleys intensive production of eight-rowed maize lags behind the emergence of complex social groups (Morse and Morse 1983; Johannessen 1984; Asch and Asch 1985; Nassaney 1987). Eight-rowed maize occurs in substantial quantities in Late Woodland (pre-A.D. 900) contexts around the core area (e.g., southern Wisconsin [Arzigian 1987], Ohio River valley [Muller 1987], eastern Iowa [Benn 1980], and the Kansas City region [Adair 1988]). Other native domesticates usually occur with maize in both core and peripheral areas, as illustrated by the horticultural complex from Initial Middle Missouri sites in South Dakota (Benn 1974; Nickel 1977: 56). Beans do not appear until after approximately A.D. 1000.

The botanical and faunal assemblages from the Priestly site (3PO490), an Emergent Mississippian hamlet in the alluvial valley of northeastern Arkansas, illustrate how diversified the Early Mississippian subsistence was. Native starchy domesticates occur in more than 70% of flotation samples, and maize is in 55% of the samples (Pearsall and Hunter 1990). Yet, a high index of nut remains and quantities of bones of native floodplain animals also are present (Kelly 1990). At Priestly, people procured fish, amphibians, water fowl, terrestrial birds, small mammals, nuts, a few deer, and probably mussels (not well preserved), and grew maize and other starchy native domesticates except beans. Maize of mostly eight-rowed and ten-rowed varieties was grown at Priestly from the beginning of the occupation at approximately A.D. 800. This maize represents a diversified, nutritionally rich, and balanced subsistence base that could have been gathered or produced within a two-mile radius of the site. After many years of surveying the Central Mississippi Valley (e.g., Phillips, Ford, and Griffin 1951), enough data exist to allow inference of a widespread pattern of Emergent Mississippian communities like Priestly. A diverse subsistence strategy with horticulture was pursued by contemporary people at the nearby Zebree site (Morse and Morse 1980). The same subsistence pattern is evident in Emergent Mississippian sites in the American Bottom (Johannessen 1984) and other locations in the Mississippi Valley (Naşsaney 1987: 140). The peoples' proportional reliance on natural and horticultural products probably depended first and foremost on local microenvironmental conditions as well as territorial and exchange relationships with neighbors.

Recent studies of stable carbon isotopes in human bones have added detail to the knowledge of aboriginal diets in the Mississippi River basin.

A study of burials from the Central Mississippi Valley found that people from Late Woodland and Emergent Mississippian contexts, including the Zebree site, did not have isotopic evidence for a diet dependent on maize, whereas people who lived after A.D. 1200 did show evidence of substantial maize consumption (Lynott et al. 1986). A similar but broader-based study of diets by Buikstra et al. (1987) found wide intersite variability in the consumption of maize by Midwesterners during the Late Woodland and Early Mississippi periods. They infer that the development of maize agriculture was not a uniform process at the community level (Buikstra et al. 1987: 72).

General agreement exists that intensive production of many varieties of maize, along with squash, beans, and native domesticates, became the dominant agricultural pattern after A.D. 1000 (Ford 1977; Smith 1978; Hall 1980; Steponaitis 1983: 170; Schroedl and Boyd 1985: 144; Peebles 1978; Nassaney 1987: 141; Watson 1988). Although foraging for natural food resources in the floodplain remained a significant part of the diet, the commitment to maize-complex production clearly included participation by all members of the community and entailed massive modification of the environment (Ford 1977; Gallagher and Sasso 1987; Woods 1987). Lathrap (1987) and others (e.g., Riley 1987: 300) stress that this intensive form of maize production was intentionally structured to produce high yields through such means as genetic manipulation of the maize plant, multiple-field plantings, fertilizing, and ridging or mounding within fields.

These studies and others undermine coevolutionary models because agricultural development cannot be shown to have been directly related through cause or effect to the appearance of complex social formations. Put simply, the timing of cultural events is not right for the model. Maize was cultivated in the Eastern Woodlands for hundreds of years before it became an important food crop, yet intensive maize cultivation postdates the initial phases of Mississippian population growth and aggregation.

Methods of Inquiry

My analysis begins with the value of human labor, that is, the social production of social subsistence use-value (Hakken 1987: 71). Marx (1906) argued that all value arises from the productive labor of human beings and that labor is produced as the social formation (society) is reproduced. Value can be construed in different ways because it is constituted in various labor contexts and is transformed through social exchange. Value in the form of material products and people (e.g., their labor and biological reproduction) is exchanged in reciprocal arrangements. When products are exchanged, the product's simple use-value is supplemented by the social relationship between exchangers, creating exchange-value, which can accumulate as a social surplus. When people are exchanged (e.g., as corvee labor, indentured servants, slaves, domestic help), their labor is put to use to create value. In the case of women, their biological potential is especially important in kin-based societies. We are indebted to Lévi-Strauss (1969) for pointing out that bride exchange is a transaction of female labor and reproductive potential. This exchange makes kinship part of the relations of production in prestate societies because kinship is the primary mechanism for reproducing labor (Godelier 1978).

Bender (1979, 1985) perceives complexity (i.e., large-scale social interaction, political control, labor mobilization, surplus accumulation) as a condition fostered by "closure" of the social environment. When movement is constrained in any way by demographic factors, social groups begin to formulate definitions of eligibility, degree of participation, and access to sources of production—the initial forms of inequality in human society (Marquardt 1985: 72). Intragroup and intergroup relationships become arenas for reciprocal exchanges—prestations (Mauss 1967)—and the creation of debt, the basis for inequality. Reciprocal exchanges are delayed-return agreements in which socially induced obligations are paid for with surplus production. The social surplus is controlled by the managers of reciprocal exchanges as they redistribute surplus products.

The preceding theoretical perspective led Sahlins (1972), Friedman and Rowlands (1978), Keesing (1981), Wolf (1982, 1984), and Saitta (1983b) to focus on the production and distribution of social surpluses as a means of explaining the history and development of complex social formations. Accumulations of social surpluses are fostered through regional exchange networks, which in turn become the arenas for the creation of social differences in the form of accumulated reciprocity or debt (Hindess and Hirst 1975: 55; Bender 1979: 210, 1985: 55). In delayed-return systems leaders ensure access to resources by exploiting the labor of kin to convert raw materials into products and by propagating alliances for the exchange of surpluses that guarantee future access to forms of value (Bender 1979: 212).

Control of surplus production and labor reproduction forms the basis for a source of power in systems where status is achieved. This theory is why Meillassoux (1972), Godelier (1978), Friedman and Rowlands (1978), Bender (1979: 212), and Clammer (1985: 101) have identified one kind of authority as the maintenance of social knowledge (e.g., alliance rules, genealogies, history, marriage regulations, customs, magic, and divination). As this type of authority is promoted through kinship, those with power will act to reproduce their influence across generations so that the aspects of authority become imbedded in the descent system. Social complexity stems from the gradual institution of inequality within the kinship and descent structures so that all members accept relationships of dominance and compliance as an inevitable condition (hegemony). When dominance relationships extend beyond the kinship network to encompass other autonomous units, they are said to be linked by politics (Service 1975: 49).

Marx viewed the processes of change in the social formation as historically constituted. Transformations of the social formation could be explained by the formation and intensification of contradictions within the economic structure through the dialectical interaction of the material forces (economic base) and the social relations of production over time (Zeidler 1987: 332). The conditions of social change certainly were present during the Late Woodland and Mississippi periods in the Mississippi River basin as intensive maize agriculture was being developed. The societies in question were largely kin-based social formations (Knight 1990), but they manifested some of the characteristics of class-stratified social formations in the form of human sacrifice, surplus accumulation, ranking in settlement patterns, differences in domestic habitations, and ascribed status as indicated by burial modes. The interpersonal and political antagonisms inherent in social formations undergoing transformation from kin-based to class-stratified structure are well known (Gailey and Patterson 1987) and will be cited later as one of the principal motivations behind the pursuit of maize agriculture.

The Role of Labor-Value in Culture Change

Origins of the subsistence pattern of harvesting aquatic and forest resources and native seed horticulture extend back to the Middle Archaic period (see Neusius 1986). The initial trajectory for the domestication of indigenous plants covered an extended period of time (about three thousand years) and occurred largely through the unconscious intervention of human foragers (i.e., the process was "stress-free" [Smith 1987: 37]). It is clear that foragers in the Midwest responded to environmental and social constraints by following a strategy of constricting their territories, intensifying allocation of local resources, and extending influence over competitors through debt transactions (Brown and Vierra 1983; Bender 1985; Brown 1986; O'Brien 1987). The one glaring contradiction in this strategy was that the economy depended on exploitation of a finite natural resource base with rudimentary technology (i.e., lithic tools and gardening). Thus, maintenance of an adequate subsistence base plus a surplus to compete in the social arena were achieved through increased labor allocations, not technical breakthroughs.

By Middle Woodland times the subsistence pattern combining intensive foraging with the gardening of squash and native domesticates was in place (Struever 1968; Styles 1981; Braun 1988: 22–23). Maize was a very minor component of gardening, perhaps merely a ritual cultigen (Hall 1980). Braun (1987: 172) listed four economic aspects of Middle Woodland society: sustained residential aggregation, changes in household organization, intensive foraging in main valleys, and intensified horticulture. I would add mound building to this list. Mounds containing ancestral bones and situated on conspicuous places near the villages were the manifestations of ritual and ideology that reinforced social solidarity (cf. Mallam 1976; Charles 1985).

The best way to describe the structure of the Middle Woodland social formation is that it was a kin-based mode of production (Wolf 1982) in which corporate descent groups functioned as the unit of social production and consumption. Braun and Plog (1982) use the concept of tribal organization to describe a parallel social structure and function, that is, social networks of exchange to distribute risks and benefits to members. Corporate kin groups carried out three basic labor processes to produce what they needed and to reproduce their society: (1) harvesting natural resources; (2) modifying the environment to produce native cultigens in gardens; and (3) producing surplus commodities for reciprocal exchange in the pan-continental interaction sphere. The social values of products from the three labor processes are different. In harvesting natural resources, people use the environment as the object of production (Wolf 1982: 91–92) and therefore are subject to the absolute limits of what nature yields. The gardening labor process uses the environment as an instrument of production because human beings intervene to modify the natural environment and select for the growth of specific plants. However, Middle Woodland gardens were not yet fully developed instruments of production because the environment was modified only enough to encourage pure stands of naturally gregarious native domesticates. Surplus commodities may be exchanged for instruments of production (human labor) when they are utilized in exchange systems and ritual to gain access to and hold potential members of the community. All of the subsistence and production processes mentioned above are labor-intensive pursuits.

At the root of the emergent Middle Woodland mode of production were syllogistic rituals that reified the status of the corporate economic group by emphasizing its links to venerated ancestors (Webb 1989: 290). This belief system established the right of the group's leaders to collect and distribute the labor-value of its members for the purpose of satisfying subsistence needs and reciprocal obligations. Rituals associated with the burial program were the most prominent institutions for ensuring social (economic) solidarity (Charles 1985, 1987). Exchange of surplus commodities is another way of expressing control over the sources of production, notably the surplus-value created by people who made the commodities.

I am placing stress on the labor formula of the Middle Woodland mode of production because it shows through in the contemporary technical achievements as well. The point has already been made that native plant gardening entailed relatively modest ecological modifications of the natural environment (Smith 1987). Increased production from gardens was achieved mostly through substantial inputs of human labor (e.g., for clearing native vegetation, planting, weeding, harvesting, winnowing, boiling food). In the case of the development of refined ceramic containers for boiling seed foods (Braun 1983), the result was an increase in the supply of food and not a change in the quality of nutrition (Buikstra et al. 1987: 79). The cost of refined ceramic containers was increased labor for the production of more and highly decorated vessels as well as more time spent processing seed foods. It is no wonder that Buikstra and her colleagues (1987: 77) argue that Middle Woodland population increases were related to improvements in food processing. I see Woodland population increases as a product of the general labor formula, which sacrificed labor efficiency for increased output (Christenson 1980: 54–55).

During the Late Woodland period the settlement pattern in much of the eastern United States became far more dispersed throughout river valleys and uplands (Braun 1988: 23). I suspect the transformation in settlement patterns was a response to contradictions in the structure of the social labor processes. My reasoning is this. In a competitive ("closed") social environment the only way to expand an economy based on natural resources is to apply more labor and more effective tools to the extraction of resources. Population increases stimulated the trend toward dispersed settlements, where production groups utilized more effective tools and crops (Braun 1988: 21–25) to extract subsistence from small territories while not radically altering the traditional economic base of natural and horticultural resources. Labor processes still favored an increase in the supply of people to do work, especially in the context of smaller-sized producer groups, because the new technology and crops were labor-intensive tools. Ford (1977) stresses that the Late Woodland period was a time of maximum redundancy in the procurement of natural and horticultural foods. The intensification of relationships between people and their tools of production contradicted the basic relations within Middle Woodland society, which focused the corporate image on the relationship between human beings and natural resources (Webb 1989: 291). A transformation in the relations of production was taking place: the previous relationship between human beings and the natural environment (as an object of production) was shifting toward a relationship between human beings and their tools of production (i.e., the artificial horticultural environment, ceramics, bow and arrow). This shift meant that authorities extended their control of the tools of production by manipulating the people who used the tools.

The changeover to agricultural (maize) production did not occur rapidly during the Late Woodland and Early Mississippi periods (Asch and Asch 1985; Watson 1988: 44), nor did people of the Mississippi period intensify maize production simply because they realized its enormous productive potential for supporting a labor-intensive, tributary system of production (cf. Boserup 1965). The combination of very productive eight-rowed Northern Flint and beans postdated the appearance of maize cultivation by more than four hundred years in the Midwest. The shift to intensive maize production had its roots in the social and political turmoil that resulted when authority figures attempted to extend their influence over the production and reproduction of autonomous kin groups other than their own. This process was resisted by kin communities, as it always is, because kin groups must retain the capacity to reproduce their relations of production, as their ancestors did, in order to maintain their traditional way of life (Gailey and Patterson 1987: 8). Maize production became a vehicle for an emerging elite to attract and hold the allegiance of people despite their attachments to kin-based production.

By A.D. 800, maize was only one of many labor-intensive tools in a system that featured increasing complexity in kin-based labor processes. Complexity in the labor process is evident in the proliferation of specialized ceramics for culinary and storage functions (i.e., bowls, jars, bottles, and plates) and for processing of raw materials like salt (i.e., pans and funnels). Decorative homogeneity seen in many regional ceramic complexes (cf. Braun and Plog 1982: 517) conveys social meaning along with the elaborated technical forms of ceramics, which is evidence for the supralocal cooperation and integration that Braun and Plog observe as characteristic of the Late Woodland period. Part of the reason for sharing ceramic technology and styles may have been the relationship with maize production. Maize and specially decorated pottery forms may be viewed as part of a tool complex; for example, maize seed was stored in hooded bottles with stoppers (Varney Red Filmed; Morse and Morse 1983), the maize crop was simmered into porridge in jars and bowls, and salt for seasoning maize was evaporated in pans.

By manipulating the social meaning inherent in tools of production, ordinary human beings can be encouraged to perform work that contributes to the social surplus. My reasoning is that sociopolitical regulations prescribe certain types of tools for tasks that produce basic needs as well as a social surplus. Without "regulation" tools, necessary rituals cannot be successfully performed nor can a social surplus be produced in the "proper" manner. At the onset of the Mississippi period an array of standardized tool forms made from particular materials appears along with maize-complex agriculture. Pottery is elaborated into specialized wares that function in both domestic and ceremonial spheres of life. Specialized vessels are forms of surplus production that convey social meaning (e.g., creation myths, themes in nature, and the deceased) and represent the control of production and exchange of the labor-value. These examples show why pottery is such a prominent part of grave furniture during the Mississippian period. Symbolic vessels represent transfer of control of the forces of production to the next generation. Specialization, social meaning, and labor-value are vested in lithic technology in the same way. For example, the Mill Creek chert hoes, Crescent Quarry chert artifacts (microdrills), and stylized triangular projectile points, which are widely traded and often replace local artifact styles and raw materials, are not technically superior tools. Their use is a manifestation of political power; that is, those who control production and distribution of special tools also symbolically control surplus production from the tools and the people who utilize them. This control is an example of political hegemony imbedded in the medium of technology.

Two socioeconomic conditions characterize emerging agricultural economies in the Midwest after A.D. 800: (1) the entire landscape was filled with a patchwork of horticultural communities, rendering these communities socially closed and circumscribed (Bender 1985); and (2) the only means, therefore, to increase food production with labor-intensive tools was to organize and expand the supply of labor within producer groups. No direct evidence of labor specialization can be found during the Early Mississippi period (e.g., Morse and Morse 1980: 6–29; Pauketat 1987). Abundant evidence of technical specialization can be found in maize-complex agriculture. People control all phases of the growth, harvesting, and storage of the maize-beans-squash complex and select the places where agricultural work will be performed. Because the crops are produced completely by human labor, authorities who control that labor ultimately exert power over labor-value invested in the crop. I believe that those people who managed agriculturally based societies encouraged maize cultivation through ritual and symbolic mechanisms because it was the most direct means of consolidating their control over all forms of surplus production. The surplus crop can be used to feed workers who produce all other surplus items. This system is why the advent of full-scale maize agriculture, which is accommodated in fixed locations, parallels the phenomenon of population aggregation in Mississippian towns, such as the American Bottom of Illinois (Kelly 1992: 190). Binford (1983: 219) noticed the same labor allocation in chiefdoms—that is, moving people instead of commodities, and Fowler's (1969: 374; 1992: 10–11) idea was not so far-fetched when he used the term "peasants" to describe the large population of farmers who supported the Cahokia polity.

Summary

In this model of agricultural development, I have tried to remove the biological imperative implicit in most explanations for growing the maize-beans-squash plant complex, that is, this group of plants is the most nutritionally effective choice for horticulturalists trying to expand their resource base (cf. Gallagher and Sasso 1987). This neo-Darwinist approach does not fit with the circumstances of culture change in preindustrial societies because this perspective relegates social relationships and ideology to secondary roles behind materialistic achievements in the economy—the reverse of the real structure of preindustrial societies.

I have emphasized, instead, the pivotal role of labor allocation throughout the model. Reproduction of labor is the central concern of all kin-based modes of production that utilize labor-intensive technology as their economic base. A modernized Marxist methodology entails an analysis of the production and distribution of labor-value to define socioeconomic relationships within society. This methodology builds on theoretical positions, such as ecological risk in subsistence pursuits, by adding the concept of dialectical process in culture change and by recognizing the existence of the exploitation of human labor.

Two phases in the modification of labor allocation strategies led to the development of cultivation and then to maize agriculture in the eastern United States. First, corporate kin groups of the Woodland periods applied increasing amounts of labor to their gardens and to the natural environment to extract a social surplus. Refinements in the instruments of production (crops, ceramics) were the consequence of increased labor allocations and through a feedback loop made possible the reproduction of additional labor supplies (population increase). In producing and distributing the social surplus, managers of corporate groups exploited the labor-value of the kinship group. Second, as competitive production and distribution of surplus products were carried through the Early Mississippi period, elite managers expended more energy through ritual and stylized artifacts to solidify, reinforce, and extend their influence over the production of social surpluses (see Ruyle 1987: 34–35). The elite utilized symbol and ritual to link themselves to the economic success of society by encouraging production with a complex of symbolically specialized tools: maize-beans-squash agriculture, diversified ceramics, chert hoes, and microdrills, for example. Nassaney (1987: 142) puts it this way: "The intensification of subsistence, including the adoption of full-scale maize cultivation, resulted from the political demands of social elites who sought to increase their hegemony and reify their positions of rank within society."

The process by which the Mississippian elite rose above the rest of society involved intensive exploitation of the labor-value of the whole population. Because individual slash-and-burn horticulturalists actually possess their own means of production in the form of seed crops and tools, political managers of prestate societies must appear to "control" the means of production in order to exploit people for their surplus labor-value. Otherwise, the elite could not exist.

Of what use is this model of Mississippian agricultural intensification to researchers working on the Plains and eastern prairies of the midcontinental United States? Its best application should be for cross-cultural comparisons with contemporary societies undergoing processes of politicoeconomic change. The phenomenon we know as the Emergent Mississippian *stage* is slowly being recognized in prairie-dwelling societies (Henning 1992) such as Great Oasis, Mill Creek, Oneota, Cambria, Glenwood, Nebraska tradition, and Steed-Kisker. These peoples utilized a great deal of maize, and most maintained contacts with the Cahokia influence sphere. None expresses evidence for the kinds of ascribed social stratification seen in Middle Mississippian societies, however. What role did maize cultivation play in the politicoeconomic development of these societies? The answers will come from careful analyses of their economic bases, especially paleobotanical studies that presently are distributed unevenly in archaeological reports from the prairies and do not compare in number and scope of coverage with studies in the Mississippi Valley.

Isotopic studies of human bone also are needed to detect the dietary strategies of prehistoric peoples. When more archaeological data have been collected, appropriate opportunities will occur to apply theories of historical process and methods of dialectical analysis to the problems of agricultural intensification in prairie societies.

7

Great Plains Mound Building

A Postprocessual View

Richard A. Krause

For more than one hundred years, American laymen and scholars pondered the authorship and use of North America's aboriginal mounds (Silverberg 1968). The builders they identified and the uses they imputed frequently reflected the spirit of the times (Vaughan 1982: 927–929). In the early years of American nationhood, when the triumph of free market capitalism was regarded as inevitable (Trigger 1984b), it is not surprising that interpretations of mound building were compatible with an ethic of manifest destiny that included territorial expansion. Native Americans were considered residues of ages past, primitives in the way of progress (Resek 1960: 13; Trigger 1986: 189–194), people incapable of the organizational effort needed for the construction of monumental works even if they were rendered in dirt. Insofar as Native Americans were responsible for the archaeological record, the record was interpreted as lacking in depth and showing little change through time. Many scholars saw North America's mounds as clear evidence for the prehistoric presence of an Old World influence (Barton 1787, 1797; Clinton 1820; Kingsborough 1830; Gallatin 1836). Using notions of hyperdiffusionism, these scholars linked North American mound builders to Egypt, Israel, and other classic civilizations. To yet other scholars an Old World link was not as clear, but it was still quite inconceivable that Native Americans could be the descendants of mound-building ancestors. Instead, the scholars posited a mysterious "mound building race" to explain the construction of North America's tumuli (Clinton 1820; Gallatin 1836).

The twentieth-century emergence of culture history broke the stasis stereotype. Stratigraphy and seriation won the day for time depth and sequencing (Ritchie 1944; Ford and Willey 1941). Archaeologists now framed refutable chronological claims and achieved a modest consensus on units of analysis, scale of measurement, and scope of inquiry. Native American marginality was a well-established fact of reservation life and Amerindians were viewed as better at receiving the wisdom of others than donating ideas of their own. Thus, transformations exposed during artifact sequencing were explained by one of several forms of diffusion from a few centers of Native American innovation (Adams, van Gerven, and Levy 1978). By the early twentieth century, the indigenous authorship of North America's mounds was firmly established, and, in order to achieve chronological goals, scholars began to sort them into classes based on observations of morphology and presumptions about use. Geometric and effigy earthworks were separated from burial tumuli and frustum-shaped or rectangular platform–shaped mounds. A systematic comparison of mound morphology and contents now indicated that geometric and effigy mounds were slightly earlier than dome-shaped mortuary tumuli and that mortuary tumuli were earlier than platform mounds (Silverberg 1968).

Although the British had made the shift in the 1920s, the move in the 1950s from an ethnological to a sociocultural or functionalist emphasis in American anthropology created the context for a challenge to the culture history approach. This challenge came in the form of a new archaeology, some of whose adherents preferred to call themselves processualists (Dunnell 1986: 29–33). At the core of this new archaeology was a view of artifacts as the products of patterned human behavior. It was assumed that this patterning reflected the organization of past social forms (see Binford and Binford [1969] for examples) and that artifactual data could be used to infer the structure of extinct cultural systems. From the perspective of this new archaeology, mounds were often assumed to be the inert residues, or crystallized reflections, of chiefdoms, the epiphenomenal indicators of an array of cultural practices that marked a stratified social order (Peebles 1974; Peebles and Kus 1977).

Truncated Mississippian stage mounds, for example, were identified as substructures for temples (mortuary and otherwise), chiefs' houses, "town houses" (i.e., council houses or public meeting places), purificatory rituals, and the presentation of world renewal ceremonies (Schnell, Knight, and Schnell 1981; Howard 1968). These same substructures were also interpreted as temple tombs, cenotaphs, markers of social ranking, and symbols of corporate identity (Jenkins and Krause 1986: 126–130). Although infrequently identified with chiefdoms, most Woodland stage mounds were considered the detritus of complex "burial programs." It became common practice to interpret the contrasts in artifact kind and quantity with the burials within the mounds as markers of rank among the deceased.

As challenging as they may be, the new archaeologists' interpretations *tend to be* both incomplete and static. They are incomplete insofar as the practice of mound building is viewed as reflecting but not participating in social action. They are static insofar as they merely correlate artifact kinds, quantities, and distributions with social forms. Those who adopt this point of view, and for a while I was one of them, seem not to realize that they limit themselves to time-isolated and context-constrained accounts of the phenomena they study. In theory, their goals are lawful or lawlike claims that are only broadly, if at all, time limited and context dependent (Watson, LeBlanc, and Redman 1971: 26, 56; Plog 1974: 14). In fact, the narrow contextual dependence and particularistic nature of their results engender a static bias (see van der Leeuw 1982: 421–457).

More recent practitioners of archaeological science have expressed a greater concern for the study of social dynamism and the role played by artifacts in human life and social interaction. Some practitioners have even attempted to transform the static perspective inhering in the new archaeology into a morphogenetic view in which time-persistent or space-persistent continuities in artifact manufacture and use are actively sought as the objects of explanation (Krause 1988). This morphogenetic view has a dynamism that springs from viewing artifacts as participating in human acts and events, and stressing the constant generation of new acts and events from previous, yet broader than site-specific or locality-specific, contexts.

When a morphogenetic perspective is applied to the search for continuity it serves as a springboard for explanation. It is with this view that I will argue that Woodland stage mound building in the Great Plains was but one case of the widespread Amerindian use of mortuary ritual to express and intensify a network of social, political, and economic transactions that had deep prehistoric roots. In so doing I will have recourse to events and processes in a restricted geographic range—the lower Republican River valley of north-central Kansas. I will treat this section of the Republican River valley as a microcosm, a restricted universe, but one within which the events and processes that shaped the broader sweep of Great Plains prehistory can be better understood. Let us now turn to the data set that will undergird our efforts.

Great Plains Tumuli

I will limit myself to the twenty-three low, circular-to-oval, dome-shaped tumuli of earth, or fieldstone and earth, built atop the bluffs or headlands fringing the east bank of the lower reaches of the Republican River between Clay Center and Junction City, Kansas (Figure 7-1). These constructions vary in length from 1.8 to 17 meters, with a mean length of 7.09 ± 3.90 meters. They vary in height from 28 centimeters to 3.7 meters, with a mean height of 69.4 centimeters ± 3.8 centimeters (Figure 7-2). All were presumably built in and over circular or oval sod-stripped basins, and all were easily visible from the surrounding lowlands. Some appear to be isolated from others of their kind, whereas others occur in clusters of two, three, or four side-by-side or partially overlapping examples (Phenice 1969: 10–53).

At one time, all of these mounds presumably contained human remains. Nevertheless, they varied considerably in the way these remains were treated and ultimately entombed. Some contained primary-extended, primary-flexed, and/or bundle burials. Some contained bones grouped by body parts, some contained pockets or clusters of burned and broken bones, and in some burned and broken bones appear to have been scattered in and over episodes of mound fill. Some contained individual burial pits, whereas others had slab-bordered or slab-lined central cores (Figure 7-2) reminiscent of the dry-wall masonry chambers typical of Kansas City Hopewell mound building. Yet others showed no discernible internal architecture. Thus indicated are postmortem practices that included skeletalization (i.e., burial and exhumation, exposure, dismemberment, and defleshing) and skeletal manipulation (i.e., bone selection and handling and then bone chopping, burning, or both [Phenice 1969: 53–60]).

The labor expended on mound construction took the form of sod-stripping; chamber digging; and the collecting, hauling, and deposition of fieldstone or digging, hauling, and deposition of skinloads or basketloads of dirt (Phenice 1969: 10–53). There are tantalizing hints that at least some of the dirt used in mound construction was scraped from camp or village sites (Wedel 1986: 83). A procedure of this kind is arguably an act of purification, indicating perhaps the periodic ritual renewal of otherwise secular contexts. Whatever their intent, the scale of these efforts varied from mound to mound. The smallest mound contained less than 10 cubic meters and the largest less than 340 cubic meters of fill (Table 7-1). Of the twenty-three measurable specimens in the sample, nine contained less than 6 meters, and eleven contained less than 30 meters of fill. Only three contained more than 150 cubic meters of fill (Table 7-1). If we posit a very modest 0.50 cubic meter effort per person per day, the smallest mounds would have required less than a four-day effort by five or so workers and the largest less than a thirty-day effort by a work force of thirty. None would have required the equivalent of corvee labor with a network of

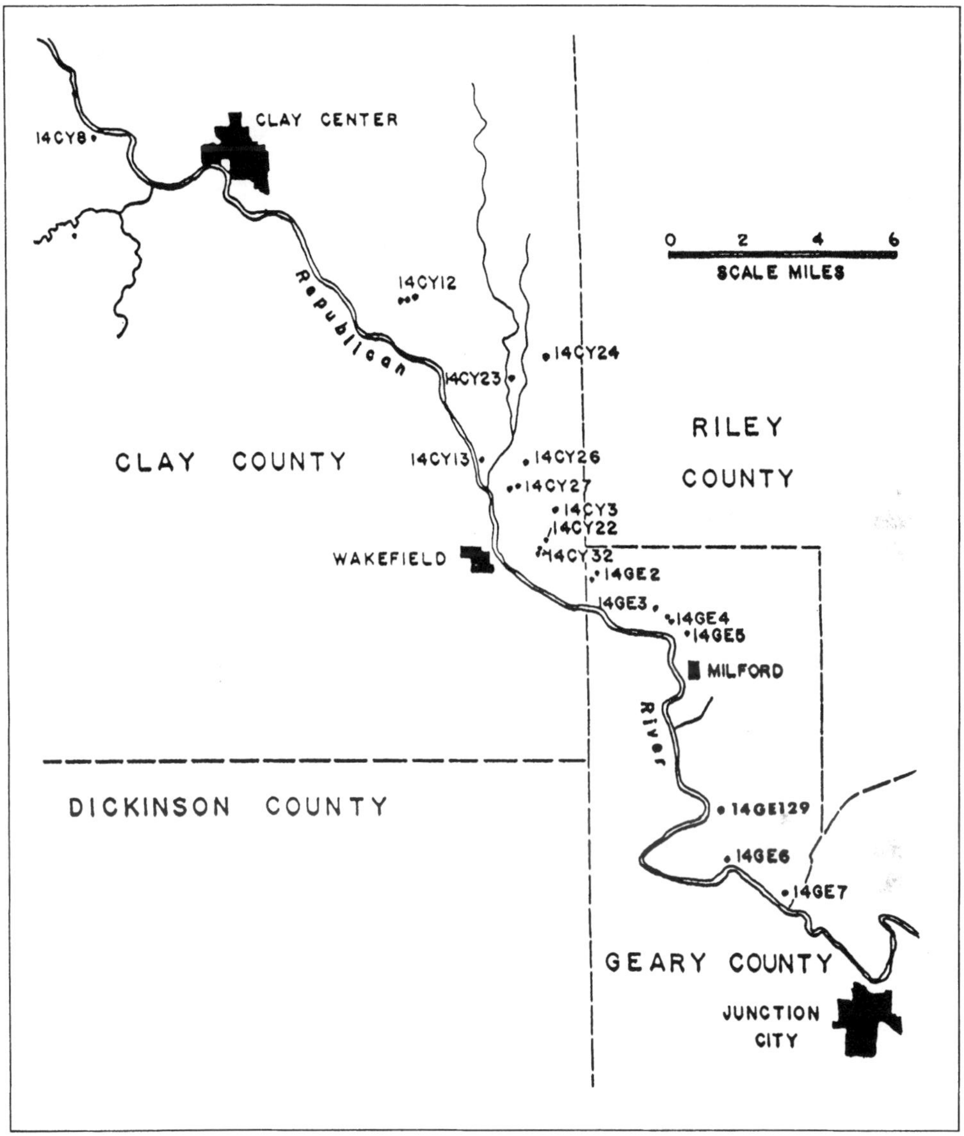

Figure 7-1. Fieldstone and Earth Mounds in Geary and Clay Counties

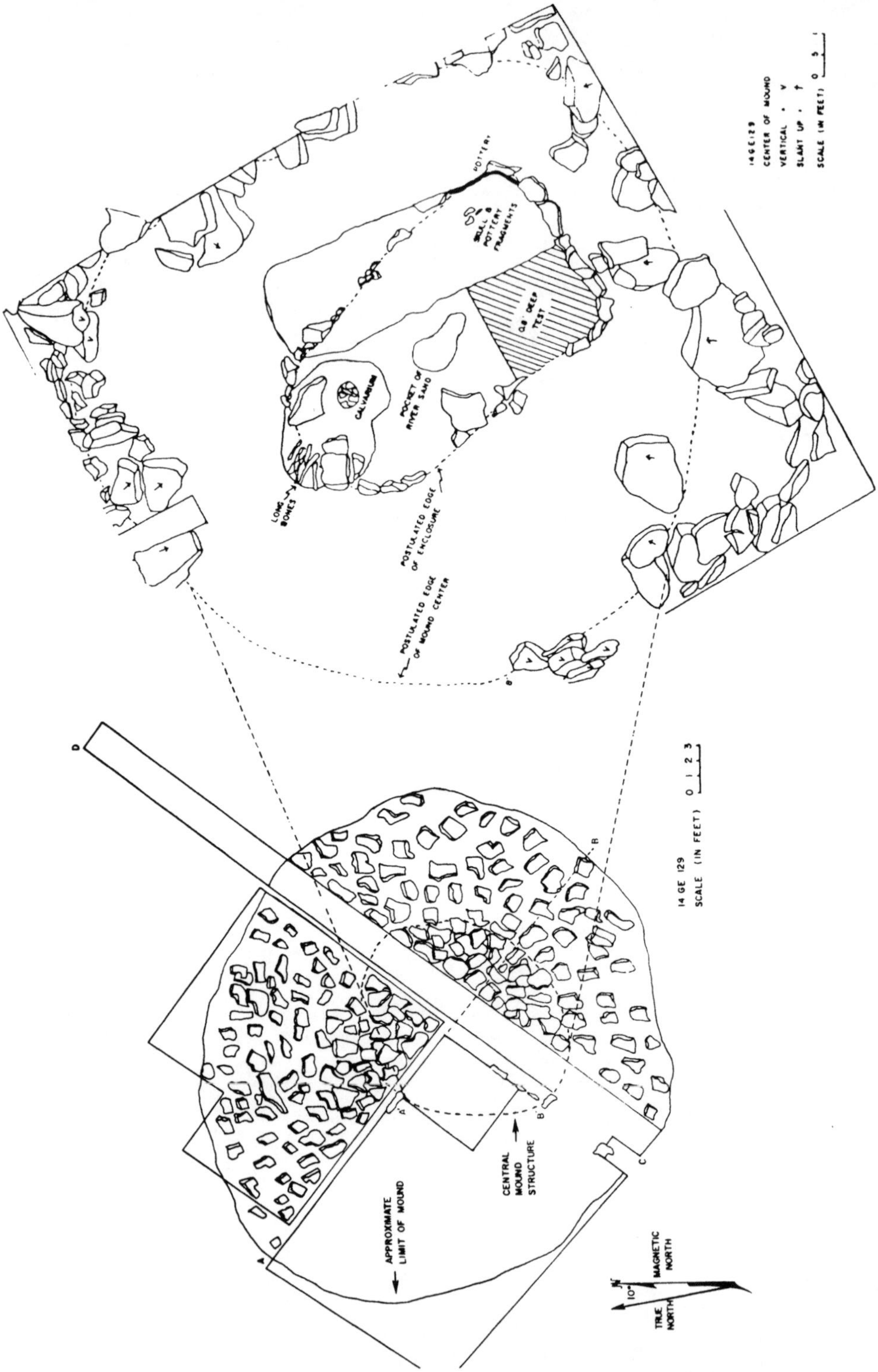

Figure 7-2. Excavated Remains of Fieldstone and Earth Mound at 14GE129.

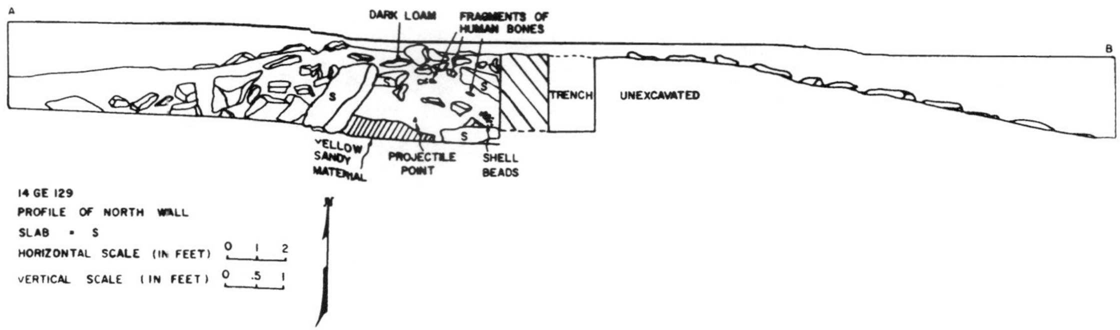
A
B
DARK LOAM
FRAGMENTS OF HUMAN BONES
S
TRENCH
UNEXCAVATED
YELLOW SANDY MATERIAL
PROJECTILE POINT
SHELL BEADS
14 GE 129
PROFILE OF NORTH WALL
SLAB = S
HORIZONTAL SCALE (IN FEET) 0 1 2
VERTICAL SCALE (IN FEET) 0 .5 1
N

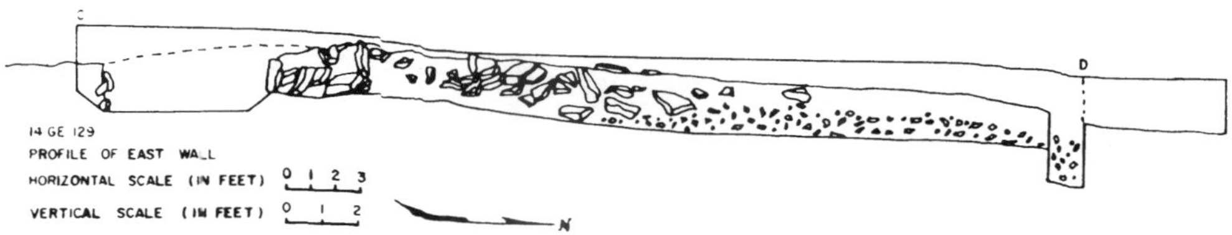
C
D
14 GE 129
PROFILE OF EAST WALL
HORIZONTAL SCALE (IN FEET) 0 1 2 3
VERTICAL SCALE (IN FEET) 0 1 2
N

Table 7-1. Mound Fill Estimated in Meters, Mound at 14GE129

Site	*Diameter*	*Length*	*Width*	*Height*	*Cu. Meters*
14CY12A	4.90	—	—	.28	7.04
14CY12B	—	4.30	2.7	.30	3.65
14CY12C	3.40	—	—	.60	7.26
14CY13	—	7.30	12.2	.41	17.82
14CY20	3.65	—	—	.53	7.36
14CY22	6.10	—	—	.82	32.00
14CY23	4.57	—	—	.76	16.70
14CY24	7.30	—	—	.76	43.60
14CY26A	3.65	—	—	.76	10.30
14CY26B	2.70	—	—	.41	3.40
14CY26C	1.80	—	—	.84	2.90
14CY26D	2.70	—	—	.69	5.67
14CY27	—	5.50	3.7	1.50	33.40
14CY30	6.10	—	—	.56	22.55
14CY31	—	—	—	—	—
14CY32A	6.10	—	—	.63	24.55
14CY32B	6.70	—	—	.71	37.99
14GE3	6.70	—	—	.30	14.11
14GE4A	5.50	—	—	.15	4.75
14GE4B	11.30	—	—	1.80	240.76
14GE5	6.40	—	—	.41	17.59
14GE6	—	14.30	17.0	1.32	334.25
14GE7	—	12.18	14.6	.91	178.14
14GE129	—	9.40	8.5	.51	42.61

overseers or equivalent administrative apparatus. I therefore tend to view them as labors of love or markers of voluntary piety that were, for the most part, self-organized and self-directed, albeit guided by tradition and custom as understood and interpreted by authorities having the status of first among equals—a status validated more by act and deed than by birthright.

The durable wealth expended in mound ritualism was either placed with the deposits of skeletal remains or spread through the mound fill. It included both utilitarian and exotic materials. Among them were shell disc beads; barrel-shaped *Columella* and sphere-shaped *Marginella* and *Olivella* beads; tubular bone beads; bone pins; dentate, rocker-stamped and cord-roughened pottery; corner-notched dart or spear points; small-stemmed or corner-notched arrow points; chipped stone knives and scrapers; and ground and polished stone pipes and pendants (Eyman 1966; Phenice 1969: 10–53; Wedel 1986: 82–85). The artifact yield from most mounds can be described as modest at best and the intramound distribution of artifacts as questionably patterned. If one judges by the ceramics and other diagnostic artifacts, some mounds contain Hopewell or Hopewell-like materials, some contain Plains Woodland specimens, some have a mixture of Plains Woodland and Central Plains Phase or Middle Ceramic period materials, and one, at least, contained only Central Plains Phase or Middle Ceramic period artifacts (Phenice 1969: 10–53). This intermound artifact diversity led Wedel (1986: 82) to question the probity of identifying them as components of a single cultural historical taxon, and for good reason. However, such taxonomic questions need not concern us. We are seeking the common theme or themes that can be seen in the diverse materials now at hand. For this task we shall use the concepts *sacra, cult institution*, and *iconic family* recently introduced by Knight (1986: 675–685) in his analysis of Mississippian ritualism in the southeastern United States.

Sacra are objects of and for ceremonial display. They derive their significance from the cult institutions for which they are produced and in which they are manipulated (Knight 1986: 675). A cult institution is "a set of rituals all having the same general goal [and] rationalized by a set of similar or related beliefs" (Wallace 1966: 75). Further, the set of all sacra associated with a specific cult institution may be termed an iconic family (Knight 1986: 676–677).

We may rightly claim that the mounds themselves, the human remains within them, and the artifacts deposited during their construction were all sacra. The artifacts deposited during mound construction, insofar as they were not coincidental inclusions, are customarily viewed as sacra by archaeologists. The identification of the mounds themselves as sacra may seem unusual to those not used to thinking of them as objects of ritual display. Nevertheless, it is quite clear that the tumuli in our sample grew in size by consuming the wealth and labor of the living as well as the bodies of the dead. They were in this sense both participants in and the consequences of communal ritual efforts. They are, therefore, no less objects of sacred display than the famous Mississippian stage embossed copper plates, engraved shell cups, and monolithic axes in the midwestern and southeastern United States. Moreover, the manipulation of the bodies and bones of the dead mark them as sacra. Their disposal, together with modest amounts of durable wealth under or in mounds, must be understood as a purely expressive act. Taken together (i.e., as sacra forming a single cult institution), burial wealth, mound building, and postmortem body and bone manipulation can be seen as elements of a single iconic family. Finally, the periodicity of the ritualism that organized them suggests a cult institution focused, in part at least, on periodic and communal rites of intensification and purification. Let us now place this cult institution in the broader sweep of Central Plains prehistory.

Discussion

As currently understood, a seriously reduced carrying capacity during the Altithermal period seems to have forced the Archaic stage inhabitants of the Great Plains into oasis areas or peripheral regions where they developed a diversified lifestyle (Wedel 1964: 88–94). It was from this diversified lifestyle that post-Altithermal differences in fauna and flora shaped a mosaic of adjustments. Among the elements of this mosaic were the following: (1) a highly mobile herd animal–hunting and High Plains foraging pattern in the Western shortgrass plains; (2) a less mobile, mixed woodland/tallgrass plains form of hunting and harvesting along the creeks and river courses in the Central Plains; and (3) a yet more sedentary, woodland-adapted pattern of hunting and gathering that focused on the broad, forested bottomlands of the major river valleys and feeder streams that edged the Plains on the east (Wedel 1964: 88–94). Mound building became bonded to the second and third elements of this pattern during Middle Woodland or Kansas City Hopewell times (Wedel 1986: 81–91).

Before this bonding, however, and perhaps as early as 5000 B.C., the Archaic stage populations in the river valleys of the Eastern and Central Plains had achieved a productive balance in using locally available resources (Wedel 1986: 72–80). To the best of our knowledge, hunting and harvesting groups used portable tools, weapons, implements, and containers (Schmits 1987: 153–173). We may reasonably argue for a division of labor by age and sex structured by and through a kin-based system of task allocation in which, theoretically at least, all held equal shares in the mode of production. Such groups are usually consensus governed, with the role of leader falling to the adult male most capable of shaping and expressing that consensus. A kind of balanced reciprocity is typically the dominant form of economic integration. In historic native North America this kind of economic integration was achieved through the custom of honoring by gift giving (Holder 1970). With communities of the size and mobility posited for Plains Archaic groups, the exchange of gifts could indeed have moved goods and services through coresident domestic groups with relative ease and efficiency.

Insofar as the goods moved by way of gift exchange were consumable (such as deer or buffalo meat, hides, and baskets), and insofar as a return in service or kind was demanded by local custom, gift giving could have formed the basis for political action in Archaic stage groups. Presents of meat and other consumables, if not immediately returned, put the receiver in the donor's debt. Hence, these exchanges could be manipulated by experienced and ambitious hunters to place consanguineal and affinal kinsmen in their debt and render them more amenable to consensus-building efforts. When decision making by consensus was focused on a daily and annual round of economic practices (i.e., when one man's interpretation of plant and animal behavior was valued above his competitors), political success could be measured by the number of domestic groups a man could attract and hold from season to season and year to year as he moved himself and his followers to food.

Although our knowledge of Archaic stage burial practices is scanty, individual mortuary rituals may have served to strengthen claims to leadership by providing the context for the disbursement or destruction of durable and consumable wealth, as limited as it seems to have been (Finnegan 1981; Fisher et al. 1985; Schmits 1987; Turpin, Hennenberg, and Risking 1986). In other words, burial rites provided intense, if periodic, opportunities for extensive gift giving. In theory, we suppose that all men had access to the means of production and distribution necessary for wealth manipulation and its investment in personalized mortuary ritual. In fact, we suspect that some men were more successful than others. We further suspect that such success was heritable in the sense that successful fathers tended to confer greater advantage to their offspring than unsuccessful ones. Even a temporary and consensual command of community resources and benefits may thus have taken the first tentative steps toward becoming focused on family lines.

Leadership by consensus is, however, ephemeral. By its very nature it can only serve a population of limited size and permanence. To build and maintain a consensus-based following greater than a few domestic groups would require extraordinary skill and effort. Thus, in consensus-based groups, authority tends to be impermanent. The strong leader of a season might, through a series of reverses, become a mere follower within the passage of a yearly round. Moreover, membership in such groups tends to be no more permanent than leadership. Separate domestic groups aggregate for common cause during greater or shorter periods of time, depending on the issues at hand and the success, or lack thereof, of those in temporary command. Groups of this kind fragment with population growth, congeal when suitable reserves of wild food are available, and dissipate when they are not. Thus, in consensus-governed groups, food and goods (locally produced or perhaps even traded in) are not used to maintain a stratified social order or codified authority structure. Continued success in providing and distributing meat and other consumables was the most stable underpinning of a political order that would have seemed flexible in the extreme to an observer steeped in the traditions of political and social affairs developed in Europe, Asia, or Africa.

The pattern of leadership typical of the Archaic stage probably continued into and through the Woodland stage. Now, however, modest population growth and decreased community mobility seem indicated (Butler 1988; Johnson 1976, 1981; Kivett 1952, 1953; O'Brien et al. 1979; Schambock 1983; Wedel 1943, 1959, 1986: 81–97; Wood 1981; Wyckoff and Brooks 1983). There are also the first reasonably widespread evidence of moderately complex mortuary practices and the first glimpse of extended periods of corpse handling as part of locally organized and ritually expressed programs of death and burial (Eyman 1966; Hill and Kivett 1941; Johnson 1976, 1981; Kivett 1952, 1953: 12; O'Brien 1971; Phenice 1969; Schultz and Spaulding 1948; Wedel 1935: 174; 1943, 1986: 81–97). What I see of importance in this development, however, is the grafting of domestically created and durable forms of wealth (admittedly restricted primarily to utilitarian goods) onto an emergent but explicit system of wealth consumption by way of burial ritual. In short, utilitarian durables could now be converted to nonutilitarian consumables, and the consequences of gift giving could be extended and more intensely focused.

Thus, although we see the Woodland stage as marked by the continuation of a well-established pattern of leadership and political action, a pattern that brought with it status mobility and shifting group and political allegiances, it now contained a new potential, a chance that the manipulation of *both* consumable and durable wealth might be used as a means to political ends. This new potential seems to have been realized in the Great Plains, albeit unevenly, in the construction of community funerary monuments. I realize that many, if not most, of these monuments have traditionally been viewed as a reflection of events and processes gathering momentum to the east and south (Wedel 1986: 81–97), events and processes that would reshape much of prehistoric native North America in a Hopewellian image. Nevertheless, these events and processes would also focus attention on the abstract idea of collective spiritual welfare (Krause 1988).

That some of the wealth committed to Great Plains mortuary monuments was supplied by an exchange network emanating from extralocal sources seems indisputable (Wedel 1986: 81–97). That this exchange network depended for its maintenance on the propagation of Hopewellian ideas about the proper treatment of the dead also seems likely. In the Great Plains, however, Hopewellian ideas seem to have been recast in the light of a strong commitment to local identity, thus providing mortuary ritualism of mixed ancestry and a markedly parochial character (Wedel 1986: 81–97). What is true of Plains burial monuments, however, is that they seem to indicate a commitment to forms of social, economic, and political life having a firmer structure than their forerunners. What is also true of them is that they bonded the production and manipulation of wealth to the abstract idea of collective spiritual welfare and allowed the conversion of durables to consumables in a quest that served *community-wide* as well as purely personal ends. For the first time in the prehistory of the Plains we have some tangible evidence that individual acts, motivated by personal goals and yielding personal benefits, could yield them in the name of community service and community well-being.

In other words, through mound building, gift giving assumes a sacramental value. Through mound building one's accumulated wealth and labor are tangibly dedicated to the group as well as to its individuals. One's wealth and labor could now transcend the limits of corporeal existence by extending the kinship ties between the community of the living and the community of the dead, drawing the two together and sealing their union much as marriage prestations might draw clusters of kin-related persons together and weave them into a community among the living. Be that as it may, what is important to my argument is that Great Plains burial mounds, despite local variations in form and construction, were among the first public monuments in the area—the first durable examples of status-seeking and prestige distribution through a commitment to manifest public works. Great Plains burial mounds grew in stature by virtue of consuming both the bodies of the dead and the labor and wealth of the living, as modest as the latter may have been. They gave in return a firmer means for creating, maintaining, and distributing those forms of status and prestige that made possible the temporary management of natural and social resources.

On the one hand, we may see Great Plains burial mounds as public monuments containing the remains of the group's ancestors and evidence of its success in manipulating both external and internal sources of durable wealth. In this light, they were community shrines and symbols of corporate identity, examples of a community's fund of prestige to which members could point with pride and in which members shared, if perhaps differentially. On the other hand, we may view them as organized and, we may suspect, managed investments of community resources that were both stage settings for public ritual and tokens of traditional forms of authority, as evanescent and potentially egalitarian as they seem to have been. Do not, however, mistake my intent. I am not claiming that Great Plains burial mounds were symbolic in the sense that they stood for something else. I view them as *actively* symbolic, as an integral and inseparable part of social reality. Instead of viewing them as passive manifestations, or epiphenomenal reflections, of power and authority, I see them as the means for creating, and the conduit for distributing, power and authority.

Summary

Mortuary monuments played an important role in Great Plains prehistory. From them we can infer the existence of an organizational theme, the public manipulation of sacra within the framework of a communal cult institution devoted to periodic rites of intensification and perhaps purification. This theme, albeit made manifest by and through different arrays of sacra, was to persist for the greater part of a millennium. It may indeed have found its ultimate expression in the veneration and manipulation of sacred bundles in the Great Plains farming villages of ethnographic record. Also, it seems that through mound building an Archaic stage tendency to focus attention on family lines may have been strengthened in Woodland stage communities. The view that the loosely stratified and family focused social orders of historic farming groups were transformations of Woodland stage authority systems also seems plausible. If, during future research, artifacts are viewed as both reflections of and participants in social action, these transformations may be systematically charted. If such transformations are then placed in morphogenetic perspective, we may expect a new and richer view of Plains prehistory.

8

Sing Away the Buffalo

Faction and Fission on the Northern Plains

James F. Brooks

> *My grandma She Kills, her brother was Cherry Necklace . . . we say Ma'suapa in Gros Ventre. This is when the Gros Ventres were at the old village [near Elbowoods]. . . . Cherry Necklace, he had wicked medicine, Ghost, Snake, Woman . . . that Ghost medicine was that he could just sing and take away your life. Everyone feared him and didn't like to come near him. One time, he got mad at the people for not respecting him in the old way. . . . This is when [in the winter] the buffalo would come down into the river timber. . . . Cherry Necklace had buffalo calling medicine too. . . . He wanted to punish those people, and he sang to the buffalo, telling them to stay away. And they stayed away. For two winters, I think . . . yes, he sang away the buffalo.*[1]
>
> —Ben Bear-Goes-In-His-Den
> Mandan, North Dakota, August 9, 1989

This narrative was just one of many told by Ben during my visits with his family at their small trailer in Mandan, North Dakota, during the summer of 1989. I had no research design in mind when we talked; our conversations were no more than the exchange of memory and meaning between two men, widely separated by age and culture, who were on their way to becoming friends. But this story never faded or merged like the others; rather, its resonance grew with time. In his closing words lay the genesis of this chapter.

In the autumn of 1971, Albers and Parker (1971) published a benchmark article titled "The Plains Vision Experience: A Study of Power and Privilege." Its enduring quality was substantiated in November 1989, when Wolf (1990) cited the work in his keynote address to the annual meeting of the American Anthropological Association in Washington, D.C. He referenced the article in a defense of the ability of the discipline "to seek explanations for cultural phenomena" (1990: 594), in this case the determination that "systematic relationships exist between the vision experience and both social-structural and ecological variables" (Albers and Parker 1971: 204). Indeed, the article is a remarkable survey and synthesis of Plains ethnology, and its persuasiveness is a testament to the care and integrity with which the authors approached their enquiry. I will suggest, however, that their argument overlooks contradictory elements of the Plains visionary and ideational world, those of conflict and dissent, of dominance and resistance, of power and paradox.

The central theme of the article by Albers and Parker (1971: 205) is that the Plains vision experience served to "solidify the individual's identification and cohesion with societal organizations." Emphasizing process and function, they argue that visions, when seen as a conjunction of quest phase and action phase, serve to stimulate and channel an individual's motivation and behavior in a socially integrative manner and have explanatory power in addressing differential power and prestige, thus justifying the visionary's social status (Albers and Parker 1971: 208). Unfortunately, by restricting their analysis to the functional elements of the vision experience, these authors fail to consider the tensions and contradictions implicit in their argument. If indeed the vision experience served to integrate and explain the interests of social cohesiveness, we must recognize that such cohesion was a contested ideal, subject to challenge by disaffected members of society. The vision experience, therefore, became the location of competition by dissidents for power and prestige; once challenged, as will be seen in the case of Cherry Necklace, disciplinary authority could counterattack in the blurred realms of snowbound winter villages and supernatural discourse.

Albers and Parker (1971) are explicit in stating their adherence to the processualist/functionalist paradigm, and they erect a positivist model in which the independent variables of ecological conditions ramify through the intervening variables of social structure to determine finally the dependent variable of the vision experience. Through the exercise of this model, they seek to confirm a traditional Marxian teleology by "demonstrating the relation of ecological and social-structural factors to ideology" (Albers and Parker 1971: 208).

My intention here is not to engage in a broad critique of the positivist/processualist paradigm but to offer an alternative (if not oppositional) perspective that emphasizes power, political conflict, and paradox in its analysis. My approach is aided by the critical archaeological theory of Hodder (1985), whose discomfort with the passivity of human beings in materialist models has led him to question not only the explanatory value of the models but also the political implications that underlie them. In

Hodder's alternative viewpoint, "people are seen as active. They actively negotiate social rules, creating and transforming the social structure that is constructed by the individual" (1985: 2). Furthermore, the social function of ideas and institutions cannot be understood independently of their cultural meaning. His call for the contextualization of function with belief is central to the argument that follows.

This chapter deals with one aspect of a society governed by consensus: factional challenge and group fissioning. I seek to place factional events within their cultural contexts and give primacy to the spiritual discourse that dominates these "political" episodes. In doing so, I concentrate on the culture history of the Hidatsa and Crow, two peoples who fit into the societal categories of Village Horticultural and True Plains tribes as described by Albers and Parker but whose histories simultaneously challenge their argument. My approach is multidisciplinary, combining evidence from the archaeological record, ethnohistory, and tribal memory with traditional ethnography. For all the ethnographic evidence Albers and Parker bring to bear in their discussion of the integrative role of visions on the Plains, I believe that abundant grounds exist for the argument that visions were often oppositional in nature, challenging traditional authority and empowering dissident members of these societies. I will argue that these Plains tribes were consensual societies deeply imbued with latent tension and conflict. At times, this internal stress and dissent resulted in the emergence of new societal expressions. For the Hidatsa and Crow, therefore, the vision experience was both disintegrative and regenerative, an exercise of power in the permeable domains of politics and the supernatural by men and women actively engaged in creating their own world. The meaning of these acts of creation will continue to elude us if we seek to find process and function at work in all cultural phenomena.

Boundaries

"He sang away the buffalo . . ." Those words lingered and echoed ever more loudly as I came to know the country of the Fort Berthold Reservation in North Dakota. The timbered bottoms into which the buffalo were called by men like Cherry Necklace have been drowned beneath 70 feet of water by the concrete bastion of the Garrison Dam, an event that has severely strained the world of the Three Affiliated Tribes (Meyer 1968; Berman 1988). The high ground on which the bison roamed, and to which they were sent by Cherry Necklace, is today the dominant feature of the reservation, especially in the southern and western segments around Twin Buttes and Mandaree. There, sacred buttes punctuate the horizon, emerging dreamlike from the gray wash of summer storms or towering like potent guardians against the backdrop of sky-fire as one watches the impossibly prolonged sunsets of the Northern Plains. Their names roll in the mind like distant thunder: Fox Singing Butte, Little Heart Singing Butte, Crow Butte, Ghost Singing Butte, Buffalo-Comes-Out, and Buffalo Home Buttes. This country is the living stage on which the drama of world building and collapse, of cohesion, oppression, and fission was created by the Hidatsa and Crow (Figure 8-1).

As is the case in any study of this nature, certain parameters and conditions constrain its scope. The first such constraint involves the tribal people from whose history this analysis is drawn. My use of "Hidatsa and Crow" is simplistic. This chapter deals with only certain subgroups of these people, not the generic tribes. From the time of the first European description of the people of the Middle Missouri River (for example, La Vérendrye [1927] in 1738), chroniclers have attempted to sort out the complex pattern of migration and settlement of the area. Current scholarship (Bowers 1965; Stewart 1974; Wood and Downer 1977; Hanson 1979; Heidenreich 1979) suggests that the Hidatsa were actually a flexible aggregation of at least three distinct groups: the Awatixa, the Awaxawi, and the Hidatsa-Proper. The Awatixa were probably the first to arrive on the Missouri from somewhere to the northeast, perhaps as early as A.D. 1300, themselves fissioning sometime around A.D. 1400, when the group known as the Mountain Crow departed to the west. The Awaxawi settled as horticulturalists near Square Buttes above present-day Mandan sometime in the fifteenth century and seem to have maintained their integrity into the "historic" period (Bowers 1965: 476–489). The last group, and the people with whom this chapter is concerned, arrived on the Missouri in the seventeenth century (Bowers suggests 1615–1650) and then split into the groups referred to as the Hidatsa-Proper and the River Crow. Prior to this split, they referred to themselves collectively as the *mir'okac*, and after the fission the River Crow become known as the *kixa'ica* by those who remained on the Missouri. In discussing these people, I range freely between "mythic" time and linear time, but for purposes of clarity cover events occurring before the mir'okac migration to the Missouri and conclude in the early years of the twentieth century.

I wish also to make clear my theoretical perspective vis-à-vis that contained in the analysis by Albers and Parker. I respect both the explanatory potential of cultural materialism and these scholars' ability to exercise the paradigm. No doubt exists that infrastructural changes on the North-

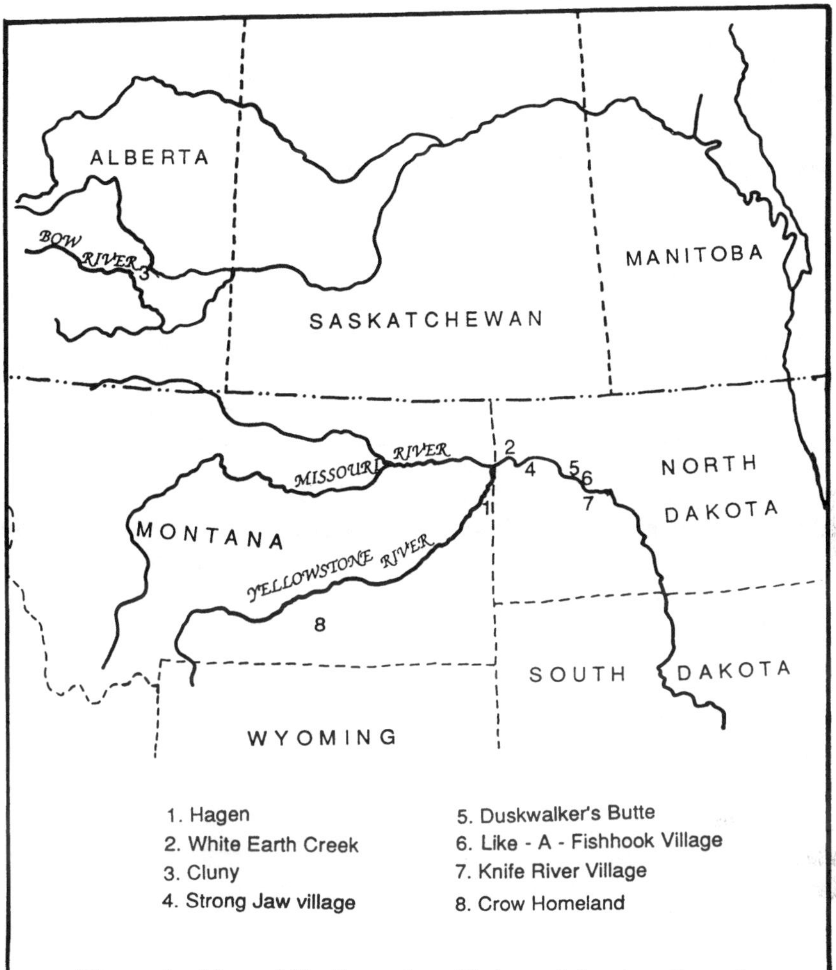

Figure 1. Map of Northwestern Plains, giving location of sites discussed in the text.

Figure 8-1. Map of Northwestern Plains

ern Plains significantly influenced the culture history of the Hidatsa/ Crow and that these changes may be identified in processual analysis. In fact, Albers and Parker touch upon oppositional visions among the Pawnee (1971: 217), but decline to pursue this critically important question. My challenge to their approach lies in whom they omit: the men and women who participated in these political disputes and who constructed alternative worlds through their intimate contact with spiritual powers. I simply argue that people create as often as they adapt and that without this recognition our interpretations of the past are rendered flat, colorless, and mechanistic. Comprehensive understanding can only derive from an approach that also considers the quixotic and unpredictable, the active, transformative, and ironic nature of human agency.

Migrations

> Crow historians tell the story that here, on the shores of this lake, two chiefs—No Vitals and Red Scout—fasted and sought the Great Spirit's guidance on their perilous journey. Red Scout received an ear of corn and was told to settle down and plant the seeds for his sustenance. No Vitals received a pod of seeds and was told to go west to the high mountains and there to plant the seeds. These were sacred and the proper way to use them would be revealed to the people when they got there someday. . . . [The *mir'okac* journeyed] and by the turn of the 17th century had reached the Missouri River and moved in with the Mandan. . . . It was probably between AD 1600 and 1625 that No Vitals, now middle aged, finally decided to go westward and to look for the promised land. Using a women's quarrel over meat *as an excuse,* No Vitals announced that as soon as spring came he planned to move away. . . . "It is time I heed the Great Spirit's instruction. I have tarried too long. Those who want to go with me are welcomed." (Medicine Crow 1979: 67; italics added).

This tribal history came to Joe Medicine Crow from Cold Wind (born around 1840), who as a young man had gone back to visit his Hidatsa relatives along the Missouri. From there, he continued his search into north-central Minnesota, where he met an elder Indian who knew the stories of the ancestors of the Hidatsa. He was taken to view the remnants of earth lodges and tipi rings where, he was told, "the forefathers of your people once lived" (Medicine Crow 1979: 66).

Although it would probably not come as a surprise to these tribal historians, contemporary scholarship finds itself in substantial agreement with their collective memory. Alfred Bowers's (1965) rendition of Hidatsa culture history, with which current analysts agree, suggests that the mir'okac came to the Missouri from a mixed nomadic/horticultural setting in the vicinity of Devil's Lake, North Dakota (1965: 486). It is also clear that these people split into two groups sometime after they had settled north of the Mandan near the Heart River, a fission that occurred during the seventeenth century (Wood and Downer 1977: 83–100). Medicine Crow's history, however, adds a significant detail to the institutional version. The latter analysis has referred to the "quarrel over the buffalo paunch" as the causal element in the split (Bowers 1965: 302) and indicative of resource depletion (Hanson 1979). Others have interpreted it as representative of "two factions, each headed by a separate, jealous, and ambitious chief" (Wood and Downer 1977: 84). Although one should keep in mind the personal and political tensions that this analysis suggests, tribal memory makes it clear that *the vision experience* lies at the heart of the schism and that the dispute over meat was tangential. Conflict lies at the heart of the split, conflict taking place in the discourse of the supernatural world.

The centrality of the ideational world is reinforced if we follow the kixa'ica (River Crow) on their exodus from the Missouri. The "mythic" history of the Crow recalls that these people (who did not yet have a name; they called themselves only "Our Side" [Medicine Crow 1979: 67]) traveled northwestward up the Missouri and into Alberta by way of the Milk River, carrying with them the sacred seeds and searching for the promised land in which to plant them (Medicine Crow 1979: 67). Lowie's (1963: 274) ethnography of the Crow suggests that these were sacred tobacco seeds, "in later times mystically identified with the stars," and from whose cultivation grew the Tobacco Society (cf. Nabokov 1988). The kixa'ica lingered long enough on the plains of Alberta to decide that "this place is too harsh; the winters are long and cold. We must move and find a better place to live" (Medicine Crow 1979: 67).

More than a century and 500 ground miles must pass before the archaeological record gives tangible evidence of the kixa'ica on the Alberta Plains. The intervening time and distance, however, are provocatively endowed with material reminders of their migration. Archaeological testimony speaks not only to their passage but also to the intensely ideational nature of this journey. Not only were they traversing a new land; No Vitals and his followers were constructing a new thought-world during their High Plains migration.

The Yellowstone River feeds into the Missouri near the present border between North Dakota and Montana. About 75 miles upstream from the confluence, on a high bluff overlooking the floodplain, is the settlement site of a people with strong ties to the Plains Village tradition (Mulloy 1942). The Hagen site has not been definitively dated, but consensus opinion places it at approximately A.D. 1675 (Wood and Downer 1977).

The Hagen site features a single excavated earth lodge structure, twenty large cache pits, and a unique circular platform mound near the north edge of the site (Figure 8-2). The earth lodge is 16 feet in diameter, smaller than its corollaries on the Missouri, and is recessed only 5 inches below the surface. Rather than the traditional four central support posts, this structure features only two supports and a single fire-hearth offset to the east, the direction of the entryway (Figure 8-3). The wear pattern of the packed floor suggests that outside the twelve vertical posts of the perimeter was the traditional *attuti* storage area, arguing for Hidatsa derivation (Gilman and Schneider 1987: 18–19). The overall design of the structure, however, is not a replication of the Missouri River form. Its architecture is simultaneously atavistic and innovative, evidence of a people in ideational transition.

This thesis is strongly supported by the mound feature at Hagen (Figure 8-4). Forty-five feet in diameter, it describes a perfect circle, its edges carefully aligned at 30° and its surface raised 2 feet above ground level by compacted humus, clay, gravel, and silt. The only mound of this sort associated with the Hidatsa is one on which the "last dance" of the Sunset Wolf ceremony was performed, a ritual that ceased with the end of the Sunset Wolf bundle line in 1837. For this ceremony, the Holy Women society and male berdaches constructed a mound on which vision aspirants fasted and danced through one hundred songs (Bowers 1965: 427–430). The Sunset Wolf ceremony provided an important outlet for group vision-seeking, and tribal members claim that it originated just prior to the arrival of the horse in the area, believed to have been around A.D. 1742 (Hanson 1986: 95). The remarkable element of the Hagen mound is that it contained the skeletal remains of at least forty individuals, some of whom show evidence of violent disarticulation with stone implements. Mulloy points to the Mandan tradition of placing skulls of the dead in a mortuary circle as a possible precursor of this mound (1942: 9–11). That this feature was a ceremonial one cannot be contested, although its precise nature remains a mystery.

The remaining material evidence from Hagen reinforces the interpretation that it had social-ceremonial significance for its builders. The occupation at the site appears to have been *outside* the perimeter of the sacred precinct, probably in temporary dwellings like wickiups or tipis (Mulloy 1942: 99). The artifact assemblages within the tested area are marked by numerous anomalies. The abundant chipped stone is of extraordinary quality and uniformity, suggesting a single "school" of artisans (Mulloy 1942: 38–39). Ground-stone assemblages contain numerous grinding stones but not of the type for food processing; rather, they appear to have been used for shaping wood or bone (Mulloy 1942: 59). The large ceramic collection (29,320 sherds) represents only ollas, food- or water-bearing vessels, with no representation of food-processing accessories like ladles, bowls, or mugs (Mulloy 1942: 15). Decorative motifs on these ollas exhibit a wide range of styles, with linkages not only to the Missouri River area but

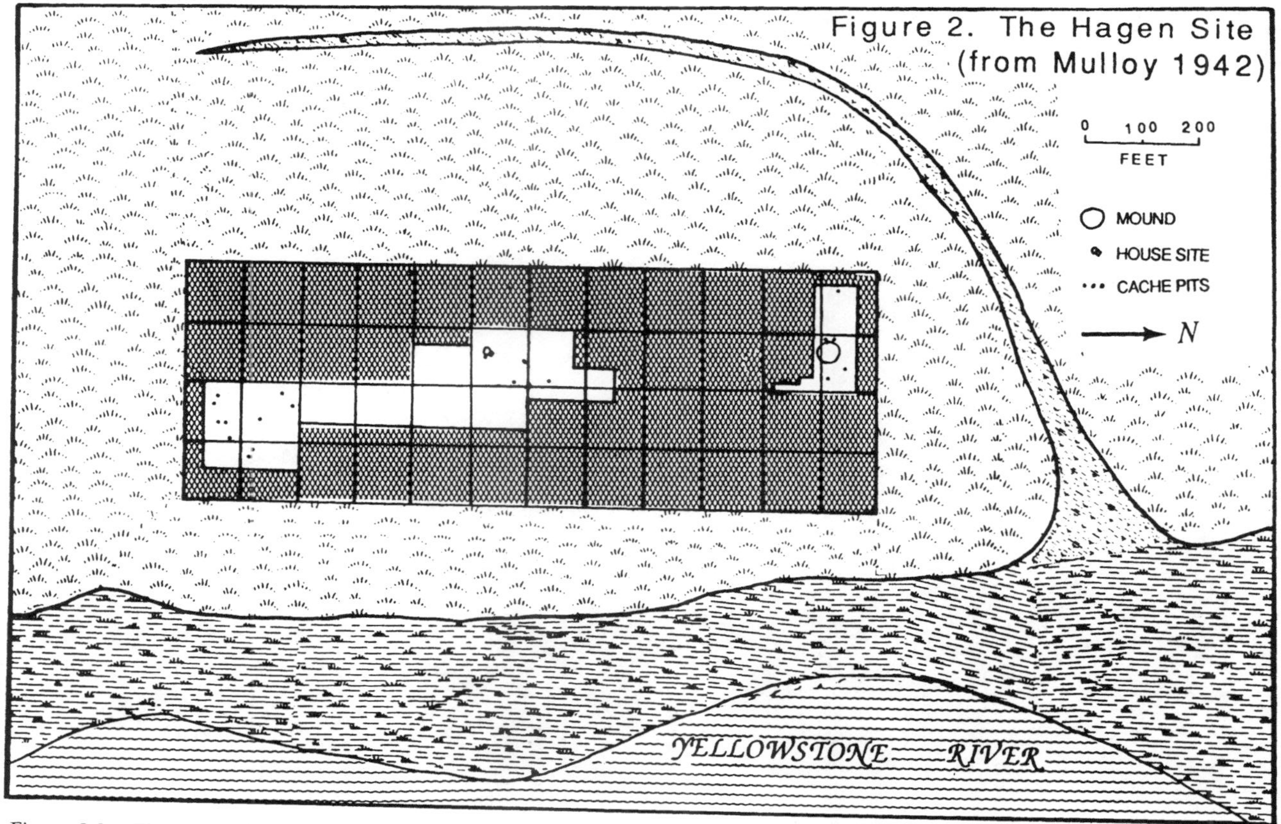

Figure 8-2. The Hagen Site

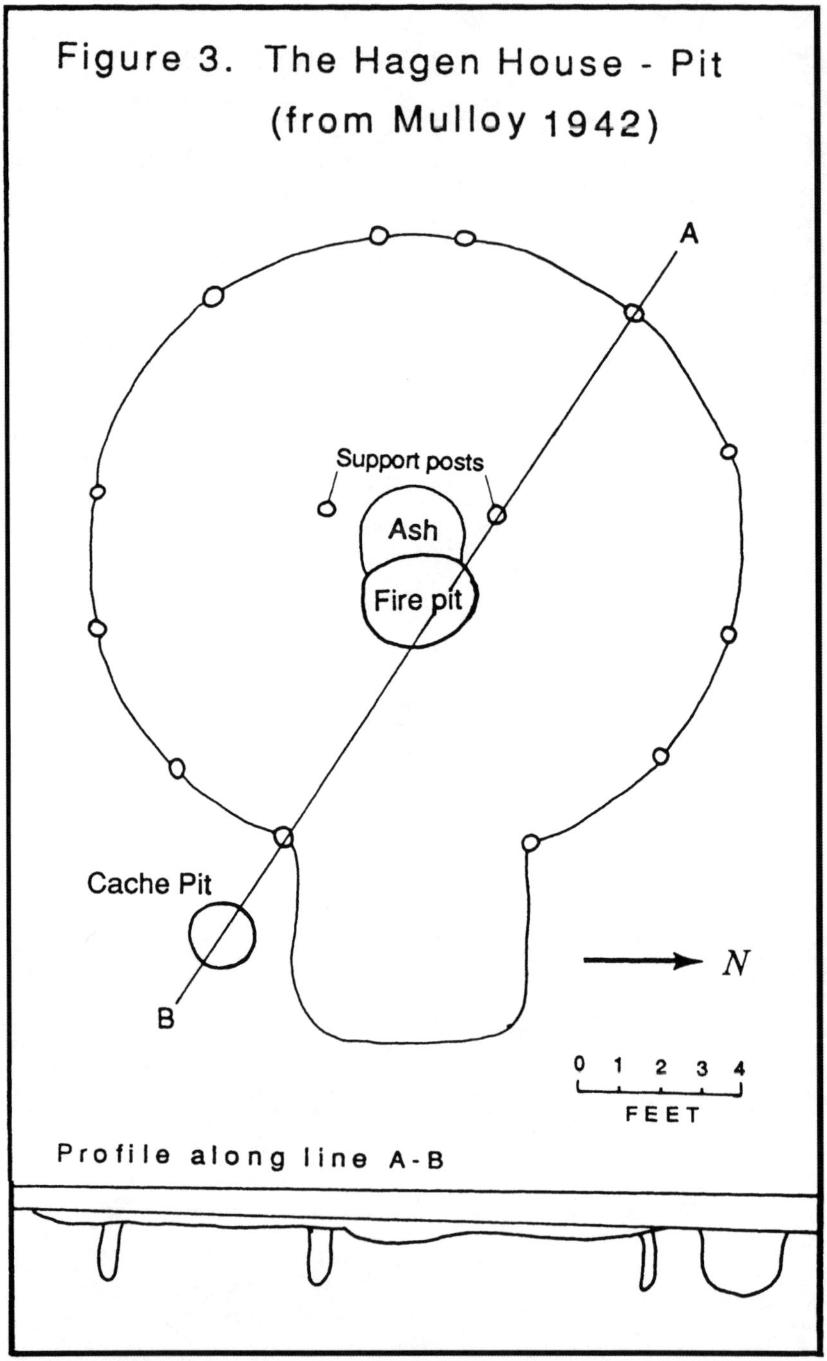

Figure 8-3. The Hagen House-Pit

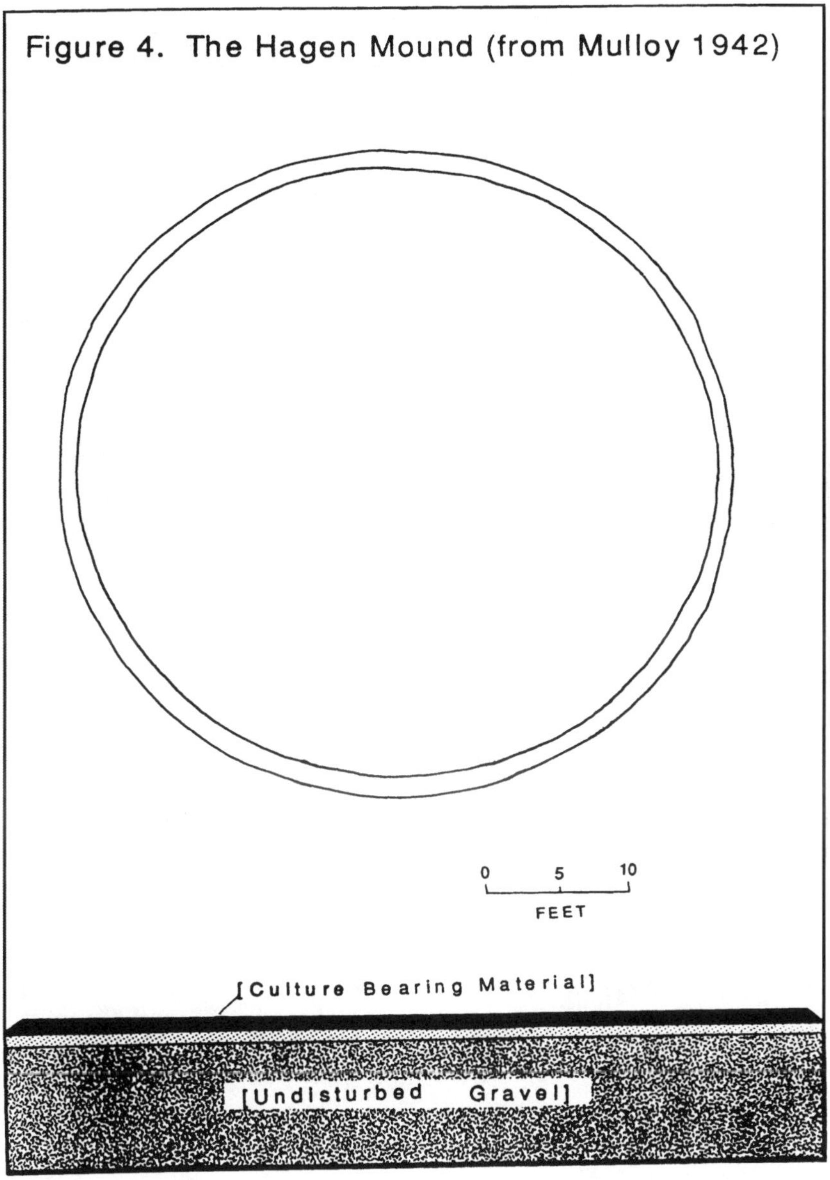

Figure 8-4. The Hagen Mound

also to northeastern North Dakota, Michigan, and the Red River valley of Winnipeg (Mulloy 1942: 37; Keyser and Davis 1982). Finally, although 45 bison-bone picks and hoes were found, no direct evidence exists for agriculture in the form of seeds or ground-stone processing equipment; instead, the remains of 341 bison argue for a hunting orientation at the complex (Mulloy 1942: 90).

It seems likely that the Hagen site represents a pause during the kixa'ica northeastward migration, where the No Vitals band experimented with their new ideational and material world. Probably dispersed in camps along the river, they retained elements of their horticultural economy while learning to hunt buffalo. Engaged in the act of creation, they constructed the site as a *center-place* that reflected their nascent thought-world, one that recalled certain ideas of the past while forcefully projecting a new vision. That new vision embraced an alternative view of the world, one which rejected the "complex and tightly organized social structure" (Albers and Parker 1971: 215) of the Hidatsa villages and replaced it with a more flexible social organization that maintained its integrity through rituals conducted at the center-place.

A more problematic site that may relate to the kixa'ica migration is located on the west bank of White Earth Creek, in extreme northwestern North Dakota (Figure 8-5). No work has been performed at the site since Thaddeus C. Hecker tested it in 1938, but certain elements of his report (summarized in Muller [1968]) suggest affiliation with Hagen and the kixa'ica. Far from the core area of the Missouri villages, this site features a fortification ditch 420 feet in diameter, inside which a timber palisade stood. No evidence of structures inside the enclosure exists, setting it apart from those villages on the Missouri, but the artifact scatter suggests that "innumerable teepee rings, fireplaces, stone drying racks, boiling pits, and rifled graves" were located outside its perimeter (Hecker, quoted in Muller [1968: 21]). Its bluff-top location is similar to Hagen's, and again with no evidence of intensive agriculture. The site's appeal as a village location is limited because what little water exists nearby is high in mineral content, and potential garden plots are too distant for effective defense. No hard dates for White Earth Creek are available; however, because no European artifacts were found, we can surmise that it was constructed prior to 1720. It seems possible that this site represents another pause on the migration, where the settlement pattern, at least, suggests a mixed ceremonial/defensive purpose.

White Earth Creek remains an enigma, but the archaeological record is again strong if we look to the northwest for signs of the kixa'ica exodus. On the north bank of the Bow River near the railstop of Cluny in Alberta,

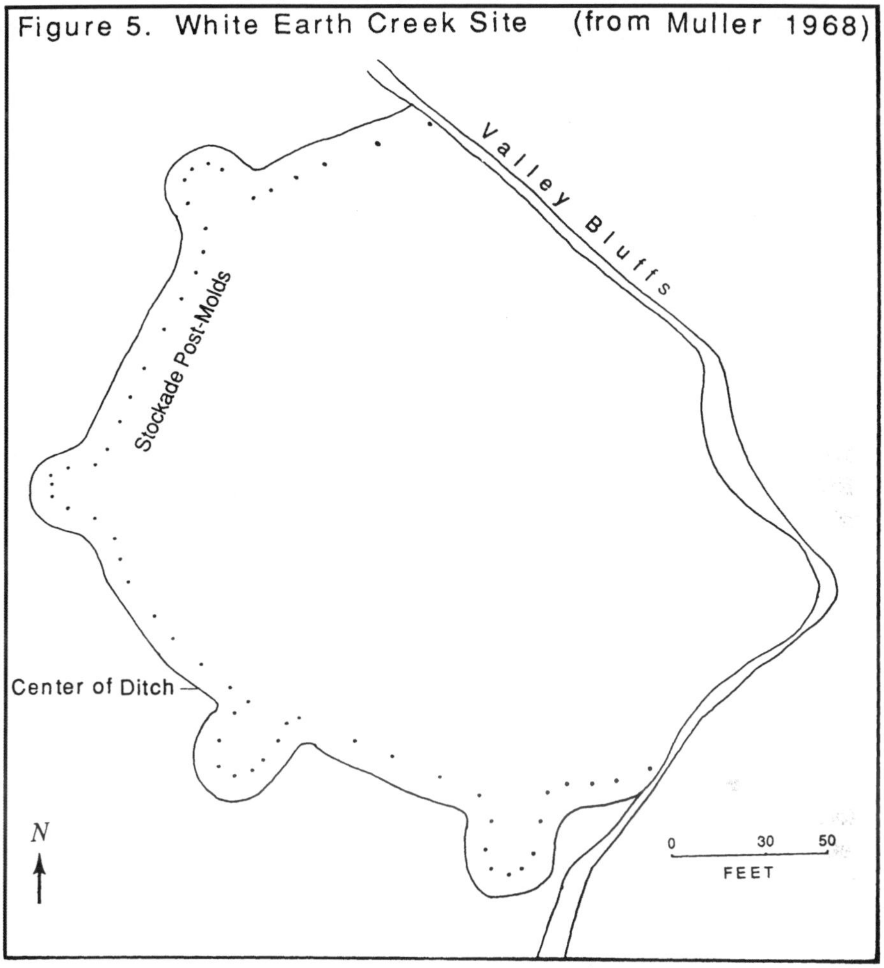

Figure 8-5. White Earth Creek Site

Canada, is an archaeological site that first excited the attention of Europeans in 1875 (Forbis 1977). Situated on an alluvial terrace above the floodplain, the site is a large, semicircular "fortified village" that, on first inspection, replicates many features of an Hidatsa earth lodge village. Surrounded on three sides by a fortification ditch more than 400 feet in diameter, the site is protected on its fourth side by the river cutbank and overlooks the Blackfoot Crossing, an important ford in the Bow River until the twentieth century. Inside the fortification ditch are eleven low depressions suggesting house-pits, and inside these lies another concentric palisade trench, the postmolds of which have been confirmed by archaeological investigation (Figure 8-6).

These features demonstrate anomalous characteristics that call into question their direct relationship to Missouri villages. The fortification trench was found to contain three major breaks within its arc, apparently part of the original design. These breaks, up to 8 feet in width, significantly impair the defensive potential of the trench. The house-pits when tested revealed no evidence of superstructure or occupation (Forbis 1977: 27–33). Their location between the outer trench and inner palisade would seem to leave them vulnerable to breach of the outer defense, if that was its intended function. Additionally, the pits are placed near the trench breaks, increasing their vulnerability. Finally, the postmolds taken from the inner palisade trench suggest that the structure leaned *inward* and was supported by ancillary posts that may have formed a covered bower (Forbis 1977: 34). An inward-leaning palisade is hardly as defensible as one that is vertical, and the suggestion of raised beds or bowers hints at a *social-ceremonial* purpose, perhaps similar to that of contemporary dance shades associated with the Plains Sun Dance or Hidatsa *Nax'Pike* (Bowers 1965: 313).

The artifact assemblage at the Cluny site is problematic and, in fact, may tell us more in terms of negative evidence than what can be learned from the collection. There was not a high concentration of ceramics at the site (two thousand sherds in all), but the ceramics appear to be of local manufacture in a Middle Missouri (Mandan/Hidatsa) tradition. Although Johnson (1979) has pointed out some real temporal disjunctions between the Cluny ceramics and Middle Missouri design elements, their closest correlation remains the Hagen assemblage and other sites peripheral to the Missouri village core area (Forbis 1977: 14). The ceramic concentration suggests that the area of the site receiving heaviest usage was inside the palisade.

The chipped-stone assemblage is sparse as well and consists predominantly of local chert. The quality is unexceptional, no doubt due to the material, and debitage at the site is not sufficient to argue for on-site manufacture of the finished pieces in the collection (Forbis 1977: 51). Some intriguing items are seen in the ground-stone assemblage, principally several grooved grinding stones whose function is unknown, although Forbis (1977: 63) suggests that they may have served to shape circular shell discs and beads.

More than a few items are conspicuously missing at Cluny. No horticultural tools were found, as occurred at the Hagen site, in spite of

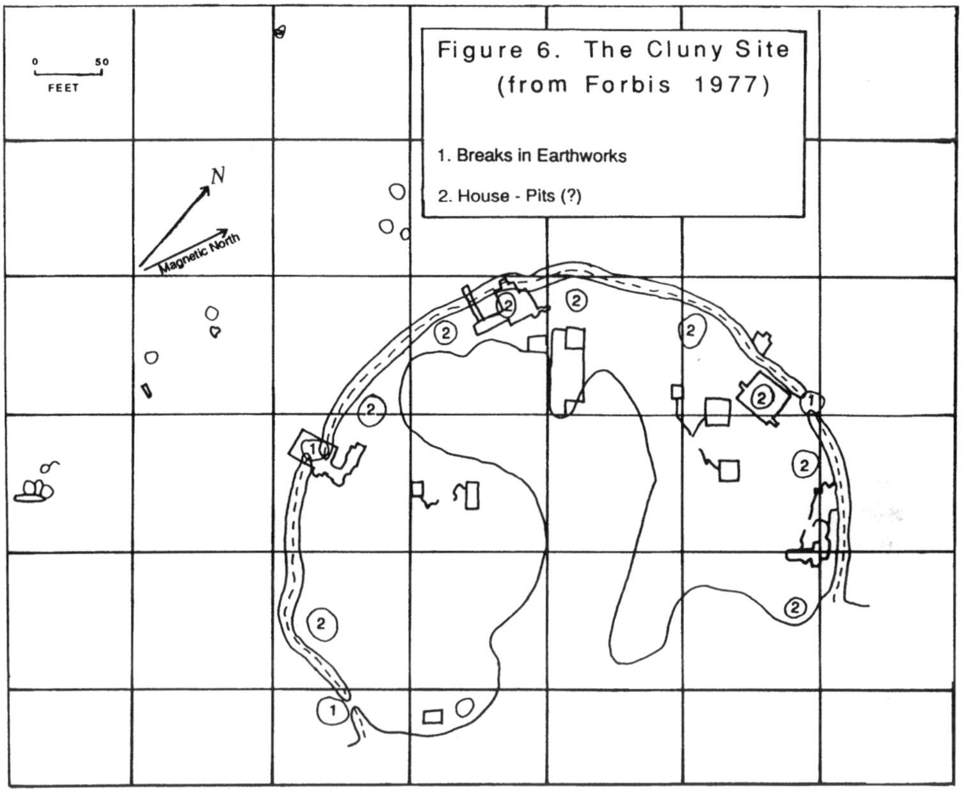

Figure 8-6. The Cluny Site

numerous grinding slabs and pestles. Although the latitude of the site makes horticulture marginal, sixty-day corn is grown in the area today and probably could have been during the occupation period. Farming aside, no digging tools were found in the excavations, a strange fact considering the amount of earth moving involved in its construction. Also, very few end-scrapers or bone fleshers were found, suggesting that hide processing was not an important activity, although bison is the major animal in the faunal remains. The bison bones indicate "a preference for certain cuts: the heavy forelegs and hindlegs, which supply the most meat" (Forbis 1977: 69). It appears that these cuts were brought to the site rather than butchered thereon. Finally, none of the simple-stamped utilitarian pottery common on the Missouri was found; nor were any pipes discovered (Forbis 1977: 67–69).

When we turn to tribal memory, insights into the questions of Cluny begin to appear. In 1911, the Blackfoot tribal historian Running Wolf, whose people controlled the area at the time of European contact, attributed the site to the Crow. There the mounted Crow had made a last stand against the pedestrian Blackfoot, who were migrating southward from the northern timber country (Forbis 1977: 7). In 1960, the Blackfoot One Gun denied that they were Crow, calling the people instead *Tsawkoyee*, "earth lodge people," and claimed that a peaceful relationship had existed between these people and the Blackfoot. He recalled that the Tsawkoyee had lived in the area for six years, residing at a different location each year, and that "these people broke off from a big tribe in the States. This little group had its own leader and broke off. The others tried to coax them not to leave, but they did. . . . They wanted to see more of the country and find out how other tribes were living" (Forbis 1977: 11). Forbis (1977: 74) believes the Cluny site was not occupied for more than a few months. This view does not deny the possibility of a longer regional occupation, however. We can explain the labor expended in construction at Cluny if we view the site as a social-ceremonial center-place where these "earth lodge people" ritualistically "touched base" with the past while pursuing the vision that would make of them the equestrian Crow of the postcolonial period.

As I have indicated, the architectural features at Cluny are reminiscent of, but quite different from, traditional Missouri villages. Additionally, the artifact assemblages do not suggest a residential usage; rather, both their content and negative evidence argue for *event-oriented* activity. The relative scarcity of artifacts, the absence of tipi rings or earth lodges, and the limited but specialized faunal remains all tend to support this interpretation. I suggest that Cluny is another pause in the kixa'ica migration where, as on the Yellowstone, these people were experimenting with their new ideational world. They now had horses with which to pursue buffalo; bones and teeth were found in some cache pits at the site (Forbis 1977: 70). On the basis of this evidence and the presence of two European trade knives, Forbis (1977: 73) dates the site at approximately A.D. 1740. Perhaps less reliant on horticulture than before, the kixa'ica did not reject that tradition entirely because the evidence of grinding stones suggests that wild plants at least were processed at Cluny.

Indeed, the kixa'ica found themselves still linked to their past, from which their original motivating vision had freed them. Although tribal memory made them seek to reproduce a tangible reminder of whence they had come, the alternative vision that drove these people caused a new idea to appear on that bench above the Bow River. Cluny was a place for powerful spiritual coalescence and renewal, where tribal identity could be confirmed through ritual without the constraints of oppressive social organization. Still driven "by the desire and dream of someday receiving the blessings of the Great Spirit when [they] reached the promised land" (Medicine Crow 1979: 67), they lingered long enough to be sure that their sacred seeds could not prosper in that locale, then turned again southward, where finally they planted their gift among "the great mountains of the west; the Beartooths, the Crazy Mountains, the Big Horns" (Medicine Crow 1979: 69). Significantly, no pipes were found at Cluny.

Homelands

The Hidatsa/Crow schism was not the only instance of vision-driven tribal fissioning on the Northern Plains. For those who remained behind on the Missouri, the burdensome weight of institutional authority was challenged repeatedly by men and women who found empowerment through communication with the supernatural and then acted out their challenge in the realm of political resistance. Three cases in the nineteenth century will be discussed here: Strong Jaw, Duskwalker, and Crow Flies High.

Strong Jaw

Following the departure of the kixa'ica, the three divisions of the Hidatsa had settled in a like number of villages around the mouth of the Knife River, where they were first visited by European travelers. This contact has been well treated in the literature (Ewers 1968; Meyer 1977; Klein 1983), but deserves a brief summary because these changes relate to the subject at hand. The appearance of the horse, the extension of the hide and fur trade, and the introduction of firearms triggered both transformation and intensification of the precontact economy. Existing trade networks expanded geographically while they contracted temporally; a greater number of goods entered the system in a shorter period of time (Wood 1980). Coupled with a series of devastating smallpox epidemics that began in 1780 and ended in 1838 (Trimble 1988), the sociocultural fabric of the Hidatsa suffered profound strains. As populations declined and production-for-exchange increased, differential accumulation of wealth was added to an already hierarchical society. Where symbolic capital had once been based on prestige and authority, real capital goods now appeared, making unequal accumulation all the more obvious. Bowers (1965: 175–178) sees the development of sophisticated kin/clan-based ranking systems and age-graded societies among the Hidatsa as an attempt to mitigate against social upheaval during this period. Albers and Parker (1971: 216) recognize this development as well, noting that "since most positions of importance were the prerogatives of specific kin groups, unrestricted competition for them would have created considerable social instability and conflict." They go on to argue, however, that "publicly recognized visions were redefined in accordance with the facts of ascription and/or inherited wealth. . . . [These standardized visions] served to stabilize and reinforce the specialized functions of corporate groups and support the differential distribution of property, privileges, and prestige in societies with formalized status inequalities and circumscribed vertical mobility" (Albers and Parker 1971: 216–219). Their argument is persuasive as far as it goes. The narrative of Cherry Necklace that began this chapter is a stellar illustration of supernatural powers applied in the interests of social control. In fact, in a version of the same story found in Bowers's ethnography, this interpretation was confirmed. In 1862, Cherry Necklace had been selected leader of the winter camp by the residents of Like-A-Fishhook village. A faction of the village, however, challenged his authority on the basis that he had filled the position just two years earlier and that several deaths had occurred during his term. Rather than submit to his leadership, this group established a rival village at some distance from the main camp. "Cherry Necklace . . . pointed his pipe to the north and invoked the gods of that direction to send the people back by sending the buffaloes only to his camp." When rumors reached the rebels that he had also "pointed his pipe to the south and directed the Sioux to attack the undefended camp," the punishment had its desired effect, and the dissidents rejoined their anxious relatives (Bowers 1965: 34–35).

Not all visions or invocations of supernatural power were aimed at the perpetuation of social order. In at least three cases during the nineteenth century, visions were the source of empowerment for individuals and their followers *against* rigid sociopolitical controls. The first of these took place around 1811 (Stewart 1974: 295), when "a very holy man named Strong Jaw" received a private vision that told him "that he and those who wished to follow him should build a new village, on high ground that could only be approached from one side" (field notes, informant's name withheld by request). In tribal memory, this schism is explained as deriving from internal conflict: "The other holy men were jealous of Strong Jaw's supernatural powers and a friend warned him that it would be best to leave the village and take the friendly families with him. . . . thirty-five families broke away and traveled westward toward the Killdeer Mountains until they reached a place on the Little Missouri where they built a new village"

(Bowers 1965: 412). Helen Wilkinson, an Hidatsa woman, recalled in 1978 that "on the west side of our territory was a very high piece of defensible land with a flat top. Up there was a large village. There was only one way to get up, and this was very narrow, so that the people came by way of the high ground when they returned. Around the village, the land was high and like a cutbank. Thus their homes were in a safe place" (Parks, Jones, and Hollow 1978: 61).

No excavations have been undertaken at the location of Strong Jaw's village near the mouth of Cherry Creek (see Kuehn, Falk, and Drybred [1982] for a brief discussion of this [the Jacobsen site]). It is, however, on a high promontory overlooking the Little Missouri, and the only access is across a narrow neck of land (Figure 8-7). This site is considered by tribal members as an intensely powerful and haunted place, an understandable attitude in light of its history in the aftermath of Strong Jaw's vision.

This breakaway settlement survived only a few years, the victim of an attack and massacre by the Shoshoni. The history of this village exemplifies both the maladaptive nature of some of these schisms and the continuing theme of supernatural influences in Hidatsa life; it was at Strong Jaw's village that the next powerful rebel obtained his spiritual weaponry, and a singular woman appeared and entered into Hidatsa mythic history.

Duskwalker

At the time Strong Jaw broke away from the main village, he had an eight-year-old daughter and a younger son whose name was Walks-At-Dusk. While his small group was searching for a site to suit his vision, they attracted the attention of "a very holy man" of the Snake (Shoshoni) Indians, who lived to the west: "[This man] was looking around to find someone to buy his sacred rites. His power was a sacred hoop through which he could look and see every tribe on the earth. . . . he looked through all the tribes until he saw Strong Jaw and his party traveling toward the Killdeer Mountains. He saw a man in the camp with something powerful looking back at him. The Snake Indian called the people together and announced that he was getting old and wanted someone to take over his medicine powers. The only one fit to do so was Strong Jaw's son, Walks-At-Dusk. 'We will go after that little boy in the middle of summer'" (Joe Ward, quoted in Bowers [1965: 412–413]).

As the Shoshoni moved toward Strong Jaw's village, his daughter began to receive powerful and frightening dreams. "I saw a big smoke in my dream. I was carrying my little brother on my back and did not know

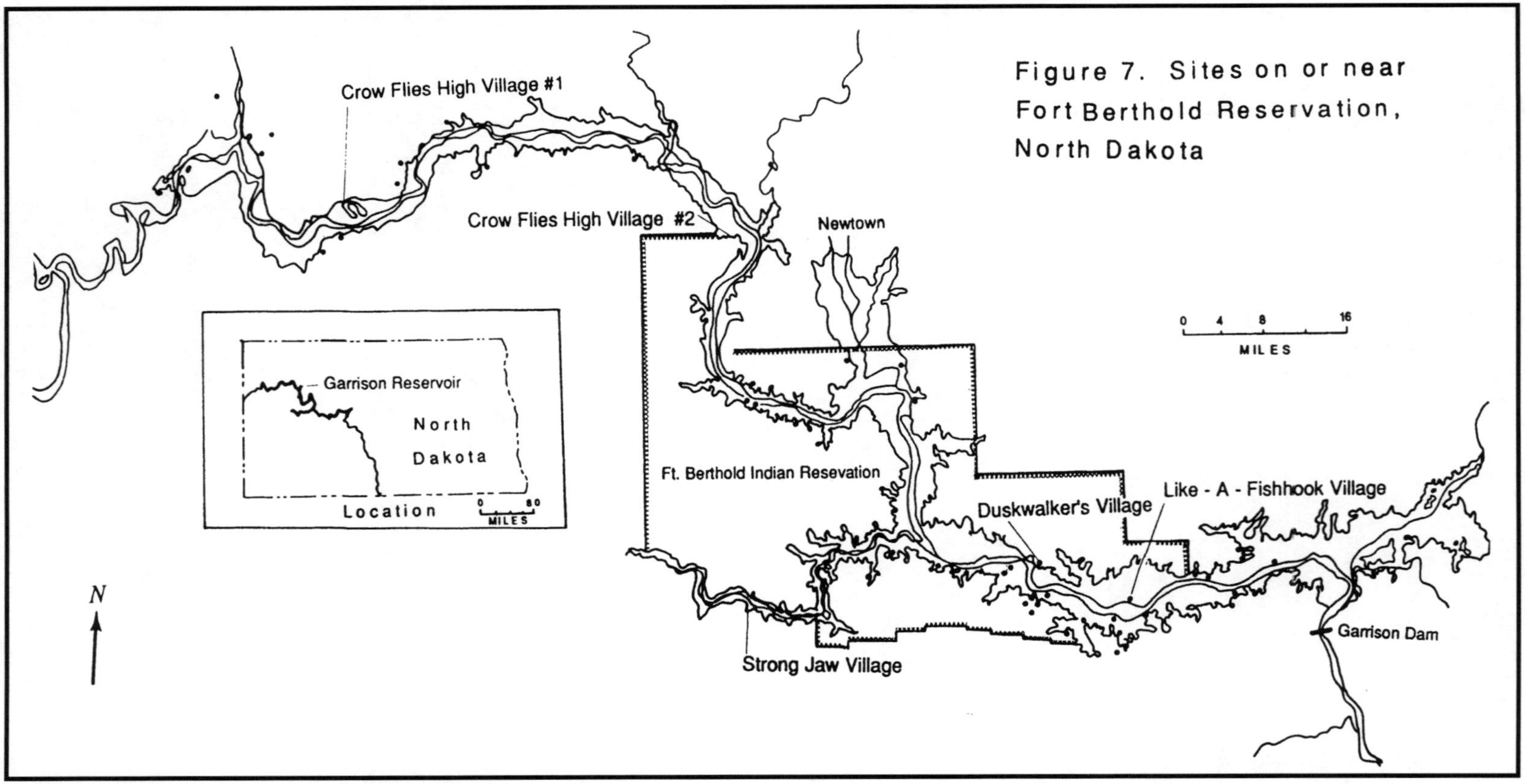

Figure 8-7. Sites on or near Fort Berthold Reservation, North Dakota

where to go. The lodges were burning and all the dogs were howling" (Bowers 1965: 413). Strong Jaw and the village elders could not bring themselves to believe that a young girl could be the recipient of such potent visions. Too late, Strong Jaw summoned up his wolf protector to investigate the danger, but by then the Shoshoni holy man was close enough to take possession of the village dogs who "drove the wolf back into Strong Jaw's lodge" (Bowers 1965: 413). When a herd of buffalo appeared on the rolling country beneath the butte, the men of the village ignored the dangerous vision and rushed out to the hunt. In their absence, the Shoshoni attacked, killing the women, burning the lodges, and taking the two children captive. After some years in captivity, an old woman to whom the young girl had been given took pity on her and offered to aid in her escape: "We will start tomorrow evening. I will take you part way. Tell your people what happened but do not urge your brother to go for he has a good home here. Some day when he is strong enough, he may come back to visit you" (Bowers 1965: 413). Once on her own, the girl was assisted in her return to the Hidatsa village by wolves who brought her food and watched over her passage. As she neared her destination, they bestowed wolf medicine on her and gave her the rights to conduct the Wolf ceremony. Known now as Wolf Woman, she became an important protector of her people, assuming the form of a wolf and accompanying Hidatsa war parties. Some years later, while she was serving in this capacity, a group of Hidatsa warriors intercepted a Shoshoni raiding party led by Walks-At-Dusk. Wolf Woman engaged in a supernatural battle of Wolf medicine with her brother and drove the raiders away, separating Walks-At-Dusk from his adopted tribe. "When Walks-At-Dusk returned to the Hidatsa he told how he had nearly lost his life because of the great supernatural powers of the Hidatsa wolf leaders" (Bowers 1965: 415). Wolf Woman had fulfilled her vision and returned her wandering brother to his people.

At this point a persistent error in the anthropological literature needs correction. A Hidatsa leader who broke from the main village in 1837 and founded a butte-top site on the north bank of the Missouri has been identified by researchers as "Nightwalker, a chief who had a reputation for breaking away and living apart from the rest of the group" (Lehmer, Wood, and Dill 1978: 66–67). My informant on these issues explained that this name resulted from a mistranslation and that the leader's name was in fact Duskwalker (field notes, informant's name withheld by request). With this clarification, it is not hard to reconstruct what really happened after Walks-At-Dusk's return.

Endowed with the Wolf bundle, the "high-butte" vision of his father, and the "full knowledge of the Snake Indians [Shoshoni] medicine rites"

(Bowers 1965: 415), Duskwalker had little chance of reintegrating with life at the main Hidatsa village. No doubt he suffered beneath the oppressive traditionalism of clan-based vision rituals and became the object of the same jealousies as his father. When the Hidatsa villages were ravaged by smallpox in 1837, he used his supernatural powers as a rallying point for others who were frightened and disaffected and led this faction to the site that now bears his inaccurate name (Figure 8-7). This site features 27 house-pits surrounded by the remains of a timber palisade. It was occupied until at least 1846, when the remnants of the Mandan and Hidatsa coalesced in a single nearby village, the one known as Like-A-Fishhook (Lehmer, Wood, and Dill 1978: 66–68). The Strong Jaw–Duskwalker line seems to end here, although more research may link it ultimately to the last schism under consideration, that of Crow Flies High in 1871.

Crow Flies High

"Wolf Chief (b. 1849) described the training of young men as equivalent to a wagon drawn along a deeply rutted road; there was no way to get out of the road except by going forward in the same path as others had done before—one could make no progress backing up, and the depth of the ruts prevented one from taking a different course. A young man . . . got along very well as long as he performed in the same way as his elders had; he was destined to be very unhappy if he attempted to stray the least little bit from the beaten path. The only effective alternative was to become a berdache" (Bowers 1965: 220).

In fact, another alternative existed. Factionalism provided release for those who had irresolvable differences with the governing hierarchy. In the last case I will discuss, a breach resulted again from political tensions that had their expression in supernatural discourse. The oppressive regimentation of life described above by Wolf Chief grew too heavy for a segment of the villagers at Like-A-Fishhook, and "under conditions approaching a civil war"(Bowers 1965: 77) they departed for the west. Twenty-five years were to pass before they returned to the reservation, but when they did so, they closed a circle that had begun with the original vision of No Vitals, for in their seminomadic hegira they reestablished close ties with the Crow, a relationship that continues today.

The Crow-Flies-High schism was related to internal power disputes that had simmered since the coalescence of the Mandan and Hidatsa in a single village in 1845. Traditionally, the highest ceremonial position in Hidatsa villages had gone to the men who held the powerful Earthnaming bundles, three of which had existed since the founding of the Knife River villages. With the smallpox epidemic, one bundle line died out; the remaining two bundle bearers found themselves coexisting at Like-A-Fishhook. In 1871, these two bundles were owned by Bobtail Bull and Poor Wolf, who was senior by ten years. When Poor Wolf was selected village chief by the elders, the younger people allied themselves with Bobtail Bull in a challenge to generational and institutional authority (Bowers 1965: 42–43). However, Bobtail Bull, by virtue of his acceptance of the traditional role of bundle bearer, did not prove radical enough to trigger a revolt. This role fell to Crow Flies High, a charismatic man whose parents had died in the epidemic of 1837. His rejection of traditional ways had begun in early manhood, for although his father was an important bearer of the Old-Woman-Who-Never-Dies bundle and he had received a vision that gave him the right to take possession of the bundle and its associated rites, he chose not to exercise this prerogative: "Instead, he made up a personal bundle of those articles seen in his dream and otherwise disregarded tribal practices of `taking up the father's gods.' Thus, the old `holy' men got neither a big feast nor fine goods and Crow Flies High received neither promises of success in warfare . . . nor the promise he would some day become a chief. Still, he was very successful whenever he went out to war" (Bowers 1965: 43).

Crow Flies High's achievements validated the oppositional power of the individual vision experience versus the carefully monitored institutional quest and posed a severe challenge to traditional authority. In an eerie echo of the first Hidatsa/Crow schism, internal tension reached the flashpoint in a dispute regarding the distribution of meat. Poor Wolf and his ally Crow Paunch had obtained two steers from the Indian agent at Fort Berthold, and when they failed to share these equitably with others, they came under attack from the dissident group. Frightened at this response, the two men planned to assassinate Crow Flies High, who was serving as spokesman for the dissidents. "Frequent rumors of the death plot had reached Crow Flies High, and it was suggested that he should leave the reservation until the animosities against him subsided" (Malouf 1963: 153). Gathering 140 followers, he left the village and headed west up the Missouri, settling initially near Fort Buford, where buffalo were still plentiful (Figure 8-7). For twenty-five years the Crow Flies High band acted out their ideational challenge. Bowers' informant, Four Dancers, claimed that "the people who split away did not have as many tribal ceremonies, but . . . [our] men were just as successful as those who stayed in Fishhook because they fasted. . . . we thought that the gods one got while fasting were just as powerful as those one bought through the fathers, for our young men got more horses and war honors than the young men of the other village" (Bowers 1965: 240, 246).

This emphasis on the personal vision experience was similar to that of the Crow and was no doubt reinforced by increasing contact with those distant cousins. It was Crow Flies High, however, who consistently demonstrated the strength of the private vision experience. "Fasting seven days at a time," he was visited by buffalo on one occasion who "taught him how to make rain. Later, when the gardens dried up, he brought rain for the women at Fort Buford" (Bowers 1965: 247). The rain-making bundles that he created from this vision have been passed down through his descendants and are still in use on the reservation today (Tressa Berman, personal communication).

Not all ties to the past were severed in this "distinct revolt against the established age-grade structure" (Bowers 1965: 250). At both major villages founded by the dissident band, ceremonial earth lodges were erected in which to continue certain traditional rituals (Fox 1982; Malouf 1963). The location and function of these lodges bear noteworthy resemblance to the Hagen site discussed earlier (Malouf 1963: 158). Although they thought of themselves as a separate group and had their own leaders, the Crow Flies High band maintained close ties with those they had left behind, and in later years significant transmigration occurred between the two factions. "Even today we visit back and forth and our young people marry into the other group" (Four Dancers, quoted in Bowers 1965: 246). Thus, the pattern of simultaneous nostalgia and innovation revealed in the earlier case studies is repeated here, more than two hundred years later.

The power of Crow Flies High's connection with the supernatural world served one last purpose. During one of his vision experiences, he was visited by the spirit of a departed Crow man, who taught him sacred songs of that tribe and the secrets of the wind (Bowers 1965: 247). This spiritual link to the Crow was acted out in the material world because the intermediate location of the dissident band reestablished communication and travel between the two tribes. The Crow and Hidatsa recommenced a vital exchange of memory and meaning. The Crow would make pilgrimages to the sacred site of Grandmother's Lodge near Red Buttes until it was inundated by the waters of the Garrison Dam, bringing with them offerings of their tobacco from No Vitals' seeds (Woolworth 1956: 80). For their part, the Hidatsa visited Crow Agency often, carrying new rituals and institutions such as the Hot Dance and the Crazy Dog Society (Lowie 1963: 206).

More than three hundred years have passed since Red Scout and No Vitals received their individual visions, but through the political and supernatural discourse of men and women like Strong Jaw, Wolf Woman, Duskwalker, and Crow Flies High, the circle is closed today. Members of each tribe can look to the horizons above Mandaree, or the Little Big Horn River, see the silhouettes of buffalo there, and sing them in with a high, trilling song of honor.

Conclusions

In this chapter I have sought to put forth an alternative way of viewing the culture history of the Northern Plains as expressed by the Hidatsa and Crow. My goal has been to find the individuals who actively engaged in the creation of that history and to allow them, as much as possible, to speak for themselves. I find myself in substantial agreement with Hodder (1985: 21) when he argues that the "passive processual view of individuals in a society, according to which there is a system behind the Indian to which the Indian is subordinate and helpless, has the result that the social analyst puts him/herself forward as having specialist knowledge and insight."

I have attempted to serve primarily as an arranger of multiple, parallel narratives, weaving these together in a single, comprehensible text. Where I venture into speculative statements of my own, I have tried to remain true to my organizing theme, which stresses the active and transformative nature of human agency. I hope this chapter has effectively challenged the viewpoint that sees the ideational world of the Plains Indians as subordinate to the forces of material change. The Plains vision experience was not (and is not) simply the superstructural validation of infrastructural conditions; rather, it was (and is) also a potent and creative tool in the minds and hands of individuals who negotiated their social locations and constructed their cultural worlds. As such, it was (and remains) *both* an instrument of domination and a weapon in political resistance. The essence of this conflict was spiritual, not material. It drew power and authority from the intimate, inseparable merging of natural and supernatural discourse. Finally, the men and women whose visions led them to challenge tradition also participated in regeneration and renewal, creating new communities from elements of the old.

Their stories could only be unveiled by a methodology that is itself fundamentally political, a critique not only of the way we understand the past but of the way we order our present. Again, I agree with Hodder's (1985: 8) position that "within the process school the individual was submerged beneath systemic exigencies perhaps because of a concern with scientific control and the desire to make a relevant contribution to the running and administration of a modern world. . . . the particularity and otherness of culture needed to be denied, to be replaced by the universally predictable character of human and animal behavior."

The subordination of human agency was the product of this framework. It follows that if people in the past were powerless in the face of material change, so too must we in the present be equally helpless. By calling on tribal members whose memories recall the innovations and actions of their forbears and merging this tradition with those of history and science, we can repopulate the past with thoughtful and creative human actors. The personal experiences of No Vitals, Strong Jaw, Wolf Woman, Duskwalker, and Crow Flies High argue emphatically for a new approach. These people were actively engaged in social critique, and from their ideas they constructed alternative ways of ordering the present. We can do no better than follow their lead.

Notes

1. The Hidatsas often self-identify as "Gros Ventres," a carryover of referents in older literature to the group known as "Gros Ventres of the Missouri." These people should not be confused with the Algonquin-speaking Gros Ventres of the Prairies, now known as the Atsina Indians.

9

The Household as a Portable Mnemonic Landscape

Archaeological Implications for Plains Stone Circle Sites

Michael C. Wilson

The cultural landscape is a medium for communication, filled with mnemonic symbols that organize cultural activities. The household is an archaeologically visible minimal cultural landscape, so household refuse is more than simply a passive residue of behavior. Ethnoarchaeological information is used here to develop new theoretical approaches to the study of Plains households represented by stone circles. Portable households of nomadic peoples are discussed in postprocessual terms as mnemonic landscapes full of codes that canalize behavior.

Stone circles ("tipi rings") probably number in the millions on the Northwestern Plains. Occurrences vary from single features to tens of circles. Although many stone circles are traces of former dwellings, low artifact yield led Burley (1990) to argue that new "baseline" theoretical studies cannot be justified for resource management. To say that baseline research is ever passé is preposterous; all the same, his concerns must be addressed. What potential do stone circles hold for archaeological inquiry, when seemingly more productive sites exist? How can one assess "productivity"?

Synthetic monographs concerning Plains stone circle sites (Finnigan 1982; Davis 1983a) provide historical reviews. Despite an early view that the excavation of these sites would be unproductive (see Kehoe 1960), recent excavations have revealed well-defined activity areas (e.g., Wilson 1983; Davis 1983b; S. Deaver 1989) and have allowed segregation of components (e.g., Davis 1983b; Stuart 1990). Even so, few excavations have completely sampled a circle and an equal (or greater) area outside; some were shoveled with only grid-square provenience (e.g., Quigg 1986). Whereas Burley (1990) concluded that past studies were unproductive because of limitations in the resource, it is equally possible that past strategies have been relatively sterile and that stone circles must be reexamined in light of new approaches and understandings (see also K. Deaver 1989).

In this chapter a discussion of ethnoarchaeology leads to consideration of space, place, landscape, and circle as landscape idealization. Studies of abandoned campsites of pastoral Tibetans provide insights relevant to Plains sites. Potential exists for consideration of the symbolic function of household space and boundaries, of the role of the household as a portable landscape evoking as well as reflecting behavior, and of markers of gender and ethnicity.

Theoretical Background

Ethnoarchaeology and Material Culture

Ethnoarchaeological models link material remains to behavior involved in their production, use and discard (Gould 1978; Tooker 1982), but they are sterile if such remains are viewed only as the passive output or residue of cultural decisions (Hodder 1985). Postprocessualists see material culture as symbol-sets (codes) actively directing, as well as being directed by, human action (Hodder 1982b), justifying efforts to reconstruct or model the social context of symbolic action. Cultural values are encoded in many media, including the cultural landscape. A key ethnoarchaeological issue is how people use space (Kent 1987: 1), but it is equally valid to ask how cultural space uses people.

Studies of feature and "refuse" distributions in modern hunter-gatherer or pastoralist camps have tended to the processual view or have focused on ethnographic analogy (e.g., Bonnichsen 1973; Robbins 1973; Binford 1978; Ammerman et al. 1978; Hole 1979; Fisher and Strickland 1989). Kent (1987: 2) argued that ethnographic analogy lies outside of ethnoarchaeology, which is "formulation and testing of archaeologically oriented methods, hypotheses, models, and theories with ethnographic data." She argues that models should be developed before ethnoarchaeological studies are made. The present chapter is in part a precursor to ethnoarchaeological studies that will continue.

Space and Place

An archaeological site is a place redolent of cultural experience. Space and place can both be mapped, yet they are difficult to define because of their basis in human experience. "Space" connotes area and can be limitless, but human activity is localized, occupying places that are, by association with activity, unique. Localization has two elements: internal characteristics (site) and external linkages (situation). Localization is fundamental to human society, but many analyses of behavior are made without due consideration of space and place. Space, in being transformed to place, acquires felt value. Biological needs (water, food, rest, procreation) are satisfied, and some argue that landscape aesthetics are only indirect reflections of biological needs; yet culture also contains an arbitrary component. One avenue for its study is the phenomenological view that experience and expectations channel perceptions of space and place. The meaning of space grades into that of place as people experience it and endow it with value (Relph 1976: 8; Tuan 1977: 3–6). Space becomes a "reality" of places that owe their meaning to the past actions of the observers. Experience, connoting feeling, is unique to the individual, but its evaluation is culturally conditioned and people share experiences to build an intersubjective identity. The element of feeling is one reason why an explicitly scientific approach need not be the only or the best analytic strategy. Alternative approaches can reveal the interplay among feeling, perception, and symbols.

Space is organized into places differently across cultures (e.g., Hall 1959, 1966). It is claimed by naming it, and thus place is tied to communication. A place is a break in space, a central point or axis for orientation. Eliade (1961: 21) equates center with the sacred, the manifestation of which "ontologically founds the world" by creating what Tuan (1971: 18) calls "reified order, a two-dimensional cosmos." A scale of sacredness exists in the landscape; centers exist within centers. A hilltop church contains an altar, within which are even more sacred places.

Experience of place, mediated by culturally influenced perception, affects a person psychologically and physically (Hiss 1990; Relph 1976). Some places are uplifting and others gloomy; some are more memorable than others. People use landmarks as devices to organize and prompt memories of past activities, the roles of actors, and their relationships (Hiss 1990). Place names (toponyms) evoke values and priorities, and they store information about landmarks. Medieval philosophers used mnemonic systems based in the landscape (Lowenthal 1979: 104), building on preexisting systems. Thus, behavior organizes the landscape, but the landscape also organizes memory and evokes behavior. The Aranda of Australia tie ancestor stories to landmarks mapped on churingas. To lose the land is to lose the connection to dream time and the shared conventions that bind people together. People are "owned" by their landscape, bound by strong sentiment (Sopher 1967: 47, 1979: 132). Through experience, place accumulates sentiment, growing ever more meaningful and powerful (Tuan 1977: 33); thus, sentimentality about places is not a mental failing of elderly people but celebrates their accumulated experience.

The Organization of Landscape

An archaeological site is a place, but it also resides in a place, a larger landscape. The term "landscape" was long associated with that portion of the natural environment modified by people (Jackson 1984: 7–8). For artists, it was also a representation, a moral idealization. In conveying ideals it was a medium in itself, not simply a depiction. With the rise of a scientific paradigm, efforts were made to "dehumanize" the definition of landscape (Cosgrove 1984: 9–20). However, the affective cultural model continues to hold meaning for geographers and archaeologists.

Societies create landscapes in their own image. The construction of artificial landscapes expresses the ideology and cosmology of a cultural group (Tanaka 1984), but natural landscapes are organized in similar fashion. Artificial landscapes can be microcosms of the larger landscape, but the larger landscape can also be conceptually organized as an extension of the artificial one. One may ask whether "landscape" can exist at all outside its cultural representation. For physical geographers, "landscape" does connote a natural phenomenon, a portion of the earth's surface "that can be comprehended at a glance" (Jackson 1984: 8). As an association of forms with objective reality (Sauer 1925; Roberts 1987: 79) it can be viewed as "outside" a cultural frame, but it is hard to define except by example (see also Hartshorne 1961: 163). This view can also lead to its characterization as a container of cultural information rather than as information in its own right (Relph 1976: 5; Wagstaff 1987: 2).

Cosgrove (1984: 269) saw landscape as a distinctively Western "way of seeing projected onto land and having its own techniques and compositional forms." As such, it was restrictive, diminishing "alternative modes of experiencing our relations with nature" (1984: 269). Such usage would require for each culture a different concept to replace "landscape" and would of necessity void cross-cultural studies. In the present study, "landscape" is used in a cross-cultural sense, and the Western perspective is taken as one of many alternative landscape models.

Maps of landscape portray cultural values, preferences, and perceptions. Toponyms are a cultural idealization of a landscape; a map locating them further idealizes that cognitive code. In a map of cultural landscape, the routes portrayed are not always optimally efficient ways of "getting from A to B" in strictly economic terms. They carry historical baggage of human experience as expressed, for example, in ritual prohibitions; within historical constraints they may prove optimally efficient, but this is not a law. One culture's map is another's distortion of reality (Hall 1959: 150); spatial behavior is elicited by the perceived environment, organized by passage through cultural and psychological filters (Tuan 1974). A society encodes in its landscape its ideal environment, no matter how imperfect or ordinary it may seem to others (Butzer 1978: 12). One should be able to "read" landscape almost like a book. "Our human landscape is our unwitting autobiography" (Lewis 1979: 12). "Its forms, proportions, orientation, and properties are meant to be the very map and pattern for correct, harmonious behavior, and to give the model by which such behavior can be learned" (Wagner 1974: 135–136; see also Meinig 1979a, b).

Meanings are not naturally inherent in a landscape but are a property of human intentions (Relph 1976: 47). Place can persist though meanings change: the Big Horn Medicine Wheel in Wyoming has served multiple functions for different groups over time (Wilson 1981) and today is taking on new meanings for New Age believers. Archaeologists, as the most recent users of these places, unwittingly serve their own national or ethnic mythologies (Leone 1973). The archaeological record of a culture arrives as a landscape, although to most archaeologists it resides within a landscape. The landscape created by archaeologists embodies their own cultural ideals and must not be arbitrarily imposed on the archaeological record. A site under excavation is itself an evolving symbolic landscape embodying the experience of its excavators and the writers of the research design, and little resembling the conceptual landscapes of past inhabitants. The sampling strategies of these excavators and writers presume certain results and obfuscate others. Circular or "pie-segment" excavation units used by some stone circle excavators (Smith 1974) seem to mimic ancient world views but actually are used to speed up the recording process, especially in impact mitigation work (Dau 1981). In fact, one measure of a posited pattern is its deviation from a standard reference pattern. Use of circular excavation units gives the illusion that ancient and modern "centers" coincide, but this idea is unprovable. Confusion of ancient and modern patterns could cloud, rather than clarify, the former.

The cultural landscape is at least in part retrievable archaeologically. Contextual studies of archaeological materials reveal patterns in the layout and geographical relationships of architectural forms and structures (Fritz 1978: 40; Oliver 1987). Ancient landscapes persist in relict place names, patternings of material culture, healing "scars" in substrate or biota, or as portrayals in paintings, written accounts, or oral traditions. Landscapes, as value-driven idealizations, can evoke behavior as well as reflect it. In the Western tradition, a "productive landscape" idealization reinforced efforts to "improve" land and produce "useful" commodities. This view was widely embodied in artistic depictions and even in "objective" scientific writing (Cosgrove 1984). At Chaco Canyon in the American Southwest, architecture identified and reinforced social aggregations; defined the economic, political, and ceremonial relations between aggregations; and beyond this conception was a metaphor for relationships of nature, society, and the sacred (Fritz 1978: 42–55). Both symmetry of buildings and sites (at three scales) and asymmetry of others held specific meaning.

Circle and Center

Stone circles are simple geometric structures with complex meanings. A circle is a maximally efficient way to delimit place and is generated from a center; therefore, circle and center possess shared meaning. This idea is the essence of the mandala cosmogram: the periphery can be subdivided (as, for example, by radiating cardinal directions) and is multiple, whereas the center is the unifying element, one. Existential space can also be ordered around center in concentric rings.

The multiple nature of the circle allows its mnemonic potential to be developed. Blackfoot elder Reg Crowshoe has told me that songs in ceremonies such as the Sun Dance are associated with specific lodge areas or structural features. The lodge thus functions as a mnemonic device to elicit songs in the correct number and order because there are many songs to be remembered. The Hopi of the Southwest use fixed landscape points surrounding the center represented by Black Mesa to organize the annual ceremonial round by orderly progress through the landscape circle (Doxtater 1981). The horizon circle, both symbolizing and directing the annual cycle, filters Hopi perceptions. The apparent horizon circle has special significance because it is uniquely perceived by the individual or group at its center. Its size and content depend on their situation and the limit of their perceptual abilities. Depending on one's understanding of the natural world, the horizon can be extended; for example, shadow streaks at sunset may come from mountains out of view. Center ("axis mundi") is therefore wherever one is situated. Zuni of the Southwest know that they are at the center of something and discuss what it might be. One person suggested that they needed a center so they "wouldn't be like the Navajos and so they would all stick together" (Tedlock 1978: 297).

As people move but remember places, the landscape becomes laced with overlapping circles defined from many centers. If people design the cosmos so that they are at its center, territoriality and defense do not merely measure the productivity of an environment and the need to protect resources (Tuan 1971: 32). They also symbolically express the centrality and integrity of the individual and the solidarity of the ethnic group. A center possesses power and is the locus for contact with the source of that power on another plane of existence. A center pole or spire in a religious structure reaches upward toward "the heavens" and so, too, can a pile of stones or even an individual or a group of people. Plains ceremonies elegantly express this relationship; for example, in an Arapaho Sun Dance rite, the Sacred Hoop is lowered over a participant's head so that the person is ritually at the center, a vertical axis to its horizontal plane (Brown 1964: 15). The sacred pipe represents the universe but also humanity; the people who fill it identify themselves with it, establishing not only the center of the universe but also their own centers (Brown 1953: 21).

Circles of people and stones are linked to center in an Ojibwa story of a boy who fasted to receive a guardian spirit. Traveling with his spirit-guide, he came to nine old men sitting in a circle. In the center sat another old man who blessed the boy and said that he had just been sent down from above. As the boy returned home, he looked in the direction his guide was going. He saw a circle of large white stones, with another in its center (Radin 1914: 365).

In possessing power and being bounded, the circle exhibits insideness and outsideness. Insideness is commemorated not only in physical structures but also in rituals and activities tied to them (Relph 1976: 141). A stone enclosure surrounding a sacred area warns people that it is dangerous to enter without purification. A doorway threshold is tied to passage from one state to the other.

For many peoples, feelings of attachment to place are based on communal territory on the one hand and household (or meeting place) on the other. Attachment of a family to a block of owned land is a different conception of place (cf. Hay 1988, 1989: 159). A landscape is a web of boundaries, not all of them simple lines. An imposed rectangular grid is a way of seeing the world, not simply a convenient way to parcel out owned land. For Western peoples, it is an attempt to produce a political landscape based on the belief that rectangular spaces are admirably suited to the creation of a just society (Jackson 1984: 153). On the Columbia Plateau, however, native groups cross-utilized resources in one another's territories so that ethnic territories overlapped. The Nez Perce exploited an area ten times the size of their core territory (Walker 1967), so their world view could not conform to a grid-based, distinct-territory model. The Columbia Plateau practice was consistent with an idealization of circular territories because tightly packed circles must overlap.

Household and Dwelling

The elementary unit of the cultural landscape is the dwelling, whereas the household is the elementary unit of social structure. The household can be viewed as a place organized around the individual as center. A dwelling may retain the natural surface as its floor, but a constructed floor still symbolizes the natural surface. Organization of elements on and above the floor both encodes and elicits human behavior (see Sopher 1979: 137–140). Archaeological household patterns can be maps of cultural values, particularly for short-term occupations with minimal mixing or overprinting. A household, defined on the basis of domestic criteria, need not fit the Western ideal of single family/single dwelling. A coresidential group is not necessarily a household; it may represent a transient or task-specific social unit (Bender 1967; Ashmore and Wilk 1988: 6). A household may be dispersed among several dwellings, whether or not in a single compound; or several households may share one dwelling. The household is nevertheless "the dominant and most fundamental form of corporate organization" (Stanish 1989: 8), a unit repeated throughout a society (Deetz 1982).

Ethnic differences may reside in such patterns as household shape and the design of task-specific features. Kent (1984) found ethnicity expressed in activity areas in Navajo, Spanish-American, and Anglo-American house lots. Correlations exist between certain social attributes (e.g., marriage pattern) and dwelling form (Whiting and Ayres 1968; Rapoport 1969). Where neighboring groups share adaptive patterns and social systems (as on the Northwestern Plains) cross-cultural similarity can exist in dwellings and in the cognitive landscapes they contain. As a caveat, in exogamous groups one spouse may not be familiar with the new cultural landscape and may even be excluded from such knowledge (Sopher 1979: 132–133).

Gender differentiation can be encoded in areal segregation of activities. A "task-differentiation" framework for ethnoarchaeological recognition of gender roles (Conkey and Spector 1984: 24–27) identifies tasks performed in a given cultural setting. It ascribes them a social dimension (gender, age, number, relationships of performers); a temporal dimension (frequency and duration of tasks); a spatial dimension (where task is performed); and a material dimension (materials associated with task). The framework emphasizes materials "left behind as byproducts of task performances," but it is equally important to consider form and distribution of materials as further eliciting behavior and reinforcing values. Ethnoarchaeological studies of lodge plans (e.g., Tanner 1979 for Mistassini Cree) indicate potential for the archaeological detection of gender differentiation.

In studies of the cognitive maps of nomadic cultural groups, short-duration archaeological sites hold greatest potential. This ranking can run counter to resource management priorities, where sites may be ranked according to "density of cultural material," "number of occupations or components," or "artifact yield." Artifact yield translates too easily into "cost-effectiveness," a bottom-line management criterion presenting pitfalls to scientific progress. I made this point before with respect to stone circles (Wilson 1983: 113), but Burley (1990) took the statement out of context and had me stating a view that science should not be fiscally responsible—a position he felt more secure in attacking. Again, raw "artifact yield" by itself is a frail and potentially misleading basis for management decisions. Few Plains managers would deny the value of single-use bison kill sites even if they yield only specialized tool kits along with a great many bones. Retrospective studies of archaeological site definitions and survey strategies in the Southwest clearly showed "user bias"; for example, in some studies a site was defined arbitrarily as having at least five artifacts per square meter—an obvious "bottom-line" productivity criterion. This definition automatically excluded most of the preceramic record (Plog et al. 1978: 387). Stone circle sites may yield relatively few artifacts (although some yield large samples) but hold potential for recovery of the domestic plan of the household and, by extension, to reveal social structures of the enclosing culture.

Artifact distributions in a site are not a "moment frozen in time." Yet the amount to which patterns are blurred can be minimized. Hull (1987) asserted that microdebitage distributions reflect activity areas in stone circle sites. Janes (1989: 854) challenged this view, citing ethnoarchaeological observations of the Slavey Dene that suggest great variability from lodge to lodge. He argued that varied activities and cleaning episodes would cause "smearing and blending," making it unlikely that repetitive cultural patterns could be retrieved. Variability observed by Janes contrasted with the standardization observed by Tanner (1979) for the adaptively similar Mistassini Cree. Tanner's observations weaken

Janes's conclusions, which are further weakened by the fact that single-lithology debitage clusters have been observed at stone circle sites (Wilson 1983: 119–120; Davis 1983b: 254–261). Metcalfe and Heath (1990) concluded that microdebitage probably would be found in its area of production, unlike the larger "refuse" observed by Janes, and the single-lithology clusters demonstrate that "smearing and blending" have not destroyed all patterns in larger material either.

The Nomadic Perspective

Mobility of nomadic peoples conditioned by a variable environment (Johnson 1978: 37) allows concentration on a limited field of productive resources. An alternative is to use a broad spectrum of resources, allowing more extended occupation of one place. The choice between the two need not be an adaptive one of "optimal efficiency" but may be arbitrary and based on historical factors. A choice of nomadism means that spatial referents in the environment are transient; "landmarks" may or may not be revisited regularly. For nomadic pastoralists, "home is a mobile space located wherever tent and herd are" (Johnson 1978: 38). The surrounding landscape must nevertheless be organized. Tanner (1979: 73) found that the partially nomadic Mistassini Cree "foster the illusion that their place of residence never changes. . . . the standardized internal arrangement is such that the dwelling seems to always occupy the same space."

The mobility of a nomadic group favors a portable landscape, its internal organization encoding cognitive percepts and precepts. The household would likely usurp the role of the greater landscape as a symbol-set reflecting cosmology and actively directing human behavior: household would become cognitive landscape. The Dakota tipi floor represented the earth, its walls the sky, and its poles the trails from earth to the spirit world (Laubin and Laubin 1957: 117). Cree storyteller Merle Tendoy told me how the tipi could also represent a person, the extended smoke-vent poles reaching like arms toward the heavens. The tipi was round like many natural phenomena, and tipis were ideally placed in circles, like the sacred hoop of the nation, the circle of the four quarters, and the cycle of the seasons (Black Elk, in Neihardt 1961: 198–200).

As place, a household could stay the same even though its situation might change, so places need not always be located unambiguously. Nomadic people can by these means have strong attachment to place despite their mobility (Relph 1976: 29–30). One would expect intensification of household organization with prescribed use of space. Gender assignment of space may be strengthened (see Tanner 1979: 77–78). The household would, by extension, become the basis for greater landscape organization so that activity areas in at least the immediate vicinity are extensions of household and organized under similar rules. The entire cultural landscape may be rationalized as a scaled-up version of the household, just as the household embodies elements of the greater landscape. Household-external landscape linkages are recognized in two ways. First, the landscape can be seen as a circle concentric with the household, in a universal system of nested circles with the individual at center. A village circle of lodges is one such circle but cannot be moved without disassembly. The circular lodges are portable modules that individually constitute households but collectively form the next higher level of circular organization. This idea explains why autonomous households appear in nomadic Plains groups despite suggestions that such units correlate strongly with Western concepts of private property and inherited land title. On the Plains a "collective" tendency is offset by the mechanism of modular portability.

In a second linkage, natural features are by analogy interpreted as "households," possibly although not necessarily part of the idealized village circle of the observer. On the Plains, "lodge" was often the name of a landmark, for example, Loge des Boeufs (Buffalo Lodge), a grove of trees, or Wolf's Tent, Snake Lodge, and Dog's Tent, all hills or bluffs (Coues 1965: 100–101, 301, 302, 396, 404, 411).

Many if not most nomadic peoples return periodically to the same places. In such cases, the external landscape would retain an agentive role in cultural codes. Landmarks for sedentary groups with fixed horizon referents, such as the Hopi of Black Mesa, are tied to the cardinal directions as viewed from that place. However, for many nomadic groups the referent is a variable one: the sun. Use of sunrise to mark "east" as a baseline for other cardinal directions would mean seasonal variations in precise orientation. Given that the sun served a utilitarian purpose (warming the lodge in the morning) as well as a symbolic one, it is likely that at temporary camps a fixed horizon referent would see less favor than the prevailing sunrise position. In this sense, cardinal directions applied by nomadic groups could differ from those of sedentary groups. Landmarks for nomadic groups might not be so strongly linked with cardinal directions but would be important in guiding the movements of people. Such Plains cultural emplacements as hilltop medicine wheels or clusters of scaffold burials would play the role of "beacons" as well as serving as centers of spiritual power. In symbolic terms, medicine wheels with radiating spokes seem to reach out from their center past the perimeter circle to grasp the enclosing landscape.

Tent Anchor Sites, Outline Features, and Related Phenomena

Classification and Function

Stone circle sites are part of a larger universe of geometric features constructed of varied materials for varied purposes. These phenomena, from sod circles through cleared stone outlines to cobble rectangles, can be classified according to crosscutting criteria: use, form, construction material, clearing versus construction, and so on. This chapter is not the place for a classificatory scheme, but examples show the place of stone circles.

Outline features can be produced by clearing (lateral displacement) or through importation (or rearrangement) and placement of material. They include utilitarian tent anchors (e.g., stone, peg, sod, or log outlines), utilitarian or symbolic perimeter markers (e.g., fences, hedges, boundary lines), and ceremonial structures, from dance lodges to funerary monuments (of many materials, including circles of human or bison skulls). Shapes run the gamut; even "circular" is a generalization hiding, for example, the tendency of tipi outlines to be oval (Laubin and Laubin 1957: 45). Although many outlines had utilitarian functions as tent anchors, most probably also served as symbolic markers of personal or household space and as requests for privacy. Given multiple functions and the likelihood that most features had simultaneous symbolic and utilitarian functions, a discussion of stone circles simply as tent anchors, although a part of the story, falls well short of their potential (Wilson and McKinnon 1989).

Use of the term "tipi ring" is dangerous in that the tipi could be a relatively recent arrival, supplanting other dwellings that could have left circular traces (Brasser 1982). Similarly, the term "medicine wheel" hinders understanding by arbitrarily excluding such related features as hilltop cairns. One class of medicine wheel is interpreted as the remains of Blackfoot death lodges (Brumley 1985), possibly having less in common with other medicine wheels than those wheels have with cairns.

As well as simply reinforcing the communication (a "claim") of space, outline features can convey implicit threats of defense, the need for purification, or both. For some societies open areas in the midst of profane, occupied territory are reserved as sacred; their emptiness conveys the contrast and the implied warning (Sopher 1967: 48). Even circles of refuse carry messages of occupation. British Gypsy camps are perceived by non-Gypsies ("Gorgios") as filthy; yet as Okely (1975) and Hodder (1982b: 62–64) indicate, the trash and dirt are a message to outsiders. Gypsies, who pick through the scraps of the sedentary Gorgios, adopt a subservient posture but preserve their self-image by explicitly distinguishing "inside" and "outside." Gypsy caravan households are spotlessly clean, and food preparation is elaborate. The trash is "the outside world as expected by Gorgios, but in a sense also, the dirt disturbs and threatens the Gorgios and thus gives Gypsies an active and powerful role in Gorgio society" (Hodder 1982b: 63). Garbage and dirt support a Gypsy strategy of social reaction, a symbolic reinforcement of ethnicity. The household, as a cultural landscape, is a vehicle for cross-cultural communication. Effective communication requires shared understanding of repetitive modules of organization. This understanding, not the convenience of the researcher, is why "normative" studies retain value. People exhibit patterned, repetitive behavior, and the search for such patterns must remain a central theme in archaeology.

Archaeological Potential

Familial relationships can seldom be directly recovered archaeologically, but domestic functions and coresidentiality are inferred through repetitive patterns in architecture, activity areas, and artifacts. Stanish (1989: 11) defined an archaeological household (equaling a minimum coresidential unit) as "the minimal architectural unit of those people who live together and who share in basic domestic economic behavior." Ashmore and Wilk (1988: 6–9) agreed that the household is a recurring module but concluded that it can be defined only after exhaustive analysis. They differentiated "household," "coresidential unit," and "dwelling" and warned of ethnocentric bias in equating archaeological dwellings with households. If a Plains stone circle is a tipi ring, it represents a dwelling, and its identification as a corporate household is inferred by ethnographic analogy. Problems of "fit" among family, household, and house may not, however, be as critical as they seem. Excessive concern with whether a household was or was not a single-family unit might prevent archaeologists from pursuing potentially valuable research (Deetz 1982: 719). The suitability of households as a source of archaeological information reflects their small, manageable size and widespread availability.

The Tibetan Connection

In search of observations to test this theoretical framework, my team traveled to the northern Tibetan Plateau of Qinghai Province, China.

Modern pastoral Tibetans leave behind, at seasonal campsites, stone outlines that are analogous to Plains stone circles. The team examined Tibetan and itinerant Han (ethnic Chinese) campsites in the Koko Nor area. Tibetans of the high steppes are pastoral nomads or seminomads with herds of sheep and yak as well as horses and goats (Ekvall 1968). They live seasonally or permanently in portable tents in which they build elongate fireplaces of stones, sod, and clay. When a tent is moved, the abandoned site retains the cultural imprint of its former occupants in its stone outline, fireplace form, and distribution of artifacts.

Others live in tents in the same territory. Political and other prisoners are sent to Qinghai and down-and-out Han might travel there for unpopular jobs. The Chinese government encourages Han settlement, swamping the Tibetans politically, if not culturally. On the high plateau, Tibetan pastoralists still are a dominant presence. Near Koko Nor other minority groups, such as the Mongols, Tu, Hui, and Salar, are also present. The Mongols, like the Tibetans, are nomadic pastoralists.

Tibetans, Mongols, and traditional Han share a Buddhist heritage and conceptualize the universe as a circle; the world is a square within it, coordinated by the cardinal directions and concentric with the enclosing circle. Square and circle also connote male and female (Oliver 1987: 158). Such symbolism is reflected in the plans of religious temples, chortens (memorials to lamas), and other structures, where squares can be seen nested in circles. Such symbolic elements rest within household patterns as well, in ethnically distinctive ways.

Ethnic Markers

Settlement pattern, tent shape, and associated ceremonial features all contribute to the ethnic recognition of tenting sites. Tibetan portable households not only serve internally to reinforce identity but also play an important role in advertising ethnicity to others. Yak-wool "black tents" are rectangular structures suspended from one or two center poles, the guy ropes and external poles resembling the legs of a giant spider (Figure 9-1). Although these tents can be labeled as the ethnic "marker" of pastoral Tibetans, this etic statement is parallel to the designation of a projectile point style as "diagnostic." Tibetan pastoralists move through a series of land allotments and return to former campsites. Improvements are made, including the building of sod and yak-dung windbreaks and excavation of pits (so that the tents become semisubterranean winter homes) and even the construction of stone houses (Goldstein and Beall 1990: 62).

The rectangular, nearly square tent covers are divided into halves by a front-to-back smoke vent. Stones or sod on up to three sides (upwind) secure the cover against the wind, and a marginal rain furrow may be present. Boxes and bales are piled inside along the rear and side walls, and stone blocks may be placed along the inside of the cover to serve both as weights and as a "shelving unit" (Wilson and McKinnon 1989: 268–269). The floor is divided in half by an elongate fireplace running nearly from front to back. This distinctive fireplace, with rectangular firebox at the front and fuel (yak dung) reservoir at the back, is a Tibetan ethnic marker. Such fireplaces do not occur in Han sites.

Orientation is important at Tibetan tent and house sites, with the doorway typically facing eastward. Strong prevailing winds and frequent extreme cold constrain the choices. Norbu (1961: 25) observed that "You could enter our homestead only from the east or lee side, which gave us protection from the weather."

Notable at Tibetan sites are prayer structures outside but not far from the household tent. Some are elaborate, with pole and prayer flags, whereas others are simple, square piles of earth. Examples examined during our fieldwork included low, square piles of sod and gravel, sod alone, stone, or small clay shapes cast from brass pyramidal or tabular molds. Use of temporary altars is typical of nomadic groups. Where ethnic religions are linked to the land by intense ecological relationships, sacred structures tend to be few and inconspicuous (Sopher 1967: 24), possibly because the landscape itself is already suffused with power.

Traditional Tibetan tents are being replaced, among more acculturated groups, by ovoid white canvas tents. Some Tibetans see these tents as a sign of wealth. In many camps both types of tents can be seen, but informants told me that a differential role exists, with canvas tents being the temporary dwellings of young women of marriageable age.

Ovoid to circular canvas tents are typical of itinerant Han, who move regularly through the Koko Nor area. Most of these people are migrants or tradesmen moving in search of work or markets. Whereas Tibetan camps are in high pastures, Han camps are along roadsides. Perimeters may be marked by cobbles, sod blocks, rain furrows, or some combination of these markers. Han travelers construct simple circular surface hearths or use small barrels for fireplaces. Fuel may be yak dung, wood, or coal.

Mongol tents, or yurts, are circular but resemble Tibetan tents in other ways. They are covered with brown felt, and a hole in the center of the roof lets the smoke escape. In the middle of the floor is a clay fireplace, usually square and outlined by wood. Along the walls are wooden chests and leather bags, and opposite the door is an altar (Migot 1955: 219–220; Oliver 1987: 158).

Figure 9-1. Tibetan Black Tent near Koko Nor (Qinghai Lake), Tibetan Plateau, Showing Support Poles and Guyropes. As viewed (from the front), women's side is to the left. In this view a woman works in front of her side of the tent; male children play on the men's side. The apparent white line on the ground is a tent pole (left) and the line made by the sun through the smoke vent (right). In the background (left) is a piled-sod winter animal shelter. (Photo by Ineke J. Dijks)

Gender Markers

Tibetan black tents are formally divided on a gender basis; as viewed from the front, the women's side is to the left and the men's side to the right, separated by the fireplace (Ekvall 1968: 63; Wilson and McKinnon 1989: 271). Artifact distributions at abandoned sites are asymmetric and reflect gender specialization: food preparation items (e.g., pot handles, jars, tins), clothing (e.g., cloth remnants, worn-out shoes), and house-cleaning items (twig brooms) are more likely on the left side, whereas butchering tools (choppers) and such items as watch bands and batteries are more likely on the right (Figure 9-2, Table 9-1). Overall, typically more artifactual material is found on the left side than on the right (Wilson and McKinnon 1989: 281). Much of the material on the left side may lie just in front of the tent. At active sites we visited, women performed many activities (especially maintenance activities such as mending of clothing) in front of the tent and usually in front of the left side. Children would also play in this area. Men's activities often occurred well away from the tent (e.g., herding) or within it (e.g., receiving visitors). Floor mats are often present on the men's side and would of course reduce the opportunity for artifacts to be left behind in activity areas.

During our field visits the above etiquette was maintained, with limited side-to-side "mixing" in front of the tent. Even there, localization of activity on the left side extended forward in narrow fanlike fashion from the tent (Figure 9-2), indicating that the formal organization of the household was being projected onto the adjacent landscape. Correlation of artifacts with gender must still be made on circumstantial grounds through linkage of the observed etiquette in active sites and the artifact distributions in abandoned sites. Children's activities seem strongly associated with the women's area. Norbu (1961: 26) recalled that in the house of his childhood (a permanent Tibetan house rather than a tent) the "greater part of the family life was lived in the kitchen."

The Plains Revisited

Household Etiquette

Like the Tibetans, Plains groups possessed codes of household etiquette that could have left gender and ethnicity markers in the archaeological record. Some of these codes are or were widespread in North America, crosscutting variations in architectural form: for example, widespread similarities in character and placement of the "seat of honour" exist (Tanner 1979: 76–80). A single pattern characterized tipi household plans in much of the Northern Plains. Ideally, the doorway was oriented to the east, toward the rising sun. The seat of honor was opposite the doorway, with the central hearth in between.

A line drawn from doorway to place of honor bisected the tipi into gender-associated halves, but groups differed as to which side went with which gender. Among the Arapaho, the owner's bed was along the southern side, with the head toward the west (Kroeber 1983: 12). In Dakota and Blackfoot tipis, men sat on the north side and women on the south, with the owner's seat against the rear south backrest and a son at the other backrest. If there was no son, this seat was for guests. When both seats were used by guests, the host moved to the right so that the guests were on his left (heart) side. On entering the tipi, a man moved to the right to his place and a woman to the left (Laubin and Laubin 1957: 118–119; Grinnell 1962: 199). As mapped by Laubin and Laubin (1957: 45), the Dakota tipi had its opening to the east, backrests on the west wall, facing the entrance, and

Figure 9-2. Abandoned Black Tent Site, Koko Nor Area, with Fireplace Remnant Dividing Women's Side (left) and Men's Side (right). Occupation debris (Table 9-1, Camp 10) shows gender-related distributional asymmetry; the fireplace form and the tent shape are ethnic markers. (Photo by Ineke J. Dijks)

beds along the north and south walls. A small rectangular altar of cleared earth was situated near the center, just west of the hearth. A pile of wood for fuel was placed just inside the tipi south of the doorway.

In many real-life situations transitions of status were marked in terms of "inside" and "outside." The doorway marked an important boundary, with a formal etiquette for entrance and exit. For some Plains tribes "it was the custom for a popular girl to receive her admirers at the door of her mother's tipi. She stood in the slanting doorway with her feet inside but from the knees up, she was actually outside" (Laubin and Laubin 1957: 122).

Camp Circle

The camp circle was viewed by many groups as a transformation of the lodge circle and thus also had its opening to the east. However, some variations occurred. The New Moon Camp circle of the Cheyenne for the Medicine Arrow Ceremony had its opening "in the direction least likely to be approached" (Dorsey 1905: 5). Despite such variations, tipis, sacred

Table 9-1. Distribution of Artifacts at Abandoned Tibetan Tenting Sites as a Possible Indicator of Gender Differentiation

Left Side (Women)	Midline	Right Side (Men)
Camp 10		
Inside tent:		
2 medicine containers	2 batteries	drink bottle
stick with streamer	twig broom	stone chopper
tin lid		paper
2 jar lids		2 medicine containers
stake		watch band
		chopstick
		jar
In front of tent:		
medicine container		stirrup
shoe		
ball		
twig broom		
sock		
tinkler		
Camp 11		
Inside tent:		
2 rubber soles	2 shoes	wire
cloth scrap		cloth scrap
tin		
broken glass		

lodges, and camp circles shared in an organizational etiquette that located a place of special importance opposite the entrance (owner's seat/seats of medicine man/location of offerings tipi), and that involved bilateral symmetry about the axis that ran from the doorway/opening, through the center (fireplace/ceremonial hearth/medicine arrow lodge) to the back (Dorsey 1905: 6–8).

Distributional Patterns

Orientation is a key to the understanding of artifact and feature distributions at stone circle sites. Gender asymmetry of distributional patterns would be in reference to a line anchored by the doorway and central hearth, and not necessarily running east–west. It should be clear from this description that test-pit programs always involving a particular quadrant,

Figure 9-3. Migrating Indians (?Blackfoot) in Calgary area, Alberta, ca. 1886. Note the use of lashed travois as sunshade (right) and drying rack for meat (left). Around the base of the tipi are what appear to be sod blocks and possibly stones (right). (Photo probably by O. B. Buell; National Archives of Canada, negative no. PA 66595; printed by permission)

or involving random placement of a one-meter-square pit in each ring, have fatal limitations. Critics of the productivity of stone circles should reflect as to the paucity of sites that have been extensively excavated (by trowel, with in situ mapping of material, and fine screening and preferably flotation of sediment) both inside and outside the stone course (see Davis 1983a). Fanlike or "butterfly" distribution of debitage marking doorway locations is suggested at the Pilgrim site (Davis 1983b). Even here, however, the search for external features or refuse distributions extending away from the circles was limited, which is important because a shade was usually erected beside the tipi in the hot season, with tipi occupants spending much of the day under the shade (Figure 9-3). A shade was roughly circular, like the tipi, but its open nature reduced the distinction between inside and outside.

If the lodge doorway is locatable at archaeological sites, intersite comparisons can be made of artifact distributions in either half. Significant amounts of artifactual material have been found both inside and outside stone circles (e.g., Schneider 1983), as have undoubted activity clusters such as single-lithology sharpening flakes (Wilson 1983). These findings indicate that stone circle sites have unrealized potential as maps of household etiquette and therefore of ancient cognitive landscapes. The extent to which archaeologists can read these maps depends on their persistence, resourcefulness, and imagination. Burley (1990) is correct in saying that stone circles typically yield fewer artifacts than do other campsites. Nevertheless, offsetting this lack is the special value of relatively short-term occupations, where "smearing and blending" have been less extensive than at campsites of long duration in which information may also have been overprinted in "palimpsest" fashion. The "Pompeii Premise" aside, stone circle sites may be the closest approach to archaeological "snapshots" of household etiquette in the open Plains.

Meaning of Stone Circles

Even if stone circles were associated with households, the stones did not necessarily serve as cover weights. Early photographs show all kinds of material placed against tipis, for whatever reason (Figure 9-4). Perhaps covers were only weighted down at night or on windy days. Perhaps, as Crow informants suggested to Lowie (1956: 89), stones were used as cover weights only in winter. Perhaps stones were used as "backstops" for logs laid against the tipi covers for security. It is unlikely, however, that stone circles were vested only with a secular function. As circles, they embodied much more because their shapes were based on that of the tipi, which itself was loaded with symbolism about world view. In outlining the tipi, stone circles demarcated household space, reinforcing symbolically the distinction between inside and outside. They could have served this important symbolic function even if they had no other use at all. Evidence exists that simple stone circles were used to demarcate sacred space used in vision quests (Hoffman 1953). As many authors have indicated, explicit separation of sacred and nonsacred is a Western cultural trait; for many other peoples sacredness resides in everything. To ask whether stone circles were sacred or utilitarian is ethnocentric and probably inappropriate.

Discussion

As Tuan (1971: 33) has pointed out, a perfect mesh between cosmology and the order of nature is seldom, if ever, realized. Cosmologies underly-

Figure 9-4. Assiniboine lodge near Fort Walsh, ca. 1876. Note the lashed-travois sunshade and presence of a variety of piled materials (including logs) around the base of the tipi. (Photo from S. T. Wood Album II; National Archives of Canada, negative no. C17621A; printed by permission)

ing the examples cited above are not ideal, however much they may be idealizations. Similarly, their day-to-day application responded to many situational exigencies, from availability of raw materials to the emotional state of the participant. The systems described here fall short of being "ideology, writ large" but contribute to an understanding of it. In the absence of written records, archaeologists must speculate about ancient ideologies. Yet some of the priorities of ancient groups can be inferred from the artifacts and features they produced. Perhaps little can be learned here because this medium of communication is so full of ambiguity. However, subjectivity and speculation have roles to play in the development of understanding; after all, the "method of multiple working hypotheses" cherished by scientists requires speculation in the original formulation of hypotheses. The problem with "reading" cultural landscapes lies in the a priori assumption that writing is more "special" than other modes of communication; even for modern groups the study of other symbolic systems lags behind study of written and verbal language. Emphasis by Western anthropologists on writing as the most reliable source of information is ethnocentric, reflecting our own unreliability in use of other media. Given widespread use by other peoples of mnemonic systems rooted in other media, we archaeologists should attempt to broaden our capabilities rather than to restrict our analytic focus prematurely, as Burley (1990) seems to recommend.

Archaeological households exist at the interface between social structure and landscape, and Plains stone circles hold great potential for the investigation of this relationship (see also S. Deaver 1989; K. Deaver 1989). Critical sampling strategies and percentages depend on the archaeological visibility of the cultural characteristic sought so that the value for optimal reconstruction of one system cannot be presumed to predict the value for another. In excavation sampling, one size does not fit all, and extensive excavation is needed for stone circle sites. Only with complete excavation inside the ring and extensive excavation for a considerable distance outside can one evaluate, for example, suggestions that tipis are better viewed as "generalized activity centers" rather than assemblages of discrete activity areas (Janes 1989).

These remarks concerning landscape seem uncannily appropriate for the archaeological record as well: "reading landscapes is not as easy as reading books. . . . First, ordinary landscape seems messy and disorganized, like a book with pages missing, torn, and smudged; a book whose copy has been edited and re-edited by people with illegible handwriting" (Lewis 1979: 12). One can nevertheless "read" the landscape to some extent, and one can "read" the archaeological record to some extent. Both are records of human behavior; both owe their reality to cultural priorities undergoing constant changes. What has not been edited already by nature will be edited and reedited by scientists, the perceptions of whom are governed by their beliefs. As my geomorphologist colleague C. B. Beaty says, "I wouldn't have seen it if I hadn't believed it." Even if much of the present chapter is speculation, such is the basis of hypothesis formation in science. An observed coincidence in itself means nothing; it is the suggested link between the observed variables that constitutes the hypothesis, and that linkage arises from the experience and the imagination of the observer. Unlike Burley (1990), I do not believe that the time for baseline theoretical studies is ever past, either in academic research or in cultural resource management.

Acknowledgments

This report arises in part from studies conducted on the Tibetan Plateau in 1987 and 1988 under a joint research agreement with colleagues in the Department of Geography at Lanzhou University, Gansu Province, China. I am deeply grateful to Professors Zhang Linyuan and Ai Nanshan, and especially to Professor Zhao He, Director-General of Science and Technology for Qinghai Province, for their encouragement and logistical support, and to the Social Sciences and Humanities Research Council of Canada and the University of Lethbridge for research funds. Graduate students Zhang Hucai (now Lecturer) and Qing Yong of Lanzhou University provided invaluable assistance in the field, as did An Shen-Hua of the Qinghai Science and Technology office, Xining. Canadian team members included Ian Robertson, Neil A. McKinnon, Ineke J. Dijks, and Darcy Dean.

The author's studies of stone circles and medicine wheels in Wyoming and Alberta were conducted under the sponsorship of several agencies. I am grateful to the U.S. Forest Service, the Wyoming Recreation Commission, ARESCO Ltd., and Fedirchuk McCullough and Associates for support, and to Professor George C. Frison, Professor Richard G. Forbis, Colin P. Poole, and Edward J. McCullough for advice. For ethnographic information and advice I am grateful to Reg Crowshoe, Martin Heavy Head, Ken Eagle Speaker, Bill Tall Bull, and Merle Tendoy.

I am grateful to Philip Duke, Ineke Dijks, Neil A. Mirau, and two anonymous reviewers for reading draft manuscripts and providing many helpful suggestions. Chester B. Beaty, Ineke Dijks, and George Zieber provided important reference material.

10

Medicine Wheels on the Northern Plains

Contexts, Codes, and Symbols

Neil A. Mirau

The most enigmatic element of the material culture of Northwestern Plains groups is contained in the archaeological category known broadly, if perhaps inappropriately, as medicine wheels. Many theories of the roles, functions, and meanings of medicine wheels have been proposed, but few have been supported by all available data. Archaeologists have lumped medicine wheel structures into a single category and in so doing have deemphasized the relevance of the variability and contexts of individual medicine wheels. Like most archaeological materials, what we do not know about these cryptic structures far outweighs what we know; however, a contextual approach to the study of medicine wheels may provide a means of gaining some insights into this aspect of Northern Plains archaeology.

A contextual approach, as Hodder (1986) has outlined, considers not only the similarities of archaeological materials but their differences. It considers the interdependency of an object's function and its symbolism, in essence denying a dichotomy between these two aspects of meaning. The approach seeks differences and similarities along several dimensions simultaneously, including the spatial, temporal, typological, depositional, and historical aspects of material culture. An emphasis on data in a contextual analysis exists, but that is not to say the approach searches for and attempts to evaluate information in a theoretical vacuum. Hodder (1986: 146) states that "within contextual archaeology a recognition of the need for general theory and for theoretical archaeology remains, but rather, the concern is to demand a closer relationship between theory and data, placing one in terms of the other, and emphasizing inductive as well *as deductive procedures."* Furthermore, such an approach recognizes that the past context in which material culture was produced is different from the context in which the archaeologists who investigate the recovered material are situated. Contextual archaeology attempts to avoid an imposition of meaning that is embedded in and dependent on the archaeologists' context by recognizing the existence of the different contexts of the past. It attempts to get at the understanding of the producers (that is, internal understanding) by evaluating and considering as many aspects of the past situation as possible. Contextual archaeology as outlined here is concerned with the "environmental and behavioral context of action" (Hodder 1986: 145). "Contextual" also refers to the fact that all archaeological material is embedded in a "text" of other material. In order to understand any item, feature, site, or other archaeological remains, we have to examine that item, feature, or site in relationship to as many other aspects of the past situation as we can. A contextual perspective is not a panacea (none exists in archaeology) and will not answer all the vexing problems that medicine wheels present; however, it may provide a base from which we can derive some of the cultural meanings that medicine wheels held for their makers. Moreover, a consideration of the contextual dimensions in which medicine wheels are situated will allow a critical examination of some of the roles and meanings that have been proposed for medicine wheels. It is beyond the scope of this chapter to examine all the relevant contexts of medicine wheels, but the ones that have been chosen will, it is hoped, illustrate the need for a close relationship between data and theory as demanded by a contextual approach.

Reading the Text: Ideas and Symbols

Any archaeological analysis should incorporate the notion of unity of action and meaning outlined by Hodder (1985). The sense in which meaning is used here is "the structured content of ideas and symbols" (Hodder 1986: 121). An analysis must strive to make inferences about how symbols evoked certain concepts, and then it must examine what roles those concepts played in the culture of the producers of the symbol. If we are able to develop reasonable and plausible inferences with respect to the symbolism of medicine wheels, we will perhaps add a fresh interpretative perspective to our knowledge of Northern Plains cultures. An examination of medicine wheels should view the structures as the material manifestations of deliberate, meaningful actions rather than viewing them as the result of regular processes embedded in the socioeconomic systems of

Northern Plains cultures. In addition, any study should look beyond singular deductions derived from the quantification of adaptive efficiency or some other economic imperative, as is often insisted on by a strictly processual approach. Many processual studies have paid scant attention to interpreting the internal cultural meanings of items of material culture (Trigger 1989a) and therefore have not been able to say much about the social effects of such items in the culture in which they were used. We may not fully understand or correctly interpret the symbolic meaning of any particular item of material culture, but interpretations can be offered and supported by examining the range of evidence and testing data against theory, thereby demonstrating the reasonableness and plausibility of an inference (Hodder 1987c: 6).

A symbol is an arbitrary coded signal in some form or other that deliberately stands for an idea or a concept of something else. In order to understand the meaning of the symbol, the code in which the symbol is embedded must be understood. Codes can change, and thus the meaning of any symbol can change through time and space even if the physical form of the symbol does not change. Interpretative problems can result; however, new codes are, in the absence of major cultural replacements or disturbances, based on previous codes. Deciphering these codes can begin only when we consider the full range of contextual data surrounding the coded material. Given the level of resolution possible in prehistoric archaeology, we may be able to draw only general inferences regarding the codes; nevertheless, these inferences can be meaningful and can help us understand the symbolic content of the material culture of the past.

I will try to incorporate available evidence and some interpretations in an assessment of the state of our knowledge of medicine wheels. Material culture necessarily has been regarded as "readable" or understandable (Hodder 1986: 122), but for a specific element of material culture to be interesting and relevant to archaeology, the circumstances of its production as well as its meaning and function have to be potentially knowable. It is in this respect that a contextual approach is crucial. Furthermore, any interpretation of meanings or functions should be subjected to self-criticism and reflexivity. The interpreter must be aware of the circumstances in which any given hypothesis is formulated and must endeavor to consider the viewpoints of human producers of the material culture being examined (Hodder 1991: 13). Although we cannot yet provide many answers, what we can say is that several theories proposed for medicine wheels are not well supported by available contextual data and that many are not sufficiently self-critical. On the one hand, many medicine wheel studies do not consider the range of information available in advancing a favored theory of functions or meanings (e.g., Eddy 1974). Such studies may be interesting, but they do not adequately consider all the contextual information. On the other hand, some studies have advanced a theory or theories supported with a range of contextual data (e.g., Wilson 1981; Brumley 1985) and in so doing have made a meaningful contribution to our knowledge of Northern Plains cultures.

On the basis of reliable ethnographic evidence, most archaeologists accept that some medicine wheels were constructed in the historic period as memorials to ethnic Blackfoot chiefs, warriors, or other notable individuals (e.g., McLean 1971; Kehoe 1954; Dempsey 1956), and good archaeological evidence exists for a similar role in the prehistoric period (see Brumley 1985). The evidence suggests that when a notable individual died his body (or possibly hers, but most evidence suggests this form of disposal of the dead was restricted to males) occasionally was deposited in his dwelling lodge. The lodge was then abandoned by living human beings and left where it was last erected. The death lodge may have been surrounded by a circle or circles of stones and radiating stone lines or other arrangements of stone. Over time, of course, all or most traces of the death lodge would disappear except the stone circle(s) surrounding the lodge itself and, if present, the group of stone lines that were said to represent a record of aspects of the dead individual's life. Sometimes the central stone circle appears to have been filled in with other stones. Only the nonperishable part of the death lodge would remain to become what is known as a Northern Plains medicine wheel. Other medicine wheel–like structures, such as the Big Horn, Majorville, and British Block medicine wheels, bear little resemblance to the Blackfoot death lodge and appear to have had other meanings, perhaps, for example, as physical manifestations of group solidarity in a region where social contact between small groups was limited. As such, these medicine wheels may have served a ceremonial role and as reminders to small, mobile population groups of their membership or participation in a larger cultural community.

A Definition of Medicine Wheels and Their Distribution on the Plains

The group of archaeological features known collectively as medicine wheels is composed of a number of complex structures located on the Northwestern Plains. Archaeologists have created this category and have placed a wide variety of stone structures and features in it. It is important to bear in mind the category is ours, not that of the makers of the structures.

We need to remember that the variability of the structures we have lumped together probably reflects the varying meanings they held for their makers and users.

Brumley (1988: 2–3) provides a review of a number of definitions and descriptions of medicine wheels developed by various researchers and proposes one of his own by listing common medicine wheel characteristics: "1. Medicine wheels are largely constructed of unmodified natural stone, possibly with some earth . . . incorporated into . . . prominent central cairns. 2. All medicine wheels consist of a combination of at least two of the following three primary characteristics: a. a prominent, centrally located stone cairn of varying size; b. one or more concentric stone rings of generally circular shape; and/or c. two or more stone lines radiating outward from a central origin point, central cairn or the margins of a stone ring. 3. Medicine wheels are made up of a generalized and radially symmetrical arrangement of the . . . primary components." Brumley goes on to state that most medicine wheels have ancillary stone features incorporated into them or associated with them, such as hearths, stone rings, anthropomorphic figures, or secondary cairns.

Brumley's definition is relatively explicit, although general enough to be workable. Again, categorization can be a thorny problem; however, in order to be able to conceptualize the phenomenon of medicine wheels some definition is useful if we remember that the category exists in our context and that our context bears no direct relationship to the contexts in which the structures were produced.

The known northern limit for medicine wheels can be drawn as a line running northwest from roughly the intersection of the Saskatchewan-Manitoba and Canada–United States borders, through Saskatchewan, to the foothills north of Calgary in south-central Alberta. The structures are scattered primarily on the Plains south of this boundary in Saskatchewan, Alberta, and Montana. A small number of other structures classified as medicine wheels are located in Manitoba, Wyoming, South Dakota, and other Plains states. Brumley (1988) lists and summarizes a total of 67 medicine wheels, although he states that others are known. Vogt (1990: 61) documents 135 reported or possible medicine wheels and like structures, 97 of which he has analyzed in some detail. A number of Vogt's 97 structures are only marginally similar to what typically are thought of as medicine wheels. Several, for example, are single large circles of stones. These stone circles are thought to be too large to be the remains of dwellings (i.e., tipi rings), have no obvious function or role, and are every bit as cryptic as medicine wheels. By including these items in the medicine wheel category, Vogt has illustrated the lack of archaeological agreement regarding what medicine wheels are, let alone what meanings they held and what roles they served for their makers. Vogt has extended the typological dimension for the medicine wheel category and in so doing has reminded us of the importance of considering differences as well as similarities in the study of these structures.

Vogt (1990: 98) suggests the known distribution of medicine wheels may be a result not of their actual distribution but of the amount and location of archaeological research conducted on the Plains to date. Certain areas of the Plains have not been as intensively surveyed as other areas; however, medicine wheels and like surface structures are usually easily visible, and few areas of the Plains exist that have not been surveyed in a manner sufficient to locate exposed medicine wheel structures. Medicine wheels are one of the more visible elements left by aboriginal Northern Plains cultures, and years of surface surveys throughout the Plains have resulted in a rather tightly circumscribed spatial distribution for known structures. Many yet-to-be-discovered medicine wheels may exist, including buried ones; again, however, given that they are generally easily visible and considering the level of archaeological survey that has been conducted on the Plains in the last several decades, their distribution in the landscape is unlikely to change significantly with the discovery of additional structures.

The relatively limited spatial distribution of medicine wheels means that they can be linked with groups that occupied this area. Despite the existence of a more or less uniform panregional Plains system of social organization and economics, they demonstrate that some differences in cultural practices and belief systems did exist within the Northern Plains, at least as far as such differences can be inferred from the remaining physical evidence. If we accept, for the moment, that the distribution of extant medicine wheels reflects their real distribution on the Plains, we can start to ask questions about the relationship between their geographic context and their place in the cultures that built them. No physical or environmental barriers seem to exist that could account for their limited distribution; that is, their distribution is not restricted to an area physically delimited from adjacent areas where medicine wheels do not exist, and therefore the distribution of known medicine wheels does not seem to be directly controlled by noncultural factors. It should be noted that the Rocky Mountains to the west and the boreal forest to the north may have constituted barriers in the sense that these areas were home to a subsistence system different from the Plains, but to the east and south no such barriers existed. Can we say then the distribution of medicine wheels is meaningful for any interpretation? The answer seems undoubtedly to be yes. I have already argued the Northwestern Plains were not unique environmentally or economically, nor apparently socio-organizationally, from adjacent areas within the greater Northern Plains region. Why then are there many medicine wheels in a relatively restricted area and so few or none in other parts of the Northern Plains or for that matter the Great Plains? That question is not yet answerable with any degree of certainty. What can be suggested is that we perhaps need not look for some general cultural process or regularity to provide an explanation; that is, perhaps at least some of the structures were the result of a minor but important single innovation that occurred on the Northern Plains and that eventually developed into one or more cultural traditions. In addition, medicine wheels may have remained restricted to this area due to cultural barriers that we do not yet recognize. As unsatisfactory as these speculations are, we cannot go further with the geographical data but neither can we propose or support any explanation that does not take this data into consideration.

A Need for Internal Consistency

The potential for archaeological research of medicine wheels on the Plains is both promising and problematic. Few known structures exist, and therefore the opportunity for acquisition of new data is limited. Having said that, it must be noted that archaeological research on medicine wheel structures has not been extensive and that the structures are potentially rich sources of information if we can "read" them. Many hypotheses have been proposed for the role or roles of medicine wheels, but few have adequately considered the range of evidence that is already available. Fewer still have paid sufficient attention to the larger context of the structures, such as their distribution in the landscape and their historical and ethnographic contexts. Undoubtedly, some new hypotheses will be proposed, and a few will be forgotten. The potential remains for virtually all hypotheses to be supported or weakened. The relatively well known astronomical alignment idea elaborated by Eddy (1974), among others, is an example of an hypothesis that has been widely discussed but that is not well supported by ethnographic, historical, or archaeological data (Haack 1987a, 1987b 1987c). As Haack (1987c: 138) says: "Not only does it appear unlikely that [medicine wheels] were used for the purpose of making astronomical observations, it also appears unlikely that structures of this nature could have been useful in this manner even if the orientations were more convincing. . . . There is no indication that the Plains Indians were ever particularly interested in establishing an accurate calendar. Any periodic event in which they were interested . . . was attended by any number of environmental clues." Actually, ethnographic evidence confirms that Plains groups did use calendric devices. Some, for example, were portable and involved the transfer of small objects from one bag to another to maintain a record of the passage of time. Such a system would be considerably more serviceable and simpler than using some large, more or less inaccessible alignment of stones to measure the precession of equinoxes and solstices in order to calculate years and seasons or some other measure of the passage of time. In addition, little ethnographic or historic data exist to support the hypothesis that medicine wheels were functional observatories. Also, as Vogt (1990: 191) notes, the variation among individual medicine wheels does not support their role as calendars dependent on the regularity of astronomical phenomena.

We should not, however, arbitrarily rule out an astronomical connection for some medicine wheels. Much of the criticism of astronomical theories is based on the failure of the structures to align accurately with equinoxes, solstices, or the heliacal rising or setting of certain prominent stars (Haack 1987c; Ovenden and Rodger 1981). It is possible that some medicine wheels, rather than being functional observatories designed to measure astronomical phenomena in an absolute sense, had a symbolic connection to such phenomena. Abundant environmental clues and indicators existed for changing seasons, bison movement, and other important cyclical events on the Plains (Haack 1987a). Therefore, the functional need for such observatories was negligible, but symbolically they may have been crucial to the ritual recognition of those events. Wilson (1981), for example, suggests that the thirst dance may have been coordinated to occur in conjunction with the season of peak rainfall on the Northern Plains. Abundant rainfall means abundant forage, and of course abundant forage is attractive to the animal resources on which Northern Plains groups so heavily depended. Furthermore, abundant resources mean that large gatherings of human beings can more easily subsist without resource stress. This season also coincides with the period of the longest daylight surrounding the summer solstice. If some medicine wheels played a role in ceremonies like the thirst or sun dance, it is conceivable that the structures might have been purposely, although not exactly, aligned with points on the horizon to mark the summer solstice or the rising or setting of certain stars during this period. Such alignments, if they existed, may have had symbolic meaning and not functional significance. Suggesting that medicine wheels are not exactly aligned to some particular solar, lunar, or stellar event and therefore not related to that phenomenon denies the real possibility that those astronomical events carried special coded meanings for the observers. When most of us look into the sky on a clear winter night, we can immediately recognize Orion and his belt and sword but only because we know the code needed to translate the stars that symbolize Orion. Neither statistical manipulation nor analysis is ever going to result in a researcher recognizing the mythical hunter if he or she is unaware of the code by which Orion is recognized. Similarly, medicine wheel structures may have encoded the meaning of some astronomical phenomena by utilizing some inexactly oriented but nevertheless culturally relevant, alignments of stone. Again, I am skeptical that medicine wheels were ever used as functional observatories; however, I am not prepared to deny a symbolic link with astronomical phenomena for some medicine wheels. In admitting this possible symbolic link, I am in agreement with Vogt (1990: 193). We will be able to pursue such a link further when we understand the code for the symbol, and we will only be able to decipher the code by "reading the text" in which medicine wheels are situated, if in fact we can decipher it at all.

In contrast to the astronomical hypothesis, contextual data for the role of some medicine wheels as memorials or grave markers are internally consistent. Similarly, evidence that supports a role for the structures in sun dance or thirst dance rituals is fairly strong (Wilson 1981; Grey 1963), whereas the evidence for other medicine wheel uses and meanings, for example, as navigational markers, is weak (Wilson 1981; Vogt 1990). The cultural "text" that surrounds medicine wheels is, as is the case with most prehistoric archaeological "texts," incomplete and difficult to understand. Nevertheless "relevant environments" (Hodder 1986: 139) exist from which medicine wheel data may be extracted and from which we may be able to get at some of the meanings of the structures.

Roles and Meanings

Gordon (1979) makes a connection between seasonal bison migrations from the open grassland to the aspen parkland on the Northern Plains and the fact that many medicine wheels are in or near the ecological transition zone between the grasslands and the parkland. He suggests that structures may have been built there in an effort by human beings to exert supernatural control over the movement and acquisition of bison. Calder (1977: 208) also links some medicine wheels to bison hunting, suggesting the structures may have been used by their builders in an attempt to influence bison through supernatural intervention. Although the ethnographic literature for the Northern Plains is silent on the issue of a connection between any medicine wheel–like structures and bison-oriented ritual, a superficial resemblance can be seen between the form of some medicine wheels and the recorded form and description of some constructed bison traps. At least ten documented medicine wheels consist of a massive central stone cairn located within one or more stone circles. The stone circles often have an opening or passageway from which run parallel stone lines. These medicine wheels are all within territory historically linked with Blackfoot, Cree, and Assiniboine groups, all of whom were known to use fairly elaborate bison traps (Wissler 1910). The circles could be seen to resemble trap walls, and the opening and parallel lines extending from it are reminiscent of the mouth and drive lanes of a bison trap. The stones of the central cairns could be understood as representing bison. None of these ten medicine wheels is adjacent to known bison traps, but that fact does not refute a link between traps and some medicine wheels (Duke 1981a).

Gordon's (1979) and Calder's (1977) hypotheses consider the geographic context of at least some medicine wheels as well as their typological dimension, and they also consider available historical and ethnographic information. The hypotheses, although interesting and plausible, are not yet well supported, but the possible link between some medicine wheels and bison acquisition magic is worthy of further investigation. Gordon and Calder have sought meanings for medicine wheels that are plausible in view of our knowledge of the environment and of the lifeways and cultural priorities of Northern Plains groups of the later Prehistoric and Protohistoric periods.

Wilson (1981) discusses various hypotheses for medicine wheel functions or meanings that have been suggested by other researchers, some of which are supportable by current archaeological and ethnographic research and some of which are not: "We are faced with the pragmatically inescapable conclusion that medicine wheels were different things to different people, long before the coming of the white man. Any single site could have been used in several different ways; and the historical documentation of one such use does not exclude others, nor does it prove that the site was constructed originally for the documented purpose" (Wilson 1981: 336). It seems, according to ethnographic and archaeological data from various sources (e.g., Oliver 1964; Calder 1977; Kehoe and Kehoe 1979; Wilson 1981; Brumley 1985; Vogt 1990), that the stone structures did serve more than one purpose and that they may have had many symbolic meanings. Vogt (1990) recognizes that medicine wheels may have had a variety of meanings but then decides that an observational role for medicine wheels played a major part in influencing the morphology, location, and construction of the structures, no matter what their individual meaning. His grouping of a wide variety of stone structures into the class "medicine wheels" appears to have affected his conclusion that most, if not all, of the structures he has examined played a role as observatories "toward the ritualistic recording of celestial motions in association with an event or ceremony, perhaps the Sun Dance" (Vogt 1990: 9). He does suggest that this posited observational role of medicine wheels was probably symbolic as opposed to functional but believes that his interpretation constitutes a general explanation of the morphology of the structures within his medicine wheel category.

We may subdivide the category of structure called medicine wheels; however, we must also be cautious in considering a division on the basis of the alleged roles played by the structures. Classificatory divisions based on inappropriate concepts held by modern observers should be avoided just as overgeneralizing should be avoided.

An ethnographic example provided by Keesing (1982) illustrates the potential pitfalls of classificatory divisions based on the use of singular as well as generalized explanations. The Kwaio people of Malaita Island in the Melanesian Solomons erect stone altars to their actual and legendary, or semimythical, ancestors. These altars serve as ceremonial sites where pigs are sacrificed to propitiate ancestors and expiate the sins of the Kwaio against their ancestors (who, in myth, provided the societal rules and regulations for the Kwaio). The sites are used to celebrate mortuary feasts, the major social affair of Kwaio society. The altars are also used to demarcate clan group and village territory. Individual Kwaio may worship at several altars, and they may also have rights in various territories. The shrines provide a physical and economic map of Kwaio territory and a socioceremonial map of Kwaio religious belief and world view. In addition, altars serve as a repository of the human remains of more recent ancestors as well as a cenotaph for ancient and legendary ancestors. When individual Kwaio move or otherwise change territory, they commonly take a stone from their former altar, which is used in the construction of a new one in another location. New altars are considered branches of the old ones, and thus the Kwaio maintain a link with their previous altar and territory, even in their new location. The Kwaio altars are, at the same time, ceremonial, social, and utilitarian.

This example illustrates that one should not attempt overarching explanations without an understanding of all the available data nor should one divide the secular and the religious when examining the archaeological record and inferring cultural practices and symbolic meanings from it. As Wilson (1981: 336) has noted: "We all have [difficulty] in understanding the ceremonial universe that surrounds any such archaeological site. It is tempting to view the site in its 'secular' and 'religious' aspects; yet an emic understanding of the problem probably requires a world view in which the secular/religious dichotomy simply does not exist."

I have suggested that the structures presently categorized as medicine wheels probably did not all have the same or even necessarily similar functions and their symbolic meanings varied in time and space. Even morphologically similar medicine wheels could have had different meanings in different circumstances. The people who used the structures obviously changed through time, and as a result of innovation and the imperfect transmission of knowledge, the meanings of the structures would in all likelihood have evolved.

This position is at least partially supported by archaeological evidence. Brumley (1988: 96) and Calder (1977: 201) believe that the Majorville, British Block, Manyberries, and Twin Peaks medicine wheels in Alberta were constructed over a long time period and were added to through time, altering their appearance and perhaps their role. Calder (1977: 201), in fact, suggests a span of approximately five thousand years of use for the Majorville medicine wheel. Wilson's (1981: 364) excavations at the Big Horn Medicine Wheel in Wyoming confirm the accretionary construction of that structure.

Many other structures appear to have been constructed in one event, and several are known to be of recent vintage. An example of a single-event, nineteenth-century Blackfoot death lodge construction is described by McLean (1971: 579), and Kehoe and Kehoe (1979: 32). Conaty and Tailfeathers (1985: 171), and Dempsey (1956: 181) describe similar structures constructed by the Blackfoot in the nineteenth and early twentieth centuries. Other apparently accretionary medicine wheels, such as Big Horn or Majorville, are the result of cultural actions spread over a considerable time span. This fact does not mean they could not have been memorials, but their accretionary nature suggests that they may have been broader cultural symbols; that is, if in fact the structures were added to over time, it is unlikely that later additions would have been meant to commemorate one long-dead individual even if that was the original meaning of a structure.

It should be borne in mind that it is archaeological research that has suggested some medicine wheel structures were added to and changed over time. Given the relatively imprecise temporal resolution of prehistoric archaeological research, any addition to a structure over one or even a few generations would be archaeologically undetectable. To the extent that we are able to discern that different elements of a structure were added through time, we must conclude that these additions took place over centuries or even longer, as was the case with the Majorville medicine wheel.

Some of the most prominent accretionary medicine wheels also appear to be considerably older than any of the dated death lodge structures. The British Block medicine wheel, a very large structure with the most massive central stone cairn of any known medicine wheel, appears to have originated at approximately the same time period as the Majorville wheel, that is, about five thousand years ago, on the basis of artifacts found in association with it. These and other medicine wheels appear to have been used repeatedly over several millennia. Whatever other roles the structures served, for example, as part of sun or thirst dance ceremonies, their primary social purpose may have been to maintain social cohesion in a region where nomadism and a sparse population would have mitigated against the level of social interaction necessary to ensure group biological and cultural survival. This view does not mean to imply that the structures did not have other meanings. In fact, if they did serve to maintain such contacts, they probably did have other important symbolic meanings that ensured social cohesion; that is, layers of meanings most likely existed for the structures, all of which were internally consistent with one another in the culture in which they existed and which were and are also understandable in and of themselves, perhaps like the example of the Kwaio altars given earlier.

Although the temporal context of medicine wheels requires much more study, some preliminary inferences may be made that make use of the limited data available. As already noted, Kehoe (1954), Dempsey (1956), and others have documented the construction of certain types of medicine wheels in the nineteenth and twentieth centuries as memorials to notable members of the Blackfoot nation. Dempsey's (1956: 177) Blackfoot informants suggest that these "memorial" medicine wheels date back at least to the prehorse days on the Northern Plains. On the basis of available archaeological evidence, Forbis (1960) suggests the Grassy Lake medicine wheel dates to the early part of the eighteenth century. The Grassy Lake wheel is similar morphologically to those described by Kehoe (1954) and McLean (1971), which were constructed by the Blackfoot. Brumley's (1985: 225) radiocarbon date range for the Ellis medicine wheel in southern Alberta is from A.D. 1270 to 1590. This structure is again very similar morphologically to those ethnographically documented as Blackfoot memorials, and Brumley (1985) concludes that Ellis is a grave marker/memorial to a member of the Blackfoot nation and suggests that this form of medicine wheel is evidence for the presence of ethnic Blackfoot in southern Alberta at least back to the period of construction of the Ellis medicine wheel in the early second millennium A.D. Of course, even if members of the Blackfoot Nation used this form of medicine wheel in the historic period, they could have borrowed it from earlier peoples in the area.

Like Brumley (1985), however, I believe that the "stone circle with radiating stone lines"–style medicine wheel can reasonably be inferred to be attributable to ethnic Blackfoot and their ancestors on the basis of ethnographic and historical data. As memorials to notable persons, these particular medicine wheels could be material manifestations of power relationships within Late Prehistoric and Historic period cultures of the Northern Plains. According to Reeves (1990), the last two thousand to three thousand years was a time of increasing social complexity brought on by technological developments, which facilitated increased social contact and interaction on the Northern Plains. It is beyond the scope of this chapter to evaluate the evidence for this increased interaction; however, such intensification and a concomitant rise in social complexity may have led to an increasing level of social inequality and the rise of individuals capable of exerting control over others. Given this scenario, reverence for a powerful individual after death may have been manifested through the construction of a physical reminder of the individual, such as what we now know as a medicine wheel. Again, although the available dating evidence is minimal, it appears that many medicine wheels were constructed in the last two thousand or so years. If this analysis is so, many medicine wheels may have had meanings related to a demonstration of power in an increasingly nonegalitarian Northern Plains social system. It may be that a specific (Blackfoot?) language group occupied this area and that the structures were manifestations of a particular set of cultural values not shared by other groups on the Northern Plains, or it may be that the presence of some very old structures, such as the British Block or Majorville medicine wheels, served as inspirations to groups that came into contact with them long after they were built. In fact no need exists to posit a population change to infer changing meanings. Old meanings were undoubtedly replaced through time, even in the absence of cultural replacement. Medicine wheels may have represented a "regional style" unique to an area by virtue of a local innovation that inspired subsequent forms but that did not spread outside of the area.

The question of style brings up another interesting aspect of some medicine wheels and their purported commemorative meanings. Kidd (1986: 62), citing a number of earlier ethnographers and using data from his own Blackfoot informants, states that some Blackfoot death lodge structures were quite intricate, incorporating concentric stone circles, radiating lines, and other features, and that some were simple stone circles without radiating lines or other elaborations. He further suggests that some groups of circles, especially those located on isolated hilltops, could have been communal burials. Many medicine wheels, for example the Majorville and British Block structures, have numerous stone circles in their immediate vicinity. If Kidd and his informants are correct, some of these may well have been death lodges that were deliberately placed near an important communal symbol in order to commemorate individuals. The meanings of the larger hilltop structures may have been forgotten in the rapidly changing social milieu of the terminal Prehistoric and Historic periods on the Plains. Some structures may incorporate one aspect of a five-thousand-year (or longer) record of culture change from small, highly mobile egalitarian societies through to the more complex social organization of later Northern Plains cultures.

If we can divide medicine wheels into distinct categories on the basis of morphology and provisionally assign different meanings to each category, can we not further subdivide them and look for different meanings under each of those categories? The answer, of course, is yes. That view does not mean we can divide them into categories that ignore the data, nor does it mean that it is legitimate to create a separate category for each structure and assign it particular meaning. The ability to assign new and particular meanings that are carefully derived from the data is a step beyond that which processualist approaches would generally permit, where adherence to general and overarching explanations are usually sought.

Medicine Wheels and Tribal Groups on the Northwestern Plains

Given the limited spatial distribution of medicine wheels on the Northern Plains, it may be reasonable to ask whether the known distribution of certain ethnic groups is in any way coincident with that area in which most medicine wheels are located. Of sixty-seven medicine wheels listed by Brumley (1988), twenty-three are located within a 200-kilometer radius of the confluence of the South Saskatchewan and Red Deer rivers, and eighteen are less than 100 kilometers from the junction of the rivers.

A series of maps has been prepared by Magne et al. (1987) that indicate the approximate territories of Plains tribal groups from A.D. 1700 to 1850. These maps are based on the journals and notes of several early European visitors to the area, including Henry Kelsey, Pierre La Verendrye, Alexander Henry, David Thompson, Peter Fidler, Alexander Mackenzie, and John Palliser, among others. The maps indicate band locations at A.D. 1700, A.D. 1750, A.D. 1800, and A.D. 1850. Interestingly, the A.D. 1700, A.D. 1750, and A.D. 1800 maps indicate that the general area surrounding the confluence of the South Saskatchewan and Red Deer rivers was occupied or otherwise used by the Blackfoot, the Gros Ventres, the Assiniboine, and possibly the Dakota or Shoshone.

If the early explorers' accounts were accurate and the area was a sphere of frequent tribal group interactions, at least some of which were violent conflicts (Ewers 1958), many of the medicine wheels in the area could well have been constructed as memorials or grave markers to individuals who died in such conflicts.

Although the ethnographic data from the Blackfoot favor the memorial theory, other hypotheses are plausible, even if they are not as well documented. One such hypothesis suggests that medicine wheel structures served as boundary markers delineating the territory of specific groups. If the structures served as border markers for an area claimed by a particular group, it would seem reasonable to place such structures in areas of potential interaction or conflict; that is, little or no reason would exist to demarcate a territory unless an enemy was infringing or threatening infringement into the zone claimed by the group. In this respect, the Red Deer River valley, around which a large proportion of known medicine wheels are located, figures prominently in accounts of Blackfoot confrontations with other groups during the eighteenth century (Ewers 1958). Perhaps the region was in dispute and groups erected markers or monuments signifying their claim to a particular area.

Dempsey (1956: 177) relates a story of interest concerning medicine wheels and the view that they could be seen as signifiers of territory or symbols of group or individual power. During a chance encounter between a Blackfoot chief and a potential enemy Crow group, the Crow were told that a medicine wheel–like structure they (the Crow) had visited on the Northern Plains indicated that a Blackfoot band under a powerful leader had recently camped on the spot the medicine wheel now occupied. The Blackfoot chief told the Crow party that the presence of the then newly constructed structure was a warning to any real or potential enemy and that they should carefully consider confronting the group who had constructed the wheel inasmuch as they were obviously powerful and led by a brave chief.

The story indicates a specific "power" role for medicine wheels. It also seems to indicate that the Crow, at the time the incident took place, were unaware of the use or function of medicine wheel structures because it was allegedly the first time they had ever seen one. This story is at least partially corroborated by the relative ubiquity of medicine wheels in historic Blackfoot territory and the paucity of such structures in historic Crow territory. As Hodder (1987a: 2) has pointed out, a symbol must be understandable if it is to be relevant, and, in this case, the fact that it had to be interpreted for an outside group may indicate that its meaning and therefore its relevance were restricted to the group that built it, in this case the Blackfoot. This account adds some weight to the argument that some of the structures were Blackfoot symbols, although it does not specifically support their role as memorials. It is, however, a short step from viewing a medicine wheel as a signifier of power of a living leader and his followers to seeing the wheel as a memorial to that leader after his death.

Conclusion

Many of the roles hypothesized for medicine wheels have failed to take one or more contextual dimensions into account and therefore have ignored available data. The various astronomical hypotheses, for example, consider the typological dimension but sometimes fail to address the historical, ethnographic, and some aspects of the geographic data available for these structures.

Some of the studies aimed at understanding the roles medicine wheels played in the cultures of the Northern Plains have sought to promote one explanation over others and, as a consequence, have used available data selectively and ignored or downplayed valid data. A commitment to a theoretical perspective that ignores human deviation, variation, and particular culture histories risks missing much of what is significant about cultures, including their ability to innovate and interpret the world around them in changing environmental and cultural contexts.

It is convenient to classify and categorize medicine wheels in order to think about them, but we must be careful when attempting to quantify and statistically analyze objects categorized on the basis of our modern, scientific world view. Such analyses can decontextualize those items, and, as all archaeologists know, an artifact out of its context is mute (Hodder 1987c: 2). We should take the optimistic position advocated by Watson, LeBlanc, and Redman (1984: 157) that the archaeological record contains crucial information that is ours if we can extract it, but we should not permit such an orientation to allow us to believe that all the information we extract is completely self-evident and conveniently quantifiable for the experienced archaeological practitioner. One interpretation does not automatically reduce the validity of others, and one interpretation in one context does not invalidate another interpretation in another context.

In addition, researchers should be aware of their own contexts. For example, they should remember the pervasive late twentieth-century attitude toward Native Americans by non-Native North Americans. The non-Native North American public views most, if not all, Natives as highly spiritual individuals with firm and somewhat homogenous metaphysical and ideological beliefs. Archaeologists should not graft this stereotype onto all North American Natives, present or past. It is inevitable that the world views of the members of past cultures varied and that their commitments to particular belief systems were equally variable. Some of the structures we call medicine wheels could have been constructed for none of the rather lofty and ideologically charged reasons that have been proposed by archaeologists. Some structures may have been the result of simple whimsy or other like actions. I am not suggesting this is so; rather, we must be aware of those types of possibilities whether they fit with our predominant views and attitudes or not.

We know that some medicine wheels were memorials to notable individuals, but some appear to have had other meanings, perhaps as symbols of power relations, monuments to the changing annual cycle, indicators of group solidarity and centers of seasonal celebrations and ceremonies, territorial markers, symbolic observatories of astronomical phenomena, or manifestations of efforts to control bison or other aspects of nature. It seems apparent that we cannot arbitrarily lump them into a single category and thereby infer a single use that ignores differences in temporal, locational, and other matrices in which they are situated.

Unidimensional explanations that purport to account wholly or even partially for a wide range of archaeological material are undoubtedly pleasing to those doing the explaining. Explanations grounded in supposed cultural regularities or systematics, as are sought after by adherents to the processual perspective, often run the risk of not paying sufficient attention to either the complete contexts of the material culture or the context in which the researchers are operating. Studies of archaeological phenomena such as medicine wheels, precisely because these structures are so enigmatic, benefit from close relationships between theory and data and a view that does not see the search for overarching generalities as the sole goal of archaeology.

Acknowledgments

I am grateful to Michael C. Wilson and Philip Duke for their encouragement, assistance, and many helpful comments in the preparation of this chapter. I also am grateful to the anonymous reviewers for their suggestions.

11

Projectile Points as Cultural Symbols

Ethnography and Archaeology

Miranda Warburton and Philip Duke

> Analogy was their explanation of relations, and the dramatic interpretation of these relations and the phenomena thereof their only logic, and so, behold, the arrow was for ages looked on as a wand of enchantment to those who made and used and lived by and loved it; was to them a symbol—a veritable portion and potency of the mightiest forces and beings that they thought the world and four waters, the sky, or the under earth held; was thus transcendent over the skill of their deftest archer; was a thing of magic, and was willful, as like to obey the wind-bird with whose feathers they had winged its shaft withal, the god in whose breath it wavered, as to obey themselves or him who wrought and loosed it; for itself would decree his luck or his fate, not he who sped it, else why all so vainly at times, however great his skill or his effort, did he speed it? Therefore it played as large a part in their theoretical and mythical as in their practical life, and must be theoretically and imaginatively, no less than practically and experimentally, studied.
>
> —Cushing 1895: 311

For the lay American, the bow and arrow evokes powerful images of the Native American. For many, it is *the* symbol of the Indian, as a present-day commercial sign reminds us (Figure 11-1). The huge arrows, placed in juxtaposition with metal Plains tipis, are found outside an Indian crafts and curio shop about ten miles from the entrance to Mesa Verde National Park, as far removed from Plains Indian culture as one could imagine. We do not believe, however, that these symbols simply demonstrate a modern American's ethnographic ignorance. Rather, they evoke a powerful image, rightly or wrongly, of "Indianness" to European Americans.

Figure 11-1. Projectile Points as Contemporary Symbols, Southwestern Colorado

In view of the powerful images the arrow evoked and still evokes for both Europeans and, as we shall show in this chapter, Native Americans, it is strange, therefore, that archaeologists have been so reluctant to investigate this aspect of the technology, concentrating instead on the tool's usefulness in constructing culture histories and particular patterns of social organization.

However, as any flint knapper will attest, many projectile points in the archaeological record demonstrate shape and care in manufacture that far exceed the requirements of function. Of the hundreds of modern-day flint knappers, few can lay claim to the skill, patience, and finesse of the flint knappers of so many projectile point types. For example, archaeologists (Frison 1978; Judge 1973; Kelly and Todd 1988) have long appreciated the flint-knapping skills in Paleo-Indian technologies. Clearly, a great deal of variation existed in the efficacy of actual techniques, which depended not only on the competence of the knapper but also on the quality of the material being used (Frison 1978: 332). Fine flaking and control are present not just on Clovis and Folsom points but also on later Plano types. A similar commitment to fine flaking is found on Avonlea points of the Late Prehistoric period.

One must therefore ponder the role of such artifacts in their prehistoric cultural contexts. With what power was the projectile point imbued to allow the investment of so much time, skill, and artistry by its fabricators? One can only deduce that these points played a social role beyond the killing of animals.

The first half of this chapter describes evidence in the ethnographic literature supporting the symbolic roles of projectiles, specifically concentrating on the Blackfoot of the Northwestern Plains. We then shift from the ethnographic literature to infer the roles that the projectile might have played prehistorically. In departing from a functional/morphological/technological approach to projectile points, we hope that our chapter will serve (symbolically, of course) to propel life force into a relatively sterile and lifeless aspect of archaeology—lithic analysis. While proposing complementary explanations for point variation and embellishment, we also support the assumption that the tools that we call points were, in fact, used for killing animals. On the Plains, this assumption seems acceptable, given the specific site contexts from which many specimens have been recovered.

Ethnographic Review

Cushing's poetic perception of the symbolic importance of projectiles, quoted at length at the beginning of this chapter, is supported by ethnographic evidence from innumerable cultures throughout the world (cf. Furst 1977; Hitchcock 1977; Obamsawin 1977). Clearly, arrows or projectiles play a role that transcends mere function; they have a symbolic aspect. As with all symbols, their message has multivocality, but the symbolic role of the projectile point seems most pronounced in the realms of hunting power, fertility, sickness, and the recurrence of life.

Because projectile points are no longer a viable part of Plains culture, their role cannot be determined by conducting further ethnographic work. Oral tradition, however, illuminates their symbolic content. A large body of Plains' oral narrative was recorded by ethnographers and observers having no apparent agenda beyond the preservation of these tales. In other words, this body of data cannot be criticized for exaggerating the role of projectiles; it is unlikely that the symbolic nature of projectile points was foremost in an observer's mind. Indeed, given the widespread use of the rifle, it is extraordinary that projectiles are mentioned so many times and in so many contexts.

Many Blackfoot traditions were compiled separately by Wissler (1911,

1912b, 1913) and Schultz (1916, 1962). The degree to which either man (Wissler or Schultz) was censoring or interpreting oral narrative as he was recording it cannot be assessed; neither man suffered from anthropological self-consciousness. Furthermore, it is likely that neither man was particularly concerned about the role of projectiles in Blackfoot culture. Moreover, these tales were told by Blackfoot people and were recorded manually by these two men. Admittedly, the tales suffer from not being exact translations and being filtered through their points of view. The role played by arrows/projectiles, nonetheless, is consistent in the different narratives.

The following analysis is primarily applicable for Blackfoot people living between approximately A.D. 1780 to 1910. Prior to this time no written records exist for them, and after this time their life was so altered that the role of the arrow becomes very difficult to analyze. It is possible that the rifle took over as the symbol in functions for which the arrow had previously been used, and the loss of such a powerful symbol as the arrow must have affected the mechanism of social discourse (Duke 1991). It should be noted that even during the period under consideration the Blackfoot already had guns, horses, and alcohol and that the following interpretations of the role of the arrow rest primarily on vestigial sources and legendary remnants. Our concern is with the *accumulated* sense of the symbolic nature of projectiles reflected in these tales.

In this analysis, we separate the "natural world" from the ceremonial/mythological or "supernatural world" and examine the role of the arrow in each realm of life. This arbitrary separation of natural and supernatural certainly did not exist for the Blackfoot. It will become evident, however, that although the arrow served a similar symbolic function in both of these realms, their differentiation is a useful heuristic device.

The natural world is reflected in children's games and socialization mechanisms; adult games; gambling; and everyday social activities, including birth, marriage, gift giving, hunting, warfare, representational art, illness, death, and life after death. The supernatural world delineated by rituals that set off sacred from profane time and space (Turner 1969) is reflected in oral narratives, medicine pipes, bundles and their songs, and dance association ceremonies and their songs.

The arrow played a role in Blackfoot life from birth: "When the child is born it is taken by the doctor and certain ceremonies follow. The child is washed in cold water. The umbilicus is cut, but not with a knife; an arrowhead must be used" (Grinnell 1896: 286). The arrowhead in this case was used to sever the new life from the old. This association of the renewal of life and recurrence of generations with the arrowhead is one that is repeated time and again in both the Blackfoot natural world and supernatural world.

After birth, naming was the first significant event in a child's life. A female child usually received only one name for life, but a male child had a series of names spanning his life from infancy to old age. A boy's first names were conferred on him by his mother (usually reflecting a physical characteristic or "cute" behavior on the child's part) and by his father or, more commonly, by a man of distinction outside the nuclear family (Wissler 1911: 17). The naming by such a person was considered very important because a name was thought to influence the child's fate; he was named after a great warrior since dead or a medicine man. If the name bestowed was not one of great power, adversities would be encountered later in life (Wissler 1911: 17). After his first war party, a youth was given a new name by his companions, generally an unflattering one and the cause of much teasing. Later, when the young man performed a worthy deed, he would change his name to something more prestigious. The word "arrow" occurred often in men's names—Long Arrow, Crow Arrow, Eagle Arrow, and White Arrow, for example; usually these names resulted from an activity in battle or hunting, or they came in a dream. The above-mentioned Long Arrow, for example, was a deaf and crazy man who regained his hearing, became chief, and brought the first horses to his people (Schultz 1916: 158–182). Although the origins of his name are unknown, Long Arrow's life represented an appropriate role model for a young man.

In the children's world, the arrow figured most prominently in games. Wissler (1911), Ewers (1958), and Grinnell (1962) mention a number of games that consisted of children throwing or shooting arrows at a target. Many variations on the game existed, but its primary goal was achieving familiarity with the weapon and a degree of skill in its use. It should be noted that children used their arrows as collateral in wagers, and the reward for hitting a target was often the capture of the losers' weapons. A ritual context to these innocuous-appearing activities may have existed; Wissler (1912b: 264) mentions, albeit in passing, that when boys were shooting arrows at a mark, they sang a special song. He notes (1912b: 263) just prior to that observation that a person never received power without receiving a song. The nature of the power associated with boys shooting arrows at targets, however, is unclear. In addition to games, boys used toy bow and arrows given them by their fathers to practice their hunting skills on squirrels and similar animals (Schultz 1962: 282).

By the age of 12 or 13 and the onset of puberty, a boy started using his bow and arrows in more serious or life-endangering pursuits, including both hunting and warfare. For some time after the Blackfoot had acquired rifles, the bow and arrow was considered a superior hunting weapon primarily because of its unique attribute of silence. The bow and arrow was used to kill every variety of game animal, including antelope, elk, deer, wolf, bear, coyote, and various kinds of birds.

Bison, of course, were their most important game animal; bison meat (*nita' pi waksin*) was "real food," whereas all other foods (*kistapi waksin*) were "nothing foods" (Schultz 1962: 30). During the days when bison were still being impounded (mid-nineteenth century), it was critical to maintain control over the herd. Any sudden noise such as a gunshot might frighten the herd and cause a stampede. The consequences of such action might be the wounding or killing of a large proportion of a particular Blackfoot group. The bow and arrow thus continued to serve as the instrument of death for the most important food resource.

Although all arrows have the attribute of silence, individuals' arrows were marked with personal insignia indicating ownership. One of a young man's obligations was providing either his parents or, if married, his parents and, of more importance, his parents-in-law, with food (bison meat) whenever he could. The buffalo were driven into pounds, whereupon the hunters shot the arrows and killed them. The arrows' insignia were then used to apportion the meat to the hunters and their families. If a young man only gave his in-laws or parents tough, undesirable portions of meat, he was disgraced. In a society that relied so heavily on a person's individual power and medicine, such disgrace constituted the worst kind of social censure possible. Therefore, for the hunter, the arrow served important functions: its silence enabled him to wound or kill an animal; and its individual markings branded the hunter as a person of power and prestige or one of disgrace. Just as the arrow could wound or kill the bison, so it could wound or kill a young man socially; alternatively, it could bring him social prestige and a better life.

The arrow served a similar dual function in Blackfoot warfare. In addition to wounding or killing one's enemy, the bow and arrow had a heraldic function (Wissler 1911; Ewers 1958; Grinnell 1962). Essentially, it was more honorable for a Blackfoot warrior to capture another warrior's weapons than to wound or kill him (Wissler 1911: 37). When a warrior captured a heraldic item from an enemy, he was then able to count coup. The coup system had a specified set of rules to which the warriors strictly adhered. Killing or wounding an enemy was not necessarily sufficient to count coup. Rather, a warrior had to scalp an enemy, make physical contact with him by striking a blow, or capture an item of heraldic significance. The heraldic items were ranked in order of importance. Unfortunately, all accounts of their ranking postdate the introduction of the gun, and the position of the arrow in the ranking system prior to contact is unknown. By the time of historic and ethnographic records, the ranking included shield, bow, arrow, gun, warbonnet, warshirt, or medicine pipe (Grinnell 1962: 248).

In the taking of another's life or dealing him a blow in the capture of his bow and arrows, a warrior was able to improve his status. Once a warrior had performed honorable deeds and counted coups, he earned respect within his group. He might be called on to name a child, lead certain sacred ceremonies, or lead other men on raids. Regardless of the specific honors conferred on a successful warrior, his life had become enriched by power and prestige involving new social responsibilities.

The Blackfoot said that it is better to die a brave warrior in battle than to die of old age. They believed that if a warrior died at the hands of the enemy in battle, his shadow (soul) would remain near the enemy camp and pester them by shooting invisible arrows, causing sickness and eventually death. This belief is a rather interesting twist on the role of the arrow in Blackfoot society; as the captured arrow of an enemy brought new life to a Blackfoot warrior, so the invisible arrow provided a lively role for one's shadow after death. The arrow thus symbolized the continuity of life, death, and life after death for the Blackfoot.

The arrow as a symbol of life and death, and as the reminder that life continued after death, can be viewed in other areas of Blackfoot life in which it has a significant role. The arrow and bow were often given together as gifts; the most common direction of exchange was either father to son or father-in-law to son-in-law at marriage. This gift giving can be viewed as a statement that the physical embodiment of a man's life and successes was handed down to the next generation. As the instruments of death provided the older man with a full and rich life, so, it was hoped, they would do the same for the younger man and his offspring. The arrow and bow, then, communicated that not only in death was there new life but that with the passing of a generation life continued; a warrior's power and glory lived on and perhaps increased in the hands of his son, son-in-law, or grandson. The bequest of one's bow and arrows to the succeeding generation symbolized the passing of one life and the consequent enrichment of another. Schultz (1916: 50) noted that a bow and arrow might be a gift from one man to another in return for a favor. Although the nature of the favor was unspecified, this powerful gift must have been in response to some vitally important action on the part of the recipient.

The arrow was also used in a men's hoop game. The hoop was a piece of young wood, the ends of which were tied together to make a circle. The hoop was then crisscrossed with strips of rawhide from which beads were hung. Someone rolled the hoop, and arrows were thrown in an effort to hit the beads. Before a man was allowed to throw an arrow, however, he had to recount a deed, usually telling of a time when he counted coup (Wissler 1911: 57; Grinnell 1962: 184). Although this activity was a gambling game, the occasions on which it was played are not clear. It was clearly a socially sanctioned opportunity to tell of one's war exploits that under other circumstances might be considered rude or boastful. The game was a symbolic reenactment of a life-and-death encounter from which came enriched life and heightened status. Before a man joined in the game, he had to prove (by a story) that he was worthy to pick up the arrow. The use of an arrow in a pastime activity that rewarded a warrior for his daring exploits clearly highlighted its significance. Once again, male power, daring, and life/death encounters are symbolized by the arrow.

A clear correlation exists between the role of the arrow in the natural world and the role of the arrow in the supernatural world. Three areas of the supernatural world allow some understanding of the role of the arrow within this realm—oral narrative, medicine bundles and pipes, and dance associations. In more than 150 Blackfoot tales, the arrow played a role similar to its role in the natural world, but with a slightly expanded symbolic function (Wissler and Duvall 1908; McClintock 1910; Schultz 1916; Grinnell 1962). Some areas of similarity include wounding and killing of one's enemies, wounding and killing of game animals (especially bison), the use of arrows as gifts, and the use of arrows in gambling games. The expanded role that arrows take on has to do primarily with a magical and tranformational aspect that they assume under certain conditions.

Grinnell (1962: 140) notes an origin myth for projectile points wherein Old Man (who appears to be the embodiment, simultaneously, of all good and bad Blackfoot qualities) "went out and began to break sharp pieces off the stones. He tried them and found that the Black flint stones made the best arrow points and some White flints" (Grinnell 1962: 140). In addition, he told the Blackfoot people to use their bows and arrows to keep their enemies off the land.

In its expanded and often more magical role in oral narrative, the arrow served as a gift. In one case, it was given by an unspecified person to a boy who became very powerful (Wissler and Duvall 1908: 122). In another case, an arrow was given to Bull-Turns-Round (a Blackfoot hero) from an "underwater father" as an honor and again to Bull-Turns-Round from his people because he was able to replenish their bison supply (Grinnell 1962: 14). In yet another situation a girl tried to placate Old Man by offering him arrows, but desirous of her body, he turned them down (Wissler and Duvall 1908: 34).

One example illustrates the role of the arrow as the symbol of a person's worthiness and standing. In this story (Wissler and Duvall 1908: 47), a chief held a contest for the honor of marrying his two daughters; the winner was the man who shot his arrow most accurately into a designated target.

There are five cases of arrows used as lures or distractions from one's goal. In three of these cases, supernatural beings left arrows as enticements for weak human beings. In one case (Wissler and Duvall 1908: 148–150), where men and wolves were living peacefully as one, a man picked up an arrow, thereby causing the men and animals to live separately. In another case, supernatural beings clearly warned people that the arrow was placed as an enticement to see if they could resist temptation and follow the dictates of the supernatural beings: "It was a beautiful arrow, the stone point long and sharp, the shaft round and straight" (Grinnell 1962: 108–109). In the final story, Scarface (a popular and important Blackfoot hero) was enticed by a warshirt, bow and arrows, and a shield to stray from his true mission, but he did not succumb (Grinnell 1962: 98). It is interesting to note that the enticements for men were not women, horses, or food, but arrows—underscoring the power and prestige accorded to the possessor of a fine or well-made arrow. This observation is further illustrated in the story of a man who went to the Sand Hills (where dead people go). On his arrival there he realized he had forgotten his arrows and, unlike other men, was allowed to return for them (Wissler and Duvall 1908: 163). He died shortly afterward and remained forever in the Sand Hills.

In some oral narratives, the arrow had a magical or transformational quality. In one story, Beaver (a Blackfoot hero) instructed his wife to take his arrows, rub them over a white bison skin—the most sacred object a warrior could possess—to make it clean and smooth, and then to throw the arrows away (Wissler and Duvall 1908: 50). The actual role of the arrows in this case is unclear, although Beaver must have considered his arrows to have a special power contributing to the care of this most sacred object.

There are two examples of arrows being shot and transforming material objects. One of these examples is in a "star myth" or a tale wherein stars have human origins. In this tale (Wissler and Duvall 1908: 40–53), one of the Twin Stars (Rock) enlisted supernatural aid from a rock and used his arrow magically to shoot at the lodge of the Old Cannibal Woman. The arrow struck near the bottom of the lodge. Water began to flow out of the hole made by the projectile, increasing in size until it carried away both the lodge and the rock (Wissler and Duvall 1908: 45–46). Another story involved supernatural aid as well; in this case, Raven helped a man fight Thunder by giving him an arrow with an elk horn shaft. The man shot this arrow through Thunder's lodge of stone and made a hole that let in sunlight; Thunder succumbed to the stronger power (Grinnell 1962: 113–116). In both of these cases the arrow was the vehicle for supernatural assistance, its physical presence symbolizing the connection with supernatural power and its ability to propel that power.

The idea of arrows embodying supernatural power is illustrated in two other stories that involve killing a bison bull with extremely strong medicine (Wissler and Duvall 1908: 112–116). In both stories, Scabby Bull could only be killed by a special arrow; in one case it was an arrow tipped with white flint, and in the other it was a blunt arrow painted yellow. Of interest here is the fact that the kind and color of the point was more important than the shaft or fletching.

Conversely, an arrow can be deflected off course and miss its intended target if the power of the person at whom it is being shot is greater than that of the archer. In one example, a kind old man, chronically mistreated by his son-in-law, had an arrow fired at him by the latter (Wissler and Duvall 1908: 53–57). That the listener's sympathies lie with the old man is implicit; he was kind and good, whereas the son-in-law was selfish and cruel and did not take good care of his in-laws. The son-in-law was doomed to failure, and his arrows which missed the target became the physical manifestation of his social failure, lack of power, and selfishness. In another story (Wissler and Duvall 1908: 94), a boy with very strong medicine was impervious to an arrow shot at him. The arrow, turned aside by his power, became both the symbol of one person's weakness and another's strength, one person's death and another's life. Hence, the admonition never to make bad weapons was given; one always had to be willing to invest the time and energy in their manufacture because one's life and future depended on them (Grinnell 1962: 157).

Two final stories illustrate the power of the arrow to bring back life into a seemingly hopeless situation. In the first case, again a star myth, an evil older sister who had been having an affair with a bear killed four of her six brothers. The youngest brother, with the aid of a little bird, shot an arrow into the air and restored life to one of his siblings. He did this four times and revived all of his brothers, whereupon they, and their kind little sister, decided they would rather live in the sky and become stars (Wissler and Duvall 1908: 68–70). The final story is of Bear Moccasin, the great medicine man, who behaved in such a way that he knew he would be killed. By prior arrangement with a friend, he hoped to be restored to life. The friend came on the disarticulated burned mass under a robe that once was Bear Moccasin. He shot an arrow three times into the sky. Each time the arrow came down and missed the robe. On the fourth shot the arrow hit the robe, and Bear Moccasin's body was restored to health (Wissler and Duvall 1908:

143–146). Once again the arrow had transformed one state of being into another; the dead were resurrected by the action of the arrow.

The close connection between the arrow as power object and arrow as personal propellant of power has been observed in oral narrative. The dual role of the arrow as carrier of life and death has also been noted. The arrow is emblematic of the unending life of the Blackfoot.

In this brief review of Blackfoot oral narrative, the correspondence between the role of the arrow in the natural world and the role of the arrow in the supernatural world has been observed. The main areas of the supernatural world that are not merely a mirrored reflection of events in the real world revolve around the tranformational aspects of the arrow. Rather than being viewed as something dissonant with what we know of the real-world role of the arrow, we may see this transformational function as being much in accord with what we have already seen as the arrow's role. The power with which an arrow is imbued is evident in myth and oral narrative; its magical and mystical aspects and thus its symbolic significance become comprehensible.

The second realm of the supernatural world—medicine pipes and bundles—is also closely tied to oral narrative. Both pipes and bundles were considered medicine. They were originally given to specific Blackfoot people by supernatural beings as help in times of need. Each bundle or pipe had its own origin myth and ritual to go with it: "In most ceremonies the origin of the ritual is regarded as the result of a personal relation between its first owner and its supernatural giver; each ceremony or demonstration of the ritual, being a reproduction of this formal transfer. Thus the myths are, in a sense, preludes to the rituals; yet, when one asks for the reason of significance of a specific part of a ritual, he is referred at once to the myth" (Wissler and Duvall 1908: 13).

Ownership of pipes or bundles was not hereditary; they could be bought or sold at any time. Tremendous responsibility, however, accompanied ownership of such objects. At every successive pipe or bundle transfer, the original transfer had to be completely and exactly reenacted. Many examples (Wissler 1912b: 272–278) of assiduous avoidance of responsibility for a particular pipe or bundle are recorded. The huge responsibility inherent both ritually and personally in the possession of these powerful items was known to all.

Each medicine bundle also had its own origin story that had to be reenacted with the transfer of the bundle. Additionally, various taboos affecting personal life were associated with the possession of a bundle. The Beaver Bundle was considered to be the oldest and most important of all the bundles (Ewers 1958: 167). The second most important one, believed to have been derived from it (Wissler 1912b: 211), was the Sun Dance or

Natoas Bundle. Interestingly, it was primarily a woman's bundle in that the husband took second place in the ceremonies (women called or dedicated themselves to a Sun Dance; men could not call Sun Dances.) The Natoas Bundle consisted primarily of a bonnet that was believed to have been given long ago to a beaver medicine man by a bull elk. Decorations on this bonnet included a blue painted leather band, a weasel skin, weasel tails, two feathers in front, two feathers behind, two plumes on each side, a flint arrowpoint, a buffalo calf tail, a snipe, and a small doll (Wissler 1918: 245).

The opening of the Natoas Bundle for the transfer took place at the Sun Dance. Indeed, this complex two-day ritual was conditional on the occurrence of the Sun Dance. The arrow mentioned above is said to have been added later by Scabby-Round-Robe (Wissler 1912b: 215). This mythical hero had a Beaver Bundle and then chose to live with the beavers to gain more of their medicine. He had been a poor, unwanted, and unsuccessful young man prior to living with the beavers, but even gaining Beaver medicine was insufficient to earn him the place in society he desired. His subsequent killing of a Snake chief, however, enabled him to marry the most desired woman in his camp and ultimately to teach his people about the Beaver Medicine. The last song in the bundle ritual contains the plea, "I want an arrow" (Wissler 1912b: 219). This ritualized expression of the arrow's importance as both a physical manifestation and symbol of successful life in Blackfoot society is personified by Scabby-Round-Robe.

The connection between oral narrative and medicine pipes and bundles is evident; dance associations are similarly linked to oral narrative. Each dance association, or men's society, had its own origin myth that described the original transfer of power from a supernatural being to a worthy human being; the origin story was reenacted at each dance.

In essence the men's societies had the responsibility of seeing that the society ran according to plan—a plan derived from the current norm and myth. Each society had its own dance and myth whereby its place within the community was made explicit. Many societies' dances—including the Pigeon Society, the Braves Society, the All-Brave-Dogs Society, the Dogs Society, the Brave Dogs Society, the Kit-Fox Society, the Catchers Society, the Bull Society, and the Horns Society—involved the use of arrows. There was one women's society, the *Ma'toki* or Buffalo Dance Society, but no bows or arrows were associated with their dance.

The role of the arrow in these dances is similar from one society to the next; the Brave Dogs dance provides an example. McClintock (1910: 462–463) describes two dancers dressed as Grizzly Bears and painted hideously:

> [They] carried bows and arrows with large points . . . while dancing, they carried their bows and arrows, pretending to aim at the dancers. The Brave Dogs kept going around in a circle, just like a dog looking for a place to lie down. When we had danced four times, the bears held the sharp pointed arrows ready to shoot, but, changing them quickly to two painted arrows without points, they took aim at the crowd, as if to shoot them, but the arrows were sent high over their heads. The rest of us ran off over the prairie, following in the direction the arrows flew, and throwing our moccasins into the air as we ran. Many boys followed us to pick them up, for we wore finely decorated dance moccasins, but no-one was allowed to pick up the two painted arrows, which the Grizzly Bears followed to recover. When the bears again returned to our ranks, we formed into line and marched through camp, singing our society song. If any of our members held back, the bears shot at them, or at any people, who might interfere with us.

In the above example—indeed for all the dance societies—the arrow is used as a physical demarcation between sacred and profane time and space. In this case, the arrow is the physical object that joins the real world with the supernatural world. It is the symbol of the connection of the origin of dance associations and thus Blackfoot Society and contemporary Blackfoot. It is once again the object that serves as the renewal of life, in this case for the entire Blackfoot society. Generation may succeed generation, but the arrow remains as the link between life, death, and rebirth; the link between father and son and son and father; and, finally, the link between the origin of the Blackfoot people and later generations.

The arrow acts as a revelatory dualistic symbol in both the Blackfoot natural world and supernatural world. It reveals a state of the world not evident elsewhere: that life and death are interconnected, that an inauspicious beginning such as that of Scabby-Round-Robe can be transformed into a successful life, and that a connection always exists between the natural and supernatural worlds. Its dualism comes from the fact that its mere physical presence is a constant reminder of the most fundamental of human concerns, the unavoidable fact of death. Alternatively, it is a constant reminder of the continuous cycle of life, afterlife, and successive generations of Blackfoot.

Points in Prehistory

It is perhaps not overly hyperbolic to state that projectile points are both the most studied and the least understood of all artifacts found on the Plains. Initially they were viewed purely as objects of culture-history significance because, almost alone in the region, these tools show sufficient change to serve as universal time markers (Mulloy 1958: 143). Regardless of any imputed cultural significance, projectile points can be used successfully as the archaeological equivalent of geological index fossils (Frison, Wilson, and Wilson 1974).

Attempts to explain morphological variation in points have centered on such processes as ethnicity, functional needs, or even sampling error (e.g., Reher and Frison 1980). For example, Kehoe (1966, 1973) took the normative view that point variation reflected different ethnic groups; thus, the temporal and spatial dynamics of points reflected the movements of prehistoric societies. The normative model is also implicit in Wheat's "mental templates" of Paleo-Indian points at the Olsen-Chubbuck site (Wheat 1972). A departure from a strict culture-history study was made by Calabrese (1972) in an examination of the mensural variation in projectile points recovered from various sites along the Middle Missouri in North Dakota. Despite the plethora of data, however, few cultural explanations were offered for this variation. Calabrese (1972: 4) assumed that the points were manufactured by males and concluded that "the possibility exists that the noted differences may be due to local manufacturing practices of different groups of people" (Calabrese 1972: 69), hinting at the ethnic origins of point variation. Problems with the traditional normative approach to Plains archaeology have been raised elsewhere (Reher and Frison 1980; Duke 1981b).

Alternative explanations for point style have been offered by Frison (1978), Hayden (1982), Bamforth (1988), Flenniken and Raymond (1986), and Kelly and Todd (1988). In a lamentably brief discussion, Frison (1978: 344) hypothesized that the elaborate flaking on Paleo-Indian points was part of a symbolism of hunting in that only certain animals were prestigious enough to deserve to be killed by these types of points: "Is the hunting concept an expression of an ideology that was concerned as much with prestige as with provisioning the group? The implements of the Plains hunter, the projectile points, appear in many cases to have been made with more than functional utility in mind. Rewards accrued to the good hunter but whether more for provisioning the group or for maintaining an ideology is not always clear. Neither is it clear whether the ideology of the hunter was dominant enough to bring forth expressions of contempt for gathered food." In this instance at least, we see the possibility of linking style to an understanding of artifacts as symbols situated within specific social and historical contexts, a theme we shall develop later in the chapter.

Hayden (1982) explained the extreme stylistic conservatism of Paleo-Indian points as the product of the need to maintain long-distance interaction networks. However, regardless of the merits of its argument,

Hayden's article did not address the important issue of why the particular messages were encoded on points at all and why they were encoded in specific attributes, in this instance shape and particular flaking patterns.

In this section of the chapter, we wish to open up a dialogue on analyzing the symbolic content of projectile points by considering alternative ways at looking at this most "well known" of all Plains artifacts. Our arguments were stimulated by the rich ethnographic documentation of the potential meanings of points. Of course, as is so often the case when a rich ethnography confronts the archaeological record, the archaeologist is dismayed by the paltry evidence left behind to analyze. We concede that the multitude of meanings recoverable from the ethnographic record will not be matched by those recoverable archaeologically. As Rogers (1990: 16) has noted, "there is no easy way to derive meaning from the physical context in the absence of native exegesis." This absence is one obvious reason why archaeologists have shied away from the symbolic and meaning content of their data. We also must concede that the numerous ethnographic references that we noted above do not, with few exceptions, refer specifically to the point alone but rather to the whole arrow. However, we still feel justified in assuming that the point itself also had symbolic power, simply because it is part of the overall object.

Needless to say, our arguments are not "processual" in nature in that they are not subject to the particular notions of testability proposed by that school of thought, although as has been pointed out (Courbin 1988; Gibbon 1989), proof has been a rather scarce commodity even among some of the processualists. Rather, our arguments are accommodative and provisional, inductive and contextual. At this stage of investigations, they can serve only as counterpoints to prevailing paradigms to demonstrate that alternative paradigms must be considered to achieve as full a knowledge of the past as possible.

Our first argument concerns the medium of artifacts. The fact that stone points preserve so well probably imbued them with added symbolic importance because of their ability to communicate messages across generations. Indeed, we can view all archaeological sites not just as loci that provided prehistoric and historic societies with the means of fulfilling certain requirements concerned with subsistence and settlement but also as loci invested with particular symbolic connotations, albeit unconscious to their participants. These meanings are explicable within the specific cultural contexts of those societies. Some sites on the Plains, such as medicine wheels, have already been viewed in this manner (Calder 1977).

We would extend this type of interpretation to "secular" sites also, not just because the profane/religious dichotomy of our society might not apply to sites of another culture but because material culture, in any situation or context, has the potential to influence and manipulate contemporary and future human behavior. Earlier point styles were not unknown to Indians, whether they were revealed in episodes of earlier use at some of the multicomponent kill sites or by other mechanisms that would keep earlier points and their "styles" visible to the Indian. To deny this possibility is to argue that Indians had no knowledge or awareness of time and their own past; clearly this proposition is unacceptable.

Our second argument is that proposing new ways for looking at the projectile point involves some discussion of style. Specifically, we conceive style as comprising two related components. The first, which follows traditional concepts, looks at the overall shape as well as the individual attributes of an artifact as representative of shared ideas about how artifacts should be made. The outcome of the individual artifact is dependent not only on its functional requirements but also on its role in signaling specific patterns of social organization (Jelinek 1976; Close 1978; Dunnell 1978; Sackett 1982; Weissner 1983). Style also consists of the meanings attached to the artifact, meanings that are partially determined by the particular context of use as well as by the particular historical trajectories of the artifact itself. As the context of use changes, so too can the meaning attached to it (cf. Hodder [1985] for an analogous interpretation of the different "styles" of diaper pins). This second use of style should not necessarily be conceived as an alternative to existing approaches because the particular meanings evoked by particular artifacts are somewhat, if not altogether, conditioned by the "roles" of the artifact in signaling social organization and the other mechanisms that have traditionally been subjected to stylistic analysis. Viewing style in this *active*, evocative sense simply adds another dimension to our analysis of artifact variation. This approach introduces the notion of historic specificity to the interpretation of points in that the specific meaning assigned to and received from the point is determined by specific cultural conditions of the society in question. In this sense, we can begin to create history not just as a series of *externally* orchestrated events but, as Collingwood (1946) intended, as an *internal* and specific history unique to its participants. Significantly, this alternative view of style looks at culture not as a unifying force in society. Rather, in eschewing a functionalist bias, it considers how artifacts can actively be used to segment society and to provide languages through which alternative social voices can be heard. This perspective, then, takes issue with prevailing notions of the essentially egalitarian, normative, and stable nature of hunting-and-gathering societies.

Our third argument is that the meanings evoked by artifacts can change as individuals redefine those meanings and as the use of the artifact changes, depending on its specific use context. The Blackfoot evidence clearly points out the different meanings evoked by the projectile point, depending on its specific context of use. One perplexing problem created by this type of analysis is that the simplistic and deterministic equation, that is, one meaning is attached to one artifact, cannot be assumed. Indeed, the very essence of the type of approach we advocate is that meanings can change, although the artifact itself remains the same.

Therefore, the different uses for points must be analyzed on a site-and-feature basis—this is the elemental procedure of any truly contextual analysis of the meanings of material culture—because these different uses provide an indicator of possible changes in meaning. The contexts of use include not only the manufacture and use of the point but, as importantly, the role of the point after it has been used and abandoned at kill sites or other locations. We need also to consider the roles of artifacts at different sites; for example, burials or cemeteries and the association of points with particular genders/sexes are areas that can profitably be explored in the future.

Fourth, we propose that the degree to which artifacts were altered by reuse and retouch must also be contextually analyzed (Duke 1991). Whether an artifact is altered or kept the same depends not only on functional considerations and the "rules" of curation but also on their roles in social discourse and therefore the degree to which artifacts were allowed to be changed. In this area, contextual analyses not only must incorporate basic rules of lithic technology in order to understand the individual "life histories" of artifacts but also must consider the potentially symbolic importance of such notions as conservatism and radicalism in artifact design.

Finally, using the direct historical approach to follow the artifacts back in time as their contexts of use and meanings change will provide a longer-term perspective on points than can be provided either by ethnographic analysis alone or by the essentially synchronic functional-adaptive arguments so often relied on by archaeologists.

Concluding Summary

The ethnographic record provides us with a view of people that includes a life rich beyond material culture. The Blackfoot life was far more elaborate than the mere hunting of bison; they enjoyed a life rich in symbolic expression. Life for all of us includes beauty, myth, pain, creativity, birth, sickness, fear of the known and unknown, joy, laughter, sadness, thoughts of an afterlife, and all the emotions that make us uniquely human. Are we really to believe that the precursors of those we identify as the Blackfoot led a one-dimensional life of hunting bison and gathering plants? Were their lives devoid of human expression and emotion? Are we, as archaeologists, so limited in our constructs and techniques that we are doomed to perpetuate a view of prehistoric people as mere automata moving across the landscape, figuring out more efficient ways to feed themselves?

Recent developments in archaeological theory give Plains archaeologists an opportunity to extend interpretation of the past into new areas. Archaeology, as William Duncan Strong observed more than fifty years ago, is "part history, part anthropology" (Willey and Sabloff 1974: 17). We suggest that it is imperative that Plains archaeologists begin to debate the symbolic content of the archaeological record. Plains archaeology runs the risk of continuing to see the past as a relatively unchanging world of hunters and gatherers that can be analyzed best through models such as optimal foraging. Examining the symbolism of historic and prehistoric cultures might reawaken our own awareness of the rich histories of aboriginal groups, histories that extend well beyond the time of first European contact.

Part III

Commentary

12

Paradigm in the Rough

Melissa A. Connor

Like a diamond cut to dazzle, culture is multifaceted. Like a well-cut diamond, culture is reflected differently in different lights. To appreciate fully all the facets of culture, it must be examined in a variety of settings, yes, through the light of different paradigms. This is the point that Duke and Wilson make in the introduction to this volume, that is, that a plurality of strategies are necessary to strengthen our interpretation of the past.

Postprocessual literature consists of a plurality of strategies and can be grouped under two schools, the first being the cognitive, structural, and symbolic approaches and the second being the Marxist approaches (Watson and Fotiadis 1990: 614). Well, here in the heartland, we never did have much to do with Marxist approaches. Chapters like Benn's, which gently introduce the Marxist labor theory of value, are important in Great Plains anthropology for showing insights gained from this point of view.

Many of the other theoretical stances gathered under the umbrella of postprocessual archaeology, however, are not totally new in the archaeology of the Great Plains although the concerns spring from different roots. Because of the wealth of Great Plains ethnographies and the time depth of Great Plains cultures, Great Plains archaeologists have always been sensitive to the cultural meanings of objects. This wealth of ethnographic data has also blurred the distinctions between the anthropological subdisciplines to a degree seen in few other places. To practice archaeology in the Great Plains, one must be familiar with the ethnologies of the Native Americans, the ethnohistory, linguistics, and physical anthropology. This cognizance of the wedding of the subdisciplines of anthropology is reflected in the name of the main regional journal, the *Plains Anthropologist*, when so many other regional and specialized journals are explicitly oriented toward a single subdiscipline (e.g., *Midcontinental Journal of Archeology*, *North American Archeologist*, *Historical Archeology*, as well as most of the state journals). Indeed, separating the anthropologist from the archaeologist has often been difficult in the careers of Great Plains anthropologists.

The contributions of both Zimmerman and Brooks in this volume demonstrate again that an intimate acquaintance with this body of knowledge only strengthens our interpretation of the past.

Although Great Plains archaeologists of the 1960s and 1970s did not have access to the vocabulary and sophisticated theoretical framework of the postprocessualists of the 1990s, many Great Plains archaeologists always had a concern with the cognitive systems, symbol systems, and structural categories of past peoples. These regular variations from the positivism of the new archaeology brought about by this concern is part of the reason the area may seem "backward" to many staunch processualists. In fact, these concerns have preadapted Great Plains archaeologists for the acceptance of postprocessualist ideas.

This concern for linking data with social concerns was reflected in a 1971 article on Valley Focus mortuary practices. The abstract states that "the implications of these burial data are examined for the insights they can give us into the *social structure* of the society" (O'Brien 1971: 165; italics added). O'Brien's concerns with how the burial complex fits into the social structure of the prehistoric society in some ways presages Krause's article in this volume. Krause combines similar mortuary data with a morphogenetic perspective to examine the social, political, and economic fabric of Woodland society.

An example of the cognizance of Great Plains anthropologists of gender-specific studies, and an article that is a personal favorite, is John Ewers's (1970) description of Great Plains Indian contraceptive systems. I do not think that those of us who came of age in the freewheeling 1970s can adequately imagine the gentleman and scholar who is John Ewers initiating the discussions with his female informants that led to the data for this article. However, surely this example suggests that there were anthropologists working in the Great Plains who were interested in, if not focused on, the gender-specific issues that interest Whelan. Although the recognition and documentation of gender roles have existed, Whelan brings a focus to these studies that has not existed before in the minds of Great Plains anthropologists.

There is no doubt, however, that the historical approach has always been the theoretical backbone of Great Plains archaeology. In one of the few recent syntheses in the area, the author makes it clear that he considers this the most useful paradigm: "I have taken up this study without setting up a specific hypothesis to be tested, since I am not convinced that interpretations based on such a proposition are necessarily any more valid or scientific or satisfying than those derived from observations not shackled by such preset procedures. The artifacts that provide the core data herein I view as cultural fossils, to be analyzed, compared, and interpreted in terms of human activity, not as commodities to be run through a computer from which arcane print-outs can be produced in order to meet a contractual deadline" (Wedel 1986: xiv).

In fact, a number of Great Plains archaeologists who never embraced the processualist paradigm suddenly find their work under the post-processual umbrella, much, I suspect, to their surprise. However, this fact does not mean that processualism passed over the Great Plains. No, I disagree with those in this volume who suggest that. Early processual studies, granted, embraced the empirical methods of processualism for historical goals (Ahler 1970; Calabrese 1972). Two decades later, however, much more sophisticated processual models are possible (Bamforth 1988), much of them in the realm of "middle-range theory" that use data from the Great Plains to examine larger questions (Bamforth 1986; Parry and Kelly 1987; Stevenson 1991). These studies are substantive contributions to the discipline, made under the processualist paradigm, and the question of whether they demonstrate that processualism is a significant paradigm on the Great Plains is rhetoric.

Many Great Plains archaeologists are not explicit in their writings about their theoretical orientation, and this ambiguity gives the impression that they are atheoretical. Rather, I see modern Great Plains archaeologists as theoretical opportunists, with both the historically oriented *Central Plains Prehistory* (Wedel 1986) and the postprocessual *Points in Time* (Duke 1991) resting on their bookshelves with the collected works of Binford.

Postprocessualism is still, however, a paradigm in the rough. This gem will need much more polishing before most archaeologists begin to glimpse reflections of their thoughts in the paradigm. As a rule, archaeologists in the United States are not well educated in structuralism or Marxist theory. Thus, archaeologists need to educate themselves in the schools of thought that make up postprocessualism. It is hoped that this education will make scholars more cognizant of their own theoretical stance and will lead to explicit statements of such in their work. A volume such as this is most useful in providing a series of "case studies," with data familiar to Great Plains archaeologists, as a guide to how these arguments may be used.

To be generally accepted by anthropologists in the Great Plains, postprocessual theory will have to prove its value in hunter-gatherer studies. Otherwise, even archaeologists who may be tempted to use postprocessual ideas will have difficulty in relating this paradigm to their hunter-gatherer data set. This volume has several examples of how postprocessualism relates to these studies. Wilson's discussion of the organization of nomadic living quarters offers new perspectives and interpretations on sites containing tipi rings. Mirau is correct in saying that medicine wheels are a site type ripe for contextual analysis. The analysis by Warburton and Duke regarding the symbolic content of projectile points shows how an artifact type intensively studied under both the historical and processual paradigms can yield yet new insights when viewed under a new paradigm. Studies such as these, which show the methods and results of postprocessual scholarship, will be responsible for bringing the paradigm into accepted use on the Great Plains.

Our knowledge of the past has been expanded by good scholarship under all three of the dominant paradigms in archaeology: culture history, processualism, and postprocessualism. Kehoe makes a solid point when she says that our paradigm of choice has much to do with the cultural milieu in which we work. We must take care not to compare examples of bad scholarship under one paradigm with good scholarship under another paradigm to show that one paradigm is better than the other. We cannot condemn the culture-historical paradigm because of archaeologists whose sole concern is fitting projectile points into preconceived stylistic pigeonholes. We cannot condemn the processualist paradigm because of archaeologists who misuse statistical methods. We cannot condemn the postprocessualist paradigm because of people who use the vocabulary without understanding the underlying principles. These people are simply bad scholars and would be under any paradigm. Conversely, we cannot afford to ignore good scholarship because we are uncomfortable with the underlying paradigm.

The strength of postprocessualism is that it recognizes that a number of strategies are necessary for a comprehensive interpretation of the past. Under any paradigm, a contribution to the discipline will result from an understanding of the relevant ethnographic and archaeological data, a knowledge of the literature, and a spark of creativity. The stress that Weimer places on a thorough knowledge of the literature is certainly relevant under any paradigm. The chapters in this volume are united in both the use of the postprocessual paradigm and the authors' creativity. Each author has taken data and examined it in a new light. It is this creativity that will give us new insights into the prehistory of the Great Plains.

13

Fighting Back on the Plains

Ian Hodder

Despite its universalist claims, processual archaeology seems to have been, at least in its early development, especially associated with the American Southwest. Whether it was Longacre and Hill testing out the matrilocal residence hypothesis or Binford developing sampling strategies, the focus seemed to be on that spectacular southwestern landscape, its archaeology, and field schools. After the move from Chicago, the most active processual archaeology departments developed in Arizona and Albuquerque. It is, in fact, often the way that certain approaches in anthropology and archaeology are associated with particular regions and problems. A whole discourse involving practicing scholars working together, influencing each other, dealing with similar problems, and producing similar ideas is often the basis for supposedly universal claims to knowledge.

For example, taphonomic studies have their homeland very much in eastern and southern Africa. Subsistence-based and ecologically driven archaeologies are associated particularly with hunter-gatherers. The main area in which claims for long-term conceptual continuities are made is Latin America. Later European prehistory has been the zone of structural-Marxist applications, especially the prestige-goods model. Many other examples could be given that reinforce the now widely accepted claim that knowledge is constructed contextually in relationship to particular problems and social networks. A clear recent example is that processual archaeology grew most successfully in North America in prehistoric contexts. It never had the same impact in Europe. As a consequence, postprocessual archaeology developed in Europe and has had less impact in North America.

This discussion is relevant to the Plains because, although they played a less central role in the development of processual archaeology, the area and its archaeological problems have been able to come into their own in a postprocessual context. The practitioners are less committed to one way of seeing, and they are more ready to be innovative in new directions. Kehoe, in an interesting chapter in this volume, adds the point that on the evolutionary ladder given such prominence by processual archaeologists, Plains archaeology seemed dull and simple. The contextual emphasis in postprocessual archaeology, however, makes the area and its problems interesting again.

Postprocessual archaeology was never well defined, deriving as it did from a critique of processual archaeology and establishing in its place a sensitivity to diversity and contextuality. It has always been better at being simply "post-" rather than establishing a new agenda. In many areas of the discipline, the term "postprocessual" is rapidly becoming redundant as processual archaeologists accommodate their views to take account of the criticisms and as postprocessual archaeologists soften their more extreme claims. The new consensus, particularly because it often recognizes a certain multivocality within the discipline, is as yet far from being worked out. It is thus of interest to see, in the particular tradition of scholarship on the Plains, what is meant by postprocessual and in what direction the participants are channeling their reactions.

One point that in particular is being developed in these chapters is that material culture is active, not passive. For example, Krause argues that mound building was actively used to transform exchange relationships and to create community solidarities and dominance. Brooks looks at vision experiences as being involved in conflict and relationships of power linked to individuals actively creating their own worlds. He shows how individuals were involved in factionalism and fission as part of the denigration of social norms. Archaeological sites in Brooks's study express the creation of difference rather than passive adaptation following cultural rules. In Benn's account of the processes of agricultural intensification, a dialectical view is taken in which the driving force for change is the control over labor and its surpluses as part of active social competition. In all these examples, the emphasis on power and action is clear. The view that material culture and individuals are actively rather than passively engaged in social life has perhaps been most easily accepted and incorporated by die-hard processualists. The writers in this volume avoid the error of assuming that the commitment to an active view can sit side by side with the central tenets of an older processual view. The very emphasis on creativity and action confronts claims for universal, adaptive, rule-bound responses to stimuli. The commitment to universal, objective generalizations as opposed to contextual interpretations is undermined. In addition, the consideration of active individuals is not meant to argue that archaeologists can "see" individuals or that "big" individuals changed the course of prehistory and history. Rather, it focuses attention on the frameworks of meaning according to which individuals in particular historical contexts constructed their world. Consideration of material culture and individuals as active rather than passive takes us from an ecologically adaptive world to one in which symbolism and meaning play a central role.

A clear example of this shift is found in the suggestion by Warburton and Duke that projectile points should be seen as symbolic as well as adaptive and technological. They argue for a program of contextual analysis of symbolic associations. Mirau discusses the meanings that can be given to medicine wheel sites, while Wilson considers Plains stone circles as having a range of locally varying symbolic and social meanings. Weimer points out that social and ideological dimensions could usefully be incorporated into predictive modeling.

Many archaeologists have now come to accept the importance of incorporating the study of mind, meaning, and symbolism. However, as in the case of the active individual, it is sometimes assumed that a processual and positivist approach can be extended to the new area of analysis without contradiction. In fact, the shift to the symbolic causes internal turmoil in a processual position. A hopeless dilemma is created by the dual attempt to maintain a commitment to universals and objective knowledge while at the same time accepting that material culture is contextually influenced by symbolic schemes. The very definition of "symbol" normally refers to the secondary (abstract, conceptual) and arbitrary nature of signs. Most people would accept that symbolic meanings are constructed within specific historical contexts. It is thus impossible to deal adequately with symbols by retaining an ecologically deterministic view and by maintaining a commitment to objectivism and positivism. Symbols open the floodgates to the contextuality of knowledge claims.

The writers in this volume avoid the tendency to be hoisted on the horns of the positivist dilemma. Mirau, for example, makes the essential point that the same or similar objects or sites can have different meanings in different contexts. The meanings of medicine wheel sites probably varied locally, and it would be necessary to conduct detailed contextual studies to gain access to these local meanings. O'Brien, in accepting the importance of ideological and social factors in cultural evolution, produces a less deterministic and universalistic picture of societal change. Warburton and Duke argue that the approach to the recovery of meaning must be accommodative, contextual, and partly inductive. Weimer recognizes that a certain amount of intuitive "thinking oneself into" an area contributes to the finding of sites. She argues for the use of history and anthropology, as well as ecology, and for the use of ethnohistoric data on nonenvironmental variables in predictive modeling. In all these ways a hermeneutic tendency is being recognized in archaeological procedures.

An acceptance of the provisional, embedded, contextual nature of our interpretations of the past does not any longer imply a slide into total relativism where subjectivity reigns unimpeded. Zimmerman shows the way in which archaeology plays a role in disputes between Indians and non-Indians. He shows that more than one past can exist and that the past is socially constructed. However, he also clearly makes the point that we do not need to set up a stark contrast between archaeology *either* as subjective politics *or* as objective science. Rather, Indian and non-Indian views can be transformed in relationship to the data, can be objectively supported, and thus can be made more powerful in the political process. The archaeological data are both subjective and objective, in a dialectical relationship, and real.

Whelan, too, in discussing feminist approaches that have burgeoned recently in the discipline, deals with alternative, multiple views on the past and with the political impact of the past in the present. Again, this impact is enhanced rather than impeded by the grounding of knowledge claims in appeals to the "hard" data. Feminists too are undermined by a total commitment to relativism and floating significance. Their political causes need to make reference to the "real" relations between genders in concrete historical circumstances. Cultural empowerment is undermined both by extreme positivism and relativism. The alternative is a hermeneutic or contextual approach that argues for the interaction between subject and object. Past and present constitute each other dialectically.

Processual and postprocessual archaeology had political and disciplinary contexts that were worked out dialectically. As already noted and as indicated in Duke and Wilson's introduction, much convergence and a greater degree of consensus now exist. O'Brien's chapter in this volume is a good example of the mixing and matching now occurring to good effect. The labels that one gives to the archaeology of the 1990s are less important than the recognition that a more mature discipline has emerged, able to countenance science and multivocality, to enlighten as well as to empower.

The progress that is represented in this volume needs to be worked through in relationship to well-argued, "thick" accounts of particular cases. In many of the chapters in this volume an agenda is set and some guidelines for achieving the new aims are discussed. However, a contextual approach that deals with meanings at the local scale and that seeks to make a contribution to the present must make its claims plausible through detailed data analysis. The claims for the authority of the archaeologist in contemporary social debate are now less related to the universality of knowledge and more to the coherence and correspondence of arguments within specific instances. The emphasis is on internal as well as external relationships. The Plains can only contribute fully to general debate when Plains archaeological data are explored in all their specificity.

References Cited

Abrams, P.
1982 *Historical Sociology*. Open Books, Shepton Mallet, England.

Adair, M. J.
1988 *Prehistoric Agriculture in the Central Plains.* University of Kansas Publications in Anthropology No. 16.

Adams, R. M.
1966 *The Evolution of Urban Society*. Aldine, Chicago.

Adams, W. Y., D. P. van Gerven, and R. S. Levy
1978 The retreat from migrationism. *Annual Review of Anthropology* 7: 483–532.

Ahler, S. A.
1970 *Projectile Point Form and Function at Rodgers Shelter, Missouri*. Missouri Archaeological Society Research Series No.8.

Albers, P.
1989 From illusion to illumination: Anthropological studies of American Indian women. In *Gender and Anthropology*, ed. S. Morgen, 132–170. American Anthropological Association, Washington, D.C.

Albers, P., and B. Medicine, eds.
1983 *The Hidden Half: Studies of Plains Indian Women*. University Press of America, Lanham, Maryland.

Albers, P., and S. Parker
1971 The plains vision experience: A study of power and privilege. *The Southwestern Journal of Anthropology* 27: 203–233.

Al-Mulk, N.
1960 *The Book of Government or Rules for Kings*. Translated by H. Darke. Routledge and Kegan Paul, London.

Ammerman, A. J., D. P. Gifford, and A. Voorrips
1978 Towards an evaluation of sampling strategies: Simulated excavations of a Kenyan pastoralist site. In *Simulation Studies in Archaeology*, ed. I. Hodder, 123–132. Cambridge University Press, Cambridge.

Anderson, D., D. Zieglowsky, and S. Schermer
1983 The study of ancient skeletal material in Iowa: A symposium. Manuscript on file, Office of the State Archaeologist, University of Iowa.

Arendt, H.
1958 *The Origins of Totalitarianism*. Meridian Books, New York.

Arzigian, C.
1987 The emergence of horticultural economies in southwestern Wisconsin. In *Emergent Horticultural Economies of the Eastern Woodlands*, ed. W. F. Keegan, 217–242. Center for Archaeological Investigations, Southern Illinois University, Occasional Paper No. 7.

Asch, D. L., and N. B. Asch
1985 Prehistoric plant cultivation in west-central Illinois. In *Prehistoric Food Production in North America,* ed. R. I. Ford, 149–204. Museum of Anthropology, University of Michigan Anthropological Papers No. 75.
Asch, D. L., K. B. Farnsworth, and N. B. Asch
1979 Woodland subsistence and settlement in west central Illinois. In *Hopewell Archaeology: The Chillicothe Conference,* ed. D. S. Brose and N. Greber, 80–85. Kent State University Press, Kent, Ohio.
Ashabranner, B.
1982 *Morning Star, Black Sun.* Dodd, Mead and Company, New York.
Ashmore, W., and R. R. Wilk
1988 Household and community in the Mesoamerican past. In *Household and Community in the Mesoamerican Past,* ed. R. R. Wilk and W. Ashmore, 1–27. University of New Mexico Press, Albuquerque.
Baerreis, D. A., and R. A. Bryson
1968 Introduction and project summary. In *Climatic Change and the Mill Creek Culture of Iowa,* ed. D. R. Henning, 1–34. *Journal of the Iowa Archeological Society* 15 (part 1).
Bahn, P. G.
1992 Review of *Engendering Archaeology: Women and Prehistory. Journal of Gender Studies* 1: 338–344.
Bamforth, D. B.
1986 Technological efficiency and tool curation. *American Antiquity* 51: 38–50.
1988 *Ecology and Human Organization on the Great Plains.* Plenum Press, New York.
Barber, B.
1952 *Science and the Social Order.* The Free Press of Glencoe, New York.
Bargielski, M. M.
1990a Test excavations of archaeological sites located during the Arkansas River R&PP sites cultural resources inventory. MS on file, Bureau of Land Management, Royal Gorge Resource Area, Cañon City, Colorado.
1990b Archaeologists in the BLM are also multiple resource managers. *Women in Natural Resources* 11: 42–46.
Barley, N.
1984 *Adventures in a Mud Hut: An Innocent Anthropologist Abroad.* Vanguard Press, New York.
Barnes, B.
1985 *About Science.* Basil Blackwell, Oxford.
Barnes, B., and D. MacKenzie
1979 On the role of interests in scientific change. In *On the Margins of Science: The Social Construction of Rejected Knowledge,* ed. R. Wallis, 49–66. Sociological Review Monograph No. 27.
Barnes, E. J.
1977 The Calovich burials (14WY7): The skeletal analysis of a Plains Mississip-

pian population. M.A. thesis, Wichita State University, Wichita, Kansas.

Barrett, R. A.
1989 The paradoxical anthropology of Leslie White. *American Anthropologist* 91: 986–999.

Barton, B. J.
1787 *Observations on Some Parts of Natural History*. C. Dilly, London.
1797 *New Views of the Origin of the Tribes and Nations of America*. John Bioren, Philadelphia.

Baugh, T. G., ed.
1986 *Current Trends in Southern Plains Archaeology*. Plains Anthropologist Memoir No. 21.

Beckerman, S.
1980 More on Amazon cultural ecology. *Current Anthropology* 21: 540–541.

Bender, B.
1979 Gatherer-hunter to farmer: A social perspective. *World Archaeology* 10: 204–222.
1985 Emergent tribal formations in the American midcontinent. *American Antiquity* 50: 52–62.
1989 The roots of inequality. In *Domination and Resistance*, ed. D. Miller, M. Rowlands, and C. Tilley, 83–95. Unwin Hyman, London.

Bender, D. R.
1967 A refinement of the concept of household: Families, co-residence and domestic functions. *American Anthropologist* 69: 493–504.

Benedict, J. B., and B. L. Olson
1978 *The Mount Albion Complex: A Study of Prehistoric Man and the Altithermal*. Center for Mountain Archaeology, Research Report No. 1.

Benn, D. W.
1974 Seed analysis and its implications for an initial Middle Missouri site in South Dakota. *Plains Anthropologist* 19: 55–72.
1980 *Hadfields Cave*. Office of the State Archaeologist, Report No. 13. University of Iowa.

Berman, T.
1988 For the taking: The Garrison Dam and the Tribal taking area. *Cultural Survival* 12: 5–8.

Binford, L. R.
1962 Archaeology as anthropology. *American Antiquity* 28: 217–225.
1971 Mortuary practices: Their study and their potential. In *Approaches to the Social Dimensions of Mortuary Practices*, ed. J. A. Brown, 6–29. Society for American Archaeology, Memoir No. 25.
1978 Dimensional analysis of behavior and site structure: Learning from an Eskimo hunting stand. *American Antiquity* 43: 330–361.
1981 *Bones: Ancient Men and Modern Myths*. Academic Press, New York.
1983 *In Pursuit of the Past: Decoding the Archaeological Record*. Thames and Hudson, New York.

1989 *Debating Archaeology*. Academic Press, New York.

Binford, L. R., and N. Stone

1988 Correspondence: Archaeology and theory. *Man* 23: 374–376.

Binford, S. R., and L. R. Binford, eds.

1969 *New Perspectives in Archaeology*. Aldine, Chicago.

Blackwood, E.

1984 Sexuality and gender in certain Native American tribes: The case of cross-gender females. *Signs* 10: 27–42.

Blanksten, G.

1951 *Ecuador: Constitutions and Caudillos*. University of California Press, Berkeley.

Bleier, R.

1986a *Feminist Approaches to Science*. Pergamon Press, New York. (editor)

1986b Introduction. In *Feminist Approaches to Science*, ed. R. Bleier, 1–17. Pergamon Press, New York.

Bloch, M.

1961 *Feudal Society*. University of Chicago Press, Chicago.

Board of Indian Commissioners

1880 *Eleventh Annual Report of the Board of Indian Commissioners for the Year 1879*. U.S. Government Printing Office, Washington, D.C.

Boehm, C.

1984 *Blood Revenge*. University of Kansas Press, Lawrence.

Bonnichsen, R. A.

1973 Millie's Camp: An experiment in archaeology. *World Archaeology* 4: 277–291.

Boserup, E.

1965 *The Conditions of Agricultural Growth*. Aldine, Chicago.

Bowers, A.

1965 *Hidatsa Social and Ceremonial Organization*. Bureau of American Ethnology Bulletin No. 194.

Braithwaite, M.

1982 Decoration as ritual symbol: A theoretical proposal and an ethnographic study in southern Sudan. In *Symbolic and Structural Archaeology*, ed. I. Hodder, 80–88. Cambridge University Press, Cambridge.

Brasser, T. J.

1982 The tipi as an element in the emergence of historic Plains Indian nomadism. *Plains Anthropologist* 27: 309–321.

Braun, D. P.

1983 Pots as tools. In *Archaeological Hammers and Theories*, ed. J. A. Moore and A. S. Keene, 107–134. Academic Press, New York.

1987 Coevolution of sedentism, pottery technology, and horticulture in the central Midwest, 200 B.C.–A.D. 600. In *Emergent Horticultural Economies of the Eastern Woodlands*, ed. W. F. Keegan, 153–182. Center for Archaeological Investigations, Southern Illinois University, Occasional Paper No. 7.

1988 The social and technological roots of "Late Woodland." In *Interpretations of Culture Change in the Eastern Woodlands during the Late Woodland Period*, ed. R. W. Yerkes, 17–38. Department of Anthropology, Ohio State University Occasional Papers in Anthropology No. 3.

Braun, D. P., and S. Plog

1982 Evolution of "tribal" social networks: Theory and prehistoric North American evidence. *American Antiquity* 47: 504–525.

Broadhead, G. C.

1880 Prehistoric evidences in Missouri. *Annual Report of the Board of Regents of the Smithsonian Institution*: 350–358.

Brown, J. A.

1976 The Southern cult reconsidered. *Mid-Continental Journal of Archaeology* 1: 115–135.

1981 The search for rank in prehistoric burials. In *The Archaeology of Death*, ed. R. Chapman, I. Kinnes, and K. Randsborg, 25–37. Cambridge University Press, Cambridge.

1986 Food for thought: Where has subsistence analysis gotten us? In *Foraging, Collecting, and Harvesting: Archaic Period Subsistence and Settlement in the Eastern Woodlands*, ed. S. W. Neusius, 315–330. Center for Archaeological Investigations, Southern Illinois University Occasional Paper No. 6.

Brown, J. A., and R. K. Vierra

1983 What happened in the Middle Archaic? In *Archaic Hunters and Gatherers in the American Midwest*, ed. J. L. Phillips and J. A. Brown, 165–195. Academic Press, New York.

Brown, J. E.

1953 *The Sacred Pipe: Black Elk's Account of the Seven Rites of the Oglala Sioux*. University of Oklahoma Press, Norman.

1964 *The Spiritual Legacy of the American Indian*. Pendle Hill Publications, Wallingford, Pennsylvania.

Brumfiel, E.

1991 Weaving and cooking: Women's production in Aztec Mexico. In *Engendering Archaeology*, ed. J. Gero and M. Conkey, 224–251. Basil Blackwell, Oxford.

Brumley, J.

1985 The Ellis Site (EcOp-4): A late prehistoric burial lodge/medicine wheel site in southeastern Alberta. In *Contributions to Plains Prehistory: The 1984 Victoria Symposium*, ed. D. Burley, 180–232. Archaeological Survey of Alberta Occasional Paper No. 26.

1988 *Medicine Wheels on the Northern Plains: A Summary and Appraisal*. Archaeological Survey of Alberta, Manuscript Series No. 12.

Buikstra, J. E., J. Bullington, D. Charles, D. Cook, S. Frankenberg, L. Konigsberg, J. Lambert, and L. Xue

1987 Diet, demography, and the development of horticulture. In *Emergent*

Horticultural Economies of the Eastern Woodlands, ed. W. F. Keegan, 67–86. Center for Archaeological Investigations, Southern Illinois University, Occasional Paper No. 7.

Burley, D.
1990 Tipi rings and Alberta prehistory: Toward a historical and critical review of legislated archaeology. *Plains Anthropologist* 35: 343–357.

Burling, R.
1974 *The Passage of Power: Studies in Political Succession*. Academic Press, New York.

Butler, W.
1988 The Woodland Period in northeastern Canada. *Plains Anthropologist* 33: 195–218.

Butzer, K. W.
1978 Cultural perspectives on geographical space. In *Dimensions of Human Geography: Essays on Some Familiar and Neglected Themes*, ed. K. W. Butzer, 1–14. Department of Geography, University of Chicago Research Paper No. 186.

Calabrese, F. A.
1969 Doniphan phase origins: An hypothesis resulting from archaeological investigations in the Smithville Reservoir Area, Missouri: 1968. Manuscript submitted to the National Park Service, Midwest Region, Omaha.
1972 *Cross Ranch: A Study of Variability in a Stable Cultural Tradition*. Plains Anthropologist, Memoir No. 9.
1974 Archaeological investigations in the Smithville area, Missouri: 1969. Manuscript submitted to the National Park Service, Midwest Region, Omaha.

Calder, J. M.
1977 *The Majorville Cairn and Medicine Wheel Site, Alberta*. Archaeological Survey of Canada, Mercury Series No. 62.

Callender, C., and L. M. Kochems
1983 The North American berdache. *Current Anthropology* 24: 443–470.

Carneiro, R. L.
1970 A theory of the origin of the state. *Science* 169: 733–738.
1981 The chiefdom: Precursor of the state. In *The Transition to Statehood*, ed. G. D. Jones and R. R. Kautz, 37–75. Cambridge University Press, Cambridge.

Cassells, E. S.
1982 Cultural resource survey of the Yellow Thunder Camp, Pactola District, Black Hills National Forest, South Dakota (Contract #53-82X8-1-169). Plano Archaeological Associates, Longmont, Colorado.

Chambers, R.
1844 *Vestiges of the Natural History of Creation*. John Churchill, London.

Charles, D. K.
1985 Corporate symbols: An interpretive prehistory of Indian burial mounds in westcentral Illinois. Ph.D. dissertation, Department of Anthropology,

Northwestern University, Evanston.
1987 Comments on O'Brien. *Current Anthropology* 28: 191.

Childe, V. G.
1950 The urban revolution. *The Town Planning Review* 21: 3–17.

Christenson, A.
1980 Change in the human niche in response to population growth. In *Modeling Change in Prehistoric Subsistence Economies,* ed. T. Earle and A. Christenson, 31–72. Academic Press, New York.

Clammer, J.
1985 *Anthropology and Political Economy*. Macmillan, London.

Clarke, D. L.
1968 *Analytical Archaeology*. First edition. Methuen, London.

Clinton, D. W.
1820 *A Memoir on the Antiquities of the Western Parts of the State of New York*. E. and E. Hosford, Albany.

Close, A. E.
1978 The identification of style in lithic artefacts. *World Archaeology* 10: 223–237.

Cobb, C. R.
1989 An appraisal of the role of Mill Creek chert hoes in Mississippian exchange systems. *Southeastern Archaeology* 8: 79–92.

Cohen, R., and E. R. Service, eds.
1978 *The Origins of the State*. Institute for the Study of Human Issues, Philadelphia.

Collier, J. F., and S. J. Yanagisako, eds.
1987 *Gender and Kinship: Essays Toward a Unified Analysis*. Stanford University Press, Stanford.

Collingwood, R. G.
1946 *The Idea of History*. Oxford University Press, Oxford.

Colson, E.
1960 *Social Organization of the Gwembe Tonga. Human Problems of Kariba, Vol. 1.* Manchester University Press, Manchester.
1962 *The Plateau Tonga of Northern Rhodesia*. Manchester University Press, Manchester.

Conaty, G., and E. Tailfeathers
1985 The Blood Tribe historic sites development project, 1984. In *Archaeology in Alberta 1984,* compiled by D. Burley, 180–232. Archaeological Survey of Alberta Occasional Paper No. 25.

Conkey, M.
1991a Does it make a difference? Feminist thinking and archaeologies of gender. In *The Archaeology of Gender: Proceedings of the University of Calgary Chacmool Conference*, ed. N. Willows and D. Walde, 24–33. Archaeological Association, University of Calgary, Calgary.
1991b Contexts of action, contexts for power: Material culture and gender in the Magdalenian. In *Engendering Archaeology,* ed. J. Gero and M. Conkey,

57–92. Basil Blackwell, Oxford.

Conkey, M., and J. Gero

1991 Tensions, pluralities, and engendering archaeology: An introduction to women and prehistory. In *Engendering Archaeology*, ed. J. Gero and M. Conkey, 3–30. Basil Blackwell, Oxford.

Conkey, M., and J. Spector

1984 Archaeology and the study of gender. In *Advances in Archaeological Method and Theory 7*, ed. M. Schiffer, 1–38. Academic Press, New York.

Cosgrove, D. E.

1984 *Social Formation and Symbolic Landscape*. Croon Helm, London.

Coues, E.

1965 *New Light on the History of the Greater Northwest: The Manuscript Journals of Alexander Henry and of David Thompson, 1799–1814*. Ross and Haines, Minneapolis (original 1897).

Courbin, P.

1988 *What is Archaeology?* University of Chicago Press, Chicago.

Creel, H. G.

1974 *Shen Pu-Hai: A Chinese Political Philosopher of the Fourth Century* B.C. University of Chicago Press, Chicago.

Cucchiari, S.

1981 The gender revolution and the transition from bisexual horde to patrilocal band: The origins of gender hierarchy. In *Sexual Meanings*, ed. S. Ortner and H. Whitehead, 31–79. Cambridge University Press, Cambridge.

Cushing, F. H.

1895 The arrow. *American Anthropologist* 8: 307–349.

Dau, B. J.

1981 Three methods of rapidly recording and testing archaeological sites. In *Megaliths to Medicine Wheels: Boulder Structures in Archaeology: Proceedings of the Eleventh Annual Chacmool Conference*, ed. M. Wilson, K. L. Road, and K. J. Hardy, 39–46. Archaeology Association, University of Calgary, Calgary.

Davis, L. B.

1983a *From Microcosm to Macrocosm: Advances in Tipi Ring Investigation and Interpretation*. Plains Anthropologist Memoir No. 19. (editor)

1983b Stone circles in the Montana Rockies: Relict households and transitory communities. In *From Microcosm to Macrocosm: Advances in Tipi Ring Investigation and Interpretation*, ed. L. B. Davis, 235–278. Plains Anthropologist Memoir No. 19.

Deaver, K.

1989 Identifying ring site occupations. In *Households and Communities: Proceedings of the 21st Annual Chacmool Conference*, ed. S. MacEachern, D. J. W. Archer, and R. D. Garvin, 256–265. Archaeology Association, University of Calgary, Calgary.

Deaver, S.

1989 Space, worldview and architectural form. In *Households and Communities:*

Proceedings of the 21st Annual Chacmool Conference, ed. S. MacEachern, D. J. W. Archer, and R. D. Garvin, 243–255. Archaeology Association, University of Calgary, Calgary.

Deetz, J.

1965 *The Dynamics of Stylistic Change in Arikara Ceramics.* University of Illinois Series in Anthropology No. 4.

1982 Households: A structural key to archaeological explanation. *American Behavioral Scientist* 25: 717–724.

Deloria, V., Jr.

1973 *God is Red.* Delta Books, New York.

1977 *A Conversation with Vine Deloria, Jr.* Words and Places, Program 8. Clearwater, New York.

DeMallie, R.

1983 Male and female in traditional Lakota culture. In *The Hidden Half,* ed. P. Albers and B. Medicine, 267–280. University Press of America, Lanham, Maryland.

Dempsey, H. A.

1956 Stone "medicine wheels," memorials to Blackfoot war chiefs. *Journal of the Washington Academy of Science* 46: 177–182.

di Leonardo, M.

1991 *Gender at the Crossroads of Knowledge: Feminist Anthropology in the Postmodern Era.* University of California Press, Berkeley.

Donley, L. W.

1982 House power: Swahili space and symbolic markers. In *Symbolic and Structural Archaeology,* ed. I. Hodder, 63–73. Cambridge University Press, Cambridge.

Donovan, A., L. Laudan, and R. Laudan

1988 *Scrutinizing Science.* Kluwer Academic Publishers, Dordrecht.

Dorsey, G. A.

1905 *The Cheyenne. I. Ceremonial Organization.* Field Columbian Museum, Publication No. 99, Anthropological Series 9: 1–55.

Doxtater, D.

1981 The Hopi ritual landscape. In *Megaliths to Medicine Wheels: Boulder Structures in Archaeology: Proceedings of the Eleventh Annual Chacmool Conference,* ed. M. Wilson, K. Road, K. Hardy, 313–332. Archaeological Association, University of Calgary, Calgary.

Duke, P. G.

1981a The use of boulder and earthen structures in palaeoeconomic reconstruction with special reference to the British Bronze Age. In *Megaliths to Medicine Wheels: Boulder Structures in Archaeology: Proceedings of the Eleventh Annual Chacmool Conference,* ed. M. Wilson, K. Road, K. Hardy, 387–396. Archaeological Association, University of Calgary, Calgary.

1981b Systems dynamics in prehistoric southern Alberta: 2000 B.P. to the Historic Period. Ph.D. dissertation, University of Calgary, Calgary.

1991 *Points in Time: Structure and Event in a Late Northern Plains Hunting Society.* University Press of Colorado, Boulder.

1992 Braudel and North American archaeology: An example from the Northern Plains. In *Archaeology, Annales, Ethnohistory*, ed. A. B. Knapp, 99–111. Cambridge University Press, Cambridge.

Dumezil, G.

1968 *Mythe et Epopée*. Editions Gallimard, Paris.

Dunnell, R. C.

1978 Style and function: A fundamental dichotomy. *American Antiquity* 43: 192–202.

1986 Five decades of American archaeology. In *American Archaeology Past and Future: A Celebration of the Society for American Archaeology 1935–1985*, ed. D. Meltzer, D. Fowler, and J. Sabloff, 23–52. Smithsonian Institution Press, Washington, D.C.

Earle, T.

1980 A model of subsistence change. In *Modelling Change in Prehistoric Subsistence Economies*, ed. T. Earle and A. Christenson, 1–29. Academic Press, New York.

Ebert, J. I., and T. A. Kohler

1988 The theoretical basis of archaeological predictive modeling and a consideration of appropriate data collecting methods. In *Quantifying the Present and Predicting the Past: Theory, Method and Applications of Archaeological Predictive Modeling*, ed. W. J. Judge and L. Sebastian, 97–171. Bureau of Land Management, Denver.

Eddy, J.

1974 Astronomical alignment of the Big Horn medicine wheel. *Science* 184: 1035–1043.

Edel, M. M.

1969 *The Chiga of Western Uganda*. Dawsons of Pall Mall, London.

Ehrenberg, M.

1989 *Women in Prehistory*. University of Oklahoma Press, Norman.

Ekvall, R. B.

1968 *Fields on the Hoof: Nexus of Tibetan Nomadic Pastoralism*. Holt, Rinehart and Winston, New York.

Eliade, M.

1961 *The Sacred and the Profane: The Nature of Religion*. Harper Torchbooks, New York.

1985 *Cosmos and History: The Myth of the Eternal Return*. Garland, New York.

Etienne, M., and E. Leacock

1980 *Women and Colonization: Anthropological Perspectives*. Praeger, New York.

Ewers, J. C.

1955 *The Horse in Blackfoot Indian Culture*. Smithsonian Institution Press, Washington, D.C.

1958 *The Blackfeet: Raiders on the Northwestern Plains*. University of Oklahoma Press, Norman.

1968 *Indian Life on the Upper Missouri*. University of Oklahoma Press, Norman.

1970 Contraceptive customs among the Plains Indians. *Plains Anthropologist* 15: 216–218.

Eyman, C.
1966 The Schultz focus: A Plains Middle Woodland burial complex in eastern Kansas. Master's thesis, University of Calgary, Calgary.

Fagan, B.
1991 Editorial. *Antiquity* 65: 186–191.

Fedigan, L. M.
1986 The changing role of women in models of human evolution. *Annual Review of Anthropology* 15: 25–66.

Finnegan, M.
1977 Osteological analysis of skeletal remains from the Chester Reeves Mound (23CL108), a Steed-Kisker Mississippian population. In *Cultural Resources Survey of Smithville Lake, Missouri,* ed. P. J. O'Brien, Appendix I, 111–163. Report submitted to U.S. Army Corps of Engineers, Kansas City District.
1981 Archaic skeletal remains from the Central Plains: Demography and burial practices. In *Progress in Skeletal Biology of Plains Populations*, ed. R. Jantz and D. Ubelaker, 82–92. Plains Anthropologist Memoir No. 17.

Finnigan, J. T.
1982 *Tipi Rings and Plains Prehistory: A Reassessment of Their Archaeological Potential.* Archaeological Survey of Canada, Mercury Series No. 108.

Fisher, A., W. Frankforter, J. Tiffany, S. Schermer, and D. Anderson
1985 Turin: A Middle Archaic burial site in western Iowa. *Plains Anthropologist* 30: 195–218.

Fisher, J. W., Jr., and H. C. Strickland
1989 Ethnoarchaeology among the Efe pygmies, Zaire: Spatial organization of campsites. *American Journal of Physical Anthropology* 78: 473–484.

Flannery, K. V.
1967 Culture history versus culture process: A debate in American archaeology. *Scientific American* 217: 119–122.
1972 The origins of the village as a settlement type in Mesoamerica and the Near East: A comparative study. *Warner Modular Publication Reprint* 1: 1–31.
1982 The golden marshalltown: A parable for the archaeology of the 1980s. *American Anthropologist* 84: 265–278.

Flenniken, J. J., and A. W. Raymond
1986 Morphological projectile point typology: Replication, experimentation, and technological analysis. *American Antiquity* 51: 603–614.

Forbis, R. G.
1960 Some late sites in the Oldman River region, Alberta. *National Museum of Canada Bulletin* 162: 119–164.
1977 *Cluny: An Ancient Fortified Village in Alberta.* University of Calgary Occasional Papers No. 4.

Ford, J. A., and G. R. Willey
1941 An interpretation of the prehistory of the eastern United States. *American Anthropologist* 43: 325–363.

Ford, R. I.
1977 Evolutionary ecology and the evolution of human ecosystems: A case

study from the midwestern U.S.A. In *Explanation of Prehistoric Change*, ed. J. N. Hill, 153–184. University of New Mexico Press, Albuquerque.

1985 The processes of plant food production in prehistoric North America. In *Prehistoric Food Production in North America*, ed. R. I. Ford, 1–18. Museum of Anthropology, University of Michigan Anthropological Papers No. 75.

Fowler, D. D.

1987 Uses of the past: Archaeology in the service of the state. *American Antiquity* 52: 228–248.

Fowler, M. L.

1969 Middle Mississippian agricultural fields. *American Antiquity* 34: 365–375.

1974 *Cahokia: Ancient Capital of the Midwest*. Addison-Wesley Module in Anthropology No. 48.

1992 The eastern horticultural complex and Mississippian agricultural fields: Studies and hypotheses. In *Late Prehistoric Agriculture: Observations from the Midwest*, ed. W. I. Woods, 1–18. Illinois Historic Preservation Agency Studies in Illinois Archaeology No. 9.

Fox, G.

1982 The Garden Coulee site. Manuscript on file, National Park Service, Midwest Archaeological Center, Lincoln.

Fried, M. H.

1967 *The Evolution of Primitive Society*. Random House, New York.

Friedman, J., and M. J. Rowlands

1978 Notes towards an epigenetic model of the evolution of "civilization." In *The Evolution of Social Systems*, ed. J. Friedman and M. Rowlands, 201–276. Duckworth, London.

Frison, G. C.

1974 *The Casper Site: A Hell Gap Bison Kill on the High Plains*. Academic Press, New York.

1978 *Prehistoric Hunters of the High Plains*. Academic Press, New York.

Frison, G. C., R. L. Andrews, J. M. Adovasio, R. C. Carlisle, and R. Edgar

1986 A late Paleoindian animal trapping net from northern Wyoming. *American Antiquity* 51: 352–361.

Frison, G. C., M. Wilson, and D. J. Wilson

1974 The Holocene stratigraphic archaeology of Wyoming: An introduction. In *Applied Geology and Archaeology: The Holocene History of Wyoming*, ed. M. C. Wilson, 108–127. Geological Survey of Wyoming, Report of Investigations No. 10.

Fritz, J. M.

1978 Paleopsychology today: Ideational systems and human adaptation in prehistory. In *Social Archeology: Beyond Subsistence and Dating*, ed. C. L. Redman, M. J. Berman, E. V. Curtin, W. T. Langhorne, Jr., N. M. Versaggi, and J. C. Wanser, 37–59. Academic Press, New York.

Furst, P. T.

1977 The roots and continuities of shamanism. In *Stones, Bones and Skin: Ritual and Shamanic Art*, ed. T. Brodzky, R. Danesewich, and N. Johnson, 1–28.

The Society for Art Publications, Toronto.

Gailey, C. W.

1987 Evolutionary perspectives on gender hierarchy. In *Analyzing Gender*, ed. B. Hess and M. Ferree, 32–37. Sage, Beverly Hills.

Gailey, C. W., and T. C. Patterson

1987 Power relations and state formation. In *Power Relations and State Formation*, ed. T.C. Patterson and C.W. Gailey, 1–26. American Anthropological Association, Washington, D.C.

Gallagher, J. P., and R. F. Sasso

1987 Investigations into Oneota ridged field agriculture of the northern margin of the Prairie Peninsula. *Plains Anthropologist* 32: 141–151.

Gallatin, A.

1836 A synopsis of the Indian tribes within the United States east of the Rocky Mountains and in the British and Russian possessions in North America. *Archaeologia Americana* 2: 1–422.

Geertz, C.

1964 Ideology as a cultural system. In *Ideology and Discontent*, ed. D. E. Apter, 47–76. The Free Press of Glencoe, New York.

Gero, J. M.

1983 Gender bias in archaeology: A cross-cultural perspective. In *The Socio-Politics of Archaeology*, ed. J. M. Gero, D. M. Lacy, and M. L. Blakey, 51–57. University of Massachusetts Department of Anthropology, Research Report No. 23.

1985 Socio-politics and the woman-at-home ideology. *American Antiquity* 50: 342–350.

1991 Genderlithics: Women's roles in stone tool production. In *Engendering Archaeology*, ed. J. Gero and M. Conkey, 163–193. Basil Blackwell, Oxford.

Gero, J. M., and M.W. Conkey, eds.

1991 *Engendering Archaeology: Women and Prehistory*. Basil Blackwell, Oxford.

Gibbon, G.

1974 A model of Mississippian development and its implications for the Red Wing Area. In *Aspects of Great Lakes Anthropology*, ed. E. Johnson, 129–137. Minnesota Prehistoric Archaeological Series No. 11, Minnesota Historical Society.

1988 The Upper Mississippi River valley and adjacent prairies: A review. Paper presented at the Forty-Sixth Annual Plains Anthropological Conference, Wichita.

1989 *Explanation in Archaeology*. Basil Blackwell, Oxford.

Gibbs, L.

1987 Identifying gender representation in the archaeological record: A contextual study. In *The Archaeology of Contextual Meanings*, ed. I. Hodder, 79–89. Cambridge University Press, Cambridge.

Gilman, A.

1984 Explaining the Upper Palaeolithic revolution. In *Marxist Perspectives in*

Archaeology, ed. M. Spriggs, 115–126. Cambridge University Press, Cambridge.

Gilman, C., and M. J. Schneider
1987 *The Way to Independence: Memoirs of a Hidatsa Indian Family, 1840–1920.* Minnesota Historical Society Press, St. Paul.

Godelier, M.
1978 Infrastructures, societies, and history. *Current Anthropology* 19: 763–768.

Goldstein, M. C., and C. M. Beall
1990 *Nomads of Western Tibet: The Survival of a Way of Life*. University of California Press, Berkeley.

Goodman, J.
1981 *American Genesis*. Berkeley, New York.

Gordon, B.
1979 *Of Men and Herds in Canadian Plains Prehistory*. Archaeological Survey of Canada, Mercury Series No. 84.

Gould, R. A.
1978 From Tasmania to Tucson: New directions in ethnoarchaeology. In *Explorations in Ethnoarchaeology*, ed. R. A. Gould, 1–10. University of New Mexico Press, Albuquerque.

Greenberg, D. S.
1967 *The Politics of Pure Science*. Times-Mirror, New York.

Greenfield, S. M.
1977 The patrimonial state and patron-client relations in Iberia and Latin America: Sources of "the system" in the fifteenth-century writings of the Infante D. Pedro of Portugal. *Ethnohistory* 24: 163–178.

Greiser, S. T.
1985 *Predictive Models of Hunter-Gatherer Subsistence and Settlement Strategies on the Central Plains*. Plains Anthropologist Memoir No. 20.

Grey, D.
1963 Big Horn Medicine Wheel site, 48BH302. *Plains Anthropologist* 8: 27–40.

Griffin, J. B.
1960 Climatic change: A contributory cause of the growth and decline of northern Hopewellian culture. *The Wisconsin Archeologist* 41: 21–33.

Grinnell, G. B.
1896 Childbirth among the Blackfeet. *American Anthropologist* 9: 286–287.
1915 *The Fighting Cheyennes*. Scribner Publishing, New York.
1962 *Blackfoot Lodge Tales*. First edition 1892. University of Nebraska Press, Lincoln.

Guenther, T. R.
1991 *The Horse Creek site: Some Evidence for Gender Roles in a Transitional Early to Middle Plains Archaic Base Camp*. Plains Anthropologist Memoir No. 26.

Gunnerson, J. H., and D. A. Gunnerson
1988 *Ethnohistory of the High Plains*. Bureau of Land Management, Cultural Resources Series No. 26, Denver.

Haack, S.
1987a A critical evaluation of medicine wheel astronomy. *Plains Anthropologist* 32: 77–82.
1987b Haack responds. *Plains Anthropologist* 32: 324–326.
1987c A critique of medicine wheel astronomy. In *Archaeology in Alberta 1986*, compiled by M. Magne, 129–139. Archaeological Survey of Alberta, Occasional Paper No. 31.

Hakken, D.
1987 Studying work: Anthropological and Marxist perspectives. In *Perspectives in U.S. Marxist Anthropology*, ed. D. Hakken and H. Lessinger, 57–80. Westview Press, Boulder.

Hall, E. T.
1959 *The Silent Language*. Fawcett Publications, Greenwich, Connecticut.
1966 *The Hidden Dimension*. Doubleday, Garden City, New York.

Hall, R. L.
1972 The Cahokia presence outside of the American Bottoms. Paper read at the Annual Meeting of the Central States Anthropological Society, St. Louis.
1980 An interpretation of the two-climax model of Illinois prehistory. In *Early Native Americans: Prehistoric Demography, Economy, and Technology*, ed. D. L. Browman, 401–462. Mouton Publishers, New York.

Handsman, R.
1990 Corn and culture, pots and politics: How to listen to the voices of Mohegan women. Paper presented at the 1990 Annual Meeting of the Society for Historical Archaeology, Tucson, Arizona.

Hanen, M. P., and J. H. Kelley
1988 *Archaeology and the Methodology of Science*. University of New Mexico Press, Albuquerque.

Hanson, J. R.
1979 Ethnohistoric problems in the Crow-Hidatsa schism. *Archaeology in Montana* 20: 73–85.
1986 Adjustment of adaptation on the Northern Plains: The case of equestrianism among the Hidatsa. *Plains Anthropologist* 31: 93–107.

Haraway, D.
1986 Primatology is politics by other means. In *Feminist Approaches to Science*, ed. R. Bleier, 77–118. Pergamon Press, New York.

Hartshorne, R.
1961 The nature of geography: A critical survey of current thought in the light of the past. Reprinted with corrections from the *Annals of the Association of American Geographers* 29 (3 and 4) (original 1939). Association of American Geographers, Lancaster, Pennsylvania.

Hay, R.
1988 Toward a theory of sense of place. *The Trumpeter* 5: 159–164.
1989 The contribution of Maori cosmology to a revision of environmental

philosophy. *The Trumpeter* 6: 156–162.

Hayden, B.
1982 Interaction parameters and the demise of Paleo-Indian craftsmanship. *Plains Anthropologist* 27: 109–123.

Heidenreich, C. A.
1979 The bearing of ethnohistorical data on the Crow-Hidatsa separation. *Archaeology in Montana* 20: 87–112.

Hellawell, J. A.
1963 A cultural ecological analysis of a cross-cultural type. M.A. thesis, University of Illinois, Urbana.

Hempel, C. G.
1965 *Aspects of Scientific Explanation and Other Essays in the Philosophy of Science.* The Free Press, New York.

Henning, D. R.
1992 Cultural interaction in the plains-prairie ecotone: An Oneota perspective. Paper presented at the 50th Plains Anthropological Conference, Lincoln.

Hill, A., and M. Kivett
1941 Woodland-like manifestations in Nebraska. *Nebraska History* 2: 146–243.

Hill, J. N., and J. Gunn, eds.
1977 *The Individual in Prehistory*. Academic Press, New York.

Hindess, B., and P. Q. Hirst
1975 *Pre-Capitalist Modes of Production*. Routledge and Kegan Paul, London.

Hiss, T.
1990 *The Experience of Place*. Random House, New York.

Hitchcock, J. T.
1977 A Nepali shaman's performance as theater. In *Stones, Bones and Skin: Ritual and Shamanic Art,* ed. T. Brodzky, R. Danesewich, and N. Johnson, 42–48. The Society for Art Publications, Toronto.

Hodder, I.
1982a Theoretical archaeology: A reactionary view. In *Symbolic and Structural Archaeology,* ed. I. Hodder, 1–16. Cambridge University Press, Cambridge.
1982b *The Present Past. An Introduction to Anthropology for Archaeologists.* B. T. Batsford, London.
1984 Burials, houses, women and men in the European Neolithic. In *Ideology, Power and Prehistory,* ed. D. Miller and C. Tilley, 51–68. Cambridge University Press, Cambridge.
1985 Postprocessual archaeology. In *Advances in Archaeological Method and Theory* 8, ed. M. Schiffer, 1–26. Academic Press, New York.
1986 *Reading the Past*. Cambridge University Press, Cambridge.
1987a *Archaeology as Long-term History*. Cambridge University Press, Cambridge (editor).
1987b *The Archaeology of Contextual Meanings*. Cambridge University Press, Cambridge (editor).

1987c The contextual analysis of symbolic meanings. In *The Archaeology of Contextual Meanings*, ed. I. Hodder, 1–10. Cambridge University Press, Cambridge.

1990 *The Domestication of Europe*. Basil Blackwell, Oxford.

1991 Interpretive archaeology and its role. *American Antiquity* 56: 7–18.

Hoffer, E.

1951 *The True Believer*. Harper & Row, New York.

Hoffman, J. J.

1953 *Comments on the Use and Distribution of Tipi Rings in Montana, North Dakota, South Dakota, and Wyoming*. Montana State University, Anthropology and Sociology Papers No. 14.

Holder, P.

1970 *The Hoe and the Horse on the Plains: A Study of Cultural Development among North American Indians*. University of Nebraska Press, Lincoln.

Hole, F.

1979 Rediscovering the past in the present: Ethnoarchaeology in Luristan, Iran. In *Ethnoarchaeology: Implications of Ethnography for Archaeology*, ed. C. Kramer, 192–218. Columbia University Press, New York.

House, J. H.

1982 Evolution of complex societies in east-central Arkansas: An overview of environments and regional data sets. In *Arkansas Archeology in Review*, ed. N. S. Trubowitz and J. D. Jeter, 37–47. Arkansas Archeological Survey Research Series No. 15.

Howard, J.

1968 *The Southeastern Ceremonial Complex and Its Interpretation*. Missouri Archaeological Society Memoir No. 6.

Hughes, S. S.

1991 Division of labor at a Besant hunting camp in eastern Montana. In *Approaches to Gender Processes on the Great Plains*, ed. M. Kornfeld, 25–49. Plains Anthropologist Memoir No. 26.

Hull, D. L.

1984 Historical entities and historical narrative. In *Minds, Machines and Evolution*, ed. C. Hookway, 17–41. Cambridge University Press, Cambridge.

Hull, K. L.

1987 Identification of cultural site formation processes through microdebitage analysis. *American Antiquity* 52: 772–783.

Ingold, T.

1992 Foraging for data, camping with theories: Hunter-gatherers and nomadic pastoralists in archaeology and anthropology. *Antiquity* 66: 790–803.

Jackson, J. B.

1979 The order of a landscape: Reason and religion in Newtonian America. In *The Interpretation of Ordinary Landscapes*, ed. D. W. Meinig, 153–163. Oxford University Press, Oxford.

1984 *Discovering the Vernacular Landscape*. Yale University Press, New Haven.

Jacobs, S., and C. Roberts
1989 Sex, sexuality, gender, and gender variance. In *Gender and Anthropology*, ed. S. Morgen, 438–462. American Anthropological Society, Washington, D.C.

Janes, R. R.
1989 A comment on microdebitage analyses and cultural site-formation processes among tipi dwellers. *American Antiquity* 54: 851–855.

Jelinek, A.
1976 Form, function and style in lithic artifacts. In *Cultural Change and Continuity: Essays in Honor of James B. Griffin*, ed. C. E. Cleland, 19–33. Academic Press, New York.

Jenkins, N., and R. A. Krause
1986 *The Tombigbee Watershed in Southeastern Prehistory*. University of Alabama Press, University.

Jochim, M. A.
1981 *Strategies for Survival*. Academic Press, New York.

Johannessen, S.
1984 Paleoethnobotany. In *American Bottom Archaeology*, ed. C. J. Baerreis and J. W. Porter, 197–214. University of Illinois Press, Urbana.

Johnsen, H., and B. Olsen
1992 Hermeneutics and archaeology: on the philosophy of contextual archaeology. *American Antiquity* 57: 419–436.

Johnson, A. E.
1976 A model of the Kansas City Hopewell subsistence-settlement system. In *Hopewellian Archaeology in the Lower Missouri Valley*, ed. A. E. Johnson, 7–15. University of Kansas Publication in Anthropology No. 8.
1981 The Kansas City Hopewell subsistence and settlement pattern. *Missouri Archaeologist* 42: 69–76.

Johnson, A. M.
1979 The problem of Crow pottery. *Archaeology in Montana* 20: 17–30.

Johnson, A. W., and T. Earle
1987 *The Evolution of Human Societies*. Stanford University Press, Stanford.

Johnson, D. L.
1978 Nomadic organization of space: Reflections on patterns and process. In *Dimensions of Human Geography: Essays on Some Familiar and Neglected Themes*, ed. K. W. Butzer, 25–47. Department of Geography, University of Chicago, Research Paper No. 186.

Johnson, E., ed.
1988 *Lubbock Lake: Late Quaternary Studies on the Southern High Plains*. Texas A & M University Press, College Station.

Judge, W. J.
1973 *Paleoindian Occupation of the Central Rio Grande Valley in New Mexico*. University of New Mexico Press, Albuquerque.

Judge, W. J., and L. Sebastian, eds.
1988 *Quantifying the Present and Predicting the Past: Theory, Method and Applica-*

tions of Archaeological Predictive Modeling. Bureau of Land Management, Denver.

Kahn, J., and J. Llobera

1981 Towards a new Marxism or a new anthropology. In *The Anthropology of Pre-Capitalist Societies*, ed. J. Kahn and J. Llobera, 263–329. Macmillan, London.

Keesing, R. M.

1981 *Cultural Anthropology: A Contemporary Perspective*. Holt, Rinehart and Winston, New York.

1982 *Kwaio Religion*. Columbia University Press, New York.

Kehoe, A.

1983 The shackles of tradition. In *The Hidden Half*, ed. P. Albers and B. Medicine, 53–73. University Press of America, Lanham, Maryland.

Kehoe, T. F.

1954 Stone "medicine wheels" in southern Alberta and the adjacent portion of Montana: Were they designed as grave markers? *Journal of the Washington Academy of Science* 44: 133–137.

1960 *Stone Tipi Rings in North Central Montana and the Adjacent Portion of Alberta, Canada: Their Historical, Ethnological, and Archaeological Aspects.* Bureau of American Ethnology Bulletin No. 173, Anthropological Paper 62: 421–473.

1966 The small side-notched point system of the Northern Plains. *American Antiquity* 31: 827–841.

1973 *The Gull Lake Site: A Prehistoric Bison Drive Site in Southwest Saskatchewan.* Publications in Anthropology No. 1. Milwaukee Public Museums.

Kehoe, T., and A. Kehoe

1979 *Solstice-Aligned Boulder Configurations in Saskatchewan*. Canadian Ethnology Service, Mercury Series No. 48.

Keller, E. F.

1985 *Reflections on Gender and Science*. Yale University Press, New Haven.

Kelly, J. E.

1985 Emergent Mississippian and the transition from Late Woodland to Mississippian: The American Bottom case for a new concept. In *The Emergent Mississippian: Proceedings of the Sixth Mid-South Archaeological Conference*, ed. R. A. Marshall, 216–226. Mississippi State University Occasional Paper No. 87-01.

1992 The impact of maize on the development of nucleated settlements: An American Bottom example. In *Late Prehistoric Agriculture: Observations from the Midwest*, ed. W. I. Woods, 167–197. Illinois Historic Preservation Agency Studies in Illinois Archaeology No. 9, Springfield.

Kelly, L. S.

1990 Faunal remains from the Priestly site. In *Excavations at the Priestly Site (3PO490): An Emergent Mississippian Community in Northeastern Arkansas*, ed. D. W. Benn, 327–361. Southwest Missouri State University Center for Archaeological Research Report No. 740.

Kelly, R. L., and L. Todd
1988 Coming into the country: Early Paleoindian hunting and mobility. *American Antiquity* 53: 231–244.

Kent, S.
1984 *Analyzing Activity Areas: An Ethnoarchaeological Study of the Use of Space.* University of New Mexico Press, Albuquerque.
1987 Understanding the use of space: An ethnoarchaeological approach. In *Method and Theory for Activity Area Research: An Ethnoarchaeological Approach*, ed. S. Kent, 1–60. Columbia University Press, New York.

Kessler, S., and W. McKenna
1978 *Gender: An Ethnomethodological Approach.* University of Chicago Press, Chicago.

Keyser, J. D.
1977 Writing-On-Stone: Rock art on the Northwestern Plains. *Canadian Journal of Archaeology* 1: 15–80.
1979 The Plains Indian war complex and the rock art of Writing-on-Stone, Alberta, Canada. *Journal of Field Archaeology* 6: 41–48.
1987 A lexicon for Historic Plains Indian art: Increasing interpretive potential. *Plains Anthropologist* 32: 43–72.

Keyser, J. D., and C. M. Davis
1982 Ceramics from the Highwalker site: A study of Late Prehistoric Period cultural systematics on the Northwestern Plains. *Plains Anthropologist* 27: 287–303.

Kidd, K.
1986 *Blackfoot Ethnography.* Archaeological Survey of Alberta, Manuscript Series No. 8 (original 1937).

Kincaid, C.
1988 Predictive modeling and its relationship to cultural resource management applications. In *Quantifying the Present and Predicting the Past: Theory, Method and Applications of Archaeological Predictive Modeling*, ed. W. J. Judge and L. Sebastian, 549–569. Bureau of Land Management, Denver.

Kingsborough, E.
1830 *Antiquities of Mexico.* Augustine Aglio, London.

Kingsland, S. E.
1985 *Modeling Nature.* University of Chicago Press, Chicago.

Kivett, M.
1952 *Woodland Sites in Nebraska.* Nebraska State Historical Society, Publications in Anthropology No. 1.
1953 The Woodruff ossuary, a prehistoric burial site in Phillips County, Kansas. Bureau of American Ethnology Bulletin No. 154. *River Basin Surveys Papers* 3: 103–141.

Klein, A.
1983 The political economy of gender: A 19th century Plains Indian case study. In *The Hidden Half*, ed. P. Albers and B. Medicine, 143–173. University

Press of America, Lanham, Maryland.

Kluckhohn, C.

1960 The use of typology in anthropological theory. In *Men and Cultures*, ed. A. F. C. Wallace, 134–140. University of Pennsylvania Press, Philadelphia.

Knight, V. J., Jr.

1986 The institutional organization of Mississippian religion. *American Antiquity* 51: 675–687.

1990 Social organization and the evolution of hierarchy in southeastern chiefdoms. *Journal of Anthropological Research* 46: 1–23.

Kohler, T. A.

1988 Predictive locational modeling: History and current practice. In *Quantifying the Present and Predicting the Past: Theory, Method and Applications of Archaeological Predictive Modeling*, ed. W. J. Judge and L. Sebastian, 19–59. Bureau of Land Management, Denver.

Kornfeld, M., ed.

1991 *Approaches to Gender Processes on the Great Plains.* Plains Anthropologist Memoir No. 26.

Kornfeld, M., and J. Francis

1991 A preliminary historical outline of Northwestern High Plains gender systems. In *The Archaeology of Gender: Proceedings of the University of Calgary Chacmool Conference*, ed. N. Willows and D. Walde, 444–451. Archaeological Association, University of Calgary, Calgary.

Kosso, P.

1991 Method in archaeology: Middle-range theory as hermeneutics. *American Antiquity* 56: 621–627.

Kottak, C. P.

1991 *Cultural Anthropology*. McGraw-Hill, New York.

Kramer, C., and M. Stark

1988 The status of women in archaeology. *Anthropology Newsletter* 29: 1, 11–12.

Krause, R. A.

1988 *The Snodgrass Small Mound and Middle Tennessee Valley Prehistory*. Tennessee Valley Authority Publications in Anthropology No. 52.

Kroeber, A. L.

1983 *The Arapaho*. Reprinted from three reports in the Bulletin of the American Museum of Natural History (1902, 1904, and 1907). University of Nebraska Press, Lincoln.

Kuehn, D. D., C. Falk, and A. Drybred

1982 *Archaeological Data Recovery at Midipidi Butte, 32DU2, Dunn County, North Dakota*. Department of Anthropology, University of North Dakota, Contribution No. 181.

Lamberg-Karlovsky, C. C.

1989 Introduction. In *Archaeological Thought in America*, ed. C. C. Lamberg-Karlovsky, 1–16. Cambridge University Press, Cambridge.

Landes, R.

1968 *The Mystic Lake Sioux*. University of Wisconsin Press, Madison.

Larrabee, E.
1966 Science and the common reader. *Commentary* 41: 43–48.

Lathrap, D. W.
1987 The introduction of maize in prehistoric eastern North America: The view from Amazonia and the Santa Elena Peninsula. In *Emergent Horticultural Economies of the Eastern Woodlands*, ed. W. F. Keegan, 345–371. Southern Illinois University Center for Archaeological Investigations, Occasional Paper No. 7.

Laubin, R., and G. Laubin
1957 *The Indian Tipi. Its History, Construction, and Use*. Ballantyne Books, New York.

La Vérendrye, P.
1927 *Journal and Letters of Pierre Gaultier de Varennes de la Vérendrye and his Sons*, ed. L. J. Burpee. Publications of the Champlain Society No. 16. Ballantyne, Toronto.

Leacock, E. B.
1978 Women's status in egalitarian society. *Current Anthropology* 19: 247–275.
1983 Interpreting the origins of gender inequality: Conceptual and historical problems. *Dialectical Anthropology* 7: 263–284.

Lefferts, H. L., Jr.
1963 Ecological limits of matrilineality in migratory hunting bands. M.A. thesis, University of Illinois, Urbana.

Lehmer, D. J., W. R. Wood, and C. Dill
1978 The Knife River phase. Manuscript on File, National Park Service, Midwest Archaeological Center, Lincoln.

Leone, M. P.
1972 Issues in anthropological archaeology. In *Contemporary Archaeology*, ed. M. P. Leone, 14–27. Southern Illinois University Press, Carbondale.
1973 Archaeology as the science of technology: Mormon town plans and fences. In *Research and Theory in Current Archaeology*, ed. C. L. Redman, 125–150. John Wiley & Sons, New York.
1978 Time in American archaeology. In *Social Archaeology: Beyond Subsistence and Dating*, ed. C. Redman, W. Langhorne, M. Berman, N. Versaggi, E. Curtin, and J. Wasner, 25–36. Academic Press, New York.
1981 The relationship between artifacts and the public in outdoor history museums. *Annals of the New York Academy of Sciences* 376: 301–314.
1982 Some opinions about recovering mind. *American Antiquity* 47: 742–760.

Leone, M. P., P. B. Potter, Jr., and P. A. Shackel
1987 Toward a critical archaeology. *Current Anthropology* 28: 283–302.

Levine, F.
1984 Ethnohistoric clues to the identifications of Plains Indian settlements. In *Papers of the Philmont Conference on the Archaeology of Northeastern New Mexico*, ed. C. J. Condie, 31–42. New Mexico Archaeological Council Proceedings No. 6.

Lévi-Strauss, C.
1969 *The Elementary Structure of Kinship*. Beacon, Boston.

Lewis, P. F.
1979 Axioms for reading the landscape: Some guides to the American scene. In *The Interpretation of Ordinary Landscapes*, ed. D. W. Meinig, 11–32. Oxford University Press, Oxford.

Littlejohn, S. W.
1983 *Theories of Human Communication*. Wadsworth, Belmont, California.

Lowenthal, D.
1979 Age and artifact: Dilemmas of appreciation. In *The Interpretation of Ordinary Landscapes*, ed. by D. W. Meinig, 103–128. Oxford University Press, Oxford.
1985 *The Past is a Foreign Country*. Cambridge University Press, Cambridge.

Lowie, R. H.
1954 *Indians of the Plains*. McGraw-Hill, New York.
1956 *The Crow Indians*. Holt, Rinehart and Winston, New York (reissued with a new preface).
1963 *The Crow Indians*. University of Nebraska Press, Lincoln (first published 1935).

Lucas, G. R., Jr.
1983 *The Genesis of Modern Process Thought*. Scarecrow Press, Metuchen, New Jersey.

Lynott, M. J., T. W. Boutton, J. E. Price, and D. E. Nelson
1986 Stable carbon isotopic evidence for maize agriculture in southeast Missouri and northeast Arkansas. *American Antiquity* 51: 51–65.

MacCormack, C. P., and M. Strathern, eds.
1980 *Nature, Culture, and Gender*. Cambridge University Press, Cambridge.

Machiavelli, N.
1952 *The Prince*. Mentor Classics, New York (first published 1523).

Magne, M. P. R., and M. A. Klassen
1991 A multivariate study of rock art anthropomorphs at Writing-on-Stone, Southern Alberta. *American Antiquity* 56: 389–418.

Magne, M., and Contributors to the Saskatchewan-Alberta Dialogue
1987 Distributions of Native groups in Western Canada, A.D. 1700 to A.D. 1850. In *Archaeology in Alberta, 1986*, compiled by M. Magne, 220–232. Archaeological Survey of Alberta, Occasional Paper No. 31.

Mallam, R. C.
1976 *The Iowa Effigy Mound Manifestation: An Interpretive Model*. Office of the Iowa State Archaeologist, Reports of Investigations No. 9. University of Iowa.

Malouf, C.
1963 Crow Flies High Village. River Basin Surveys No. 29. *Bureau of American Ethnology Report* 185: 132–166.

Marcus, G. E., and M. M. J. Fischer
1986 *Anthropology as Cultural Critique: An Experimental Moment in the Human Sciences*. University of Chicago Press, Chicago.

Markman, C. W.
1986 Above the American Bottom: The Late Woodland-Mississippian

transition in Northeastern Illinois. Paper presented at the Society for American Archaeology Meeting, New Orleans.

Marquardt, W. H.

1985 Complexity and scale in the study of fisher-gatherer-hunters: An example from the Eastern United States. In *Prehistoric Hunter-Gatherers*, ed. T. D. Price and J. A. Brown, 59–98. Academic Press, New York.

Marshall, Y.

1985 Who made the Lapita pots? A case study in gender archaeology. *Journal of the Polynesian Society* 94: 205–233.

Martin, M. K., and B. Voorhies

1975 *Female of the Species*. Columbia University Press, New York.

Marx, K.

1906 *Capital: A Critique of Political Economy*. Kerr, Chicago.

1973 *Grundrisse*. Vintage Books, New York.

Mauss, M.

1967 *The Gift*. W. W. Norton, New York.

Mayr, E.

1972 The nature of the Darwinian revolution. *Science* 176: 981–989.

1982 *The Growth of Biological Thought*. Harvard University Press, Cambridge.

McClintock, W.

1910 *The Old North Trail or Life, Legends and Religion of the Blackfeet Indians*. Macmillan, London.

McDonald, J. D., L. J. Zimmerman, A. L. McDonald, W. Tall Bull, and T. Rising Sun

1991 The Northern Cheyenne outbreak of 1879: Using oral history and archaeology as tools of resistance. In *The Archaeology of Inequality*, ed. R. H. McGuire and R. Paynter, 125–150. Basil Blackwell, Oxford.

McGhee, R.

1977 Ivory for the Sea Woman: The symbolic attributes of a prehistoric technology. *Canadian Journal of Archaeology* 1: 141–149.

McGuire, R. H.

1992 *A Marxist Archaeology*. Academic Press, New York.

McHugh, W. P., G. D. Gardner, and J. Donahue

1982 Before Smith's Mill: Archaeological and geological investigations, vol. 1. Report submitted to the U.S. Army Corps of Engineers, Kansas City District.

McLean, J.

1971 *Canadian Savage Folk: The Native Tribes of Canada*. Coles Publishing, Toronto (first published in 1896).

Mead, M.

1935 *Sex and Temperament in Three Primitive Societies*. William Morrow, New York.

1950 *Male and Female: A Study of the Sexes in a Changing World*. William Morrow, New York.

Medicine, B.

1983 Warrior women: Sex role alternatives for Plains Indian women. In *The Hidden Half*, ed. P. Albers and B. Medicine, 267–280. University Press of

America, Lanham, Maryland.

Medicine Crow, J.

1979 The Crow migration story. *Archaeology in Montana* 20: 63–72.

Meighan, C. W.

1985 Archaeology and anthropological ethics. *Anthropology Newsletter* 26: 20.

Meillassoux, C.

1972 From reproduction to production. *Economy and Society* 1: 93–105.

Meinig, D. W.

1979a Introduction. In *The Interpretation of Ordinary Landscapes*, ed. D. W. Meinig, 1–7. Oxford University Press, Oxford.

1979b Reading the landscape: An appreciation of W. G. Hoskins and J. B. Jackson. In *The Interpretation of Ordinary Landscapes*, ed. D. W. Meinig, 195–244. Oxford University Press, Oxford.

Metcalfe, D., and K. M. Heath

1990 Microrefuse and site structure: The hearths and floors of the Heartbreak Hotel. *American Antiquity* 55: 781–796.

Meyer, R. W.

1968 Fort Berthold and the Garrison Dam. *North Dakota History: Journal of the Northern Plains* 35: 217–335.

1977 *The Village Indians of the Upper Missouri: The Mandans, Hidatsas, and Arikaras*. University of Nebraska Press, Lincoln.

Migot, A.

1955 *Tibetan Marches*. Translated from French by P. Fleming. Rupert Hart-Davies, London.

Miller, D., and C. Tilley, eds.

1984a Ideology, power and prehistory: An introduction. In *Ideology, Power and Prehistory*, ed. D. Miller and C. Tilley, 1–15. Cambridge University Press, Cambridge.

1984b *Ideology, Power and Prehistory*. Cambridge University Press, Cambridge.

Minnich, E.

1982 A devastating conceptual error: How can we NOT be feminist scholars? *Change Magazine* 14: 7–9.

Mitchell, W. P.

1973 The hydraulic hypothesis: A reappraisal. *Current Anthropology* 14: 532–534.

Moore, H.

1988 *Feminism and Anthropology*. University of Minnesota Press, Minneapolis.

Moore, J. H.

1989 The myth of the lazy Indian: Native American contributions to the U.S. economy. *Nature, Society and Thought* 2: 195–215.

Morgan, A. E.

1976 *Nowhere was Somewhere*. Greenwood Press, Westport.

Morgan, L. H.

1963 [1877] *Ancient Society*. Meridian Books, World Publishing Co., New York.

Morgen, S., ed.

1989 *Gender and Anthropology*. American Anthropological Association, Washington, D.C.

Morse D. F., and P. A. Morse, eds.
1980 Zebree archaeological project. Manuscript on file, Arkansas Archaeological Survey, Fayetteville.
1983 *Archaeology of the Central Mississippi Valley*. Academic Press, New York.
Mukhopadhyay, C. C., and P. J. Higgins
1988 Anthropological studies of women's status revisited: 1977–1987. *Annual Review of Anthropology* 17: 461–495.
Muller, J.
1968 Notes on the White Earth Creek site. *Plains Anthropologist* 13: 18–25.
1987 Lower Ohio Valley emergent horticulture and Mississippian. In *Emergent Horticultural Economies of the Eastern Woodlands*, ed. W. F. Keegan, 243–276. Southern Illinois University Center for Archaeological Investigations, Occasional Paper No. 7.
Mulloy, W.
1942 *The Hagen Site: A prehistoric village on the Lower Missouri*. University of Montana Publications in the Social Sciences No. 1.
1958 *A Preliminary Historical Outline for the Northwestern Plains*. University of Wyoming Publications No. 22.
Murdock, G. P.
1949 *Social Structure*. Macmillan, New York.
Nabokov, P.
1988 Cultivating themselves: The inter-play of Crow Indian religion and history. Ph.D. dissertation, University of California, Berkeley.
Nassaney, M. S.
1987 On the causes and consequences of subsistence intensification in the Mississippi alluvial valley. In *Emergent Horticultural Economies of the Eastern Woodlands*, ed. W. F. Keegan, 129–152. Southern Illinois University Center for Archaeological Investigations, Occasional Paper No. 7.
Neihardt, J. G.
1961 *Black Elk Speaks: Being the Life Story of a Holy Man of the Oglala Sioux*. University of Nebraska Press, Lincoln.
Neusius, S. W., ed.
1986 *Foraging, Collecting, and Harvesting: Archaic Period Subsistence and Settlement in the Eastern Woodlands*. Southern Illinois University Center for Archaeological Investigations, Occasional Paper No. 6.
Nickel, R. K.
1977 The study of archaeologically recovered plant materials from the Middle Missouri subarea. In *Trends in Middle Missouri Prehistory: A Festschrift Honoring the Contributions of Donald J. Lehmer*, ed. W. R. Wood, 53–58. Plains Anthropologist Memoir No. 13.
Norbu, T. J.
1961 *Tibet is My Country*. As told to Heinrich Harrer, translated from German by E. Fitzgerald. Readers Union, Rupert Hart-Davies, London.
Obamsawin, A.
1977 Sounds and voices from our people. In *Stones, Bones and Skin: Ritual and Shamanic Art*, ed. T. Brodzky, R. Danesewich, and N. Johnson, 49–57. The

Society for Art Publications, Toronto.

O'Brien, M. J.

1987 Sedentism, population growth, and resource selection in the Woodland Midwest: A review of coevolutionary developments. *Current Anthropology* 28: 177–197.

O'Brien, P. J.

1971 Valley Focus mortuary practices. *Plains Anthropologist* 53: 165–182.

1972a Steed-Kisker Mississippian and labor specialization. Paper presented at the 37th Annual Meeting of the Society for American Archaeology, Miami.

1972b Urbanism, Cahokia, and Middle Mississippian. *Archaeology* 25: 188–197.

1974 A seriation of Steed-Kisker ceramics. Paper presented at the 39th Annual Meeting of the Society for American Archaeology, Washington, D.C.

1977 Cultural resources survey of Smithville Lake, Missouri, vol. 1: Archeology. Report submitted to U.S. Army Corps of Engineers, Kansas City District.

1978a Steed-Kisker and Mississippian influences on the Central Plains. In *The Central Plains Tradition: Internal Development and External Relationships*, ed. D. S. Blakeslee, 67–80. Office of the Iowa State Archaeologist, Reports of Investigations No. 11, University of Iowa.

1978b Steed-Kisker: A western Mississippian settlement system. In *Mississippian Settlement Patterns*, ed. B. D. Smith, 1–19. Academic Press, New York.

1981 Steed-Kisker: A cultural interpretation. *Missouri Archaeologist* 42: 97–108.

1988 Ancient Kansas City area borders and trails. *Missouri Archaeologist* 49: 27–39.

1989 Cahokia: The political capital of the "Ramey" state? *North American Archaeologist* 10: 275–292.

1991 Evidence for the antiquity of women's roles in Pawnee society. In *Approaches to Gender Processes on the Great Plains*, ed. M. Kornfeld, 51–64. Plains Anthropologist Memoir No. 26.

1992 The world-system of Cahokia within the Middle Mississippian tradition. In *Precapitalist World Systems*, ed. C. Chase-Dunn, 389–417. *Review* 15.

1993a Cultural taxonomy, cross-cultural types, and Cahokia. In *Highways to the Past: Essays on Illinois Archaeology in Honor of Charles J. Bareis*, ed. T. E. Emerson and R. B. Lewis. *Illinois Archaeology* 5: 481–497.

1993b Steed-Kisker: The western periphery of the Mississippian Tradition. *Mid-Continental Journal of Archaeology* 18: 61–96.

n.d. Bordermarkers and the boundaries of the Cahokia site. Manuscript accepted for publication in *Gateway Heritage*.

O'Brien, P., M. Caldwell, J. Jilka, L. Toguren, and B. Yeo

1979 The Ashland Bottoms site (14RY603): A Kansas City Hopewell Site in North Central Kansas. *Plains Anthropologist* 23: 1–20.

O'Brien, P. J., and W. McHugh

1987 Mississippian solstice shrines and a Cahokian calendar: An hypothesis based on ethnohistory and archaeology. *North American Archaeologist* 8: 227–247.

O'Connell, B., M. Whelan, and R. Withrow
1989 The Blackdog burial site: Evidence for culture change at an historic Dakota Indian cemetery. Paper presented at Annual Meeting of the American Association of Physical Anthropologists, San Diego.
Okely, J.
1975 Gypsy women: Models in conflict. In *Perceiving Women*, ed. S. Ardener, 55–86. Malaby Press, London.
Oliver, P.
1987 *Dwellings: The House Across the World*. University of Texas Press, Austin.
Oliver, S.
1964 *Ecology and Cultural Continuity as Contributing Factors in the Social Organization of the Plains Indians*. University of California Publications in American Archaeology and Ethnology No. 48.
Ong, W. J.
1982 *Orality and Literacy: The Technologizing of the World*. Methuen, London.
Opler, M. E.
1971 Pots, Apache and the Dismal River culture aspect. In *Apachean Culture History and Ethnology*, ed. K. H. Basso and M. E. Opler, 29–33. University of Arizona Press, Tucson.
Ortner, S. B., and H. Whitehead
1981 Introduction: Accounting for sexual meanings. In *Sexual Meanings*, ed. S. Ortner and H. Whitehead, 1–27. Cambridge University Press, Cambridge.
Ovenden, M., and D. Rodger
1981 Megaliths and medicine wheels. In *Megaliths to Medicine Wheels: Boulder Structures in Archaeology: Proceedings of the Eleventh Annual Chacmool Conference*, ed. M. Wilson, K. Road, and K. Hardy, 371–386. Archaeological Association, University of Calgary, Calgary.
Pailes, R.
1981 On the archaeology of the absurd and green slimy frogs: A plea for civility and mutual respect. Guest editorial. *American Antiquity* 46: 468.
Parks, D. R., W. Jones, and R. C. Hollow
1978 Earth lodge tales from the Upper Missouri: Traditional stories of the Arikara, Hidatsa, and Mandan. Manuscript on file, Mary College, Bismarck.
Parry, W. J., and R. Kelly
1987 Expedient core technology and sedentism. In *The Organization of Core Technology*, ed. J. K. Johnson and C. A. Morrow, 285–304. Westview Press, Boulder.
Patrik, L. E.
1985 Is there an archaeological record? In *Advances in Archaeological Method and Theory*, ed. M. B. Schiffer, 8: 27–62. Academic Press, New York.
Patterson, T. C.
1989 History and the postprocessual archaeologies. *Man* 24: 555–566.
Pauketat, T. R.
1987 Mississippian domestic economy and formation processes: A response to

Prentice. *Midcontinental Journal of Archaeology* 12: 77–81.

Paynter, R.

1989 The archaeology of equality and inequality. *Annual Review of Anthropology* 18: 369–399.

Pearsall, D. M., and A. A. Hunter

1990 Analysis of plant remains from the Priestly site. In *Excavations at the Priestly Site (3PO490): An Emergent Mississippian Community in Northeastern Arkansas* , ed. D. W. Benn, 362–419. Southwest Missouri State University Center for Archaeological Research Report No. 740.

Peebles, C. S.

1974 Moundville: The organization of a prehistoric community and culture. Ph.D. dissertation, University of California, Santa Barbara.

1978 Determinants of settlement size and location in the Moundville Phase. In *Mississippian Settlement Patterns,* ed. B. D. Smith, 369–416. Academic Press, New York.

Peebles, C. S., and S. Kus

1977 Some archaeological correlates of ranked societies. *American Antiquity* 42: 421–429.

Peristiany, J. G.

1939 *The Social Institutions of the Kipsigis.* The Humanities Press, New York.

Phenice, T.

1969 *An Analysis of the Human Skeletal Material from Burial Mounds in North Central Kansas.* University of Kansas Publications in Anthropology No. 1.

Phillips, P., J. A. Ford, and J. B. Griffin

1951 *Archaeological Survey in the Lower Mississippi Alluvial Valley, 1940–1947.* Papers of the Peabody Museum of American Archaeology and Ethnology No. 25.

Plath, D. W., ed.

1971 *Aware of Utopia.* University of Illinois Press, Urbana.

Plog, F.

1974 *The Study of Prehistoric Change.* Academic Press, New York.

Plog, S., F. Plog, and W. Wait

1978 Decision making in modern surveys. In *Advances in Archaeological Method and Theory,* ed. M. Schiffer, 1: 384–421. Academic Press, New York.

Powers, W.

1977 *Oglala Religion.* University of Nebraska Press, Lincoln.

Preucel, R. W.

1991 The philosophy of archaeology. In *Processual and Postprocessual Archaeologies: Multiple Ways of Knowing the Past,* ed. R. W. Preucel, 17–29. Southern Illinois University Center for Archaeological Investigations Occasional Paper No. 10.

Price, J. E., and C. R. Price

1984 *Phase II Testing of the Shell Lake Site, 23WE627, near Wappapello Dam, Wayne County, Missouri, 1984.* Center for Archaeological Research, Southwest Missouri State University and St. Louis District Cultural Resource Management Report No. 11.

Quick, P. M.
1986 *Proceedings: Conference on Reburial Issues.* Newberry Library, Chicago, June 14–15, 1985. Society for American Archaeology, Washington, D.C.

Quigg, J.M.
1986 *Ross Glen: A Besant Stone Circle Site in Southeastern Alberta.* Archaeological Survey of Alberta, Manuscript Series No. 10.

Quimby, G.I.
1979 A brief history of WPA archaeology. In *The Uses of Anthropology*, ed. Walter Goldschmidt, 110–123. American Anthropological Association Special Publication No. 11. Washington, D.C.

Quinn, N.
1977 Anthropological studies on women's status. *Annual Review of Anthropology* 6: 181–225.

Radin, P.
1914 Religion of the North American Indians. *Journal of American Folk-Lore* 27: 335–373.

Rapoport, A.
1969 *House Form and Culture.* Foundations of Cultural Geography Series. Prentice-Hall, Englewood Cliffs, New Jersey.

Rappaport, R. A.
1971 The sacred in human evolution. *Annual Review of Ecology and Systematics* 2: 23–44.

Reeves, B. O. K.
1990 Communal bison hunters of the Northern Plains. In *Hunters of the Recent Past*, ed. L. B. Davis and B. O. K. Reeves, 168–194. Unwin Hyman, London.

Reher, C. A.
1977 Adaptive processes on the shortgrass plains. In *For Theory Building in Archaeology*, ed. L.R. Binford, 13–40. Academic Press, New York.

Reher, C. A., and G. C. Frison
1980 *The Vore Site, 48CK302: A Stratified Buffalo Jump in the Wyoming Black Hills.* Plains Anthropologist Memoir No. 16.

Reidhead, V. A.
1980 The economics of subsistence change: A test of the optimization model. In *Modeling Change in Prehistoric Subsistence Economies*, ed. T. K. Earle and A. L. Christenson, 141–186. Academic Press, New York.

Reiter, R. R., ed.
1975 *Toward an Anthropology of Women.* Monthly Review Press, New York.

Relph, E.
1976 *Place and Placelessness.* Pion, London.

Resek, C.
1960 *Lewis Henry Morgan: American Scholar.* University of Chicago Press, Chicago.

Reynolds, B.
1968 *The Material Culture of the Peoples of the Gwembe Valley.* Praeger, New York.

Rhodd, B.
1990 Reburial in South Dakota: Two perspectives. In *Preservation on the Reservation: Native Americans, Native American Lands and Archaeology*, ed. A. Klesert and A. Downer, 369–375. Navajo Nation Papers in Anthropology No. 26.

Riley, T. J.
1987 Ridged-field agriculture and the Mississippian economic pattern. In *Emergent Horticultural Economies of the Eastern Woodlands*, ed. W. F. Keegan, 295–304. Southern Illinois University Center for Archaeological Investigations, Occasional Paper No. 7.

Ritchie, W. A.
1944 *The Pre-Iroquoian Occupations of New York State*. Rochester Museum of Arts and Sciences Memoir No. 1.

Robbins, L. H.
1973 Turkana material culture viewed from an archaeological perspective. *World Archaeology* 5: 209–214.

Roberts, B. K.
1987 Landscape archaeology. In *Landscape and Culture: Geographical and Archaeological Perspectives*, ed. J. M. Wagstaff, 77–95. Basil Blackwell, Oxford.

Rogers, J. D.
1990 *Objects of Change: The Archaeology and History of Arikara Contact with Europeans*. Smithsonian Institution Press, Washington, D.C.

Rosaldo, M. Z., and L. Lamphere, eds.
1974 *Woman, Culture and Society*. Stanford University Press, Stanford.

Roscoe, W., ed.
1987 Bibliography of berdache and alternative gender roles among Native American Indians. *Journal of Homosexuality* 14: 81–171.
1988 *Living the Spirit: A Gay American Anthology*. St. Martin's Press, New York.

Ross, D.
1991 *The Origins of American Social Science*. Cambridge University Press, Cambridge.

Ross, R., and E. Stutzman
1984 Two views of archaeology. Paper presented at the 49th Annual Meeting of the Society for American Archaeology, Portland, Oregon.

Rossignol, J.
1992 Concepts, methods, and theory building: A landscape approach. In *Space, Time, and Archaeological Landscapes*, ed. J. Rossignol and L. Wandsnider, 3–16. Academic Press, New York.

Rowe, J. H.
1963 Urban settlements in ancient Peru. *Nawpa Pacha* 1: 1–27.

Rudner, R. S.
1966 *Philosophy of Social Science*. Prentice-Hall, Englewood Cliffs, New Jersey.

Ruyle, E. E.
1987 Rethinking Marxist anthropology. In *Perspectives in U.S. Marxist Anthro-*

pology, ed. D. Hakken and H. Lessinger, 24–56. Westview Press, Boulder.

Sackett, J. R.

1982 Approaches to style in lithic archaeology. *Journal of Anthropological Archaeology* 1: 59–112.

Sahlins, M.

1961 The segmentary lineage: An organization of predatory expansion. *American Anthropologist* 66: 332–345.

1972 *Stone Age Economics*. Aldine-Atherton, Chicago.

Saitta, D. J.

1983a The poverty of philosophy in archaeology. In *Archaeological Hammers and Theories*, ed. J. A. Moore and A. S. Keene, 299–304. Academic Press, New York.

1983b On the evolution of "tribal" social networks. *American Antiquity* 48: 820–824.

1992a Theory in Colorado archaeology. In *The State of Colorado Archaeology*, ed. P. Duke and G. Matlock, 61–94. Colorado Archaeological Society Memoir No. 5.

1992b Radical archaeology and middle-range methodology. *Antiquity* 66: 886–897.

Salmon, M.

1982 *Philosophy and Archaeology*. Academic Press, New York.

Sanders, W. T., and B. Price

1968 *Mesoamerica*. Random House, New York.

Sanders, W. T., and D. Webster

1978 Unilinealism, multilinealism, and the evolution of complex societies. In *Social Archaeology: Beyond Subsistence and Dating*, ed. C. L. Redman, W. Langhorne, M. Berman, N. Versaggi, E. Curtin, and J. Wasner, 249–302. Academic Press, New York.

Sandoz, M.

1953 *Cheyenne Autumn*. McGraw-Hill, New York.

Sauer, C.

1925 The morphology of landscape. *University of California Publications in Geography* 2: 19–53.

Scaglion, R.

1980 The Plains culture area concept. In *Anthropology on the Great Plains*, ed. W. R. Wood and M. Liberty, 23–34. University of Nebraska Press, Lincoln.

Schambock, F.

1983 The archaeology of the Great Bend region in Arkansas. In *Contributions to the Archaeology of the Great Bend Region*, ed. F. Schambock and F. Rackerby. Arkansas Archaeological Survey Research Series No. 22.

Schlesier, K.

1990 Rethinking the Midewiwin and the Plains ceremonial called the sun dance. *Plains Anthropologist* 35: 1–27.

Schmits, L.

1987 The Williamson site and the Late Archaic El Dorado phase in Eastern

Kansas. *Plains Anthropologist* 32: 153–174.

Schneider, F.

1983 Artifact distribution at tipi ring sites: A cautionary tale. In *From Microcosm to Macrocosm: Advances in Tipi Ring Investigation and Interpretation*, ed. L. B. Davis, 93–100. Plains Anthropologist Memoir No. 19.

Schnell, F., J. Knight, and S. Schnell

1981 *Cemochechobee: Archaeology of a Mississippian Ceremonial Center on the Chattahooche River*. University of Florida Press, Gainesville.

Schroedl, G. F., and C. C. Boyd, Jr.

1985 Mississippian origins in East Tennessee. In *The Emergent Mississippian: Proceedings of the Sixth Mid-South Archaeological Conference*, ed. R. A. Marshall, 137–148. Mississippi State University Occasional Papers No. 87-01.

Schultz, F., and A. Spaulding

1948 A Hopewellian burial site in the Lower Republican Valley, Kansas. *American Antiquity* 13: 306–313.

Schultz, J. W.

1916 *Blackfeet Tales of Glacier National Park*. Houghton Mifflin, Boston.

1962 *Blackfeet and Buffalo: Memories of Life among the Indians*. University of Oklahoma Press, Norman.

Scott, J. W.

1986 Gender: A useful category of historical analysis. *The American Historical Review* 91: 1053–1075.

Sebastian, L., and W. J. Judge

1988 Predicting the past: correlation, explanation and the use of archaeological models. In *Quantifying the Present and Predicting the Past: Theory, Method and Applications of Archaeological Predictive Modeling*, ed. W. J. Judge and L. Sebastian, 1–18. Bureau of Land Management, Denver.

Service, E. R.

1962 *Primitive Social Organization*. Random House, New York.

1971 *Cultural Evolutionism*. Holt, Rinehart and Winston, New York.

1975 *Origins of the State and Civilization*. W. W. Norton, New York.

Shanks, M., and C. Tilley

1987a *Reconstructing Archaeology: Theory and Practice*. Cambridge University Press, Cambridge.

1987b *Social Theory and Archaeology*. Polity Press, Cambridge.

Shippee, J. M.

1972 *Archaeological Remains in the Kansas City Area*. Missouri Archaeological Society Research Series No. 9.

Silverberg, R.

1968 *Mound Builders of Ancient America: The Archaeology of a Myth*. New York Graphic Society, New York.

Simberloff, D.

1982 A succession of paradigms in ecology: Essentialism to materialism and probabilism. In *Conceptual Issues in Ecology*, ed. E. Saarinen, 63–69. D.

Reidel, Dordrecht.

Sioux Falls Argus Leader

1982 Historian says hills not Indian holy land. *Sioux Falls Argus Leader*, December 3, p. C1.

Sjoberg, G.

1960 *The Preindustrial City, Past and Present*. Free Press, Glencoe, Illinois.

Smith, B. D.

1975 *Middle Mississippi Exploitation of Animal Populations*. Museum of Anthropology, Anthropological Papers No. 57. University of Michigan, Ann Arbor.

1978 Variation in Mississippian settlement patterns. In *Mississippian Settlement Patterns*, ed. B. D. Smith, 479–503. Academic Press, New York.

1987 The independent domestication of indigenous seed-bearing plants in eastern North America. In *Emergent Horticultural Economies of the Eastern Woodlands*, ed. W. F. Keegan, 3–48. Southern Illinois University Center for Archaeological Investigations, Occasional Paper No. 7.

Smith, M. B.

1974 Rapid method for recording stone circles. *Archaeology in Montana* 15: 47–54.

Sopher, D. E.

1967 *Geography of Religions*. Prentice-Hall, Englewood Cliffs, New Jersey.

1979 The landscape of home: Myth, experience, social meaning. In *The Interpretation of Ordinary Landscapes*, ed. D. W. Meinig, 129–149. Oxford University Press, Oxford.

South Dakota Writers Project

1987 *Legends of the Mighty Sioux*. Badlands Natural History Association, Interior, South Dakota (original 1941).

Spector, J. D.

1983 Male/female task differentiation among the Hidatsa: Toward the development of an archeological approach to the study of gender. In *The Hidden Half*, ed. P. Albers and B. Medicine, 77–99. University Press of America, Lanham, Maryland.

Spector, J. D., and M. K. Whelan

1989 Incorporating gender in archaeology courses. In *Gender and Anthropology*, ed. S. Morgen, 65–94. American Anthropological Association, Washington, D.C.

Spriggs, M., ed.

1984 *Marxist Perspectives in Archaeology*. Cambridge University Press, Cambridge.

Stands-In-Timber, J.

1967 *Cheyenne Memories*. Yale University Press, New Haven.

Stanish, C.

1989 Household archaeology: Testing models of zonal complementarity in the South Central Andes. *American Anthropologist* 91: 7–24.

Stark, B. L.

1986 Origins of food production in the New World. In *American Archaeology*

Past and Future: A Celebration of the Society for American Archaeology, 1935–1985, ed. D. J. Meltzer, D. D. Fowler, and J. A. Sabloff, 277–321. Smithsonian Institution Press, Washington, D.C.

Stark, M.

1991 A perspective on women's status in American archaeology. In *The Archaeology of Gender: Proceedings of the University of Calgary Chacmool Conference*, ed. N. Willows and D. Walde, 187–194. Archaeological Association, University of Calgary, Calgary.

Steponaitis, V. P.

1983 *Ceramics, Chronology, and Community Patterns*. Academic Press, New York.

Stevenson, M. G.

1991 Beyond the formation of hearth-associated artifact formation processes. In *The Interpretation of Archaeological Spatial Patterning*, ed. E. M. Kroll and T. D. Price, 269–300. Plenum Press, New York.

Steward, J. H.

1938 *Basin-Plateau Aboriginal Sociopolitical Groups*. Bureau of American Ethnology Bulletin No. 120. Washington, D.C.

1942 The direct historical approach to archaeology. *American Antiquity* 7: 337–343.

1955 *The Theory of Culture Change*. University of Illinois Press, Urbana.

1960 Evolution principles and social types. In *Evolution After Darwin, Vol. 2*, ed. S. Tax, 169–186. University of Chicago Press, Chicago.

1977 Determinism in primitive society? In *Evolution and Ecology*, ed. J. C. Steward and R. F. Murphy, 180–187. University of Illinois Press, Urbana.

Steward, J. H., R. McAdams, D. Collier, A. Palerm, K. A. Wittfogel, and R. Beals

1955 *Irrigation Civilizations: A Comparative Study*. Social Science Monographs No. 1. Washington, D.C.

Steward, J. H., and R. F. Murphy

1977 Tappers and trappers: Parallel processes in acculturation. In *Evolution and Ecology*, ed. J. C. Steward and R. F. Murphy, 151–179. University of Illinois Press, Urbana.

Stewart, F. H.

1974 Mandan and Hidatsa villages in the 18th and 19th centuries. *Plains Anthropologist* 19: 287–301.

Stewart, O. C.

1943 Notes on Pomo ethnogeography. *University of California Publications in American Archaeology and Ethnology* 40: 29–62.

Stoffle, R. W.

1984 Toyavita Piavuhuru Koroin: Ethnohistory and Native American religious concerns in the Ford Carson-Piñon Canyon maneuver area. Manuscript on file, National Park Service Interagency Archeology Services, Denver.

Strong, W. D.

1935 An introduction to Nebraska archaeology. *Smithsonian Miscellaneous Collections* 93(10).

Struever, S.

1968 Woodland subsistence-settlement systems in the Lower Illinois Valley. In *New Perspectives in Archaeology*, ed. S. R. Binford and L. R. Binford, 285–312. Aldine, Chicago.

Stuart, G. S. L.

1990 *The Cranford Site (D1Pb-2): A Multicomponent Stone Circle Site on the Oldman River*. Archaeological Survey of Alberta, Manuscript Series No. 17.

Styles, B. W.

1981 *Faunal Exploitation and Resource Selection: Early Late Woodland Subsistence in the Lower Illinois Valley*. Northwestern University Archaeological Program, Scientific Papers No. 3.

Sundstrom, L.

1989 Archaic hunting practices depicted in a Northwestern Plains rock art style. *Plains Anthropologist* 34: 149–169.

Taaffe, E. J.

1974 The spatial view in context. *Annals of the Association of American Geographers* 64: 1–16.

Tainter, J.

1978 Mortuary practices and the study of prehistoric social systems. *Advances in Archaeological Method and Theory*, ed. M. Schiffer, 1: 105–141. Academic Press, New York.

Tanaka, H.

1984 Landscape expression of the evolution of Buddhism in Japan. *Canadian Geographer* 28: 240–257.

Tanner, A.

1979 *Bringing Home Animals: Religious Ideology and Mode of Production of the Mistassini Cree Hunters*. Social and Economic Studies No. 23, Institute of Social and Economic Research, Memorial University of Newfoundland, St. John's.

Taylor, W. W.

1948 *A Study of Archaeology*. American Anthropologist Memoir No. 69.

Tedlock, D., trans.

1978 *Finding the Center: Narrative Poetry of the Zuni Indians. From Performances by Andrew Peynetsa and Walter Sanchez*. University of Nebraska Press, Lincoln.

Thoms, A. V.

1988 A survey of predictive locational models: Examples from the late 1970s and early 1980s. In *Quantifying the Present and Predicting the Past: Theory, Method and Applications of Archaeological Predictive Modeling*, ed. W. J. Judge and L. Sebastian, 581–645. Bureau of Land Management, Denver.

Tiffany, S., ed.

1979 *Women and Society: An Anthropological Reader*. Eden Press, Women's Publications, Montreal.

Tooker, E., ed.

1982 *Ethnography by Archaeologists*. 1978 Proceedings of the American Ethnological Society, Washington, D.C.

Trigger, B. G.
1978 *Time and Tradition*. Edinburgh University Press, Edinburgh.
1980 Archaeology and the image of the American Indian. *American Antiquity* 45: 662–676.
1984a Archaeology at the crossroads: What's new? *Annual Review of Anthropology* 13: 275–300.
1984b Alternative archaeologies: Nationalist, colonialist, imperialist. *Man* 19: 355–370.
1986 Prehistoric archaeology and American society. In *American Archaeology Past and Future: A Celebration of the Society for American Archaeology 1935–1985*, ed. D. Meltzer, D. Fowler, and J. Sabloff, 187–215. Smithsonian Institution Press, Washington, D.C.
1989a *A History of Archaeological Thought*. Cambridge University Press, Cambridge.
1989b Hyperrelativism, responsibility, and the social sciences. *Canadian Review of Sociology and Anthropology* 26: 776–796.

Trimble, M. K.
1988 Chronology of epidemics among Plains Village horticulturalists: 1738–1838. *Southwestern Lore* 54: 4–31.

Truener, C.
1880 Indian pictographs in Missouri. *Kansas City Review of Science and Industry* 6: 208–210.

Tuan, Y.-F.
1971 *Man and Nature*. Association of American Geographers, Commission on College Geography, Resource Paper No. 10.
1974 *Topophilia: A Study of Environmental Perceptions, Attitudes, and Values*. Prentice-Hall, Englewood Cliffs, New Jersey.
1977 *Space and Place: The Perspective of Experience*. University of Minnesota Press, Minneapolis.

Tuck, J.
1976 *Ancient People of Port au Choix: The Excavation of an Archaic Indian Cemetary in Newfoundland*. Newfoundland Social and Economic Studies No. 17.

Turner, V.
1969 *The Ritual Process*. Aldine, Chicago.

Turpin, S., M. Hennenberg, and D. Risking
1986 Late Archaic mortuary practices of the Pecos River region, Southwest Texas. *Plains Anthropologist* 31: 295–315.

United States Air Force
1985 Conference on reburial. Norton Air Force Base, California.

Van der Leeuw, S.
1982 How objective can we become: Some reflections on the nature of the relationship between the archaeologist, his data, and his interpretations. In *Theory and Explanation in Archaeology*, ed. A. C. Renfrew, M. Rowlands, and B. Segraves, 431–457. Academic Press, New York.

Vaughan, A. T.
1982 From white man to red skin: Changing Anglo-American perceptions of the American Indian. *American Historical Review* 87: 917–935.

Vita-Finzi, C., and E. S. Higgs
1970 Prehistoric economy in the Mount Carmel area of Palestine: Site catchment analysis. *Proceedings of the Prehistoric Society* 36: 1–37.
Vogt, D. E.
1990 An information analysis of Great Plains medicine wheels. Ph.D. dissertation, Simon Fraser University, Burnaby, British Columbia.
Voorhies, M. R.
1969 *Taphonomy and Population Dynamics of an Early Pliocene Vertebrate Fauna, Knox County, Nebraska*. University of Wyoming, Contributions to Geology, Special Paper No. 1.
Wagner, P. L.
1974 Cultural landscape and regions: Aspects of communication. *Geoscience and Man* 10: 133–142.
Wagstaff, J. M., ed.
1987 *Landscape and Culture: Geographical and Archaeological Perspectives*. Basil Blackwell, Oxford.
Walde, D., and N. D. Willows, eds.
1991 *The Archaeology of Gender: Proceedings of the 22nd Annual Chacmool Conference*. Archaeological Association, University of Calgary, Calgary.
Walker, D. E., Jr.
1967 *Mutual Cross-Utilization of Economic Resources in the Plateau: An Example from Aboriginal Nez Perce Fishing Practices*. Washington State University, Laboratory of Anthropology, Report of Investigations No. 41.
Wallace, A. F. C.
1966 *Religion: An Anthropological View*. Random House, New York.
Watson, N., L. J. Zimmerman, and P. M. Peterson
1989 The present past: An examination of archaeological and Native American thinking. In *Thinking Across Cultures*, ed. D. Topping, 33–42. Lawrence Erlbaum, Hillsdale, New Jersey.
Watson, P. J.
1988 Prehistoric gardening and agriculture in the Midwest and Midsouth. In *Interpretations of Culture Change in the Eastern Woodlands during the Late Woodland Period*, ed. R. W. Yerkes, 39–67. Department of Anthropology, Ohio State University Occasional Papers in Anthropology No. 3.
1989 Postprocessualist archaeology: Comments on the new dissonance. Paper prepared for the 88th Annual Meeting of the American Anthropological Association, Washington, D.C.
1991 A parochial primer: The new dissonance as seen from the midcontinental United States. In *Processual and Postprocessual Archaeologies: Multiple Ways of Knowing the Past*, ed. R. W. Preucel, 265–274. Southern Illinois University Center for Archaeological Investigations Occasional Paper No. 10.
Watson, P. J., and M. Fotiadis
1990 The razor's edge: Symbolic-structuralist archaeology and the expansion of archaeological inference. *American Anthropologist* 92: 613–629.
Watson, P. J., and M. C. Kennedy
1991 The development of horticulture in the Eastern Woodlands of North

America: Women's role. In *Engendering Archaeology*, ed. J. Gero and M. Conkey, 255–275. Basil Blackwell, Oxford.

Watson, P. J., S. LeBlanc, and C. Redman

1971 *Explanation in Archaeology: An Explicitly Scientific Approach*. Columbia University Press, New York.

1984 *Archaeological Explanation: The Scientific Method in Archaeology*. Columbia University Press, New York.

Watson, R.

1976 Inference in Archaeology. *American Antiquity* 41: 58–66.

1990 Ozymandias, king of kings: Postprocessual radical archaeology as critique. *American Antiquity* 55: 673–689.

Webb, M. C.

1989 Functional and historical parallelisms between Mesoamerican and Mississippian cultures. In *The Southeastern Ceremonial Complex: Artifacts and Analysis*, ed. P. Galloway, 279–293. University of Nebraska Press, Lincoln.

Wedel, W.

1935 Contributions to the archaeology of the Upper Republican valley. *Nebraska History Magazine* 15: 133–209.

1938 *The Direct-Historical Approach in Pawnee Archaeology*. Smithsonian Miscellaneous Collections Vol. 97 (7).

1941 *Environment and Native Subsistence Economies in the Central Great Plains*. Smithsonian Miscellaneous Collections Vol. 100 (3).

1943 *Archaeological Investigations in Platt and Clay Counties, Missouri*. United States National Museum, Bulletin No. 183.

1953 Some aspects of human ecology in the Central Plains. *American Anthropologist* 55: 499–514.

1959 *An Introduction to Kansas Archaeology*. Bureau of American Ethnology Bulletin No. 174.

1961 *Prehistoric Man on the Great Plains*. University of Oklahoma Press, Norman.

1964 The Great Plains. In *Prehistoric Man in the New World*, ed. J. D. Jennings and E. Norbeck, 193–220. University of Chicago Press, Chicago.

1977 The education of a Plains archaeologist. *Plains Anthropologist* 22: 1–11.

1986 *Central Plains Prehistory: Holocene Environments and Culture Change in the Republican River Basin*. University of Nebraska Press, Lincoln.

Weissner, P.

1983 Style and social information in Kalahari San projectile points. *American Antiquity* 48: 253–276.

Weist, K.

1983 Images of women. In *The Hidden Half*, ed. P. Albers and B. Medicine, 29–52. University Press of America, Lanham, Maryland.

Welbourn, A.

1984 Endo ceramics and power strategies. In *Ideology, Power and Prehistory*, ed. D. Miller and C. Tilley, 17–24. Cambridge University Press, Cambridge.

Wenke, R. J.

1990 *Patterns in Prehistory*. 3rd ed. Oxford University Press, New York.

Wheat, J. B.
1972 *The Olsen-Chubbuck Site: A Paleo-Indian Bison Kill.* Society of American Archaeology Memoir No. 26.

Whelan, M. K.
1991 Gender and historical archaeology: Eastern Dakota Indian patterns in the nineteenth century. *Historical Archaeology* 25: 17–32.

Whelan, M. K., R. M. Withrow, and B. H. O'Connell
1989 The Blackdog burial site (21DK26): Evidence for culture change at an historic Dakota Indian cemetery. Paper presented at the 54th Annual Meeting of the Society for American Archaeology, Atlanta, Georgia.

Whelpley, H. M.
1914 An unusual Indian flint notched hoe. *Missouri Historical Society Collections* 4: 352–355.

White, L. A.
1949 *The Science of Culture.* Grove Press, New York.
1959 *The Evolution of Culture.* McGraw-Hill, New York.

Whitehead, H.
1981 The bow and the burden strap: A new look at institutionalized homosexuality in native North America. In *Sexual Meanings,* ed. S. Ortner and H. Whitehead, 80–115. Cambridge University Press, Cambridge.

Whiting, J., and B. Ayres
1968 Inferences from the shape of dwellings. In *Settlement Archaeology,* ed. K.-C. Chang, 117–133. National Press Books, Palo Alto.

Whorf, B. L.
1956 *Language, Thought, & Reality: Selected Writings,* ed. J. B. Carroll. M.I.T. Press, Cambridge.

Wildesden, L. E.
1974 Archaeologists and planners: The uses and misuses of predictive models. Paper presented at the 1974 Annual Meeting of the Society for California Archaeology, Riverside, California.

Wilk, R. R.
1985 The ancient Maya and the political present. *Journal of Anthropological Research* 41: 307–326.

Willey, G. R.
1953 *Prehistoric Settlement Patterns in the Viru Valley, Peru.* Bureau of American Ethnology Bulletin No. 155.
1956 *Prehistoric Settlement Patterns in the New World.* Viking Fund Publications in Anthropology No. 23.

Willey, G. R., and P. Phillips
1958 *Method and Theory in American Archaeology.* University of Chicago Press, Chicago.

Willey, G. R., and J. A. Sabloff
1974 *A History of American Archaeology.* Thames and Hudson, New York.

Williams, W.
1986 *The Spirit and the Flesh: Sexual Diversity in American Indian Culture.* Beacon Press, New York.

Wilson, D.
1862 *Prehistoric Man*. Macmillan, Cambridge.

Wilson, M.
1949 Nyakyusa age-villages. *Journal of the Royal Anthropological Institute* 79: 21–25.

Wilson, M. C.
1981 Sun dances, thirst dances, and medicine wheels: A search for alternative hypotheses. In *Megaliths to Medicine Wheels: Boulder Structures in Archaeology: Proceedings of the Eleventh Annual Chacmool Conference*, ed. M. Wilson, K. Road, and K. Hardy, 333–370. Archaeological Association, University of Calgary, Calgary.
1983 A test of the stone circle size-age hypothesis: Alberta and Wyoming. In *From Microcosm to Macrocosm: Advances in Tipi Ring Investigation and Interpretation*, ed. L. B. Davis, 113–137. Plains Anthropologist Memoir 19.

Wilson, M. C., and N. A. McKinnon
1989 Modern tent anchor sites (stone circles and related features) on the Tibetan Plateau, Qinghai Province, China: Implications for the Plains archaeologist. In *Households and Communities: Proceedings of the 21st Annual Chacmool Conference*, ed. S. MacEachern, D. J. W. Archer, and R. D. Garvin, 266–273. Archaeological Association, University of Calgary, Calgary.

Wissler, C.
1910 Material culture of the Blackfoot Indians. *Anthropological Papers of the American Museum of Natural History* 5: 1–175.
1911 The social life of the Blackfoot Indian. *Anthropological Papers of the American Museum of Natural History* 7: 1–64.
1912a Social organization and ritualistic ceremonies of the Blackfoot Indians. *Anthropological Papers of the American Museum of Natural History* 7.
1912b Ceremonial bundles of the Blackfoot Indians. *Anthropological Papers of the American Museum of Natural History* 7: 65–289.
1913 Societies and dance associations of the Blackfoot Indians. *Anthropological Papers of the American Museum of Natural History* 11: 359–460.
1914 Material cultures of the North American Indians. *American Anthropologist* 16: 447–505.
1918 The sun dance of the Blackfoot Indians. *Anthropological Papers of the American Museum of Natural History* 16: 223–270.

Wissler, C., and D. C. Duvall
1908 Mythology of the Blackfoot Indians. *Anthropological Papers of the American Museum of Natural History* 2: 1–163.

Wittfogel, K.
1957 *Oriental Despotism*. Yale University Press, New Haven.

Wobst, H. M.
1978 The archaeo-ethnology of hunter-gatherers or the tyranny of the ethnographic record in archaeology. *American Antiquity* 43: 303–309.

Wolf, E. R.
1982 *Europe and the People Without History*. University of California Press, Berkeley.

1984 Culture: Panacea or problem? *American Antiquity* 49: 393–400.

1990 Facing power—old insights, new questions. Distinguished lecture. *American Anthropologist* 92: 586–596.

Wolf, E., and E. C. Hansen

1967 Caudillo politics: A structural analysis. *Comparative Studies in Society and History* 9: 168–179.

Wolfe, A. W.

1977 The supranational organization of production: An evolutionary perspective. *Current Anthropology* 18: 615–635.

Wood, W. R.

1968 Mississippian hunting and butchering patterns: Bone from the Vista Shelter, 23SR20, Missouri. *American Antiquity* 33: 170–179.

1980 Plains trade in prehistoric and protohistoric intertribal relations. In *Anthropology on the Great Plains*, ed. W. R. Wood and M. Liberty, 98–109. University of Nebraska Press, Lincoln.

1981 The Poole Site, 36A3. *The Arkansas Archaeologist* 22: 7–65.

Wood, W. R., and A. S. Downer

1977 Notes on the Crow-Hidatsa schism. *Plains Anthropologist* 22: 83–100.

Wood, W. R., and M. Liberty, eds.

1980 *Anthropology on the Great Plains*. University of Nebraska Press, Lincoln.

Woods, W. I.

1987 Maize agriculture and Late Prehistoric: A characterization of settlement location strategies. In *Emergent Horticultural Economies of the Eastern Woodlands*, ed. W. F. Keegan, 275–294. Southern Illinois University Center for Archaeological Investigations, Occasional Paper No. 7.

Woolworth, A. W.

1956 Archaeological investigations at site 32ME59. *North Dakota History: Journal of the Northern Plains* 23: 78–102.

Wright, R.

1991 Women's labor and pottery production in prehistory. In *Engendering Archaeology*, ed. J. Gero and M. Conkey, 194–223. Basil Blackwell, Oxford.

Wyckoff, D., and R. Brooks, eds.

1983 *Oklahoma Archaeology: A 1981 Perspective of the State's Archaeological Resources, Their Significance, Their Problems and Some Proposed Solutions.* Oklahoma Archaeological Survey. Archaeological Resource Survey Report No. 16.

Wylie, M. A.

1982 Epistemological issues in structuralist archaeology. In *Symbolic and Structural Archaeology*, ed. I. Hodder, 39–46. Cambridge University Press, Cambridge.

1985 Putting Shakertown back together: Critical theory in archaeology. *Journal of Anthropological Archaeology* 4: 133–147.

1991a Gender theory and the archaeological record: Why is there no archaeology of gender? In *Engendering Archaeology*, ed. J. Gero and M. Conkey, 31–54. Basil Blackwell, Oxford.

1991b Beyond objectivism and relativism: Feminist critiques and archaeological challenges. In *The Archaeology of Gender: Proceedings of the University of Calgary Chacmool Conference*, ed. D. Walde and N. Willows, 17–23. Archaeological Association, University of Calgary, Calgary.

1992 The interplay of evidential constraints and political interests: Recent archaeological research on gender. *American Antiquity* 57: 15–35.

Yellen, J. E.

1977 *Archaeological Approaches to the Present: Models for Reconstructing the Past.* Academic Press, New York.

1983 Women, archaeology, and the National Science Foundation. In *The Socio-Politics of Archaeology*, ed. J. Gero, D. Lacy, and M. Blakey, 59–65. Department of Anthropology, University of Massachusetts, Amherst, Research Report No. 23.

1991 An update on gender differences in funding from the National Science Foundation. In *The Archaeology of Gender: Proceedings of the University of Calgary Chacmool Conference*, ed. D. Walde and N. Willows, 201–210. Archaeological Association, University of Calgary, Calgary.

Zeidler, J. A.

1987 The evolution of prehistoric "tribal" systems as historical process: Archeological indicators of social reproduction. In *Chiefdoms in the Americas*, ed. R. D. Drennan and C. A. Uribe, 325–343. University Press of America, Lanham, Maryland.

Zihlman, A.

1987 Sex, sexes and sexism in human origins. *Yearbook of Physical Anthropology* 30: 11–19.

Zimmerman, L. J.

1982 Indians, archaeologists, and bones: Cooperation and compromise in South Dakota. Paper presented to the Executive Committee of the Society for American Archaeology, Minneapolis, Minnesota, April 13, 1982.

1985 A perspective on the reburial issue from South Dakota. In *Proceedings: Conference on Reburial*, ed. P. Quick, 1–4. Newberry Library, Chicago, June 14–15, 1985. Society for American Archaeology, Washington, D.C.

1987 The impact of the concept of time on the concept of archaeology: Some lessons from the reburial issue. *Archaeological Review from Cambridge* 6: 42–50.

Zimmerman, L. J., and J. B. Gregg

1989 A history of the reburial issue in South Dakota. *South Dakota Archaeology* 13: 89–100.

Contributors

David W. Benn is Research Coordinator for Bear Creek Archeology, a firm conducting cultural resource management studies in the Upper Mississippi River Basin. He has published two books and several articles about the Woodland cultural period in Iowa and currently is bending his interests toward the political economies of late prehistoric peoples.

James F. Brooks is a graduate of the University of Colorado and a Ph.D. candidate in history at the University of California, Davis. His dissertation, "Captives and Cousins: Violence, Kinship, and Community in the New Mexico Borderlands, 1780–1880," continues his investigations into the historical construction of identities in the American West.

Melissa A. Connor is an Archaeologist for the National Park Service's Midwest Archeological Center. Her research interests include the hunter-gatherers of the Central and Northern Rocky Mountains and the Plains/Mountain interface.

Philip Duke is an Associate Professor of Anthropology at Fort Lewis College, in Durango, Colorado. His research interests include the archaeology of hunter-gatherers of the American West, and he is currently conducting fieldwork in the Colorado Rockies. His recent publications include *Points in Time: Structure and Event in a Late Northern Plains Hunting Society.*

Ian Hodder is Reader in Prehistory at Cambridge University, England, and Director of the Cambridge Archaeological Unit. Currently he is conducting excavations at the Neolithic site of Çatalhöyük, Turkey. He is the author of *Symbols in Action* (1982), *Reading the Past* (1986 and 1991), *The Domestication of Europe* (1992), and *Theory and Practice in Archaeology* (1992).

Alice B. Kehoe is Professor of Anthropology, Marquette University; she received her Ph.D. from Harvard University in 1964. Her research interests include American Indian history and prehistory, history of archaeology and archaeological theory; and the Northwestern Plains Indians. Among her publications are the following: *North American Indians: A Comprehensive Account* (revised edition 1992); *The Ghost Dance: Ethnohistory and Revitalization* (1989); *Francois' House, an Early Fur Trade Post on the Saskatchewan* (1978); "'In Fourteen Hundred and Ninety-two, Columbus Sailed . . .': The Primacy of the National Myth in American Schools" in *The Excluded Past*, ed. P. Stone and R. MacKenzie (1989); *Powers of Observation: Alternate Views in Archeology* (1990, with Sarah M. Nelson); "The Invention of Prehistory," *Current Anthropology* 32(4): 467–476 (1991).

Richard A. Krause is Professor of Anthropology at the University of Alabama, in Tuscaloosa, Alabama. He received his B.A. and M.A. at the University of Nebraska and his Ph.D. from Yale University. He has conducted ethnographic and archaeological research in the Great Plains of North America, Alaska, South Africa, and the Southeastern United States. His published works include *The Leavenworth Site: Archaeology of an Historic Arikara Community; The Clay Sleeps: An Ethnoarchaeological*

Study of Three African Potters; The Tombigbee Watershed in Southeastern Prehistory; and *The Snodgrass Small Mound and Middle Tennessee Valley Prehistory.*

Neil A. Mirau is an Assistant Professor of Archaeology at the University of Lethbridge and a graduate student at the University of Calgary. He has published articles and conducted fieldwork on the cultural implications of Northern Plains environmental changes during the early Holocene. He is continuing his research of the roles played by medicine wheels in Plains Native cultures.

Patricia J. O'Brien is Distinguished Professor of Anthropology at Kansas State University. She has conducted archaeological research in Kansas, Illinois, and Missouri with particular emphasis on the Central Plains tradition and the Cahokia site, and has written extensively on both. She has recently completed the editorship of *Plains Anthropologist.*

Miranda Warburton, Office Manager of the Navajo Nation Archaeology Department–Northern Arizona University Branch Office, is a graduate of Prescott College and Washington State University. She coordinates a variety of cultural resource management projects on the western Navajo Reservation and supervises a student-training program that provides a means for Native American students to pursue anthropology degrees while receiving on-the-job training. Her publications and research interests focus on technology, specifically stone tool manufacture and vernacular architecture.

Monica Bargielski Weimer has been with the Bureau of Land Management as the Royal Gorge Resource Area Archaeologist since 1988. She has also held positions at the Anasazi Heritage Center and with the BIA in northeastern Arizona. In 1985, she received an M.A. from Southern Illinois University in Carbondale and has had fieldwork experience in Illinois, Israel, the Four Corners, and eastern Colorado.

Mary K. Whelan is an Assistant Professor of Anthropology at the University of Iowa. She is interested in feminist archaeology and has completed research on gender relations and colonization in nineteenth-century Minnesota. She is currently trying to examine changing labor and gender relations during the Middle and Late Woodland periods.

Michael C. Wilson received his M.A. in Anthropology in 1975 from the University of Wyoming and a Ph.D. in Archaeology from the University of Calgary in 1981. He taught in Geology and Geophysics at the University of Calgary from 1980 to 1986, and in the Department of Geography at the University of Lethbridge, Alberta, from 1986 to 1992. His research centers upon geoarchaeology in arid lands, ethnoarchaeology of nomadic peoples, and Quaternary vertebrate paleontology, especially *Bison*. He has undertaken field studies in West Africa, northwest China, and northern Japan, in addition to the Great Plains and Plateau of North America. He is now Adjunct Associate Professor at the University of Calgary.

Larry J. Zimmerman is Distinguished Regents Professor of Anthropology and Chairperson of the Department of Social Behavior at the University of South Dakota. He has published widely on Plains archaeology. A past editor of *Plains Anthropologist* and associate editor of *American Antiquity,* he is executive secretary of the World Archaeological Congress and editor of *World Archaeological Bulletin.*

Index